EXORCISM AND ITS TEXTS

SUBJECTIVITY IN EARLY MODERN LITERATURE OF
ENGLAND AND SPAIN

Exorcism and Its Texts

Subjectivity in Early Modern
Literature of England and Spain

Hilaire Kallendorf

UNIVERSITY OF TORONTO PRESS
Toronto Buffalo London

National Library of Canada Cataloguing in Publication

Kallendorf, Hilaire
    Exorcism and its texts : subjectivity in early modern literature of
England and Spain / Hilaire Kallendorf.

    (University of Toronto romance series)
    Includes bibliographical references and index.
    ISBN 0-8020-8817-1

    1. Demoniac possession in literature. 2. Exorcism in literature.
3. English literature – Early modern, 1500–1700 – History and criticism.
4. Spanish literature – Classical period, 1500–1700 – History and
criticism.   I. Title.   II. Series.

    PR149.D47K34 2003   809'.9337   C2003-903627-8

Permission is gratefully acknowledged to reprint parts of chapters 1, 4, and 5 from the
following:

'Exorcism and the Interstices of Language: Ruggle's *Ignoramus* and the Demonization
of Renaissance English Neo-Latin.' From *Acta Conventus Neo-Latini Cantabrigiensis:
Proceedings from the Eleventh International Congress of Neo-Latin Studies*, edited by
Rhoda Schnur, MRTS vol. 259 (Tempe, AZ, 2003). Copyright Arizona Board of
Regents for Arizona State University.

'Intertextual Madness in *Hamlet*: The Ghost's Fragmented Performativity,'
Renaissance and Reformation / Renaissance et Réforme 22.4 (1998): 69–87.

'The Diabolical Adventures of Don Quixote, or Self-Exorcism and the Rise of the
Novel,' *Renaissance Quarterly* 54.1 (2002): 193–223.

University of Toronto Press acknowledges the financial assistance to its publishing
program of the Canada Council for the Arts and the Ontario Arts Council.

University of Toronto Press acknowledges the financial support for its publishing
activities of the Government of Canada through the Book Publishing Industry
Development Program (BPIDP).

To my husband Craig

Vide quam mihi persuaserim te me esse alterum.

– Cicero, *ad Familiares* 7.5

Contents

Illustrations follow p. 138

Acknowledgments

I would like to express gratitude to the Renaissance Society of America for a research grant and to the UCLA Center for 17th and 18th Century Studies for an Ahmanson-Getty Postdoctoral Fellowship, which allowed me the leisure to revise this manuscript. I would also like to thank the editors of *Renaissance Quarterly, Renaissance and Reformation / Renaissance et Réforme,* and *Acta Conventus Neo-Latini Cantabrigiensis: Proceedings of the Eleventh International Congress of Neo-Latin Studies* for permission to incorporate into this book material from articles published first in those venues. My heartfelt thanks go to Dr Miriam Skey of the University of Toronto Press for her careful copy editing of the manuscript.

On the personal level, my debts are more numerous. I would like to thank my parents for giving me life, my husband for giving me love, and my son for being this book's 'twin.' To my thesis director, mentor, and friend Alban Forcione go my warmest thanks and appreciation. To Tony Grafton I offer most sincere thanks for doing much more than you had to (and let's have another beer at the Hispanic Society sometime). To Ron Surtz, well, what can I say? You are a 'full service' DGS. ... To Douglas Brooks for reading part of the manuscript and for being the best colleague I could hope to have. Thanks also to Meg Greer for her generous hospitality. To Bob Hollander for the smell of his pipe. To Carol Szymanski for the butterflies. And to God for sending me a guardian angel to protect me from all the demons!

HORATIO: O day and night, but this is wondrous strange!
HAMLET: And therefore as a stranger give it welcome.
There are more things in heaven and earth, Horatio,
Than are dreamt of in your philosophy.

(*Hamlet* 1.5.164–7)

Prologue – A Force Within:
The Importance of Demonic Possession
for Early Modern Studies

Why should demonic possession matter to all students and scholars of the early modern period? One answer – and, I believe, the most important one – is that potential possession by a demon both threatened and enhanced the integrated notion of selfhood which scholars from Jacob Burckhardt to Stephen Greenblatt have pointed to as a hallmark of the Renaissance.[1] This early modern attention to the self and the individual identity has been contrasted broadly with the medieval insistence on anonymity: the emphasis in medieval manuscripts copied by anonymous scribes was on what was being said, not on who was saying it. Thus medieval literature was largely communal or anonymous (at least by conventional distinction),[2] while the new-found preoccupation with authorship may be understood to be linked closely with the advent of the printing press and the economic concept of private ownership.[3]

The idea of a coherent self is central to emergent notions of individuality and subjectivity in the early modern period.[4] From Montaigne and Machiavelli to Castiglione and Queen Elizabeth, early modern people carefully fashioned and scrutinized both their private selves and their public images.[5] It is only logical that any external force, supernatural or otherwise, which was perceived as a possible threat to – or enhancement of – the self was potentially viewed with extreme interest combined with at least moderate (if not hysterical) alarm.

Demons were a threat to the self in that they were believed by some to have the ability to take over a person's identity – body, mind, and soul. As Nancy Caciola asserts: 'It is the primal ability of the body to maintain its borders, to recognize the self and keep other things out, that defines identity';[6] when this ability is lost, as in the case of demonic possession, then so is identity. For this reason, exorcisms addressed individual adjurations to each body part, sealing them against diabolical incursion.[7] In fact, the idea of identity was so inextricably bound up with notions of possession that the early modern self, in the face of a demon, could fear 'the total transformation of her own essence, rather than the integration of a supplemental spirit into her heart or soul.'[8] In this sense, demonic possession could mean a complete loss of, or change of, identity. The possessed person could even conceivably fluctuate between identities as a result of the demon's inconstant visitations: 'the devil's mark is a cloud gliding through the flesh in an "inconstant" manner, a text erasing itself and rewriting itself at random.'[9]

Once inside a person, what else could a demon do? The Inquisitors Heinrich Krämer and James Sprenger, in their infamous *Malleus maleficarum*, assert that

> devils can, with God's permission, enter our bodies; and they can then make impressions on the inner faculties corresponding to the bodily organs. And by those impressions the organs are affected in proportion as the inner perceptions are affected in the way which has been shown: that the devil can draw out some image retained in a faculty corresponding to one of the lenses; as he draws from the memory, which is in the back part of the head, an image of a horse, and locally moves that phantasm to the middle part of the head, where are the cells of imaginative power; and finally to the sense of reason, which is in the front of the head.[10]

This passage describes the demons' use of the sense of sight to torment their victims. Demons could also take over a person's hearing: 'victims are often unable to hear the priest's words because the devil is whispering, mumbling, or screaming in their minds.'[11] In other words, demons are like an 'invisible miasma'[12] which infect the inner faculties, the bodily organs, the memory and imagination, and finally even the seat of reason. Harold Skulsky has compared metaphors of cannibalism with metaphors of demonic possession and concluded that they bear some striking similarities: 'the would-be "demon's" wish dream of parasitism is the would-be "cannibal's" nightmare of taking in a parasite – of finding oneself the container of something malignant, intelligent, and alive.'[13] Caciola describes the experience of demonic possession with sensitivity and detail:

> This literal sense of physical openness within the interior of the body – like a network of interconnected caverns criss-crossing beneath the surface of the earth – leads to a vision of the demon hibernating inside the human body as an animal might live within a cave. Yet this incursion is disruptive and violent, the cause of torments: the surface imprint of possession displays the interior penetration of the body in somatic changes such as bloating, boils, or convulsions ... [T]he original spirit of the victim remains within the body, but it is as if held captive, surrounded by demonic influ-

ences that do not allow it to access its ... senses or to control its limbs. This sense of spirits playing at hide-and-seek within the caverns of the body also is elaborated symbolically ...[14]

This picture of the early modern self as 'porous or frangible'[15] to demonic penetration is unambivalent in its consequences: demons could eliminate free will and make a person less than responsible for his or her actions.

On the other hand, demons were a potential enhancement to the self because of the revival during this time period of ancient Greek notions of prophecy and poetic frenzy.[16] Socrates had a *daimon* who advised him on weighty matters of philosophy, and Neoplatonists such as Marsilio Ficino, Tommaso Campanella, and Giordano Bruno, citing ancient precedents, revived the hermetic tradition and practice of 'white' or beneficial demonic magic.[17] This magic, often connected to astrology and frequently leading to charges of heterodoxy by ecclesiastical officials, was a synthesis of several competing traditions. As this white or 'angelic' magic was practised by such early modern *magi* as Cornelius Agrippa and John Dee, it invoked *daemones* who were ambiguous figures with primarily positive attributes:

> Pythagorean souls of departed good and wicked men, cherished and perpetuated by the Stoics, still flit about the earth, persecuting or ministering to mortals; Socrates' good daemon and Plato's sons of gods by nymphs or other mothers, intermediaries between men and gods, meet themselves after centuries transformed and fused with the Roman genius or with the creatures of the Neo-platonic imagination.[18]

Even in the realm of ecclesiastical orthodoxy, possession was often confused with enthusiasm, a more 'positively' perceived label which was nonetheless used to condemn religious dissidents.[19]

Medical interest in (and the positive perception of) demons also reached its zenith in this period because while melancholy was widely regarded as a physical and spiritual state triggered by demonic intervention, it was also seen as a prerequisite of artistic genius.[20] This kinship of melancholy to genius is thought to have originated with the pseudo-Aristotelian Problem XXX,1 and been continued by Democritus, who believed that no great minds existed without the inspiration of *furor*.[21] These conflicting early modern attitudes toward the specific interrelated phenomena of possession, melancholy, enthusiasm, etc. will be explored in my epilogue.

It is, more generally, the ambivalent feelings toward demons and their intrusions into human affairs that I have tried to explore in depth in this study. Demonic possession appears in so many genres of early modern literature since attitudes toward demons at this time were polyvalent and variously textured. If early modern people had always made fun of demons, then devils might have appeared only in satirical or picaresque fiction. On the other hand, if early modern people had always been afraid of demons, then devils would have appeared as fatalistic or determining factors in tragedies but would not have participated in other sorts of drama. It is a testament to the pervasiveness of demonic possession in early modern literature that demons appear in almost every genre cultivated in Europe during this period.

Since it would have been impossible to survey the literature of all European countries, I have chosen to focus on England and Spain as two representative nations to serve as case studies until the rest of early modern literature has been surveyed with this topic in mind. Why study exorcism in these two countries and not others? Aside from my interest in their close historical connections and clashes during the period 1550–1700, I decided to study exorcism in England and Spain because this choice of one Protestant country and one Catholic country gave me the opportunity to explore the differences (and a surprising number of similarities) between Protestant and Catholic laws, liturgies, and literatures on exorcism.

The charge of bewitchment was introduced into cases of possession much more frequently in England than in Spain. I believe the reason was that England had no effective official way of dealing with demonic possession: 'Reformers only combatted the doctrine of possession upon strictly theological grounds, and did not go on to suggest any substitute for the time-honoured practice of exorcism as a means for getting rid of the admittedly obnoxious result of diabolic interference.'[22] If Anglicans could conduct exorcisms at all, they were only allowed to pray to God to expel the demon; they were not permitted to presume to do so themselves. Bishop Joseph Hall complained of the resultant ineffectuality of the clergy: 'We that have no power to bid must pray.'[23] Keith Thomas calls this English problem 'the Anglican Church's confessed impotence in this sphere.'[24] In England, where exorcism was officially condemned and the occasional exception proved ineffectual, the solution for the problem of demonic possession became the search for and execution of the witch responsible for causing it.

In contrast, exorcism was sanctioned in Spain and was usually more effective there than in England. It has been noted that despite the negative stereotypes shrouding the Spanish Inquisition, its rational control and regulation actually served to channel religious belief away from witchcraft.[25] Fewer witches were burned in Spain than in England, in part, I believe, because fewer witches were accused in the first place.[26] As David Gentilcore points out in the similar case of Spanish southern Italy: 'Because exorcism could be employed against both suspected witch and victim to chase away demonic influences, it served as a further escape valve for the perceived witchcraft threat.'[27] Spanish Catholics had effective exorcisms to deal with the situation of demonic possession whenever it arose, as it did frequently.

Unlike my choice of countries to study, my choice of genres was less deliberate. I did not set out to explore some genres in this study and not others, but simply included those genres where exorcistic material appeared. The glaring omission in my lineup of genres is the epic, and I would hypothesize that demonic possession and exorcism do not appear as often in this genre because they would violate either the obligatory epideictic rhetoric praising the epic hero or even the integrity of that hero's identity.[28] Demons would threaten the epic hero's selfhood or they would enhance it, but either way, by virtue of their supernatural 'largeness,' they would then have to become protagonists in the epic on the level of the hero they influenced (just as did the Greek and Roman gods of Homer and Virgil). The classic example of this literary process of elevation of demons to heroic stature is, of course, Milton's epic *Paradise Lost*.[29] This entire epic poem could be read symbolically as Satan's progressive possession of the snake, and then Eve, and then Adam, who is himself exorcized from the Garden of Eden upon his expulsion therefrom.[30] Instead of studying demons who loom so large in the imagination as Milton's Satan and his minions, I have chosen instead to concentrate on the more subtle demons who appear in literature only through the actions they induce in human beings. Another criterion I have used is that demonic possession, the ritual of exorcism, or the language of exorcism had to be incorporated specifically into the works of various literary genres in order to be included in this study.

Demonic possession is linked to so many supernatural activities and paranormal phenomena of the early modern period that it has been difficult to draw these distinctions consistently. What distinguishes an exorcism from a conjuration?[31] And what separates an exorcist from a wizard or witch? For that matter, what is the difference between bewitchment and possession, and are they not sometimes to be cured in the same way? In order to facilitate a widely intuitive, nontechnical understanding of the pages that follow, a few generalizations may be made here on the condition that they are understood as only the broadest brushstroke view of what is happening in literature about demons.

An exorcism is an attempt to expel a demon or demons from a person or object which has been possessed by it or them. It is a highly formalized, ritualistic ceremony with common characteristics found in its Catholic, Protestant (Anglican, Puritan, or dissident), Jewish, and pagan (including, but not limited to, Greek) variations. For our purposes here it does not always matter which particular kind of exorcism is being portrayed. Sometimes the specific details are important for ideological or partisan reasons, but often the only point is that a demonic presence inhabits the person (I have for the most part foregone the study of possessed objects and animals), and someone is trying to remove it. The exorcism ceremony almost always involves ritualistic language and – especially in its Catholic variations – includes the use of 'props' such as a cross, relics, holy water, or rope to bind the limbs of the possessed. But because these 'props' were often the object of intense sectarian divisiveness, it is better to leave them out of our most basic general definition.

The figure of the exorcist is likewise a highly variable one. The most obvious distinction to be made is that an exorcist expels demons, while a conjurer summons or calls them up. Witches and wizards fall into this latter category as well. Exorcists may be male or female, clerics or laymen, although a male priest or minister is the most typical exorcist figure during this time period. In Catholic countries the role of 'exorcist' was one of the minor orders which could serve as a stepping stone to the priesthood but could also be taken by a layman. In fact, students in medieval universities were ordained to the lower orders as a matter of course;[32] that is why all university students, such as those referred to as exorcists in *Hamlet* and Quevedo's *Buscón*, were expected to know how to perform an exorcism.[33] Every such student who did become a priest would receive a book of exorcisms at the ordination ceremony.

Theoretically, a possession and a bewitchment produce the same symptoms in the patient: convulsions, loss of free will, manifestation of a different personality, and the feeling of being subjected to benign or malign spiritual influence. Technically, however, a possession arises spontaneously or through the agency of the demon only, while a bewitchment is always the result of human plus demonic intervention. In other words, a demon must use a human being to reach another human being in the case of bewitchment, instead of acting upon the person directly, as in demonic possession. Because the literature of witchcraft is so vast, and the complicating factors of the witch's culpability and subsequent prosecution so distracting, I have chosen to focus on demonic possession to the more or less total exclusion of bewitchment.

Having made these distinctions, I have of course felt free to ignore them when the literature itself conflates these categories. Most literary authors were not such experts in these matters as the demonologists, although the degree of their particular knowledge about demons could be extraordinary. Later I will develop more fully a pattern of what I call the component 'theologemes' of the exorcism ritual, but for now it is necessary simply to lay out these basic distinctions by way of introduction for the supernaturally uninitiated.

After a thorough (indeed, almost exhaustive) study of possession and exorcism in early modern literatures of England and Spain, I shall end this study with some concluding remarks about early modern literary theory and its treatment of the legitimate marvellous. It has often been commented on how little early modern authors and poets seemed to follow the prescriptions laid out for them in contemporaneous poetics manuals.[34] While it certainly remains true that, in the realm of literature, theory did not always equal *praxis*, it is amazing to see how literary treatments of demons did seem to derive from, or at least agree with, poetical theory of the period. The discussion of demons (commonly perceived by postmodern scholars as 'medieval' entities) in the Renaissance not only pushes us to make flexible the rigid boundaries of period distinctions but also forces us to concede that poets occasionally followed the advice of those who would instruct them on how to compose perfect examples of the different literary genres they chose to tackle. This maxim falls apart when confronted with the novel, a 'new' literary genre for which no theory existed previously, but as we shall see, the appearance of a unique kind of exorcism in this unique genre seems to be the exception which proves the rule.

It is my hope that after reading this study, you will start to see demons everywhere. They are lurking in some of the most obscure as well as the most familiar works of early modern literature. In the many genres in which they appear, with the often-conflicting authorial attitudes these reflect, they reveal the early modern fascination with the idea of a supernatural 'force within.'

A Paradigm of Theologemes for Literary Exorcism

This notion of a paradigm is essential, apparently, if we are to understand the structuralist vision: the paradigm is a group, a reservoir – as limited as possible – of objects (of units) from which one summons, by an act of citation, the object or unit one wishes to endow with an actual meaning....

—Roland Barthes, 'The Structuralist Activity'

	1. Demon enters	2. Symptoms	3. Polyglossia	4. Coach	5. Exorcist	6. Lovers' ruse	7. Mock exorcism	8. Bind body	9. Props	10. Success	11. Body politic
Vega, *La duquesa de la rosa*	#	#									#
Jonson, *Devil is an Ass*		#	#	#				#	#		#
Ruggle, *Ignoramus*	#		#	#	#		#				#
Jonson, *Volpone*		#		#							
Shakespeare, *Errors*					#		#	#	#		
Bugbears		#		#	#	#	#		#		#
Shakespeare, *12th Night*					#	#	#	#	#		#
Timoneda, *Menemnos*					#		#	#			
Shadwell, *Lancashire Witches*	#	#	#		#				#		#
3 authors, *El pleyto*	#	#	#		#				#	#	#
Middleton, *Phoenix*					#			#	#	#	#
Zamora, *Hechizado*	#	#			#				#		#
Lazarillo		#			#		#		#		#
Quevedo, *Buscón*		#			#		#		#		
Quevedo, *Entremés*		#			#		#	#	#		
Quevedo, *Alguacil*		#			#			#	#		
Cervantes, *Persiles*		#			#	#	#	#	#	#	
Lope, *La endemoniada*	#	#	#	#	#	#					
Cervantes, *Rufián*	#	#	#		#				#	#	
Calderón, *Cadenas*	#	#			#			#		#	#
Lope, *El divino africano*	#	#			#		#	#		#	
Shakespeare, *Lear*	#	#					#				#
Yorkshire Tragedy	#	#									#
Shakespeare, *Othello*	#	#									#
Shakespeare, *Macbeth*	#	#									#
Shakespeare, *Hamlet*	#	#									#
Cervantes, *Quijote*	#	#			#					#	

1. The demon's entrance into the body. 2. Symptoms of possession. 3. Demonic polyglossia. 4. The coach. 5. The exorcist. 6. The lovers' ruse. 7. The (mock) exorcism. 8. Binding the body and other exorcistic procedures. 9. Relics, holy water, and other 'props'. 10. The successful exorcism (a serious rite performed in earnest). 11. Exorcism as a synecdoche for curing the body politic.

EXORCISM AND ITS TEXTS

SUBJECTIVITY IN EARLY MODERN LITERATURE OF
ENGLAND AND SPAIN

Introduction: The Morphology of Exorcism, or a Grammar of Possession in Spanish and English Literature, 1550–1700

Exorcism and demonic possession appear as recurrent motifs in early modern Spanish and English literature. This fact is not surprising, given the dramatic appeal of sensational details of actual exorcism cases. These exorcisms were conducted by both orthodox authority figures and illegitimate charlatans upon both suffering demoniacs and cynical masters of illusion. Unfortunately, the claims of postmodern scholars such as some so-called New Historicists that early modern thinkers could not ever have believed in the literal possibility of demonic possession have prevented readers from appreciating the power of many exorcism scenes in early modern literature. It is important not to make too many generalizations about this 'school' of critics, as Richard Halpern observes:

> Because the new historicism shuns overt allegiance to any single authorizing model (for example, Marx or Foucault), because it draws its inspiration from a variety of disciplines including social history and anthropology, and because its leading practitioners tend to resist both incorporation into a movement and, sometimes, the name 'new historicism' itself, one must be careful in ascribing one particular model of power to all its exponents and productions.[1]

Nevertheless it is possible to identify a few salient features of this trend in scholarship.

Postmodern New Historicist scholars often approach literature from the perspective of what Paul Ricoeur has called a 'hermeneutics of suspicion.' In his essay 'The Critique of Religion,' Ricoeur accuses Marx, Freud, and Nietzsche of practising this hermeneutics in an earlier generation:

Each of them ... cooperates in a *general exegesis* of false-consciousness and belongs by this fact in a *hermeneutics*, in a theory of interpretation, under the negative form of demystification. But with Marx, Nietzsche, and Freud, beyond their economism, biologism, and psychiatrism respectively, demystification is characterized in the first place as the exercise of suspicion. I call suspicion the act of dispute exactly proportional to the expressions of false-consciousness. The problem of false-consciousness is the object, the correlative of the act of suspicion. Out of it is born the quality of doubt, a type of doubt which is totally new and different from Cartesian doubt.[2]

What these practitioners of the 'hermeneutics of suspicion' do not acknowledge is that early modern intellectuals could doubt some instances of fraudulent possession while still believing in the potency of some exorcisms as practised under the aegis of sanctioned ecclesiastical authority. This is part of the paradox of the early modern period. It is true that particularly in non-Catholic countries such as England, John Darrell and other 'upstart' exorcists were trying to usurp the cultural authority previously invested in priests by the common folk in cases of madness or possession. But it is also true that exorcism as practised by Saint Ignatius, Saint John of the Cross, and others was one of the most dangerous weapons in the arsenal of the Counter-Reformation.

Some erudite (and even pious) members of early modern societies did ridicule what they deemed to be superstition about exorcism in the uneducated classes. They lamented the common person's credulity when it came to the supernatural:

How manie stories and bookes are written of walking spirits and soules of men, contrarie to the word of God; a reasonable volume cannot conteine. Therefore no mervell, though the common simple sort of men ... be deceived herein ...[3]

These sceptics verged on suggesting that the lower classes were mad to believe that alleged supernatural phenomena were unquestionably valid: 'Who seeth not that they are witlesse, and madde fooles to mainteine it?'[4] But were all early modern sceptics and intellectuals denying every belief in the supernatural?

The answer is, most certainly not. Consider this bizarre factoid: at least four printed accounts (obviously written by educated men) exist from between 1594 and 1673 in England of a stage production of *Dr Faustus* which came to its terrifying conclusion when an extra devil appeared onstage.[5] True, one opinion circulating at the time was that '[d]iuels are none other thing else, but those ... euill motions in men, which doe maruellously ... afflict their minds.'[6] A modern atheist (or at least 'ademonist') would probably agree. But even sceptics whose books were being burned[7] did not often dare to question the theoretical possibility that demons could appear to and possess human beings. The sceptic Reginald

Scot (the same author quoted above) pronounces that he believes demons exist and emphasizes his awareness of the seriousness of his topic: 'There is no question ... so difficult to deal in, nor so noble an argument to dispute upon, as this of divels and spirits. For that being confessed or doubted of, the eternitie of the soule is either affirmed or denied.'[8] Scot was of course an Anglican, but the equivalent Catholic belief was that denying the presence of a possessing demon was equivalent to denying the literal truth of transubstantiation in the Eucharist. As Fray Mateo Bonilla wrote at about this same time: 'It is as much a matter of faith to believe that the said women ... are possessed by the devil as it is to believe in the Most Holy Sacrament of the altar.'[9] This belief was summed up by the maxim *Nullus Deus sine diabolo* (i.e., without proof of the devil, there could be no proof of God).[10] Even scientists and mathematicians argued for the plausibility of demonic possession until well into the eighteenth century. William Whiston, an associate of Newton who succeeded him in the Lucasian chair of mathematics at Cambridge, wrote in 1737 in *An account of the daemoniacks, and of the power of casting out daemons*:

> [The assaults of invisible demons are] no more to be denied, because we cannot, at present, give a direct solution of them, than are Mr. Boyle's experiments about the elasticity of the air; or Sir Isaac Newton's demonstrations about the power of gravity ... because neither of them are to be solved by mechanical causes.[11]

Many scholars and intellectuals of the early modern period routinely affirmed their belief in at least the theoretical possibility of demonic possession, although they did not always agree upon which form of exorcism should be deemed appropriate.

In sum, belief in demonic possession and exorcism extended to all levels of society – commoners and noblemen, erudite and uneducated. There were of course still some sceptics, and various degrees of belief and disbelief coexisted messily within individual perspectives, let alone entire groups or classes of people. As John Cox remarks incisively: 'The cynicism of con men coexists with fear of the devil.'[12] A telling example of the conflicted attitudes held by individuals toward the supernatural at this time is the self-proclaimed 'atheist' Thomas Fineux of Dover (thought to have been influenced by Marlowe), who set out to prove that the devil did not exist by going into a forest at night to pray to the devil – a 'gesture that buys heavily into the very reality it attempts to disprove.'[13]

This study takes us back to the early modern world, where order was in tension with disorder and belief was challenged by scepticism. Even if we set aside the question of the conflicting views early modern authors themselves held about demons, we must still confront the issues of what they chose to write about, under what cultural authority, and for which audiences. I intend to expose the tensions (sometimes even within the corpus of a single author) in early modern fiction, drama, and poetry written about demonic possession and exorcism. In Fredric Jameson's terms, exorcism is my 'identical mechanism at work on all the levels of discourse and expressing itself at some points as action, at others taking the form of an image, at still others being articulated as a psychological percep-tion or a stylistic mannerism.'[14] The thesis of this book is that closer attention to the many different early modern genres which incorporated scenes of exorcism or exorcistic language will demonstrate the adaptability of this *topos* to a broad range of authorial purposes, audience responses, cultural paradigms, and patterns of belief.

Exorcistic terminology is one linguistic register through which early modern authors could make convincing portrayals of extraordinary religious phenomena. These phenomena could include demonic possession and exorcism, but they could also include madness or murder presented in an exorcistic context. These phenomena, which were also seen within categories of the neo-Aristotelian 'legit-imate marvellous,' were approached from many different perspectives by early modern writers. Each of these approaches results in a different formal treatment. My study is organized according to the (sometimes conflicting) genres through which early modern writers envisioned their world.

The works in which exorcism or exorcistic terminology appear are best studied within a generic framework because authors writing in the venues of comedy, picaresque, satirical poetry, satire, romance, interlude, hagiography, tragedy, or novel wrote with different purposes in mind, for different audiences at hand, under different cultural paradigms, and within different patterns of belief. Generic constraints both shaped fiction about demonic possession and provided a beginning place from which authors could depart radically. Demonic possession could become an object of satire or a tragic metaphor for madness, depending on the context. The satirical treatments of exorcism are not so biting, nor the tragic moments so touching, if we as postmodern readers refuse to accept the generic premises of early modern authors and their readers. Finally, I will show how all of the genres were open, in some way, to the inclusion of neo-Aristotelian theories of the 'legitimate marvellous' as they were applied to the appearance of the super-natural in literature.

Organizing the book in this way accounts for the fact that some genres are more susceptible than others to New Historicist and/or structuralist analysis. The arrangement of chapters presents a spectrum ranging from those genres which conform to a New Historicist model for exorcism in literature to those which defy it. A New Historicist approach works well with comical, theatrical material where the exorcisms (usually fraudulent) are staged performances manipulated by authority figures. It even works reasonably well with picaresque, satire, and to a limited degree, romance. But there is much in the early modern literary assimilation of the rituals of exorcism that the New Historicist model fails to account for. Where is the dark baroque mystery? The obsession with demons and hell? The Counter-Reformation use of exorcism as propaganda for the faith? These are found primarily in hagiographical drama, in tragedy, and in the novel. Surely it is possible to find a third term between a structuralist ideal of literature aloof from the world of culture and authority and a New Historicist ideal of literature that is totally engaged politically – and, almost by definition, areligious.[15]

In this study, I use the work of the structuralists as a useful corrective to work done by some New Historicists, and vice versa. As the editors of *True Rites and Maimed Rites* warn about the New Historicists:

> Even where newly historicized critics are not explicitly addressing ritual, the major shift in literary criticism away from formalist approaches toward historicized, political reading, effected by thinkers from Gramsci to Foucault to Greenblatt, has inevitably affected the study of ritual ... New historicists have been interested in magical thinking ... Yet Greenblatt more typically argues that in adopting the forms of magical rites, the Renaissance 'evacuated' them of magical meaning ('Exorcists'), and this seems to me to lean too far toward the triumph of rationalism, making Shakespeare and his contemporaries more 'modern' than they were.[16]

New Historicists have attempted to study the ritual of exorcism as it appears in literature without paying close attention either to religious ritual or to literary genre. I shall try to show how the work of the structuralists might offer a corrective to what I see as shortcomings in some New Historicist approaches. Meanwhile, I shall also try to answer some New Historicist critiques of structuralism by using New Historicist methods to generate historical components for my discussions of literary texts.[17] By demonstrating the historicity of these texts and the textuality of this history, I hope to avoid the structuralists' potential fallacy of focusing on synchrony to the detriment of diachrony.

Structuralism is out of fashion today, in a postmodern world which prefers chaos. Nonetheless it cannot be ignored, for 'the achievement of the formalists, like that of Aristotle, will be permanent because it will have to be incorporated in any later poetics of fiction.'[18] This is especially true for a poetics of early modern fiction written about demonic possession and exorcism. This study of structural order in literature about exorcism has been influenced to some degree by the work of Claude Lévi-Strauss and Vladimir Propp. Again, I use the work of these structuralists as a useful corrective to the work of some New Historicists, and vice versa.

As Roland Barthes has implied, these two schools of thought would appear to be almost diametrically opposed: 'The chief resistance to structuralism today seems to be of Marxist origin and ... it focuses on the notion of history (and not of structure).'[19] One such Marxist (as well as Hegelian) critique of structuralism is Fredric Jameson's *The Prison House of Language*. Jameson objects that 'the Formalistic model is essentially synchronic, and cannot adequately deal with diachrony, either in literary history or in the form of the individual work.'[20] As a structuralist, Barthes answers Jameson and his New Historicist critics, whose work he says 'has been done a thousand times' already:

> Structuralism does not withdraw history from the world: it seeks to link to history not only certain contents (this has been done a thousand times) but also certain forms, not only the material but also the intelligible, not only the ideological but also the aesthetic.[21]

I will argue that it is precisely their inattention to aesthetic structure (such as genre) which makes some of the New Historicists' work so potentially misleading.

The structuralists have taught us that when ritual (such as exorcism) is integrated into narrative (of a certain literary genre), the result is always a hybrid structure: a ritualized narrative. In other words, a ritualized narrative is a repetitive, paradigmatic narrative which becomes sacralized in nature. Mircea Eliade describes sacralized narrative as 'a periodical return of the same primordial situations and hence a reactualization of the same sacred time.'[22]

Belief in exorcism is a form of sacralized or mythical thought. In *The Symbolism of Evil*, Paul Ricoeur defines myth in the sense that I mean here:

> Myth will here be taken to mean what the history of religions now finds in it: not a false explanation by means of images and fables, but a traditional narration which relates to events that happened at the beginning of time and which has the purpose of providing grounds for the ritual actions of men of today and, in a general manner, establishing all the forms of action and thought by which man understands himself in his world.[23]

Exorcism is just such a tradition-fraught cultural narration – just such a ritualistic, authorized action. Exorcism is just such a 'myth.' There is not necessarily an implication of falsehood in this definition: 'myth,' when used in this sense, is a technical term.

If we allow this definition of exorcism as a form of mythical thought, then we will be able to take advantage of the work of theorists who have studied other categories of mythical thought. A key essay in this field is Lévi-Strauss's 'The Structural Study of Myth.'[24] Here Lévi-Strauss explains his method in surprisingly precise detail: 'The technique ... consists in analyzing each myth individually, breaking down its story into the shortest possible sentences, and writing each sentence on an index card bearing a number corresponding to the unfolding of the story.'[25] He later notes that a 'variant of average length requires several hundred cards to be properly analyzed.'[26] After he has made these cards, he divides them into columns and rows in a highly purposeful way: 'The synchronic-diachronic structure of the myth permits us to organize it into diachronic sequences (the rows in our tables) which should be read synchronically (the columns).'[27] He analyses these many versions to arrive at a group of 'combinational variants of the same function in different contexts,' with his goal being 'to organize all the known variants of a myth into a set forming a kind of permutation group.'[28]

This type of almost mathematical analysis can be extended to a study of exorcism in literature. In Lévi-Strauss's terms, exorcism is our 'myth' and the many genres in which it appears are our 'variants.' The 'set' or 'permutation group' would be the master narrative of a demonic possession and exorcism with all its possible ingredients or 'mythemes.' The word 'mytheme' comes from Lévi-Strauss: 'Myth, like the rest of language, is made up of constituent units ... These constituent units presuppose the constituent units present in language when analyzed on other levels – namely, phonemes, morphemes, and sememes ... we shall call them gross constituent units ... or mythemes.'[29] I prefer the term 'theologeme' coined by Algirdas Julien Greimas to refer to the constitutive units of myths bearing theological content.[30] When each author in this study exploits the exorcism material, he picks and chooses the 'mythemes' or 'theologemes' which he (alas, all of my texts have male authors) wants to use from this permutation group. The result, in each case written within early modern generic constraints, is a variant of the exorcism myth which chooses to highlight some aspects of demonic possession and exorcism and to downplay others. Which aspects of the exorcism experience are highlighted or emphasized usually depends on which genre the writer is working within.

To understand how mythical thought about exorcism is incorporated into literature of various genres, we must understand a concept devised by Lévi-Strauss called 'bricolage.' Lévi-Strauss sees mythical thought as 'a kind of intellectual "bricolage,"' a concept which he develops in some detail. He describes the 'bricoleur' thus:

> His universe of instruments is closed and the rules of his game are always to make do ... with a set of tools and materials which is always finite ... but is the contingent result of all the occasions there have been to renew or enrich the stock or to maintain it with the remains of previous constructions or destructions ... He has to turn back

to an already existent set made up of tools and materials, to consider or reconsider what it contains and finally and above all, to engage in a sort of dialogue with it and, before choosing between them, to index the possible answers which the whole set can offer to his problem ... The elements which the 'bricoleur' collects and uses are 'pre-constrained' like the constitutive units of myth ...[31]

This last statement reinforces the idea that the concept of bricolage applies especially to mythical thought. Lévi-Strauss in fact believes that

mythical thought, that 'bricoleur,' builds up structures by fitting together events, or rather the remains of events ... Mythical thought for its part is imprisoned in the events and experiences which it never tires of ordering and re-ordering in its search to find them a meaning.[32]

He even explains the eventual transformations of bricolage in new contexts in a way which helps us to understand what happens when the exorcism material is 'recycled' in the new contexts of different genres:

In the continual reconstruction from the same materials, it is always earlier ends which are called upon to play the part of means: the signified changes into the signifying, and vice versa. This formula, which could serve as a definition of 'bricolage,' explains how an implicit inventory or conception of the total means available must be made in the case of mythical thought also ...[33]

It is this inventory that I have attempted to reconstruct in my 'Paradigm of Theologemes for Literary Exorcism' at the beginning of this study (see p. xxi). In this chart a pattern of genres emerges, ranging from the types of theologemes appropriated by more humorous genres, near the top, to the types of theologemes appropriated by less comical genres, toward the bottom.

The notion of genre is an important one for the structuralists. Roland Barthes explains why in a discussion of form, which in this case is really just another word for literary genre. For Barthes, forms or genres are 'rules of combinations.'[34] The content is always the same for these tales of exorcism. It is the presentation, or 'rule of combination,' which is different in each successive (or concurrent) literary form or genre.

The question of the structuralists' concern with genre naturally brings us to the work of Vladimir Propp on the genre of the wondertale.[35] My work departs from his significantly in the very fact that while he studies one genre, I study many, but he makes certain methodological pronouncements which make it easy to envision extensions of his work into other fields: for example, 'form usually means genre;

therefore, the same plot can take the form of a novel, a tragedy, a film script, etc.'[36] In my case, this 'same plot' is the exorcism ritual. Propp states clearly that 'any folklorist knows that plots very often migrate from genre to genre.'[37] In this study I show how the exorcism 'plot' migrates through the genres of comic drama, picaresque, satirical poetry, satire, romance, interlude, hagiography, tragedy, and the novel. To do this, I use the fundamental categories established by Propp for his study of the 'wondertale.'

For Vladimir Propp, all fairy tales or 'wondertales' contain thirty-one identifiable elements called 'functions.' A 'function' is a verbal or action-oriented element (as opposed to an attributive or character-oriented element):[38]

> Fairy tales exhibit thirty-one functions, not all of which may be found in any one fairy tale; however, the absence of certain functions does not interfere with the order of appearance of the others. Their aggregate constitutes one system, one composition. This system has proved to be extremely stable and widespread.[39]

Some examples of these 'functions' would be 'the hero leaves home,' 'the hero is pursued,' 'a difficult task is proposed,' or 'the villain ascends the throne.'[40] In addition to 'functions,' there are identifiable character types in the fairy tale. One example is the 'donor,' who is 'the actor who furnishes the hero with the magical tool.'[41] Finally, there are also characteristic elements such as props and places (for example, the hut on chicken legs which rotates in a forest) that appear frequently enough in fairy tales to be called hallmarks of the genre.[42]

These identifiable elements of the fairy tale – 'functions,' character types, and props or places – undergo various 'transformations' in the course of multiple retellings of the same story. A 'transformation' of the aforementioned magical place might be, for example, a hut on chicken legs in the forest which now rests on pancakes and is shingled with cookies.[43] Propp lists twenty 'transformations' of the same subject matter that may occur in its various iterations, including reduction, expansion, contamination, inversion, intensification, attenuation, and confessional substitution.[44]

I have found Propp's methodology helpful in studying the recurrence and transformations of exorcism rituals in literature. There are certain identifiable verbal 'functions' – to possess, to exorcize, to trick, to confess – which remain constant in all literary works where exorcism appears. When I say they remain constant, it is only in the Proppian sense of this phrase, remembering that 'the absence of certain functions does not interfere with the order of appearance of the others.'[45] The order of appearance is important because the nature of the exorcism ritual is by definition diachronic and teleological. Likewise, there are certain character types – demoniac, exorcist, fake demoniac, fake exorcist, coach, student, credulous spectator, possessing demon, guardian angel, God, the Virgin Mary, and the saints – who appear over and over in these literary portrayals of demonic possession and exorcism. Finally, there are 'props' (holy water, cross, rue, salt, stole, whip, etc.), symptoms (body writhing, teeth gnashing, eyes bulging, etc.), and exorcistic procedures (binding, blessing, whipping, and cajoling) which also recur time and time again in various literary adaptations of the exorcism *topos*. I prefer the more general term 'theologemes' to denote any or all of these recurring elements because it includes not only these verbal 'functions' but also these character types, props, symptoms, and procedures.

The first chapter on comic drama is the key to the rest of this study. Because I found exponentially more material to work with here than in any other genre, I have used this chapter as the place to establish a structuralist paradigm for exorcism in literature. Using twelve early modern plays written in Spain and England about exorcism, I identify common 'theologemes' or ingredients of the exorcism ritual. I use each play to illustrate one theologeme which it incorporates in a particularly emphatic way. I then extend the resultant table of theologemes to each of the other genres as represented by each of my subsequent chapters. For now, let us look briefly at each of the genres and their representative works in turn, with the goal of exploring how the exorcism paradigm proves flexible enough to adapt to each set of generic conventions.

Some New Historicists have pointed to the theatricality of exorcisms as their primary attraction for Renaissance authors. A basic premise for these scholars is that the exorcisms were always fabrications and that their fictionality provided their major attraction for dramatists. As professional writers who also created fictions, dramatists would have admired any new and convincing form of acting. This explanation probably works best when comic theatrical subject matter is at issue. For example, some of these scholars have identified the influences of Samuel Harsnett's *The Discovery and Confutation of John Darrell* on *Twelfth Night*; these critics view Malvolio as a parody of this Protestant exorcist who was arrested, tried, and condemned by Elizabethan ecclesiastical officials. These critics have made a valuable contribution to early modern scholarship with this interpretation. Their approach also works admirably when applied, for instance, to the comedia *El hechizado por fuerza* by Antonio de Zamora. This play is a dangerously direct parody of the politically manoeuvered exorcisms performed upon the king of Spain, Carlos II ('El Hechizado'), in the Alcázar Real. In the play, as in the historical situation it reflects, several women convince a man that he is possessed so that they can manipulate him more easily. In the case of the Spanish king, this crisis of political intrigue and manipulation of the weak monarch reverberated throughout the country, as we know from contemporaneous accounts by ambassadors who witnessed it. These plays and other comic dramas like them do make direct topical allusions to concrete historical cases of exorcism. This genre is characterized by an historical immediacy (and for many of these plays, an ephemerality) which makes it more susceptible to New Historicist analysis than other genres.

A New Historicist model is still fairly convincing for the genre of the picaresque. In the second chapter we see how the sceptical demonologists' attitude is absorbed and repeated with little adaptation in this genre, with little complexity and much blunt caricature of fraudulent exorcists and fake demoniacs. There is little or no character development of the parodied figures, although there is development of the picaresque protagonists who encounter these charlatans in the course of their journeys. For Lazarillo, his master the *buldero* provides him with yet another educational spectacle as he conspires with the *alguacil* to sell more *bulas*. The *alguacil* feigns demonic possession during a church service and creates a sensation with his writhing, foaming, and gesticulation. The *buldero* then pretends to exorcize him successfully, forcing him to declare that all the slanderous complaints he had made previously about the inefficacy of the *bulas* were inspired by the devil to interfere in the holy man's work. This darkly satirical portrait of the devious partnership of demoniac and exorcist leaves little room for speculation as to the attitude of its anonymous author. The often-cited anticlerical bias of this writer extends here to encompass staged exorcism performances as some of the most flagrant abuses attacked in his wide-ranging social criticism.

A New Historicist analysis would at first glance appear to work well with satire also, but a closer look shows that there are serious demonic elements which it fails to account for. For example, in this chapter we see how Francisco de Quevedo's burgeoning interest in exorcistic material, as evidenced by his satirical poetry and by a youthful foray into the picaresque genre, attained a new maturity in his satirical *Discurso* of the 'Alguacil endemoniado.' In this work, Quevedo as narrator surprises an exorcist, Calabrés, in the act of exorcizing the *alguacil endemoniado* of the title. In the ensuing dialogue, he questions a demon (who speaks through the mouth of the demoniac) about the fates of various classes of persons in hell. At its beginning and end Quevedo jokes that he himself is demon-possessed, perhaps to distance himself from such a heterodox and potentially dangerous piece of writing. In the course of the dialogue the *alguacil* and the exorcist are both mercilessly satirized, along with representatives of many other occupations.

In addition to seeing rich opportunities for parody, however, Quevedo found something serious to think about in the often ridiculed ritual of exorcism. In the course of his work, Quevedo (in his role as narrator) indulges in the single most dangerous kind of curiosity against which all the demonologists warn most vigorously: he wants to use the exorcism ritual as a way to discover occult information from the devil. It is the attraction of forbidden knowledge which proves most fascinating for Quevedo. Even though his attitude toward the rites of exorcism appears as the most darkly cynical of any of our authors, it is nonetheless possible to glimpse the not-altogether-impious passion with which he seeks demonic knowledge not available to human beings. Not available, that is, except through the exorcism ritual, which provides a window to the world beyond – a place of contact between the natural and the supernatural, where illicit questions are asked and sometimes answered.

The third chapter is a synthesis of two very different genres, romance and hagiographical drama, both of which 'humanize' the experience of demonic possession and exorcism. At first glance, these genres may seem to form an unlikely pair, but they – along with the related genre of the interlude or *entremés* – were both utilized to create literary portraits of exorcism (albeit with radically different results) by two of the same authors, Miguel de Cervantes and Lope de Vega. Thus they illustrate the tension between, and the potential reconciliation of, quite conflicting views of exorcism within the complete works of at least two individual writers. For example, Cervantes' attitude toward exorcism in his prose romance, the *Persiles*, is light-hearted and fun-loving without risking irreverence. The Isabela Castrucha episode, while symbolic of the work's overall pattern of deliverance from demonic bondage, is nonetheless a mischievous wink at the credulity of the old uncle who is fooled by his niece's pretended possession. But a serious undertone may be glimpsed when the characters make numerous philosophical comments about how being in love is very similar to being possessed by a demon. This humanization of the experience of demonic possession is related to Cervantes' humanization of exorcism in an entirely different work of his, *El rufián dichoso*. In this hagiographical drama, Cristóbal de la Cruz is summoned to the deathbed of a wealthy, dying young woman named Ana de Treviño. When Ana is surprised by death, she despairs of God's mercy and declares that for her, there is no God. Other clergymen have been unable to prevail upon her to receive absolution in the sacrament of confession. Cruz performs a beautifully Cervantine, humanized version of the exorcism ritual by reasoning with Ana and even making a bargain with her to save her soul. A more 'serious' depiction of demonic possession and exorcism would hardly be possible. Lope de Vega's works reiterate this tension between scepticism and belief, demonstrating that authors' attitudes toward supernatural phenomena were far from consistent during this period. By humanizing both the experience of demonic possession and the experience of exorcism in their fictions, Cervantes and Lope de Vega contribute to the durability of this *topos* as it remains relevant to literature of widely different genres.

The next chapter, on tragedy, represents the diametrical opposite of the successful exorcism in hagiography. Most commonly, exorcism is absent from tragedy; when it does appear there, it fails. In *King Lear*, the exorcism ritual does indeed appear, but while it succeeds as a metatheatrical metaphor of catharsis, it fails within the text as an effective redemptive process. In *A Yorkshire Tragedy*, there is a sort of exorcism, but it also fails within the text as a path to ultimate redemption. In the other tragedies discussed in this chapter, exorcism never even appears. But the topos of demonic possession is exploited in three of the plays to create a 'demon as scapegoat' pattern which attempts to explain the inexplicable act of murder. Finally, even the 'demon as scapegoat' pattern fails in *Hamlet*, where demonic possession proves to be only one possible explanation for the protagonist's madness. The Ghost and Hamlet try on the 'masks' of demon and demoniac, but only as part of their endless series of roles to perform. Thus in these plays I will show a progression of decreasing potency, efficacy, or pervasiveness of the exorcism ritual. Demonic possession resonates through the genre of tragedy, but the hope for an ultimate exorcism is forever raised and then dashed to pieces. It is the nature of the tragic experience that exorcism cannot succeed.

Finally, we come to the chapter on the novel. Unlike many other works in which the exorcism material appears, in *Don Quijote* its inclusion is not limited to a single episode or incident. Instead the linguistic register of the diabolical permeates both volumes of the work, creating a cumulative effect of powerful parody. Many of the other parodic linguistic registers – such as that of the chivalric romance – employed to describe the protagonist's madness have been taken into account by critics who have demonstrated the polyvalent richness of this text. As every reader knows, Don Quixote's mind is a mass of intertextual confusion. This chapter explores the intertextuality between this novel and contemporaneous popular manuals of demonology, written in the vernacular and thus providing a register of specifically Spanish terminology being used in the Golden Age to describe the phenomena of apparitions, diabolical pranks, demonic possession, and exorcism. Throughout the book Don Quixote senses that he is being followed and persecuted, and he speaks of this sensation in specifically demonological terms. Cervantes utilizes the linguistic register of diabolical mysteries as one of multiple narrative techniques which lend verisimilitude to Don Quixote's madness. But he also allows his character to act as his own exorcist, even reciting·the words of the *Rituale Romanum*, 'fugite, partes adversae!' By granting this sort of autonomy to his character, Cervantes contributes both to the rise of the autonomous early modern character in general and to the birth of the novel.

It may be argued today that demonic possession is a 'myth.' Some would even use this word in both the technical and nontechnical senses of the term. But diabolical possession is also connected quite closely to other 'myths,' on both the micro- and macrolevels, of human religious life. On the microlevel, the great drama of the psychomachy has been one of the central myths – again defined technically as foundational stories or master narratives, without implication of falsehood – of the Christian religion. Exorcism may be seen (as it was repeatedly in the early modern period) as simply an extreme case of the normal struggle between God and Satan for the soul of every Christian. On the macrolevel, the exorcism 'myth' or narrative has also been connected by scholars such as Stuart Clark to the futurizing 'myths' of early modern Christian eschatology:

> Only demoniacs could serve in this way as symbols of the inner dynamic of Christian history. In an age accustomed to polarize the moral categories on which this history ultimately rested, possession and its treatment were the most vivid possible demonstration of the relative strengths of good and evil in the world ... At two moments in time Christ and the devil came into direct confrontation and on both occasions demoniacs were, in effect, the battleground. The natural expectation was that the pattern established in the gospels would be repeated in the 'last days', that possessions would multiply both as a sign of Christ's impending arrival and as an appropriate focus for the apocalyptic events that were due to follow.[46]

Exorcism did, in fact, create an arena where religious and cultural values and beliefs – about such diverse topics as the individual soul or the end of the world – could be tested, affirmed, or denied. Nowhere was this truer than in the realm of literature.

Recognizing (and re-cognizing) another age's preoccupations requires a certain respect for them. The rituals, beliefs, and signs of exorcism may not carry today the stability they sometimes embodied for early modern readers, but the fact that early modern writers incorporated them into their literature – in many different and sometimes conflicting generic variations – confirms that in their controversial historical context, these rituals, beliefs, and signs were often still effective purveyors of artistic *and* religious tension, emotion, and power.

Chapter One

Demoniacs in the Drama: Theatricalities of Comic Possession and the Exorcism of the Body Politic

I begin my study of exorcism in literature with a chapter on comic drama, where – I will argue – the greatest emphasis falls on the theologeme of exorcism as a synecdoche for curing the body politic. Just as early modern people could feel threatened by demons, so by extension entire societies could feel threatened by epidemics of demonic possession. Just as exorcism was a way of restoring the equilibrium of the internally coherent self in the private sphere, so in the public sphere exorcism on the stage could function as a therapeutic restoration of the spiritual equilibrium of an entire society. Ernst Kantorowicz has demonstrated that, during this period, the king's body was seen as a synecdoche for the body politic.[1] So too the demoniac's body (particularly, as we shall see, in the cases of *El hechizado por fuerza* and *The Phoenix*, when the demoniac or exorcist *is* the king himself) was considered to be the locus of supernatural forces which, if they disturbed this one individual, were bound to menace the larger society of which this individual was a representative.

The recent interest of some New Historicists in the theatricality of exorcism and its comic treatments in stage plays has led to a number of articles about exorcism in English Renaissance comedies. There is a reason why New Historicists have focused on English Renaissance comic drama, for the reality is that there is more material available for study in this genre and its first cousin, the Spanish *comedia*, than in all the other genres together. This wealth of material makes this chapter the perfect place for generating a Proppian paradigm for the component theologemes of literary exorcism in general. As with Propp's 'functions,' not every theologeme appears in every comic play, nor does every theologeme appear in every genre, as we will see later when we extend this paradigm to encompass the other genres as well. But these theologemes are the structural 'building blocks' from which literary treatments of exorcism are constructed.

Thus my purpose in this chapter is twofold: to discuss demonic possession and exorcism in the genre of comic drama, and to draw from that discussion a set of theologemes which will be transferable (in various permutations) to discussions of other genres. For now, a set of eleven theologemes will help us to see the components of the exorcism ritual (I refer the reader to my 'Paradigm of Theologemes for Literary Exorcism,' p. xxi):

1 The demon's entrance into the body
2 Symptoms of possession
3 Demonic polyglossia
4 The coach
5 The exorcist
6 The lovers' ruse
7 The (mock) exorcism
8 Binding the body and other exorcistic procedures
9 Relics, holy water, and other 'props'
10 The successful exorcism
11 Exorcism as a synecdoche for curing the body politic.

This set of theologemes was generated from many comic dramas containing episodes of demonic possession or exorcism, including (among others) Alonso de la Vega's *La duquesa de la rosa*, Jonson's *The Devil is an Ass* and *Volpone*, Ruggle's *Ignoramus*, Shakespeare's *Twelfth Night* and *Comedy of Errors*, Timoneda's *Los menemnos*, the anonymous *The Bugbears*, Shadwell's *The Lancashire Witches and Tegue o Divelly the Irish-Priest*, Middleton's *The Phoenix*, Zamora's *El hechizado por fuerza*, and the play *El pleyto que tuvo el diablo con el cura de Madrilejos* by Vélez de Guevara, Mira de Amescua, and Rojas Zorrilla. Although these are all comic dramas, the set of theologemes generated by these examples will be transferable to other genres once it undergoes certain permutations. For example, the theologemes of the mock exorcism, the fraudulent coach, or the lovers' ruse are emphasized more often in humorous genres such as the romance and the interlude, while the theologemes of the demon's entrance into the body, the symptoms of possession, and the successful exorcism may be emphasized in more serious genres such as tragedy and hagiography.

While many of these theologemes or elements of exorcism are corroborated by historical accounts of actual dispossessions, it is essential when analysing literature to pay closer attention to literary accounts than to historical ones. What interests us here is precisely the process of selection that occurs when each author draws from the historical materials available and picks or chooses only those elements which seem worth emphasizing. Just as the author chose to use exorcism instead of, say, kidnapping or some other 'building block' to move the plot along, so those theologemes which will advance the drama in the desired direction are selected from the exorcistic paradigm. Let us examine each of these theologemes in turn, illustrating each element of the exorcism ritual with a play or plays which emphasize that element in particular.

The Demon Enters the Body: Alonso de la Vega's *La duquesa de la rosa*

The theologeme of the demon's entrance into the early modern body is often marked by fear, watchful defensiveness, and the failure of an attempt to prevent the demon from entering a new human habitation. Many early modern people tried vigilantly to guard against succumbing to demonic penetration by being careful about what they ate, about who looked at them or had an opportunity to curse them, and – most importantly – about guarding against specific sins which were thought to give demons greater opportunity for entrance into the human soul. We shall analyse this theologeme in a comical literary context in order to understand just how specific the demonological knowledge of even uneducated early modern people was. We must keep in mind that the demon's entrance into the body, although it could be portrayed comically on the stage in order to generate a few laughs, was often viewed in the 'real' world with terror or at least great alarm.

The comic drama which demonstrates most playfully the demon's entrance into the body is Alonso de la Vega's *La duquesa de la rosa* (*The Duchess of the Rose*) (1560–3). This piece was written by a Sevillian actor of Lope de Rueda's company, and it is written in prose, according to the manner of Rueda. It was inspired by Matteo Bandello's novella *Amore di Don Giovanni di Mendozza e della Duchessa di Savoja*,[2] as was the seventh *patraña* of Juan de Timoneda.[3] The titular character is a princess who is saved from her brutal husband by a paladin, Dulcelirio. The playwright converts the historical figures (nobles from the houses of Savoy and Mendoza) into heroes from the more distant past with names derived from the tradition of the *romance*.

At the play's opening, we discover that the princess of Denmark has been given in marriage to the Duke of the Rose. Before her marriage, however, she had been courted by the Castilian prince Dulcelirio. She had given him a ring as a farewell gift. After her marriage, her steward (major-domo) lusts after her, but she rejects his advances. The major-domo concocts a scheme to avenge his wounded pride: he hides his brother in the duchess's bedchamber. He proceeds to show the duke how a strange man has entered his wife's bedroom, convincing him that she is an adulteress. The duke stabs the brother and throws his wife into prison. Within three months, she must find a champion who will enter combat with the major-domo to determine her guilt or innocence. The allegorical figures Truth, Consolation, and Remedy enter her jail cell and suggest that she send a message to Dulcelirio. At first he refuses the request, but then he arrives on the scene disguised as a monk to hear her last confession and decide for himself whether she is innocent (this motif of a ruler disguised as a monk to learn the secrets of his subjects also appears in Shakespeare's *Measure for Measure*). Her funeral pyre, on which she is to be burned alive, has been prepared. But at the last moment Dulcelirio presents himself as her champion and kills the major-domo in armed combat. A sudden illness comes upon the duke, who dies conveniently so that the hero and heroine may wed each other. The ring serves as a token of identity and a remembrance of their past love.

The demonic possession trope appears in the secondary plot as pure fun in its light, comic treatment. The major-domo sends some jellied preserves to his brother via a simpleton, Thomé Sanctos. In an attempt to prevent the simpleton from eating the preserves on the way, the major-domo tells him that the preserves are demon-possessed and that he will die if he eats them. Thomé sets out on his journey and encounters a page, and both of them are tempted to eat the preserves. They give in to temptation and then believe they are demon-possessed and dying. The major-domo finds them in this state and discovers what has happened. Upon seeing that they have eaten his preserves, he punishes them. The simpleton and the page ultimately receive blows in a typical *entremés*-like ending designed to please the crowd.

A closer look at this episode will reward us with a specialist's knowledge of early modern jokes about how demons could enter bodies. The major-domo explains that the preserves are inhabited by demons, a statement to which the simpleton reacts in fear. In fact, he voices a garbled version of 'Satan, avoid,' a command which is central to the exorcism ritual:

MAYORDOMO: Conseruas son espiritos.

THOMÉ: Mas par dios? y es cosa de morir?

MAYORDOMO: Mira que si llegas a ellas luego te moriras.

THOMÉ: *Tirte a fuera*, paño espritado, no seas diabro que me engañes.

(MAJORDOMO: Preserves are spirits.

THOMÉ: But by God? and is it a fatal thing?

MAJORDOMO: Look, if you go near them, then you will die.

THOMÉ: Throw yourself out, spirit-possessed cloth,[4] that you not be a devil who deceives me.)[5]

When he encounters the page on the road, Thomé convinces him that the preserves are in fact demon possessed by pointing out how they seem to jump about of their own volition:

THOMÉ: Aua que son espritos, aua que bullen: no ves como saltan?
PAGE: Que no son: ven acá, quies que nos espritemos los dos?

(THOMÉ: Look, they are spirits; look, they jump: don't you see how they leap?
PAGE: They are not: come here, do you want the two of us to bespirit ourselves?)[6]

Here we see how the page tempts the simpleton to eat the preserves, challenging him to test the theory that the preserves are demon-possessed by experiencing their effects for himself. He accepts the challenge, eats the preserves, and immediately suspects that he is possessed. In fact, he cries, the bells might as well already be tolling for his death:

THOMÉ: Bien, a tu cargo vaya: sus, encomiendo me a dios, ya me voy espritado, ya me muero, ya pueden tocar a mí los badajos, din dan, din dan, ha que me toma, ha que me fino.
PAGE: Tente, tente, qué descolorido que te has parado!
THOMÉ: Mas par dios.
PAGE: Cómo estás?
THOMÉ: Espritado dulce.
PAGE: Pues aguarda que yo me quiero espritar.
THOMÉ: No hagas, aua que te moriras.
PAGE: No haré.
THOMÉ: A qué espritazo tan grande tomas! ... A que te paras amarillo, ya te descoloras!
PAGE: Ha que me toma, ha que me muero.

(THOMÉ: Well, go to your charge: ay, I commend myself to God, already I go bespirited, already I die, already the bell clappers can ring for me, ding dong, ding dong, ay! that it takes me, ay! that I end myself.
PAGE: Hold on, hold on, how discoloured you have become!
THOMÉ: But by God.
PAGE: How are you?
THOMÉ: Sweetly bespirited.
PAGE: Well wait, for I want to bespirit myself.
THOMÉ: Don't do it, for you will die.
PAGE: I will not do it.

THOMÉ: What a great bespiriting you take! For you become yellow, already you discolour yourself!

PAGE: Ay, that it takes me, ay, that I die.)[7]

This episode rehearses an oft-repeated medieval tradition in which a demon entered the body of a nun when she ate a head of lettuce without blessing it first. The first account of this case appears to be the one by Gregory the Great. It is included in the fourth chapter of the first book of Gregory's First Dialogue:

> One day a nun of this same convent, on entering the garden, found some lettuce there which appealed to her taste. Forgetting to say the customary blessing, she began to eat of it greedily. Immediately the Devil threw her to the ground in a fit of pain. The other nuns, seeing her in agony, quickly sent word to Abbot Equitius to come with all speed and help them with his prayers. As soon as the holy man entered the garden, the Devil, using the nun's voice, began to justify himself. 'I haven't done anything!' he kept shouting. 'I haven't done anything! I was sitting here on the lettuce when she came and ate me!'[8]

Bodily processes such as sex and eating are often associated with comic treatments of demonic possession because they emphasize the low bodily humour of the carnivalesque world.[9]

These bodily processes are not always treated comically, however; sometimes women's bodies in particular become demonized through double association with sexual and diabolical activity. The Black Queen's Pawn in Thomas Middleton's *A Game at Chess* (a play written in the historical context of the Spanish match) decries the Black Bishop's Pawn for having impregnated a young woman and then spread the rumour that she was really demon possessed:

> Whose niece was she you poisoned with child, twice,
> Then gave her out possessed with a foul spirit
> When 'twas indeed your bastard?[10]

Peter Dinzelbacher has studied the historical associations of pregnancy with demonic possession in *Heilige oder Hexen?*[11] This association of demonic possession with pregnancy is repeatedly invoked by Shakespeare, as for example in *Richard III*. Demonic associations resonate in the deformity of Richard, described in terms of paternity by an incubus devil in the lines of Queen Margaret:

> Thou elvish-mark'd, abortive, rooting hog!
> Thou that was seal'd in thy nativity
> The slave of nature and the son of hell![12]

We can better understand the concept of the succubus devil through the Elizabethan notion that outer deformity must indicate moral depravity – in this case, on the part of the mother. Another reference in another play to Richard as a monster again confirms his demonic paternity. In *3 Henry VI* this birth of Richard, duke of Gloucester, is described. An owl shrieked, and his mother bore

> To wit an indigest deformed lump,
> Not like the fruit of such a goodly tree.[13]

Likewise, Jacqueline E.M. Latham, in an article on *The Tempest*, discusses Caliban's demonic paternity through the intercourse of his mother, Sycorax, with an incubus.[14] All of these examples show how the sexual penetration of the body was associated with spiritual penetration by a demon.

In both comic and not-so-comic contexts, the entrance of the demon into the body was a recurrent trope exploited by early modern dramatists. The fear exploited by this dramatic commonplace was real: that a demon could invade you, take over your personality completely, and rob you of all sensation and choice of action. This fear was particularly acute when it was associated with the human body. Just as an exorcist could drive a demon into a single hair, a toe, or some other extremity, so too were the various orifices of the (particularly female) body seen as potential points of entrance for spirits: 'The twin emphases of transgressive ecstacy and internal union ... centering as they do around issues of physical access and egress, portray the surface of the female mystic's body as frangible, breachable, in short, as *open*.'[15] A female saint might invite the divine penetration of mystical union, but these same openings or breaches of the body which could harbour the Holy Spirit had to be guarded with great vigilance to keep the ever-menacing demons at bay.

Symptoms of Possession: Jonson's *The Devil is an Ass*

The theatre-going public attending a performance of comic drama may have considered possession to manifest both supernatural *and* theatrical aspects, but in either case, as Stephen Greenblatt observes, they would have recognized 'the types of cries appropriate to the occasion, the expected violent contortions, the "decorum" ... of the trance state.'[16] The purpose of this section is to describe the symptoms of an attack of demonic possession as playwrights of this period conceived them.

The raw material of real-life cases upon which these playwrights drew was undoubtedly very rich. The demoniac Will Sommers's symptoms were repeated many times in the exorcist John Darrell's *Apologie*: he stared with his eyes, his face and his mouth were fearfully distorted, his head was turned directly backward, and his neck doubled under him.[17] John Deacon and John Walker describe his behaviour in similar terms: 'His bodie doubled, his head betweene his legges, suddenly plucked round, like a round browne loafe: he was cast up like a ball from the bed.'[18] Reginald Scot likewise describes a demon's power over a young female victim:

> But he [the demon] would not speake, but rored and cried mightilie ... striuing, and gnashing of teeth; and otherwhile with *mowing*, and other terrible countenances ... [the demon] was so strong in the maid, that foure men could scarse hold hir downe ...[19]

Other symptoms of possession included abhorring relics, prayers, and holy water; crying without knowing why; speaking incessantly and senselessly; being deprived of the senses; tearing the hair; foaming at the mouth; feeling as if insects, snakes, or frogs were moving through the body; having a cold or burning gust rush through the entrails; sensing something like wool in the stomach or throat, but being unable to vomit it up; and feeling that the heart was being bitten by snakes or dogs.[20]

This raw material proved completely suitable for a comic dramatist like Ben Jonson, whose unforgettable fake demoniac speaks in rhyme to parody the theatre of the time. In Jonson's *The Devil is an Ass*, Fitzdottrel feigns demonic possession – with a little coaching from Meercraft and Everill – in order to recover his lost estate. The emphasis here is on the symptoms of possession as exemplified in the recent performance of an historical personage, John Smith, a thirteen-year-old boy whom King James himself had exposed as a fake:[21]

> Sir, be confident;
> 'Tis no hard thing t' outdo the devil in:
> A boy o' thirteen year old made him an ass
> But t'other day.[22]

The symptoms of demonic possession which Pug suggests to Fitzdottrel in the play are belly swelling, eyes turning, mouth foaming, face staring, teeth gnashing, limbs beating, loud laughing, and the feigning of multiple voices.[23] These and similar symptoms had been documented earlier by John Darrell's pamphlets, which Jonson specifically satirizes:

> It is the easiest thing, sir, to be done.
> As plaine as fizzling: roll but wi' your eyes,

And foame at th' mouth. A little castle-soap
Will do 't, to rub your lips: and then a nutshell,
With toe and touchwood in it to spit fire.
Did you ne'er read, sir, little Darrel's tricks,
With the boy o' Burton, and the seven in Lancashire,
Somers at Nottingham? All these do teach it.[24]

Clearly the widely circulated pamphlet accounts of the symptoms displayed by demoniacs enabled any charlatan or amateur actor to imitate the telltale signs of demonic inhabitation. Later Fitzdottrel, stricken by a qualm of conscience, admits to having followed his coaches' instructions for counterfeiting. He even produces his props, including a pair of bellows, a false belly, and a mouse that was to have come forth from his throat.

Through his chosen vehicle of comic drama Jonson satirizes both John Smith and John Darrell, whom he considered to be frauds, as well as the credulity of his fellow Englishmen for believing the antics of these men and their 'demoniac' pupils or accomplices.[25] This credulity is exemplified in the character of the Justice of the Peace, Sir Paul Eitherside, who accepts Fitzdottrel's performance unquestioningly. Various historical figures have been suggested as Jonson's model for this character (and thus, the butt of his most vicious satire), including Lord Chief Justice Edward Coke,[26] Lord Chief Justice Popham,[27] Sir Humphrey Winch (Justice of the Common Pleas), and Seargeant Randal Crew.[28] Various interpretations of this satire have also been suggested in light of Jonson's situation with regard to his patron. Scholars viewing the same evidence have come to the diametrically opposite conclusions that Jonson was insulting King James I[29] or that he was actually offering him a compliment.[30] Jonson was probably poking fun at a panoply of current events in a wide ranging satire which defies reduction to any one level of meaning. John D. Cox offers the most even-handed recent assessment of the play: 'Jonson's explicit satire of popular tradition coexists with his debt to it in *Devil Is an Ass*, and nothing in the play challenges the real existence of devils or their association with human evil.'[31]

This reading of the play, which honours its complexity, seems even more valid when we consider that Jonson added a remarkable twist to his satire. This deft touch prevented his audience (and should prevent modern critics as well) from labelling him too quickly as a sceptic vis-à-vis demonology: he included Satan and Pug, a junior demon, in his cast of characters. The significant irony here is that the human characters concoct their hoax about demonic possession without any help from the demon assigned to them by Satan. Reed points out the further irony that Pug engages in a performance as a 'Tom o' Bedlam' or madman at one point in the play when he is trying to escape punishment for stealing a cutpurse's clothes.[32] The result is a demon pretending to be a madman in a play about a man pretending to be demon-possessed.

Jonson has the last laugh in this comedy, as his audience is left with the star-tling message that demons exist, but human beings remain unaware of their pres-ence because they are corrupt enough to create their own ruin; in effect, they are truly possessed by demonic impulses. Jonson's treatment of the possession phe-nomenon is far too complex to be reduced to mere satire, just as his attitude toward exorcism is too complicated to be dismissed as only that of a sceptic. In any event, his incorporation of the symptoms of possession into his drama for comic effect illustrates this theologeme of exorcism in early modern literature.

Demonic Polyglossia: Ruggle's *Ignoramus*[33]

In addition to physical symptoms, the state of demonic possession is character-ized either by extraordinary speech or extraordinary absence of speech. These two possibilities are explained in Reginald Scot's *Discourse upon divels and spirits* as the different conditions resulting from inhabitation by two different kinds of demons:

> And if it be a subterrene diuell, it doth writh and bow the possessed, and speaketh by him, using the spirit of the patient as his instrument ... when *Lucifugus* possesseth a man, he maketh him dumbe, and as it were dead: and these be they that are cast out ... onelie by fasting and praier.[34]

The second condition, involving the extraordinary absence of speech, is not altogether unknown in the comical dramatic genre. Thus Troilus speaks of 'a still and dumb-discoursive devil / That tempts most cunningly' in Shakespeare's *Troi-lus and Cressida*.[35] Likewise, in *Gammer Gurton's Needle*, Gammer Gurton and Tib 'sit as still as stones in the street, / As though they had been taken with fairies, or else with some ill sprite.'[36] Other lines of the play bespeak demonic possession, as when Hodge threatens to cut open Gib, the gasping cat: '[I will] see what devil is in her guts.'[37] This line is a fulfilment of an earlier one, where Hodge curses the cat Gib: 'a foul fiend might on her light!'[38] Although they are simply perturbed about the missing needle, Diccon assumes that the silent Gammer Gurton and Tib must be afflicted by a demon: 'What devil aileth Gammer Gurton and Tib her maid to frown?'[39]

More often, however, silence is not the problem in comic drama that features demonic possession. Usually, in fact, the opposite affliction prevails: an abundance of speech, of extraordinary speech (in fact, a parody of speaking in tongues), infuses the comic drama with hilarious vitality. Sometimes this abundance of speech may include prophecy or clairvoyance. Often this demonic proliferation of speech involves multiple foreign languages, to the point that the association of possession with polyglossia becomes a commonplace. We see this symptom in Marston's *The Malcontent*: 'Phew! the devil: let him possess thee; he'll teach thee to speak all languages most readily and strangely.'[40]

This association is developed further in George Ruggle's neo-Latin university play *Ignoramus*, based on Giambattista della Porta's *La Trappolaria*.[41] Performed before King James I at Cambridge in March 1615, this five-hour play drew an audience of 2,000 to Trinity College. This performance is perhaps one of the best documented to have occurred in Jacobean England; we even have the report of King James's reactions to the play from a contemporary witness: 'his maiestie was much delighted with ye Playe and laughed exceedingly and offentymes with his handes and by wordes applauded it.'[42] John Chamberlain reported in a letter that King James found it impossible to forget the play after this performance and, in fact, that he returned to Royston, a town near Cambridge, in May of the same year for an encore:

> The King went again to Cambrige to see the play *Ignoramus* which hath so netled the Lawiers that they are almost out of all patience, and the Lord Chiefe Justice [Coke] both openly at the Kings Bench and divers other places hath galled and glaunced at schollers with much bitternes, and there be divers ynne of court men have made rimes and ballades against them, which they have aunswered sharply enough ...[43]

Evidently the play had been not merely a college production, but a political event which came to represent the whole university; students at its major rival, Oxford, also soon produced a torrent of satirical ballads about the play.

What were all the lawyers, including Lord Chief Justice Coke, so upset about?[44] And why the proliferation of ballads (clear adaptations of the play's subject which have survived to this day) against the legal establishment?[45] The play *Ignoramus* presents the story of the lovers Antonius, whose father is Theodorus, and Rosabella, whose custodian is Torcol (a pander). Theodorus sends Antonius from Bordeaux to London to bring back the rest of his family, whom he has not seen in nearly twenty years: his mother Dorothea, his twin brother Antoninus, and his stepsister Catherina (his remaining stepsister has been lost during childhood). Antonius, however, has other plans: with the help of his father's servant, Trico, he escapes from the ship bound for London. His purpose in escaping is to prevent the pander Torcol from giving his love Rosabella in marriage to Ignoramus, an English lawyer who speaks only in silly legal jargon with copious borrowing from Anglo-Norman French. Antonius and Trico enlist the help of Cupes and Friar Cola to trick the pander and Ignoramus. Following the idea of Polla,

Cupes's wife, they convince other characters that Ignoramus is really possessed by a demon and in need of exorcism. During the exorcism ritual Ignoramus continues to pour forth jargon, so that each time he uses a legal phrase, the 'exorcists' deliberately mistake it for the name of a familiar demon. Finally the 'exorcists' pronounce him incurable and remove him to a monastery where he will be tortured with fire. Antonius's long-lost family arrives from London, and they end up helping him to achieve his goal: they recognize that Rosabella is really his long-lost adopted sister, who had been promised to him in marriage so many years ago. The good servant Trico is rewarded, and Ignoramus is left in disgrace.

The main point of interest for us here is that the other characters are persuaded that Ignoramus is demon-possessed because of his elaborately fantastical language. They mistake his legal phrases for the names of demons who possess him. Some examples of this ridiculous language and its deliberate misapprehension are the following exchanges:

> IGNORAMUS: Descedite vos, nebulones ut estis, cum vestra *Riota & Rowta*.
> COLA: Duplex Daemon, *Riota & Rowta* ...

> IGNORAMUS: Et praeter juncturam, si maritasset me, habuisset *Francum Bancum*.
> COLA: Profuge sis *Francum Bancum*, separa te *Francum Bancum* ...

> IGNORAMUS: Ignis ardeat vos: si dagarias capio, rumpam calvas coronas vestras.
> COLA: Conjuro te, prodi dagarias.[46]

These lines were rendered into English by Robert Codrington in the generation after Ruggle:

> IGNORAMUS: Be you gone like two Knaves as you are, what a foul *Riota*, what a *Rowta* do you make here?
> COLA: Two Divels, *Riota*, and *Rowta* ...

> IGNORAMUS: And besides her Joynture, If she had married me, she had *Francum Bancum* too.
> COLA: Be gone *Francum Bancum*; Separate thy self from her *Francum Bancum* ...

> IGNORAMUS: The fire consume you all. *Si dagarias capio rumpam calveo coronas vestras*; If I take my Daggers once, I will break both your bald crowns in an instant.
> COLA: *Dagarias*, I conjure you to come forth *Dagarias*.[47]

From these snippets of the exorcism scene, we can see that the main butts of the play's satire are the Jesuits conducting exorcisms and the lawyers babbling legalese jargon. Other objects of satire were the Cambridge deputy recorder, Francis Brackyn, and a foreigner named Schioppius who had attacked King James I in writing. The thrust of the play is that all of these entities are associated with the devil, and university audiences at the time were frustrated enough with lawyers to seize upon this particular association and make much of it. Playwrights and poets continued to be suspicious of lawyers and other pedants in ensuing years, as is evidenced by the success of the various progeny of this play, such as Samuel Butler's satirical poem *Hudibras* (which also incorporates a 'demon'-haunted pedant).[48] The fact that the lawyers' characteristic language was being widely compared to one of the symptoms of demonic possession shows that people were used to seeing demoniacs and could use their performances as a point of reference, especially for recognizing demonic polyglossia.

Polyglossia is one of those ambiguous indicators of demonic possession which can be (and was, in the early modern period) viewed either positively or negatively, depending on one's perspective. The ability to speak multiple languages was often viewed as an asset, and in this sense polyglossia illustrates the potential for demonic possession to enhance the social stature or intellectual ability of the early modern person. However, it is the coherence or integration of this self which polyglossia also threatens, for in its evocation of the Tower of Babel and the confusion resulting from a proliferation of different languages, polyglossia threatens the ability of the self to signify or receive and interpret signals in any meaningful way.[49] Polyglossia threatens to erupt into linguistic chaos, and in this sense it is one of the most terrifying theologemes to appear in the paradigm of literary exorcism. By threatening to undermine the system of signs on which literature itself must necessarily depend,[50] polyglossia is the theologeme which offers at the same time the greatest threat and the greatest enhancement to the early modern notion of the coherent self.

The Coach: Jonson's *Volpone*

The next theologeme we need to consider in the paradigm of early modern literary exorcism is the figure of the coach who instructs a fake demoniac in the particulars of his performance. Twenty years ago, Stephen Greenblatt coined the now-famous term 'self-fashioning.'[51] The 'coach' figure in the exorcism ritual at once fashions himself and is a fashioner of other selves, a designer of identities who provides instruction in the art of feigning demonic possession. This figure is particularly prominent in the comic drama, where tricksters, charlatans, and mountebanks proliferate.

The presence of the figure of the coach, of course, presupposes a scenario where the demonic possession and exorcism are feigned or staged. This scenario is by no means universal; many demonic possessions in history were experienced and witnessed as real, not feigned. In literature, likewise, many demonic possessions and exorcisms were narrated or enacted as real, not staged. Feigned possessions and exorcisms did occur, but the very presence of the counterfeit presupposes the prior existence of the genuine article. The figure of the coach is one theologeme that is absent from literary exorcism as often as it is present.

As Thomas Lodge describes him, the coach was the instructor of 'that Demoniack, who when he would, could counterfeit to beé dead, faine blindnesse, seéme lame, or resemble a man troubled with the dropsie.'[52] The best example of the coach figure is Ben Jonson's Machiavellian *Volpone*. The titular character is a Venetian charlatan whose name means 'the fox,' and in fact Jonson structures his play around an Aesopian fable about the fox that was repeated (and Christianized) in medieval bestiaries.[53] The fable goes something like this: to catch his prey, the fox pretends to be dead and smears his body with red clay to resemble blood. Scavenger birds, believing him to be dead, circle and descend upon him, thus coming within his reach; the fox then catches the birds and devours them instead. Jonson's Volpone reenacts this fable when he pretends to be wealthy, dying, and childless as part of a greedy scheme. With the help of his parasite Mosca (the Fly), he attracts the scavengers (bounty hunters) Voltore (the Vulture), Corvino (the Raven), and Corbaccio (the Crow), who respectively promise to give him legal aid, a wife to borrow, and the inheritance formerly promised to a son if he will name them as his beneficiaries. Like the fox, Volpone then pretends to die. But he overreaches himself in leaving his property to Mosca, and the whole plan backfires as the enraged suitors seek 'justice.' Voltore the lawyer takes the matter to court, where Mosca turns upon his master and seeks to inherit his money in earnest. Volpone is forced to discredit Voltore and then to reveal his identity. After admitting that he is not dead after all, he must receive punishment.

The exorcism scene takes place at the point when Volpone seeks to discredit Voltore by seizing upon an accusation already made by one of the other angry suitors, Corvino, who exclaims that Voltore must be demon-possessed.[54] Volpone immediately fixates on this idea, seeing its potential usefulness to his purpose. If he can only show Voltore to be a demoniac, then the court will perhaps ignore his claims upon the estate. (This plan would only work if Mosca remained loyal, which in fact he does not, but it is Volpone's last hope.) Volpone acts as a coach in telling Voltore how to perform the part of a demoniac, convincing him that it is in his own best interest to do so. Then he proceeds to interpret the performance for the onlookers, in this case the Avocatori (Advocates) and the other suitors, in a way designed to convince them that they are witnessing an exorcism as well.

As we have stated, Volpone pursues an idea originally voiced by Corvino, who exclaims of Voltore that 'he is possessed' and 'the devil has entered him!'[55] Corvino is attempting to discredit Voltore so that his own claim on the estate will become more viable: he asks the Avocatori to 'credit nothing, the false spirit hath writ: / It cannot be, but he is possessed, grave fathers.'[56] Later he repeats:

Grave fathers, he is possessed; again, I say,
Possessed: nay, if there be possession,
And obsession, he has both.[57]

Volpone seizes upon this idea by revealing his identity to Voltore, showing him that he is not dead after all, and convincing him to play along with a little charade:

VOLPONE: Sir, you may redeem it –
   They said, you were possessed; fall down, and seem so:
   I'll help to make it good.   [*Voltore falls*]
                                   God bless the man!
   [*Aside*] Stop your wind hard, and swell – See, see, see, see!
   He vomits crooked pins! his eyes are set,
   Like a dead hare's, hung in a poulter's shop!
   His mouth's running away! do you see, signior?
   Now, 'tis in his belly.
   CORVINO: Ay, the devil!
VOLPONE: Now, in his throat.
   CORVINO: Ay, I perceive it plain.
VOLPONE: 'Twill out, 'twill out; stand clear. See, where it flies! In shape of a blue
   toad, with a bat's wings! Do you not see it, sir?
CORBACCIO: What? I think I do.
CORVINO: 'Tis too manifest.
VOLPONE: Look! he comes t'himself!
VOLTORE: Where am I?
VOLPONE: Take good heart, the worst is past, sir.
   You are dispossessed.[58]

Yumiko Yamada suggests the significance of this scene for the play as a whole by focusing on St Mark, the tutelary saint of Venice who banishes Plutus, the mock saint of the city.[59] I would like to suggest, however, that the latent potential of this critical insight for a political interpretation of exorcism in the play remains unexplored. A political interpretation of the play rests upon the assumption that Volpone and Mosca represent a threat to the social order, one which must be expelled or 'exorcized' through the vehicle of comic drama:

Final disintegration threatens when the fourth Avocatore moves to match Mosca with his daughter; but within moments Venetian order is resumed with the judicial cry 'Disrobe that parasite!' The conventional comic servant discarding his master's robes becomes the symbol of Venice restored to its 'honoured fathers' – at least for the time being.[60]

This reading begins to sound as if it might fit well with our last theologeme, the exorcism as a synecdoche for curing the body politic.

Philip Brockbank and others have suggested a political interpretation of the play as a whole, but they have neglected to integrate the exorcism scene into this reading. The best political reading I have found is a recent one by James Tulip:

> Jonson's *Volpone* is what may be termed a Respublica play, having resonances and allusions to this strong line of plays dramatising the usurpation of the State ... Jonson in the charged atmosphere of the context of the Gunpowder Plot of November 1605 dared to present a subject of this kind[61] ... Jonson in *Volpone* was attempting by his farce to purge the hysteria in London and England following the [Gunpowder] Plot and to deflect or deflate the English paranoia regarding this threat to the State ...[62]

'Purge the hysteria,' 'deflect or deflate the ... paranoia' – these phrases would seem to be synonymous with 'exorcize the body politic.' Tulip does not, however, integrate the exorcism scene into this reading.

The key to such an integration is the statement by the first Avocatore that demonic possession is a metaphor for societal ills: 'These possess wealth, as sick men possess fevers, / Which, trulier, may be said to possess them.'[63] Following this metaphor to its logical consequences, the exorcism scene, appearing as it does at the end of the play, does illustrate the functioning of the last theologeme we shall discuss in this chapter.

Now, ultimately, Volpone's fake exorcism does not work very well, but neither did the efforts of Catholics like Jonson to 'deflect or deflate the ... paranoia' of the English people about the Gunpowder Plot. In fact, English people to the present time celebrate Guy Fawkes's Day with a sort of exorcism ritual, as James Tulip observes: 'Guy Fawkes has entered English folk history as a demonic figure of early winter rituals, the burning of his effigy being as much an exorcism of the encroaching winter as any patriotic recognition of saving the nation.'[64] Tulip even speculates that Jonson was punning on Guy Fawkes's name when he chose for his play the title of *Volpone, or the Fox*. As we shall see later on, it is rituals such as this one – and plays such as *Volpone* – that best serve what I argue to be one of the goals of comic drama: the exorcism of the body politic. But for now, *Volpone* serves to illustrate the theologeme of the coach, one of the components of the exorcism ritual most often emphasized in comic drama.

The Exorcist: Shakespeare's *Twelfth Night*

An especially significant theologeme for the paradigm of literary exorcism is, of course, the figure of the exorcist. In the more serious genres, the exorcist is the great healer, the restorer of the early modern self to tranquil stability. But in comic drama, as we have seen, demonic possession is often feigned, and in these situations, the exorcist is of course a 'quack.' Shakespeare plays upon this association in *All's Well That Ends Well*, when the king of France sees Helena, whom he believes to be dead, and exclaims: 'Is there no exorcist / Beguiles the truer office of mine eyes?'[65] There are many different variations on this scenario: the demoniac may be a fake, but the exorcist is in earnest; the demoniac may be convinced (or the characters around him may be told) that he is really possessed, while the exorcist takes advantage of this credulity, etc. A classic caricature of the exorcist figure may be found in the character of Feste (also known as Sir Topas) in Shakespeare's *Twelfth Night*.

Recent critics have identified the influence of Samuel Harsnett's *The Discovery of the Fraudulent Practices of John Darrell* (1599) on *Twelfth Night*[66] (probably performed before Elizabeth on Twelfth Night of 1601).[67] In this scholarship, Feste is a parody of John Darrell, a Protestant exorcist who was arrested, tried, and condemned by the ecclesiastical officials.[68] Moreover, Malvolio, the alleged demoniac, is a parody of John Darrell as well; like Darrell, Malvolio is called a Puritan and is treated harshly while imprisoned.[69] Stephen Greenblatt observes an evolution in Shakespeare's thinking about exorcism in this play as opposed to *The Comedy of Errors*, a play (to be discussed later in this chapter) in which exorcism had appeared briefly: 'In *Twelfth Night*, written some ten years later, Shakespeare's view of exorcism, though still comic, has darkened. Possession now is ... a fraud, a malicious practical joke played on Malvolio.'[70] Following the basic outlines of a New Historicist interpretation, I will first discuss this practical joke to understand the context in which the exorcist figure emerges.

The point of the joke alludes to one of our other theologemes, the lovers' ruse, in that Malvolio is treated as demonically possessed because he is in love with Olivia. Possession is thus equated with love madness, as we shall see in our discussion of *The Bugbears* in this chapter and again later in chapter 3 with the genres of romance and the interlude. As part of the lively subplot of *Twelfth Night*, Maria, Toby, and Feste lure Malvolio to engage in an absurd performance of madness before Olivia, ostensibly because Malvolio deserves a comeuppance, being 'the dev'l a puritan that he is.'[71] Olivia is convinced of his madness, even though he suffers from no such malady, and the conspirators discuss the hypothetical possibility that 'all the devils of hell ... and Legion himself possessed him' and that 'the fiend speaks within him.'[72] The conspirators also want to test the urine of the 'possessed' to see if it is black, for this was one of the telltale signs of demonic possession: 'Carry his water to th' wise woman.'[73] Other signs of demonic possession are bandied about through the course of the play; for example, like Hamlet, Malvolio appears with his garters crossed. Crossed garters were mentioned specifically in the treatises on exorcism as one of the telltale signs of possession.[74] In what is interpreted as another manifestation of possession, Malvolio becomes angry when the conspirators instruct him to pray. Ironically, his refusal only corroborates their accusations. Then Sir Topas begins to question him, as K.M. Briggs explains, 'to uncover the heresies of the fiend and to see if the patient showed any unnatural knowledge, such as he had not been in a position to acquire.'[75] Malvolio cannot extricate himself by answering questions correctly because Darrell claimed that demoniacs could not be held responsible for the questions they answered – since it was the devil who was really talking. In this vein, Feste asks Malvolio: 'But tell me true, are you not mad indeed, or do you but counterfeit?'[76] The irony, of course, is that no answer he gives can be the 'correct' one.

After the conspirators have amassed suitable 'evidence' for Malvolio's 'possession,' the stage is set for the exorcist to appear. Sir Toby Belch gives instructions for the handling of the 'demoniac,' ordering that he be placed in a dark room and bound. Feste then pretends to be the exorcist Sir Topas,[77] a Calvinist minister, and he comments on the role which he is instructed to play: 'I would I were the first that ever dissembled in such a gown.'[78] From this comment, we see that the exorcist's costume is one of his distinguishing features; as for the topical reference, he probably alludes to exorcists such as Darrell (whom many believed to be fraudulent) running rampant in England at the time. The counterfeiting of this fraudulent exorcist becomes another of his salient features in this literary portrait as Sir Toby, speaking to Maria, compliments Feste: 'The knave counterfeits well; a good knave.'[79] To counterfeit well, the exorcist must know what jargon to use; in creating this scene, Shakespeare may have remembered John Darrell's exorcisms of Nicholas Starkey's children, as described in his *True Narration* (1600), in which we find the words 'bible bable ... prittle prattle.'[80] Shakespeare borrowed these words of the children for his bogus exorcist Feste, acting as Sir Topas, who urges Malvolio to leave his 'vain bibble-babble.'[81] Acting well in his function, Feste goes on to conduct staged exorcisms, replete with ritualistic language: 'Out, hyperbolical fiend, how vexest thou this man!'[82] He defies Satan in the manner of the self-righteous exorcists: 'Fie, thou dishonest Sathan! I call thee by the most modest terms, for I am one of those gentle ones that will use the devil himself with courtesy.'[83] Presumably, the 'gentleness' and 'courtesy' mean he will refrain from the harsher whipping sometimes used upon the demoniacs, although these words are extremely ironic, considering how cruelly Malvolio is treated by the conspirators. Schleiner thinks that both 'references to gentleness parody Darrell, since they allude to his refusal to deal harshly with the subjects of his exorcism, particularly Sommers.'[84] Finally Feste sings a song at the end of the scene which contains the words, 'adieu, goodman devil,' presumably to signal the departure of the demon and thus, the end of the exorcism. In the same song, he says to Malvolio: 'I am gone, sir and anon, sir, / I'll be with you again.'[85] Hamilton has noticed that these words echo the usual message of devils departing from demoniacs and gives George More and John Darrell (particularly his *True Narration*) as specific sources.[86]

The character Feste/Sir Topas displays many of the qualities inherent in any fully realized portrait (or mock portrait) of the exorcist figure. He dresses as an exorcist and uses ritualistic language. Since the comic genre is partial to fake exorcists instead of real ones, this representative exorcist figure counterfeits exceedingly well. He knows all the right jargon to use, even to the point of singing a song about the demon's departure. He is also self-righteous in his attitude toward the demoniac, even boasting of 'gentleness' and 'courtesy' where clearly there are none. He speaks authoritatively, defying the demon and commanding him to depart. Finally, to show his control of the situation, he bids the devil goodbye and signals that the exorcism has ended. The qualities he exemplifies are at least the broad brush strokes in the portrait of an (in this case, fake) exorcist figure. When he appears in less comically cynical contexts, this is the figure who offers the greatest hope to the disintegrated people of the early modern period – hope that they might someday be restored to spiritual peace and sanity.

The Lovers' Ruse: The *Bugbears*

Another theologeme commonly found in portrayals of exorcism in literature, especially in the genre of comic drama, is that of the lovers' ruse. This theologeme may be defined as either two lovers' appropriation of exorcistic language or their performance of the roles of demoniac and exorcist. This theologeme, like prophecy or poetic furor, demonstrates another situation in which 'possession' is seen as something that is positive or even desirable. The highly charged erotic atmosphere of plays about both demonic possession and romantic love provides a space for exploration of the possibility of being 'possessed' completely by one's lover.

The decision to include this topos as an actual theologeme in the paradigm of literary exorcism is a debatable one. It occurs so frequently, and in so many genres, that – while it would probably not be found in a paradigm for historical exorcism – this theologeme would seem to take a rightful place in the paradigm for literary exorcism. This theologeme appears in the genre of romance, as we shall see in the chapter on romance and hagiography; in drastically altered form, it may even appear in such genres as the closet drama or the *acción en prosa*. In such cases all humour is removed from the theologeme, which then becomes a very serious equation of demonic possession with love madness, of spiritual with sexual penetration. Even though it appears in radically altered form, the theologeme is still recognizable then as the metaphor of a lover who 'possesses' the beloved. This topos appears more frequently in comic drama than in other genres, however, because it is often a humorous trick played upon the older generation by a pair of young lovers. These young characters pretend to be possessed by demons when they are really possessed by love. We shall explore the basic outlines of this theologeme as it appears in the comedy *The Bugbears*.

The Bugbears was probably written by John Jefferay at some point between 1563 and 1570. It is an adaptation of Anton Francesco Grazzini's *La Spiritata* (1561).[87] Jefferay took a play which was already full of demonology and adapted it to include even more of the same: after borrowing fifteen demons' names from Grazzini, he added fifty-three more, and he also added two charms (of unknown origin) and parts of three charms (which scholars have traced back to Weyer's *De praestigiis daemonum*).[88] Of even more significance for our purposes, he interpolated a lengthy Greek and Latin exorcism which he probably composed himself.[89] We know from references within the text that minimal props were used for the performance of this play, but that among them there figured three devil's masks. With this wealth of demonological and exorcistic material at our disposal, let us see how this play helps to illustrate the theologeme of the lovers' ruse.

Iphigenia and Manutius are in love. Iphigenia's father Brancatius favours the match; Manutius's father Amedeus, however, demands an unreasonably high dowry. Iphigenia's father Brancatius decides that instead he will wed her to Cantalupo, an old man who is wealthy and thus asks for no dowry. Iphigenia pretends to be demonically possessed to avoid a marriage which is not to her liking. Meanwhile, Manutius's friends Trappola and Biondello devise a plan to steal the dowry money from Amedeus's house: they use devils' masks to make him believe his house is haunted, and then explain that the devils have stolen his money. They pronounce exorcisms over the greedy old men, Amedeus, Brancatius, and Cantalupo, and over Iphigenia. Amedeus ultimately receives his money back when the lovers wed, except that he does not realize the 'dowry' really came from his coffers in the first place.

The exorcisms are obviously the element which interests us the most. The playwright mixes conjurations, charms, and exorcisms in a comical witches' brew designed to confuse and frighten the greedy old men. When the old men come to

Biondello and Trappola – thinking they are great conjurors – for help with their scheme of marrying Iphigenia to Cantalupo, Trappola writes charms on pieces of paper for them and bids them fall to their knees as they cast the charms into the fire:

> And while they are burning, on your knees you must fall,
> Till they be consumed, speaking these words withal:
> 'To limbo lakes ye hellish hags begone,
> To Styx and Cocytus, to Acheron and Phlegethon.'[90]

This is meant to be one sort of exorcism, but it is only the beginning of the many exorcisms in the play. Another exorcism occurs when Trappola casts the 'devils' out of Amedeus's house; he later reports: 'They are gone and dispatched I warrant you of my honesty. / I have taught them their daddy's dance, they will never come there more.'[91] Later, Trappola also 'exorcizes' Iphigenia using suffumigation and a charm or written exorcism hung around her neck (see fig. 3):

> But touching her disease, certain things must be preparèd
> As I will prescribe. We will make suffumigation,
> Then will I gather herbs to make a fomentation,
> And then an incantation. Then I'll hang about her neck
> This writing that shall give the falling ill a countercheck:
> *Gaspar fert Mirrham, Thus Melchior, Balthazar aurum.*
> It is writ in virgin parchment. You shall see a strange cure
> Yet before it be night I dare you assure.[92]

The Latin refers to the gifts of gold, incense, and myrrh brought by the Wise Men from the East when the baby Jesus was born. Supposedly the myrrh and incense are ingredients in the suffumigation. The 'exorcism' appears to be effective; as the maids report of Iphigenia: 'suddenly she stert up – / 'Now blessèd be Jesu,' / Quoth she, 'I am whole. Go, gentle nurse, go –.'[93]

The longest and most interesting exorcism in the play is pronounced in Greek and Latin by Trappola over the old men. This exorcism basically serves to list their sins in corrupt Greek (the sins are the alleged 'demons') without their being aware of the meaning of the litany. A string of Latin verbs comes next, followed by commands in English:

> ... yet shall they want power to come nigh
> After this conjuration, it shall bind them so mightily!
> *Miastor, Agniptos, Anturgos, Dolicoschios,*

Theostygis, Cantilios, Chrismodos, Inoflyx, Paramoschos,
Frenomoses, Gereos, Aphron, Licnos, Phalacros,
Parachros, Sapros, Hypnilos, Phylargros:
Vos claudo in hoc circulo, constringo et vincio,
Vos arguo, increpo, objuro, jubeo, impero,
Et omnes daemones a Sathana usque ad Saraboth.
I conjure and bind you, be you lief or loth,
That you touch not these gentlemen, nor once come in place,
Nor the hardest of you all once dare to show his face
To hinder or trouble them until they have done –
Now fear not, you are safe.[94]

The Greek words mean crime stained, uncleansed, opposer, caster of the long shadow, hated by God, a great pack ass, oraclemonger, one of besmeared baldness, drunken, heifer chaser or adulterer, maddening, filthy minded, old, fool, glutton, bald-headed, sallow, rotten, sluggardly, and covetous. The Latin verbs are typical of those addressed to the demons as part of the Catholic exorcism ritual.

The exorcistic context of this play, both in its Italian and English versions, is undoubtedly Catholic. James D. Clark comments on the significance of Jefferay's giving 'the religious aspect in his own play sympathetic rather than satirical treatment':

> There is remarkable restraint in this ... [play] ... [A] Roman Catholic priest is treated without satire by an Elizabethan playwright, and this handling constitutes an extensive readjustment of the attitude toward the clergy which Jefferay found in *La Spiritata* where there is a good deal of rather heavy-handed satire on clerical abuses ... That a dramatist in Protestant England just after the Marian persecutions and during the time of the Huguenot suppressions did not choose to amplify Grazzini's satire into a more virulent anti-catholicism but instead chose to represent the church favorably, seems to show that the author had something more essentially serious in mind than gibing at papists.[95]

And what is this 'something more essentially serious'? The play seems to contrast two different kinds of imaginary possession with two different kinds of 'real' possession. Clark points out that the lengthy Greek and Latin exorcism in the play, which Trappola pronounces over the old men Amedeus, Brancatius, and Cantalupo, 'amounts merely to a long list of their sins. Trappola is, in effect, exorcising the evil spirits, the sins, in the old men themselves.'[96] Amedeus believes his house is haunted by devils, when he himself is really haunted by avarice.

The other imaginary possession in the play is, of course, really love madness.

The young girl pretends to be possessed by demons but is really possessed by love. Like Rosalind in *As You Like It*, she could say from experience that 'love is merely a madness, and ... deserves as well a dark house and a whip as madmen do.'[97] Or she could identify with Romeo in *Romeo and Juliet* who, when asked by Benvolio whether he is mad, replies: 'Not mad, but bound more than a madman is, / Shut up in prison, kept without my food, / Whipt, and tormented.'[98]

This contrast of imaginary possession with real possession is characteristic of the theologeme of the lovers' ruse. Even the title of this play points to the contrast between bugbears – imaginary monsters used to scare little children – and real demons or moral entities. As Biondello says in the play: 'Sprites know our deeds and our thoughts.'[99] Moral entitites, deeds, or thoughts such as avarice or love may in truth 'possess' people, as this theologeme demonstrates.

Early modern people were constantly being invaded by various emotions, and they saw analogies between these feelings and the influx of the spirit world. Thomas Hobbes would write in *Leviathan* in the seventeenth century that he understood the Greeks to have worshipped the various passions or emotions as deities within ancient religion:

> [The Greeks] filled almost all places with spirits called *Daemons* ... They have also ascribed Divinity, and built Temples to meer Accidents, and Qualities; such as are Time, Night, Day, Peace, Concord, Love, Contention, Vertue, Honour, Health, Rust, Fever, and the like ...[100]

Although early modern people did not worship the emotions as the Greeks had done, they nonetheless understood and partook of the Greek notion that emotions could 'invade' the self. These invasions are further evidence that sometimes early modern people could view possession as something positive or even desirable. Many people, especially the young, wanted to be in love, and if that meant being 'taken over' by a force beyond themselves, then the experience sounded even more rapturous and exhilarating. It may not be an exaggeration to say that part of the early modern fascination with demonic possession stemmed from this linguistic and metaphorical association with love madness. Early modern selves could be at once (and ambiguously) repelled and attracted by possession, and this theologeme may be the best place to witness that ambivalence.

The (Mock) Exorcism: Shakespeare's *Comedy of Errors*

The exorcism ritual itself is clearly the central theologeme in any grammar of literary demonic possession. The ritual can take many different forms, including Catholic, Protestant, or vaguely superstitious ones, but it is usually still recognizable as an effort to cast out the offending demons and calm or soothe their disturbed victim, thereby restoring the integrity, coherence, and balance of the early modern self. Even when the exorcism is a mocking or parodic derivation of the formal ritual, it normally still contains many of the recognizable ingredients of a proper exorcism. For a play which alludes to several different variations of the exorcism procedure, let us look briefly at Shakespeare's *Comedy of Errors* (1592–4), a familiar adaptation of Plautus's *Menaechmi*.[101]

In *The Comedy of Errors* the long separated twin brothers Antipholus of Syracuse and Antipholus of Ephesus are constantly mistaken for each other after the former is shipwrecked in Ephesus. Adriana, the wife of Antipholus of Ephesus, runs into his twin brother and assumes he is her husband. He, of course, does not recognize her. At this point Doctor Pinch, a schoolmaster, is called in by Adriana to act as an exorcist – to cast the devil out of her husband, Antipholus of Ephesus, whom she believes to be possessed. As Donna Hamilton points out, 'the charge [of demonic possession] is delivered within a context of misunderstanding and exaggerated accusations.'[102] Stephen Greenblatt likewise comments:

> The false presumption of demonic possession in *The Comedy of Errors* is not the result of deception; it is an instance of what Shakespeare's source calls a 'suppose' – an attempt to make sense of a series of bizarre actions gleefully generated by the comedy's screwball coincidences. Exorcism is the straw people clutch at when the world seems to have gone mad.[103]

Specifically, exorcism is the straw people clutch at in a place such as Ephesus. As K.M. Briggs notes, it was a place known for witchcraft:

> Ephesus had a reputation for witchcraft, and the strangers from Syracuse were the readier to accept whatever happened to them because of this. Antipholus' first reference to it reminds one of the opening of the *Golden Ass*, when Lucius arrives in witch-haunted Thessaly ... This is in the vein of classical witchcraft, but Christianity soon begins to put its mark on the beliefs.[104]

Given the mistaken premise (one of the play's many 'errors') that Antipholus becomes possessed in Ephesus, how will he be exorcized? The answer is, in many different ways. First his wife brings in a 'conjuror' or exorcist (the two terms were often 'erroneously' conflated in Shakespeare's day) to perform a traditional exorcism in what turns out to be the Catholic style. She begs: 'Good Doctor Pinch, you are a conjurer, / Establish him in his true sense again.'[105] Dr Pinch attempts to do so in a speech which follows the form of Catholic episodes of exorcism:

I charge thee, Satan, housed within this man
To yield possession to my holy prayers.
And to thy state of darkness hie thee straight;
I conjure thee by all the saints in heaven![106]

The charge of authority commanding Satan to depart and the reference to the saints are clear indicators that it is a Catholic-style exorcism which Shakespeare has in mind here.

Antipholus protests this attempt to exorcize him with: 'Peace, doting wizard, peace! I am not mad.'[107] But Pinch makes his diagnosis: 'the fiend is strong within him.'[108] He recommends:

Mistress, both man and master is possess'd;
I know it by their pale and deadly looks,
They must be bound, and laid in some dark room.[109]

This plan is executed, and later Antipholus complains:

This pernicious slave,
Forsooth, took on him as a conjuror,
And, gazing in mine eyes, feeling my pulse,
And with no face, as 'twere, out-facing me,
Cries out, I was possess'd. Then, altogether
They fell upon me, bound me, bore me thence,
And in a dark and dankish vault at home
There left me and my man, both bound together;
Till, gnawing with my teeth my bonds in sunder,
I gain'd my freedom ...[110]

Even though this new strategy of binding the 'demoniac' and placing him in a dark room is the suggestion of Dr Pinch himself, it nonetheless represents a major shift of focus from the Catholic method of exorcism to the Protestant one. Robert Reed explains this shift to a different method of exorcism:

But the devil is not to be budged by the hocus-pocus of holy phrases. Dr. Pinch is compelled to discontinue the attempt at exorcism and suggest a more conventional remedy: he orders that Antipholus 'be bound and laid in some dark room' ... [To] be bound 'in a dark room' conforms with the Protestant treatment of the devil-possessed and evokes no ostensible criticism.[111]

As we see from his own words, Antipholus of Ephesus manages to gnaw his way free and escape this harrowing second attempt at exorcism. Ironically, in light of what we know is happening to his brother, Antipholus of Syracuse encounters his twin's mistress and imagines that she is the devil: 'Sathan, avoid. I charge thee tempt me not.'[112] This is a third form of exorcism alluded to in the play; this kind is more of a protection against evil spirits that any believer could use when he felt the need to do so. This form of exorcism is more ecumenical, as the injunction to Satan not to tempt the believer was a trope found in both Catholic and Protestant accounts of exorcism. This injunction might even be seen to border on self-exorcism, a phenomenon which we shall explore later in the final chapter on exorcism in the novel.

We have seen traces of Catholic, Protestant, and ecumenical exorcisms in this play. There is yet another form of exorcism in the play, and this one is the more medical version of the exorcistic ritual. Protestants were more likely to suggest a medically oriented remedy than were Catholics, but there were certainly also some common-sense Catholics who insisted that at the very least the patient visit a doctor first before seeing an exorcist. The Abbess, the figure of common sense in this drama, plays the part of the exorcist in this fourth version of exorcism – quite an innovative move on Shakespeare's part, enough to delight feminist critics today. Females were rarely allowed to conduct real exorcisms in the early modern period. St Teresa of Avila, for example, always preferred to bring in men such as St John of the Cross to exorcize her nuns. Ironically, more medieval women, especially saints and mystics, were exorcists than in Shakespeare's time.[113] As was so often the case, he was ahead of his time in this instance. Again it is Adriana who initiates the exorcism, asking the Abbess for help in curing her husband, although this time she asks that he be allowed to recover at home instead of in a dungeon. The Abbess asks Adriana her purpose in coming, and Adriana responds:

> To fetch my poor distracted husband hence.
> Let us come in, that we may bind him fast,
> And bear him home for his recovery.[114]

We are presented with specific methods of the exorcists as the Abbess makes her objections:

> Be patient; for I will not let him stir
> Till I have us'd the approved means I have,
> With wholesome syrups, drugs, and holy prayers,
> To make of him a formal man again.[115]

The Abbess combines medical with religious elements in a sort of holistic exorcism procedure which might be seen to anticipate the New Age therapies of today.

The four exorcisms in this play give us a fairly broad spectrum of what the exorcistic procedure could look like when presented in different contexts. K.M. Briggs notices some differences among the various methods of exorcism attempted upon Antipholus:

> The conjuror fully believes that the devil is in his patient. The women and servants attempt the remedy in good faith; only the Abbess, who represents wisdom and common sense in the play, believes that the madness comes from natural causes.[116]

I must take exception with this last statement, however, because the Abbess does mention 'holy prayers' as one of the remedies she will use. If Antipholus's madness were only natural, then prayers *of this sort* would not be necessary (other prayers, of course, were often used in the context of physical illness). In fact Shakespeare went to great pains to introduce the topos of demonic possession in a story that formerly contained only generic or 'natural' madness. Robert R. Reed confirms that the demonic possession motif is Shakespeare's addition: 'The episode of Antipholus' alleged madness in *The Comedy of Errors* (c. 1590) is borrowed from Plautus's *Menaechmi*; but Shakespeare makes one notable alteration: in the attempt to cure the distracted man, he substitutes exorcism for the Roman playwright's "acre of hellebore."'[117] Shakespeare added the demonic possession 'twist' to the madness theme he found in his source, Plautus's *Menaechmi*. He clearly had a purpose in doing so; the question is, what could it have been?

Early critics saw this play as a mild satire that did not target any one group in particular, except perhaps the Catholic exorcists, as Reed observes:

> The satire of this episode is directed neither against belief in devil-possession nor against the 'dark room' theory, both of which almost every Elizabethan accepted; it is aimed, instead, at the Roman Catholic pretense to the power of exorcism, a capacity which the Church of England ascribed only to the apostles of the first two centuries of the Christian era. The fact that the youthful Shakespeare's satire of exorcism is extremely mild, and not scornful, suggests that he had, at least in 1590, no strong religious prejudice.[118]

More recent commentaries by some New Historicists have stressed a radically different view:

> The position that Adriana takes is analogous to the positions taken routinely by those who levelled charges against the puritans ... This practice of charging the non-

conformists with heresy and possession is replicated metaphorically in Adriana's assumption that her husband requires exorcism. When Adriana turns Antipholus of Ephesus over to Pinch, the 'conjuror' ... and orders him to 'Establish him in his true sense again' ... she uses the same style of demonizing that Cosin and Bancroft had used on the puritans. By making it clear that Adriana is mistaken on this point too, Shakespeare critiques and undisguises one more aspect of the conformist rhetoric. Whatever Adriana may think, Antipholus is not mad; and the nonconformists were neither heretical nor traitorous.[119]

To assume on the basis of this play that Shakespeare was a defender of the non-conformists seems odd, or at best a 'stretch' or extrapolation which should be labelled clearly as pure conjecture.[120] To transpose the rhetoric of Cosin and Bancroft onto the lines of the literary character Adriana seems even stranger; in doing so, perhaps Hamilton might be politicizing Shakespeare in a way that the text does not fully support.

Whether Shakespeare was satirizing the Catholics, the Puritans, or no one in particular, *The Comedy of Errors* remains a perfect illustration of several different forms of exorcism. An exorcism ceremony may be Catholic or Protestant, ecumenical or medical, but it must have as its primary goals the casting out of demons and the soothing of the possessed. The early modern self could either welcome being taken over by demonic influence or abhor it, but when the latter reaction predominated, the exorcism ritual was seen as an effective means of purification and reintegration.

Binding the Body: Timoneda's *Los menemnos*

The next theologeme demonstrates the ambiguity not just of the state of demonic possession, but also of its cure. Just as being 'possessed' could have both positive and negative connotations, so the process of exorcism could include both positive and negative elements. Exorcism was rarely as relaxing a procedure as, say, going to the day spa and getting a massage. It might more aptly be compared to modern misconceptions about acupuncture. Often it included harsh or even painful elements which had to be suffered through before relief could be realized.

These elements were actions taken by the exorcist, such as binding the demoniac's body, beating it with candles, or whipping it with a stole. The significance of binding the body (with a stole, for example) had to do with the tradition that Jesus had captured the 'ancient snake' and tied it up with a chain (see fig. 1).[121] There were also actions taken by the demoniac at the exorcist's instruction, such as symbolic breathing (insufflatio[n] and exsufflatio[n]),[122] the drinking of holy water or other liquids, the inhaling of gases produced by burning substances (suffumigation), and forceful verbal renunciation of the devil and his ways (abrenunciation). Abrenunciation followed a different form in the Eastern Church from that used in the West: 'In the Eastern Church he was required to thrust out his hand toward the west, as if in the act of pushing away an object in that direction. This was a token of his abhorrence of Satan and his works, and his determination to resist and repel them.'[123]

These (originally Catholic) components of the exorcism ritual were often appropriated even by non-Catholic exorcists. These actions became such hallmarks of the exorcism ritual that they served as grist for the mill of sceptics such as Reginald Scot, who described exorcism thus:

> The right order of exorcisme in rebaptisme of a person possessed or bewitched, requireth that exsufflation and abrenunciation be doone toward the west. Item, there must be erection of hands, confession, profession, oration, benediction, imposition of hands, denudation and unction, with holie oile after baptisme, communion, and induition of the surplis ...[124]

Reginald Scot assures us that non-Catholic exorcisms follow this same general outline: 'The papists you see, have their certeine generall rules and lawes ... and even so likewise have the other conjurors ... Even so doo common conjurors ... even in the same papisticall forme.'[125] The 'forme' was a ritual or formula that had to be spoken in precisely the right way: 'I conjure thee *Peter* or *Barbara* being sicke ... that everie fantasie and wickednesse of diaboticall deceipt doo avoid and depart from thee, and that everie uncleane spirit be conjured ... And this order must alwaies be followed ...'[126] In a more modern (but still sarcastic) account, the basic ingredients of an exorcism were as follows:

> The patient, seated in a 'holy chair,' specially sanctified for the occasion, was compelled to drink about a pint of a compound of sack and salad oil; after which refreshment a pan of burning brimstone was held under his nose, until his face was blackened by smoke. All this while the officiating priest kept up his invocation of the fiends ... under such circumstances, it is extremely doubtful whether the most determined character would not be prepared to see somewhat unusual phenomena for the sake of a short respite. Another remarkable method of exorcism was a process termed 'firing out' the fiend.[127] The holy flame of piety resident in the priest was so terrible to the evil spirit, that the mere contact of the holy hand with that of the body of the afflicted person in which he was resident was enough to make him shrink away into some more distant portion; so, by a judicious application of the hand, the exorcist could drive the devil into some limb, from which escape into the body was impossible, and the evil spirit, driven to the extremity, was obliged to depart, defeated

and disgraced. This influence could be exerted, however, without actual corporal contact.[128]

Thus we see how early modern people could sometimes feel more threatened by the arduous process of expelling the demon than by the frightening internal actions of the demon itself.

To demonstrate how one of these specific procedures was exploited by a comic dramatist for theatrical effect, we shall look at Juan de Timoneda's *Los menemnos*, a Spanish adaptation of Plautus's *Menaechmi* (the same Roman play Shakespeare was adapting in *The Comedy of Errors*). Just as Antipholus of Ephesus is bound and laid in a dark room in Shakespeare's play, Menemno Casado is bound and led away because he, too, is believed to be mad. In Timoneda's play especially, the binding of the body happens onstage and is meticulously detailed. The theatrical emphasis on the physicality of restraining the body gives this play a sensationalism that must have been entertaining to watch.

Let us look at the scene where the binding of the body occurs. Auerroys, the doctor/exorcist, binds Menemno Casado before he realizes what is happening:

AUERROYS: Coge assi los brazos.

MENEMNO CASADO: Ya estan cogidos. ¿Qué es lo que hazes?

AUERROYS: Sufrete, que por tu bien se haze, que estés atado un poco con este cordel, porque assi lo dize Auicena que se deue hazer ... Oh cómo acotaste bien, rapaz! Es menester, señor Casandro, que desta manera atado lo lleuen a mi casa, porque alli, con aquel emplasto aureo, te lo daré sano en tres dias.

(AUERROYS: Take thus the arms.

MENEMNO CASADO: Already they are taken. What are you doing?

AUERROYS: Suffer it, for it is done for your good, that you be tied a little with this cord, because thus says Avicenna that it should be done ... Oh how you bound yourself well, rapacious one! It is necessary, Mister Casandro, that in this manner, tied, they take him to my house, because there, with that golden plaster, I will give it to you healthy in three days.)[129]

The reference to Avicenna, of course, is an allusion to the important medieval tradition in Spain of Arabic medicine and philosophy. In binding the body of Menemno Casado, the character Auerroys (named for Averroës, the medieval Arabic philosopher from Córdoba) thus claims to be following the directions of an ancient authority. After Menemno Casado is tricked into allowing himself to be bound, his servant Tronchón secretly tries to find a way to free his master. Tronchón and Casandro discuss with Auerroys what to do next:

TRONCHÓN: Está assombrado y endemoniado.
AUERROYS: Endemoniado? Ariedro vaya Satanas.

(TRONCHÓN: He is astonished and demonically possessed.
AUERROYS: Demonically possessed? Satan, avoid.)[130]

Here the exorcist utters the exact words of the Catholic exorcism ritual. But this is not a very official exorcism, for the slave Tronchón soon decides that he would like to try to conduct the exorcism too (with the real goal of freeing his master and escaping this entanglement with him):

TRONCHÓN: De los demonios publicos es; a bozes quiero hablarle. Yo te mando de parte de Dios, que te vayas a los infiernos sin dañar ni atormentar a este hombre.

(TRONCHÓN: Of the public demons it is: I want to speak to it out loud. I order you on behalf of God, that you go to hell without damaging or tormenting this man.)[131]

Notice the very Catholic-style commandment to depart, followed by the typical injunction that the demon return to hell without harming the patient or damaging him irreparably on his way out.

These are the only words spoken in this very physical exorcism ritual. Just as he was tricked into allowing his hands to be tied, Menemno Casado devises a physical manoeuver that will free him from bondage before the very eyes of the audience. Pretending to speak as the possessing demon, he demands to see a cross before he will depart, knowing full well that the only cross available under the circumstances is the top of Tronchón's sword that he spies nearby: 'No saldre si primero no veo la cruz, o señal della' (I will not leave unless I see first the cross, or a symbol of it).[132] In what must have been an outrageously funny piece of staged action when it was performed, he then uses the sword to cut himself free from his bonds.

The binding of the body is only one of the specific procedures used in the exorcism ritual, but it is one normally favoured by comic dramatists at least in part because of its potential for staged spectacle. Requiring actions over words, physicality over textuality, this theologeme emphasizes the violence inflicted on the body and the sensational spectacle inherent in the exorcism ritual. Early modern selves were inordinately concerned, even obsessed, with early modern bodies.[133] The violence inflicted upon the body during the exorcism ritual was very much a threat to the integrated, coherent self.[134] In effect, violence against the body *was* violence against the self; and when violence came from the hands of the exorcist, it was possible for early modern patients to feel more threatened by a human being than by the invisible supernatural force which he was allegedly trying to expel. Not all exorcists were violent, to be sure; in fact, the majority of them were probably not. As we shall see in the next chapter on the picaresque and satire (especially in Quevedo's *Sueños*), the violence of the exorcism ritual is a theologeme which appears in literature primarily, if not exclusively, in the more comical genres. When it does appear, however, this theologeme presents the real threat as coming from a different quarter: the most severe threat to the early modern self could stem more from natural (i.e., human) than from supernatural forces.

Relics, Holy Water, and Other Props: Shadwell's *The Lancashire Witches*

Another theologeme in the paradigm of literary exorcism is the group of various 'props' used in the exorcism ritual: holy water, a cross, a stole, an *Agnus Dei* (wax figurine of the Lamb of God), sulfur, relics of the saints, written *ensalmos* or *rescritos*, and so on. The list of these props is seemingly endless and often creative: for example, Thomas Lodge informs us that some people of his day erroneously thought devils could be expelled through the use of a fish liver (as with Tobias in the Bible).[135] Such 'props' most often appeared as part of the Catholic version of the exorcism procedure. As such, they were often the target of satire by Protestant dramatists in England who wished to ridicule 'popish superstition.' The best example of this specific type of satire occurs in a Restoration play performed in 1681, Thomas Shadwell's *The Lancashire Witches and Tegue o Divelly the Irish-Priest*.

The plot of this play is so paradoxical as to have inspired much critical puzzlement over the years. Isabella and Theodosia, two noble and vivacious young women, are about to be forced into arranged marriages little to their liking. They belong to two wealthy families, the Hartforts and the Shackleheads respectively, who wish to form a dynastic alliance by marrying off their daughters to their sons. The girls are in love with Belfort and Doubty, two other gentlemen of equal rank but not their parents' choices for them. The young ladies playfully 'bewitch' their lovers simply by charming them with womanly wiles. Sir Edward Hartfort is a sympathetic figure of rational scepticism in the play, and the action takes place in and around his estate.[136] His household curate is a superstitious high Anglican named Smerk,[137] who quickly allies himself with Tegue O'Divelly, the Irish priest summoned by the Shackleheads. These two clerics are called in to help when strange acts of witchcraft begin to take place in Hartfort's cellar. The ironic premise behind much of the play's humour is the fact that while Sir Edward Hartfort does not believe in witchcraft, there are real witches holding their rituals in his basement. The audience is fully aware of this fact, seeing (as they do) the witches flying about the stage on elaborate contraptions engineered specifically for this theatrical production. First the priest tries to exorcize the witches; then he exorcizes the Anglican Smerk after the latter becomes convinced that the witches have cast a spell on him. After many comic mishaps – including a night full of confused sexual intrigue – the girls are permitted to marry their lovers, and the two charlatan clerics are tried and executed along with the witches.

This play was based on actual events, the 1612 and 1634 Lancashire witch trials. Accounts (both 'historical' and 'fictitious') of these trials were available in several forms, primarily Thomas Potts's court records in *The Wonderfull Discoverie of Witches in the Countie of Lancaster* (1613) and an earlier play by Thomas Heywood and Richard Broome titled *The late Lancashire Witches* (1634).[138] In addition to these sources, Shadwell read (and cited) standard works of demonology such as the *Malleus maleficarum*, Remy's *Demonolatreiae*, Del Río's *Disquisitionum magicarum*, Le Loyer's *De spectris*, Bodin's *De la démonomanie des sorciers*, Guazzo's *Compendium maleficarum*, and Agrippa's *De occulta philosophia*. He cited these and other demonological works in the copious notes (over 100) on intricate details of witchcraft that he added to the version of his previously performed play which he prepared for publication in 1682. Shadwell wrote in his 'To the Reader': 'I had no hopes of equalling Shakespear in fancy, who created his Witchcraft for the most part out of his own imagination ... and therefore I resolved to take mine from Authority. And to that end, there is not one action in the Play, nay scarce a word concerning it, but is borrowed from some antient, or Modern Witchmonger.'[139]

The 1682 edition of the play reinstated the lines (primarily Smerk's) that had been expurgated by the censor from the stage version.[140] Censorship of this play occurred mainly as a result of Shadwell's conflation of the beliefs of an Anglican minister with those of an Irish Catholic priest and even with the witches in the title.[141] The censorship was probably not a result of the obvious Whig and anti-Catholic sentiment in the play, which Shadwell exploited in a timely fashion considering that the Popish Plot had failed only three years earlier.[142] The result of the censorship controversy was that Shadwell remained absent from the stage for the next seven years, spending his time instead writing political pamphlets.

Shadwell is still inciting controversy among critics who discuss his plays. First of all, the appearance of 'real' witches in a Restoration drama is unexpected enough to stretch our notions of periodicity. How could a serious treatment of witchcraft appear in a play this late? Jessica Munns calls the supernatural 'an intrinsic, if disturbing, part of the play' and explains that 'the witches have to be "real" – as are Catholicism, absolutism and invasion – to demonstrate the "real" dangers facing England.'[143] Shadwell himself, in his prologue 'To the Reader' (37), justifies the inclusion of 'real' witches thus:

> For the actions, if I had not represented them as those of real Witches, but had
> show'd the ignorance, fear, melancholy, malice, confederacy, and imposture that con-
> tribute to the belief of Witchcraft, the people had wanted diversion, and there had
> been another clamor against it, it would have been call'd Atheistical ... and by this
> means the Play might have been Silenced.

There does seem to be some cognitive dissonance here. Shadwell at once apolo-
gizes for making use of real witches and, at the same time, justifies their inclusion.
Clearly his society was not yet ready to relinquish altogether the belief in some
forms of supernatural activity. Even Richard Steele, writing a review of a later
performance of this play in 1711 for *The Spectator*, could not relinquish the idea
that the supernatural was a legitimate province of dramatic expression. He did,
however, show the tide beginning to turn toward secularism by restricting the
appropriate realm of the supernatural to tragedy rather than comedy:

> The Gentleman who writ this Play ... appears to have been mis-led in his Witchcraft
> by an unwary following the inimitable *Shakespear*. The Incantations in *Mackbeth*
> have a Solemnity admirably adapted to the Occasion of that Tragedy, and fill the
> Mind with a suitable Horror; besides, that the Witches are a part of the Story it self,
> as we find it very particularly related in *Hector Boetius*, from whom he seems to have
> taken it. This therefore is a proper Machine where the Business is dark, horrid and
> bloody; but is extreamly foreign from the Affair of Comedy.

J.M. Armistead attempts to explain the appearance of witches in a comedy rather
than a tragedy by discussing this play in relation to Restoration drama in general:

> The important thing is to recognize that the intellectual outlook in any age com-
> bines an awareness of both the visible and the invisible worlds, the known and mys-
> terious, so that to speak of the decline or decay of supernaturalism in the later
> seventeenth century is both inaccurate and counter-appreciative.[144]

It may safely be said that both Shadwell's ambivalence toward the supernatural
and critics' ambivalence toward his play may be explained in terms of the tensions
and inconsistencies between conflicting attitudes regarding the marvellous in
literature.

Although the supernatural in the play deals primarily with witchcraft, it also
includes one important exorcism scene.[145] Unlike its sources (both historical and
literary) which in fact do not contain instances of exorcism, this play introduces
the exorcism topos and exploits it to fullest effect. As stated earlier, the most
prominent theologeme which this play illustrates is the use of 'props' during the

exorcism procedure. Let us see how Tegue O'Divelly's exorcism of Smerk using multiple 'props' allows this theologeme to emerge clearly.

The Priest, Tegue O'Divelly, proposes to exorcize Smerk and then proceeds to do so:

> PRIEST: *Exercizo te Conjuro te in Nomine, &c* ... Hold him, and I vill taak some course vid him, he is possess'd, or obess'd, I vill touch him vid some Relicks.
>
> SUSAN: Oh, good Sir, help him, what shall I do for him?
>
> LADY SHACKLEHEAD: Get some Lead melted (and holding over his body) power it into a Poringer full of Water, and if there appear any image upon the Lead, then he is bewitch'd. [*Shadwell's note: This experiment is to be found in* Malleus maleficarum.]
>
> PRIEST: Peash, I shay, here is shome of St. *Phaatricks* own Whisker, and some of the Snuff he did use to taak, dat did hang upon his Beard; here is a Tooth of St. *Winifred*, indeed, here is a Corn from de Toe of St. *Ignatius*, and here is de paring of his Nails too. [*He rubs him with these Relicks.*]
>
> SMERK: Oh worse, worse, take her away.
>
> PRIEST: By my shoule it is a very strong Devil, I vill try some more, here is St. *Caaterine* de Virgins Wedding-Ring, here is one of St. *Bridgets* Nipples of her Tuggs, by my shoule, here is some of de sweat of St. *Francis,* and here is a piece of St. *Laurence's* Gridiron, dese vill make Cure upon any shickness, if it be not ones lasht shickness ... By my shoule it is a very strong Devil, a very aable Devil, I vill run and fetch shome Holy-vater ...
>
> LADY SHACKLEHEAD: But I do not know what to think of his Popish way, his Words, his Charms, and Holy Water, and Relicks, methinks he is guilty of Witchcraft too, and you should send him to Goal for it.[146]

From this exchange it is clear that the 'props' of the exorcism ritual are satirized as being akin to witchcraft. The ridiculous relics and dialects, in particular, generate a perverse hilarity. As we have seen, Shadwell's attitude toward the authenticity of the phenomena he describes must be labelled ambiguous at best. Not wanting to dismiss witches and other supernatural phenomena as inauthentic, for fear of being accused as 'Atheistical,' he writes during a transitional period when rituals are not entirely devoid of meaning and relics are not completely consigned to ridicule. By studying the 'props' of the exorcism ritual in this play we can see both how they are satirized and how, in a different context, they might be taken seriously. Let us move now to this more serious context.

The Successful Exorcism: *El pleyto que tuvo el diablo*

In many ways the most important theologeme in the paradigm of literary exorcism is the successful exorcism, for it makes the teleology of the other theologemes viable. Whether it is accompanied by a victorious shout, a final violent convulsion, or the stillness of peaceful silence, the success of an exorcism is cause for great rejoicing. The successful exorcistic ritual orchestrates a return to sanity, a renewed vitality, and a reinforced vigour associated with the spiritual rebirth of the early modern self. Obviously, this theologeme is not present in every work of literature in which exorcism appears. In those where it does not appear (such as in tragedy, for example), its presence is nonetheless felt as the negative of its absence.[147]

Perhaps the most illustrative example of this theologeme may be found in a *comedia* almost unknown today, *El pleyto que tuvo el diablo con el cura de Madrilejos* (The lawsuit that the devil had with a priest of Madrilejos).[148] This *comedia* was composed ca. 1639[149] by a team of playwrights, Luis Vélez de Guevara, Antonio Mira de Amescua, and Francisco de Rojas Zorrilla, who each wrote an act. The play is remarkable in several aspects, not least of which is its direct relationship to what may be the only surviving news pamphlet (*suelta*) from Spain printed exclusively for the purpose of publicizing an exorcism. Much work remains to be done in establishing the relationship of the play to this pamphlet, Pedro de Salazar Treviño's *Relacion de vn caso raro, en que fueron expelidos de vna muger casada muchos demonios, en la villa de Madrilejos, a los 14. dias del mes de Otubre deste año passado de 1607* (Relation of a rare case, in which were expelled from a married woman many demons, in the village of Madrilejos, on the 14th day of the month of October of this past year 1607).[150] For now, however, some salient points may be summarized here.

The play bears some close resemblances to the pamphlet, but it also differs in some key aspects, such as the fact that it isolates the demonic possession to remove any traces of bewitchment. The woman in the play becomes demon-possessed as a result of a faulty baptism, not through eating an enchanted orange (as in the pamphlet). In the play this woman, Catalina Sánchez (called La Rosela), experiences many characteristic symptoms of demonic possession: she cannot approach the altar or pray, she faints or alternatively tears her clothes furiously, she threatens suicide after blaspheming and despairing, she sees visions of fiery serpents and swords, she flies through the air and passes through doors, and she prophesies about events of which she could have had no foreknowledge. Her acquaintances become familiar with her demonic powers when she takes them on aerial journeys with her; she does this both for the peasant Mateo who wishes to marry her, and for the sexton and Maria, a servant girl. The sexton and the servant girl, in fact, make a grand entrance – they are covered with soot, having just passed through a chimney – at the feast which the mayor of Tembleque has prepared for the *comendador* and the curate of Madrilejos. Soon the sexton is dropped into a well, the food for the banquet vanishes into thin air, and the villagers swarm around Catalina's house to apprehend her as a witch – all in Act 1 (written by Vélez de Guevara) of this unusual drama.

In Act 2, written by Rojas Zorrilla,[151] Catalina moves away from the village to live in isolation. The priest of Madrilejos, passing through the wilderness, is suddenly attacked by her and almost murdered, but just as suddenly, she falls at his feet in a fit which he recognizes as demonic possession. The villagers, believing her to be dead, insist on burying her at once, but the sexton and Mateo rescue her upon hearing her cries from within the burial vault. She is severely afflicted by demons and does not recognize her friends or her village.

In Act 3, written by Mira de Amescua, the priest conducts what may be the most elaborate exorcism ever performed on stage. He begins by summoning the possessing demons to a trial (the 'pleyto' of the title), complete with official legal documents and pronouncements:

Yo indigno Ministro, y Sacerdote de Dios, por la autoridad q[ue] de la Iglesia te[n]go, mando, fuerço, y compelo a los espiritus infernales, q[ue] luego que este nuestro ma[n]damiento os fuere notificado, intimado, y leido, declareis, manifesteis, y descubrais todo aquello que por nos os fuere preguntado. Lo primero, que confesseis como estais en esse cuerpo, y quantos, y porque entrasteis en el. Y desde luego citamos, ma[n]damos, y compelemos, y forçamos a Lucifer, Principe de los demonios a Leviatan, Beelzebut, Asmodeo, Behmot, y Astarot, y Belial, y a todos los demas Capitanes, y Ministros infernales; que oyda esta nuestra notificacion dentro de tres instantes, y el vltimo por peremptorio, trina Canonica munitione praemissa, atorme[n]teis a los demonios, que estàn en la dicha Catalina molestandola, y los forceis con penas inte[n]sissimas de cien mil años, las quales executela en cada momento que dexaren de cumplir nuestro mandamiento. Y si por obstinacion no obedeceis, os excomulgo, y anatematiço, y os mando no atorme[n]teis mas a la dicha Catalina. Y digais la causa porq[ue] la molestais; y passados tres instantes de la notificacion, incurrais en las dichas penas.

(I unworthy minister, and priest of God, by the authority that I have from the church, command, force and compel the infernal spirits, that after this our commandment be notified, intimated, and read to you, you declare, manifest, and discover all that which be asked by us of you. The first thing, that you confess how you are in that body, and how many there are of you, and why you entered it. And from that point we cite, command, and compel, and force Lucifer, prince of the demons, and Leviathan, Beelzebuth, Asmodeus, Behemoth, and Astaroth, and Belial, and all the other captains, and infernal ministers; that this our notifications being heard, within three moments, and the last one for peremptory, the triune canonical entrenchments being set forth, that you torment the demons, who are in the said Catalina molesting her, and that you force them with the most intense penalties of a hundred thousand years, which you should execute in each moment that they refrain from completing our commandment. And if by obstinacy you do not obey, I excommunicate you, and I anathematize you, and I command that you do not torment more the said Catalina. And that you say the cause for which you molest her; and three moments after the notification, you will incur the said penalties.)[152]

This extended legal trial of the demons according to inquisitorial procedure had its origins in Roman law.[153] The demons in the play are commanded to answer all questions put to them, namely, how they came to enter the body of the possessed, how many of them are present, and why they inhabit the demoniac. Later, in the chapter on tragedy, we shall see in *King Lear* another play in which exorcism is 'staged' as a trial on the heath.

In response to the demand for judicially correct responses, the demons in the Spanish play give their obstinate answer. Their chief Asmodeo speaks for them, forcing Catalina to sign his name to a piece of paper, admitting that there are legions of demons within her but refusing to answer the priest's other questions:

Dezimos nosotros Satanas, Barrabas, Belzebut, y Asmodeo, espiritus infernales q[ue] estamos en Catalina la Rosela muchas legiones, de quie[n] somos Capitanes los quatro: Y en quanto à salir de su cuerpo, y co[n]fessar porque entramos en èl, negamos, y no podemos obedecer; y lo firmè en nombre de todos: Yo Asmodeo.

(Thus say we Satan, Barrabas, Beelzebuth, and Asmodeus, infernal spirits who are in Catalina la Rosela many legions, of whom we four are captains: And as for leaving her body, and confessing why we entered it, we refuse, and cannot obey; and he signed it in the name of all: I Asmodeus.)[154]

Then Catalina draws from her breast a piece of paper which, when it is read aloud, is found to contain the names of other specific demons possessing her. The priest responds by having the scribe write a condemnation of these demons, an 'auto,' on a piece of paper. They are condemned to excommunication and 100,000 years of infernal torment. Next the priest passes this piece of paper, along with a crucifix, over Catalina's forehead, mouth, and breast. He then sprinkles holy water upon her with a branch of hyssop.

At this point further tests are performed to see whether she is still possessed. One of these tests is to command her to speak in languages unknown to her, something which demoniacs were said to do spontaneously (the reader will recall the theologeme of polyglossia discussed earlier in this chapter in connection with

George Ruggle's neo-Latin play *Ignoramus*).[155] Earlier, before the exorcism procedure actually started, the priest had heard her speak Greek. Prompted by more
questions, the demons finally reveal that they entered her body after a faulty
baptism in which the godmother failed to speak the name of the Holy Spirit as
part of the baptism ritual. They claim to number one million devils and to have
possessed her for twenty-six years.

Once he has forced the demons to reveal this much, the priest has the key piece
of information he needs: a faulty baptism was the open door through which the
demons entered. To close that door, he must simply rebaptize Catalina in the
appropriate manner for the exorcism to be complete. This theory that a faulty
baptism could lead to demonic possession was common in the Renaissance; Reginald Scot explains that 'it is possible that the ... midwife hath not baptised him
well, but omitted some part of the sacrament ... [W]ho or whatsoever is newlie
exorcised must be rebaptised.'[156] In England, although baptismal exorcism was
retained in the First Prayer Book of 1549, by 1552 it had been entirely elimi-
nated. Nevertheless, after the exorcism ritual was omitted from the baptism service, generations of the faithful believed that babies who cried during baptism
were releasing the devil through their mouths.[157] In this case, when the priest
announces his plan for a formal rebaptism, the demons 'appeal' the 'sentence'
which has been imposed upon them, for they know that soon they will have to
depart. Relentlessly the priest leads Catalina to the church and performs the baptism, at which time she becomes completely free of the demons' control.

This play shows that the occurrence of exorcism in literature is not limited to villains or other 'bad' characters. According to early modern popular belief, any person, however blameless, was liable to be struck down into the throes of possession
at any moment, as King James I observed: 'Being persones of the beste nature per-
aduenture, that yee shall finde in all the Countrie about them, GOD permittes
them to be troubled in that sort, for the wakening up of their zeale.'[158] Demonic
possession was a very real threat to early modern people, and one which these playwrights clearly took very seriously. There is not a single hint of scepticism or sar-
casm about the exorcism ritual in this play. Its authors were serious about their
religion, and if there is any propaganda in the play at all, it is fervent and devout
support of the Catholic Church and its sacred rituals. One of the playwrights, Mira
de Amescua – a writer famous for his interest in the supernatural, most notably
expressed in *El esclavo del demonio*, a play about a demonic pact – was a priest who
took his vows even more seriously toward the end of his life, when this play was
written. As for the other two playwrights, Rojas Zorrilla was a knight of the
religious Order of Santiago who enjoyed the favours of King Philip IV; Vélez de
Guevara, who followed the court to Valladolid and then to Madrid, and served
both the count of Saldaña and the duke of Veragua, also wrote other works about

the supernatural.[159] These were men of position and prestige who did not hesitate to use their pens to express their Catholic devotion. Vélez de Guevara was a skillful lawyer, and it may be to his influence that we owe the 'exorcism as trial' scene of the last act. Together this team of dramatists, each one famous in his own right in the history of the Spanish Golden Age *comedia*, created the most enduring literary monument to the theologeme of the successful exorcism.

What are the salient features of this theologeme as it is presented in this play? In this play it becomes apparent just how great a threat demonic possession was to the average early modern person. If a reasonably virtuous person could fall prey to the wiles of crafty demons through a detail so seemingly trivial as whether her god-mother ran out of breath at her baptism, then everyone was potentially at risk. This play also illustrates the escalating efforts on the parts of early moderns to contain and restrict this otherwise boundless threat. The attempt to bring demons to trial is a way of trying to retaliate rationally against a force that is completely irrational (William Christian has shown how locusts were similarly indicted and then excommunicated for the crime of ruining crops).[160] In Christian's excommunica-tion of the locusts, even saints and the Virgin Mary were called in as witnesses and/or advocates to participate in the trial of the offending malign entity. These invo-cations of authority confirm the impression of early modern minds who are grasp-ing for reassurance in a hostile and threatening spiritual ambience. They need to feel that they are still 'in charge' when faced with calamity or catastrophe.

In this play the theologeme of the successful exorcism at once affirms both divine and human power, for it is through the exorcist (the successful prosecuting lawyer) that the situation is reversed. Similar representations of the exorcist as a successful (but still human) power will be discussed later, in the chapter on romance, the interlude, and hagiography. As in the longer literary treatments of exorcism we shall examine later in these genres, the theologeme of successful exorcism in this play offers to the early modern self the hope for restoration. In this sense this play is simply a foretaste of the humanization of possession and exorcism that which we shall see more fully in these other genres. This restora-tion, here experienced in the private sphere, will be extended to the public sphere in the next theologeme we shall discuss before concluding this chapter. This theologeme is the healing or cleansing of the body politic.

Exorcizing the Body Politic: Zamora's *El hechizado por fuerza* and Middleton's *The Phoenix*

The final theologeme in the paradigm of literary exorcism – one which is particu-larly relevant for the genre of comic drama – is exorcism used as a synecdoche for curing the body politic. At first glance, this theologeme has less to do with the early modern self seen as an individual construct than it does with the totality of early modern selves seen as a corporate entity. There is a sense, however, in which demonic possession is relentlessly individualistic: it is on the microlevel that specific demons choose specific human beings to torment. Exorcism, likewise, is persistently individualized: no two demons are exactly alike, and the exorcist must proceed with care to respond to the eccentricities of each particular demon. Thus when we are speaking in an exorcistic context about early modern society as a whole, or at least about the totality of early modern England or Golden Age Spain, it is only possible to speak of the group as a rhetorical extension of the individual demon-tormented body. There is no incongruity here: John D. Cox has argued similarly that 'the role of stage devils ... was to enact whatever opposed individual wellbeing *and* the sacramental community ... [D]evils were a way of imagining how and why the sacred needed to function redemptively in the life of the individual *and* the community.'[161] It is only through our understanding of demonic possession as both a potential enhancement and a potential threat to the early modern self that we can begin to understand the dramatic metaphor of exorcism as a process of curing the body politic.

Wherever this theologeme appears in early modern literature, the exorcism ritual symbolizes a larger intention on the part of the author to engage actively in the problems of his society. This theologeme only appears overtly in literature that is self-consciously socially conscious – in other words, literature which is peculiarly susceptible to a New Historicist analysis. It appears most often in comic drama because, as we have stated, this genre is more ephemeral than many others and is more likely to contain direct references to the world outside the theatre.

This theologeme is most apparent in plays written specifically for performance before a monarch. Indeed, the two plays we will use to illustrate this theologeme, Antonio de Zamora's *El hechizado por fuerza* (The one bewitched by force) and Thomas Middleton's *The Phoenix*, were both performed before kings. What is more, they both depict directly the kings who were invited to view them. In both cases, this situation produced fascinating dynamics (of which we have traces in the texts) whereby the 'king's playwrights,' themselves royal subjects, turned their rulers into 'apprehending subjects' by forcing them to view themselves being portrayed on stage.[162] The 'regal phantasms'[163] created by these dramatists were the king acting as demoniac (in the case of Spain) and the king acting as exorcist (in the case of England), respectively.

Zamora's *El hechizado por fuerza* is, on one level, a *comedia de figurón* ridiculing a pretentious fool, Don Claudio, who is tricked into believing he is bewitched by women who conspire to force him to marry. On another level it is a direct satire of King Carlos II, nicknamed 'El Hechizado,' who also believed he was bewitched by malicious women plotting to harm him. The subject matter of the play has long been recognized for what it is – a carnivalesque satire of the monarch before whom it was performed on a Carnival holiday – but the few scholars who have studied this now-obscure play remain hesitant to comment about the political context that might have engendered it.[164] We know from the title pages of the earliest editions that this play was performed twice before King Carlos II and his wife Mariana de Neoburgo, first in the theatre of the Buen Retiro on 26 May 1697 and then again on the Tuesday of Carnival 1698.[165] It is absolutely certain that the play was performed before the king, incredible as that may seem, considering how direct the satire of him really is.[166] The playwright, Antonio de Zamora, was a government official, having been appointed to a position in the Secretariat of the Indies (in the section of New Spain) in 1689. The fact that he would dare to ridicule the monarch in such a relatively straightforward fashion requires at least an attempt at explanation through the theory of carnival as elucidated by Mikhail Bakhtin and Michael Bristol.[167]

In the play, Don Claudio (the dramatic figure symbolizing King Carlos II), is a cleric of minor orders. He is contracted to marry Leonor, whose brother Diego is also contracted to marry Luisa, Claudio's sister. Claudio is attempting to escape from this arrangement by giving the excuse that he cannot afford to give up the small benefice he receives from his clerical position. To force him to comply with his obligation, Leonor enlists the help of Picatoste (Claudio's disaffected servant) and, more importantly, Lucigüela, a Guatemalan servant woman who allegedly knows black magic. Together they devise a plot so complicated that it eventually envelops all the other characters in the play (all of whom are 'in the know' except for Claudio, the butt of the satire). Playing on his natural hypochondriacal tendencies, they convince Claudio that he is dying because Lucigüela has bewitched him: 'Pues amigo, vos estáis maleficiado' (Well, friend, you are bewitched).[168] They bring in doctors who produce a long list of Latin terms for the symptoms of bewitchment which, they convince him, he manifests. Many of these symptoms are the same ones which Carlos II himself suffered from.[169] The conspirators produce as evidence for this diagnosis a wax doll in Claudio's image stuck through with needles;[170] this doll sewn into a blanket is a direct allusion to the diabolical charms discovered in the king's bedchamber, under his doorpost, and under his pillow.

As another ruse to scare him, the conspirators show Claudio a lamp burning black oil which will end his life as soon as the oil runs out. At one point he becomes so terrified by the ghostly sound of a chain rattling that he spills some of the oil himself, exclaiming:

Válgame aquí la piedad
de diáconos y exorcistas,

y los cuatro evangelistas,
Fe, Esperanza y Caridad.

(Let it avail itself to me, the piety
Of deacons and exorcists,
And the four evangelists,
Faith, Hope and Charity.)[171]

These lines were immortalized by the eighteenth-century Spanish painter Francisco de Goya, who illustrated them in his painting *La lámpara descomunal* (now called *La lámpara del diablo*; see fig. 2). The conspirators even go so far as to dress up like demons, wearing masks and carrying candles along with the lamp, dancing and chanting a diabolical litany as they go. Convinced that Leonor has hired Lucigüela to cast a spell on him, Claudio offers to marry her rather than die from bewitchment. Leonor accepts, the 'spell' is broken in the most rapid exorcism the stage has ever seen, and both couples give this comedy the traditional happy ending of marriage.

One of Zamora's purposes in writing this play appears to have been to satirize belief in possession and bewitchment, as Caro Baroja speculates:

La comedia de Zamora, tanto por el tono con que se alude a la Inquisición, como en la manera de exponer las creencias en hechizos, dándolas más bien como expresión de estupidez que como 'creencias populares' (al estilo de Feijoo), supone, sin duda, una apertura ... [P]arece que bastantes conciencias debieron irritarse cuando el mismo palacio, el viejo alcázar madrileño, se vio dominado por la noción de hechizo o los hechizos, que se decía tenían achicado hasta grados inverosímiles a Carlos II y creo muy posible ... que ... se hiciera una campaña contra la credulidad, popular o popularizada.

(The comedy of Zamora, as much by the tone with which the Inquisition is alluded to, as in the manner of exposing the beliefs in spells, giving them more as an expression of stupidity than as 'popular beliefs' (in the style of Feijóo), supposes, without doubt, an opening ... It appears that enough consciences should have been irritated when the palace itself, the old Madrileñan castle, saw itself dominated by the notion of bewitchment or spells, which it was said had belittled Carlos II to nonverisimilar degrees; and I believe it very possible ... that ... there was made a campaign against credulity, popular or popularized.)[172]

But Zamora's purpose was also to ridicule King Carlos II as an ineffective ruler with the intention of furthering the cause of his successor, Felipe V, as Caro Baroja also observes:

> En esta obra ... había una intención política: la de oponer la amplitud de criterio de los partidarios de la dinastía triunfante, a un oscurantismo y arcaísmo que se atribuiría a los secuaces del Archiduque y a los hombres 'chapados a la antigua' que seguían las modas y usos más comunes en tiempo de Carlos II. Todos los rumores que corrieron en torno a los hechizos de palacio, a los conjuros a los demonios que tenían desasosegado al rey etc., etc., podían darse como un símbolo del pasado inmediato, frente a la 'modernidad' del presente. Zamora reflejaría esta modernidad desde un punto de vista.

> (In this work ... there was a political intention: that of opposing the amplitude of criteria of the partisans of the triumphant dynasty, to an obscurantism and archaism that was attributed to the followers of the archduke and the old-fashioned men who followed the most common modes and usages in the time of Carlos II. All the rumours that ran surrounding the bewitchments of the palace, and the conjurings of the demons who had the king disturbed, etc., etc., could be given as a symbol of the immediate past, facing the 'modernity' of the present. Zamora would reflect this modernity from one point of view.)[173]

Alva Ebersole believes the king was so ill and unaware of his surroundings that he would not even have recognized himself being thus satirized.[174] Surely this could not have been the case. In a more theoretically grounded argument which still does not overtly invoke Bakhtin, John Dowling believes that the overriding power of the farcical genre of the play would have silenced any more sinister political insinuations it might have contained.[175] The second recorded performance of this play did take place in an atmosphere of Carnival, however, and this fact should not remain overlooked. We shall see how this satire does not overstep the bounds of traditionally permissible carnivalesque humour.

According to Michael Bristol's *Carnival and Theater*, the Bakhtinian 'elements of festive uncrowning, debasement and renewal' to be found in English drama about kings do not seriously threaten the 'political doctrine of *dignitas non moritur*: the king's mystical identity or dignity never dies.'[176] We could see the prospect of a demon-possessed king as one of Bristol's 'images of uncrowning'; like physical death, demonic possession is one situation in which 'the identity of the king's natural body with the body politic is disrupted.'[177] If the identity of the king's natural body with the body politic were preserved, then the body politic would also be possessed by demons – a thought not likely to be embraced by even the most loyal of royal subjects. Once the king or his theatrical symbol is exorcized on the stage, his royal aura becomes tarnished, and his crown begins to slip off his head. But comical dramatic representations of such a disruption in the royal identity are possible because the fool or other humorous theatrical persona has the advantage of looking at the situation with godlike detachment and omniscience. He sees this disruption, disjunction, or uncrowning (in this case, the rite of exorcism) as simply a normal transition from one ruler to the next. As Bristol explains concerning the porter, who is the comical fool figure witnessing the deposition of one king and the ascendence of another in *Macbeth*:

> In the porter's interpretation of political reality, the difference between a good king and a bad king is relatively slight and inconsequential. The slaughter that goes on as each succession is disputed is understood to be business as usual.[178]

Thus we see how the exorcism of a king on the stage, like similar theatrical depictions of a king's death, is permissible within early modern social order because it does not seriously threaten the dignity of the kingly office. It may even help to ease the transition from one monarch to another.

Even if the satire may be explained within the framework of carnivalesque behaviour, however, we cannot be sure that the king responded to it magnanimously. The answer to the mystery of the king's response to the play could potentially be found by studying the 'emendations' which the 1703 title page claims had been made to the manuscript – presumably after at least one of the performances, but before publication. According to Dowling, the earliest *suelta* of this play, found in Madrid's Biblioteca Nacional, bears the following information on the title page: *Comedia famosa. El hechizado por fuerza. Fiesta que se hizo a sus Magestades martes de Carnestolendas,*[179] *del año de 1698, enmendada en el año 1703. De Don Antonio de Zamora. Impresa en Valladolid, en la Imprenta de Alonso de Riego* (Famous comedy. The one bewitched by force. A festival that was made to their Majesties the Tuesday of Carnival, of the year of 1698, emended in the year 1703. By Don Antonio de Zamora. Printed in Valladolid, in the Press of Alonso of Riego).[180] But until a manuscript of the play is discovered which is notably different from the printed version, the question of the emendations will remain as mysterious as the question of whether the performance of the play caused a cloud to fall upon the king's countenance.

Whatever the play's immediate reception, it remained popular throughout the eighteenth century. From 1708 to 1750, it boasted over 114 productions.[181] The painter Francisco de Goya must have seen one of these, for – as was mentioned earlier – he depicted a scene from the play in a painting which now hangs in the National Gallery in London.[182] Perhaps this healthy *Nachleben* demonstrates that the play filled a need for Spanish intellectuals: to ease the transition from the rule of a feeble and superstitious ruler into the reign of the perceptibly more 'modern' Philip V. Perhaps the emergent, collective Spanish early modern consciousness could identify more readily with a robust, wilful ruler than it could with a pathetic coward who was the evolutionary biological result of too many generations of aristocratic inbreeding. By ridiculing the old superstitions and hailing the new Enlightenment rationality,[183] the play 'exorcized' the body politic of its embarrassments and fears.

In a similar way, as the title demonstrates, Middleton's *The Phoenix* also smoothed the transition from one ruler to the other. In English Renaissance parlance, the monarch was the phoenix who was reborn from the ashes as long as the monarchy continued. In this case, the transition was from the reign of Elizabeth to that of James. This play was probably performed before King James on 20 February 1604.[184] Ostensibly set in Ferrara, the play catalogues the evils of Middleton's London, all of which the duke's son Phoenix uncovers as he tours the realm in disguise prior to ascending the throne. Most of these evils had been detailed the year before the play was performed in King James's book of advice to his son, *Basilikon Doron*.[185] In the play, the old duke has been in power forty-five years, exactly the length of Elizabeth's reign.[186] The play is a thinly disguised compliment, and perhaps also a word of advice to James on how to govern his new kingdom, or *Respublica*. Moreover, it may also be an attack – in the character of the traitor Proditor – on Sir Walter Raleigh, who was imprisoned in the Tower at the time the play was being performed after having been brought to trial on charges of plotting the king's death.[187]

In the play, Proditor and other nobles, hoping to murder the duke and seize power, suggest that the duke's son Phoenix travel abroad. Phoenix agrees to leave and then really travels not abroad, but in his own kingdom. While travelling in disguise he encounters every manner of vice; in fact, some critics have seen the drama as heavily influenced by the morality play as well as other allegorical traditions. By meeting various figures with allegorical names, he uncovers abuses of marriage (the Captain), law (Tangle), justice (Falso), the court (Proditor), the nobility (Lussurioso and Infesto), the gentry (the Knight), and the citizenry (the Jeweller's Wife).[188] These characters are all described in terms of the disease imagery which runs throughout the play, and their exposure to the light is described using the imagery of seeing and sight.[189] The good citizens Phoenix encounters along the way also have allegorical names, such as Castiza, Fidelio, and Quieto.

The prince's disguise[190] is so convincing that he is even hired by Proditor to assassinate his father the duke. Phoenix details all the abuses in the kingdom in a letter to his father, which he has Fidelio deliver. In a bold dénouement, he enters the presence chamber of the ducal palace as the letter is delivered and, still disguised as the would-be assassin, announces that the contents of the letter (just read aloud) are true. He then professes such profound loyalty to the duke that his conscience will not allow him to raise a hand against his lawful ruler. The evil characters are exposed and pardoned after they promise to reform; the one exception is Proditor (the Raleigh figure), who is banished forever. The play ends in a strange but moving tableau scene in which Tangle the lawyer, representing the laws of the realm, falls into a fit of demonic possession after losing two lawsuits. The good citizen Quieto exorcizes him in what is clearly meant to be a synecdoche for curing the body politic:

PHOENIX: He's been so long in suits that he's law-mad.

TANGLE: A judgment, I crave a judgment, yea! Nunc pro tunc, corruptione alicujus. I peep'd me a raven in the face, and I thought it had been my solicitor: oh, the pens prick me! ...

PHOENIX: You see th' unbounded rage of his disease.

QUIETO: 'Tis the foul fiend, my lord, has got within him.
   The rest are fair to this, this breeds in ink,
And to that color turns the blood possess'd ...
The power of my charm come o'er thee,
Place by degrees thy wits before thee;
With silken patience here I bind thee,
Not to move till I unwind thee ...

PHOENIX: Oh, do you sluice the vein now? ...
   Pray, let me see the issue ...

QUIETO: [*Opens Tangle's vein over a basin.*] Now burst out,
Thou filthy stream of trouble, spite, and doubt!

TANGLE: Oh, an extent, a proclamation, a summons, a recognizance, a tachment, and injunction! a writ, a seizure, a writ of 'praisement, an absolution, a quietus est.

QUIETO: You're quieter, I hope, by so much dregs.
   Behold, my lord. [*Holds up basin to Phoenix.*]

PHOENIX: This! why, it outfrowns ink.

QUIETO: 'Tis the disease's nature, the fiend's drink ...
The balsam of a temperate brain
I pour into this thirsty vein, [*pours fluid from bottle*]
And with this blessed oil of quiet,
Which is so cheap that few men buy it,
Thy stormy temples I allay: [*rubs fluid on Tangle's forehead*]
Thou shalt give up the devil, and pray;
Forsake his works, they're foul and black ...

TANGLE: Hail, sacred patience! I begin to feel
I have a conscience now; truth in my words,

Compassion in my heart, and, above all,
In my blood peace's music.[191]

The 'pens pricking' are a clever adaptation of the 'pins pricking' the skin of demoniacs in the historical accounts of the time (demoniacs, like witches, were believed to feel only numbness when pierced with sharp objects; we shall see this 'litmus test' for demonic possession again later in *King Lear*). As we have seen earlier with *Ignoramus*, there was a long tradition in England of demon-possessed lawyers on the stage.[192] The peculiar manner in which this lawyer was exorcized may owe something to Jonson's *Poetaster*, in which Horace gives Crispinus pills to make him vomit his eccentric words into a basin, or to Spenser's *Faerie Queene*, in which Mother Error vomits ink and letters of type.[193]

The medical procedure of bleeding, although not common in literary accounts of exorcism, is not altogether unknown. The medical metaphor is appropriate to this play because metaphors of disease abound throughout the drama. It is clear from the text, however, that this bleeding is more than simply a medical procedure; it is also an exorcism. The exorcism of Tangle by Quieto is, by extension, the exorcism of the body politic by the young prince Phoenix. It is also, by further extension, the exorcism of England by the dramatist Middleton. By having Quieto serve as Phoenix's hand-chosen proxy in performing the exorcism, Middleton implicitly ordains King James as exorcist for the body politic of his new kingdom.

Satirists have traditionally seen the purging of the ills of society as their civic responsibility. By portraying kings on stage either as demoniacs or as exorcists, early modern comic dramatists also created a powerful synecdoche for curing social ills. While this theologeme is more concerned with group dynamics than with emergent notions of early modern selfhood, the rhetorical figure of synecdoche only works when it starts out on the level of the individual. In these two plays and others like them, *the* early modern individual *par excellence* was the king. It is through exploration of the 'regal phantasm' of a king acting as demoniac or exorcist that the early modern dramatist attains the fullest insight concerning the polyvalence of demonic possession for both the individual and the state. The psychodrama of demonic possession and exorcism must always be played out on the level of the individual first. Then it can be extended to encompass an entire society.

The foremost New Historicist, Stephen Greenblatt, has postulated that

the boundaries between the theater and the world are never fixed, nor can they be deduced logically; rather, they are themselves a blend of institutional regulations, unspoken assumptions, evolving moral and aesthetic commitments, ideological interests – in short, a sustained collective enterprise ... [S]ince exorcism involves an unusually self-conscious conjunction of ritual and theater, it is a particularly straight-forward instance of the negotiation of cultural power.[194]

This is how one of the New Historicism's most distinguished practitioners views exorcism in literature, and for the genre of comic drama, it is one with which I can agree. While there has been much fertile and interesting work done recently under the banner of the New Historicism, however, some of the New Historicists' notions about power negotiations and the poetics of culture[195] were foreshadowed by the work of powerful precursors. For example, critics such as Northrop Frye and C.L. Barber have long viewed comedy as a social ritual.[196] M.M. Mahood's essay on *A Midsummer Night's Dream* as exorcism has nothing to do with exorcism but instead argues that the play performs a dramatic ritual designed to chase away social evils.[197] Mahood suggests that in this particular comedy, the evils are the anxieties experienced before making the marriage commitment, but by extension, any comedy could be seen as a dramatic ritual designed to exorcize social anxieties.

In choosing the genre of comic drama, the early modern playwright sublimated the concerns and fears of his audience (seen as a group of early modern playgoers) through the healing power of laughter, offering along the way a social commentary on the political situation as the author saw it. Whatever the topic of the play in which exorcistic motifs appear, these motifs offer a release for the frustrations of the early modern self toward the topic – especially if the topic is, for example, a contemporaneous instance of exorcism or a new monarch's ascension to the throne. The social phenomena of private exorcism (which was nonetheless often very public)[198] and public theatre in the early modern period met the needs of both participants and witnesses by responding in some way to severe pressures, be they political or spiritual.

Whether we choose to see them as caused by evil spirits or political machinations, there is no doubt that exorcisms in literature – particularly comic drama – help to release these pressures in somewhat the same way that private exorcisms did. Bruno Bettelheim's theories about the therapeutic value of children's fairy tales could apply also to literature containing supernatural motifs or elements. While enjoying this literature, the early modern self, like the child of Bettelheim's scenario,

can achieve understanding, and with it the ability to cope, not through rational comprehension of the nature and content of his unconscious, but by becoming familiar with it through spinning out daydreams – ruminating, rearranging, and fantasizing about suitable story elements in response to unconscious pressures.[199]

Although these therapeutic benefits to the self may apply to all instances of exorcism in literature, they apply especially and more communally to the genre of comic drama. The emphasis in the genre of comic drama is on the humorous aspects of a (usually fake) spectacle of demonic possession and exorcism. For example, the demon's entrance into the body is usually by way of something comical, such as eating preserves or a head of lettuce. The symptoms of possession are usually exaggerated for comic effect, and the phenomenon of polyglossia usually appears as comical nonsense. The lovers' ruse is common in this genre as one of many ways in which feigned demonic possession and exorcism can be used to gull the unsuspecting; the culmination of this theologeme in the traditional happy ending of marriage coincides well with this recognized feature of comedy as a genre in which weddings proliferate. The mock exorcistic procedure, conducted by a fake exorcist, includes such elements of interlude-like farce as whipping, beating, binding, and yelling. Because comic drama is a theatrical genre, the 'props' used in this procedure are given special emphasis: relics, holy water, cross, and stole are used (and misused) to comic effect. The successful exorcism is cause for rejoicing, and once again, this theologeme coincides well with the traditional happy ending of comedy. Finally, the exorcism as a synecdoche for curing the body politic provides the comic drama with an apt vehicle for fulfilling its role as a politically engaged genre with a function for society.

These theologemes may also be present in exorcism scenes or motifs in other genres, but with different emphases according to different genres. In more 'serious' genres the theologemes of the symptoms of possession and the successful exorcism will assume greater importance. Demonic possession in less comical genres will assume a more sinister face – a greater threat to the early modern notion of the fully integrated self. Accordingly, we will shift our discussion to the genres of the picaresque and satire, which still retain some features of the more comical genres but partake of some of the more serious theologemes as well.

Chapter Two

Possessed *Pícaros* and Satanic Satire

Oftentimes, to win us to our harm,
The instruments of darkness tell us truths ...   *Macbeth* 1.3.123–4

The same evil spirits who are responsible for every wickedness, namely the 'demons' ...
were given their name because it means 'those who know' in Greek.

Erasmus, *Praise of Folly*

The experience of demonic possession, real or feigned, seen as a source of knowledge – that is the common denominator for the works to be discussed in this chapter. This chapter emphasizes a more positive side of demonic possession, its desirability as a state in which access to knowledge can be gained. This knowledge may be the 'school of hard knocks' sort of common sense of the *pícaro*, or the enticing glimmer of dark, evil knowledge gleaned through the satirical descent into hell. Either way, this new and fascinating knowledge is a potential enhancement to the early modern self – a heightened awareness of the surrounding dangers and entrapments or of an alluring substratum of diabolical lore.

This chapter highlights once again the fundamental ambiguity of the experience of demonic possession during the early modern period. Never seen as a phenomenon which was flatly and unequivocally 'bad,' demonic possession – like sorcery, witchcraft, and other marginal or heterodox activities – could provide entrance into a realm of shadows where mortals seldom dared to tread. As such, it was guarded against by some; it was just as frequently invoked by others. In this chapter we will examine two of these 'marginal' perspectives: that of the picaresque hero and that of the satirist. The purpose will be to hold up to the light yet another facet of demonic possession in literature. In doing so, we are once again reminded of the enduring appeal of this literary topos.

The picaresque and the satirical genres are two distinct but related literary forms which both play a variation on the theme of knowledge:[1] the painfully acquired 'way-of-the-world' knowledge of the *pícaro*, or the critical knowledge about social types and *mores* generated through satirical antithesis.[2] For the picaresque, the anonymous *Lazarillo de Tormes* provides a humorous instance of exorcism as part of the picaresque experience. For satire, Quevedo's *Discurso del alguacil endemoniado* (Discourse of the demoniac constable) reveals the scorn with which more intellectual writers viewed unorthodox superstitions about possession. For these and other works in both of these genres, the attitude of the sceptical demonologists is absorbed and repeated with few adaptations, with little complexity, and with much blunt caricature of fraudulent exorcists and fake demoniacs.

This caricature emphasizes certain theologemes from our paradigm of literary exorcism, while clearly downplaying others. The symptoms of demonic possession receive much attention, particularly as they can be replicated at will and manipulated to full satirical effect. The symptom of clairvoyance is the one most exploited by the satirist who wishes to gain access to diabolical knowledge. The figure of the exorcist is also a locus of interest in these two genres, especially the version of this figure who is a charlatan or a hypocrite. The exorcism ritual itself is also an object of scrutiny, as are the props which are utilized in the course of this procedure. All of these elements or theologemes combine to form a sometimes humorous, often bitter portrait of possession and exorcism as sources of knowledge in the picaresque and satire.

An Erasmian View of *Lazarillo*'s Fifth *Tratado*

The fifth *tratado* or treatise of *La vida de Lazarillo de Tormes* (*The Life of Lazarillo of Tormes*) has elicited little praise from critics. Almost universally condemned as an artistic failure,[3] this *tratado* is the only one in which the protagonist Lazarillo is relegated to the status of mere observer instead of active participant.[4] Scholars have focused not on the subject matter of this *tratado* (it is about exorcism),[5] but instead on the stylistic discontinuities between this section and the rest of the work.

One important exception to this critical consensus is voiced by Raymond S. Willis:

[T]he author did indeed manage to relegate Lazarillo to the background in the ... fifth *tractado* ... [T]his fact is a common complaint in criticism of the book. But it is not generally recognized how apposite and skillfull this treatment really is. In some ways Chapter V is one of the most interesting of the little book. Throughout the first 43 words the first person singular continues to occur at the customary frequency, or no less than six times; but thereafter it virtually disappears from the text until the last 40 ... On the other hand, the first person plural makes an important appearance, by which device Lazarillo submerges himself among the mass of bystanders ... The first person plural further serves to efface Lazarillo as merely an unholy acolyte of the Pardoner ... The disengagement of Lazarillo from the recollected anguish of experience is accomplished with exquisite neatness; and the objectified style corresponds perfectly to the matured and 'educated' personage who, at this stage intermediate between childhood and manhood, is viewed by the narrator as moving immune among the wiles and deceits of the world.[6]

Just as time seems to move more quickly as people grow older, so the flanking of this *tratado* with two exceedingly short *tratados* (of less than a page each) serves to give the reader a sense of time moving more quickly from Lazarillo's perspective.

Willis also points out that this triptych[7] of *tratados* IV, V, and VI serves as the key transition from Lazarillo's highest moral point – feeling humane compassion for the squire – to his moral nadir of sharing his wife with the archpriest.[8] Willis argues convincingly that the anonymous author already had the ending in mind after he penned the third *tratado*. The ironic reversal he envisioned for his protagonist would offer a perfect contrast of human goodness in the midst of poverty with human corruption in the midst of ill-gotten wealth. But a problem presented itself to the author: how to bridge the enormous moral distance between these two states of being?[9] The bridge had to be very short, or else the power of the irony would be lost upon the reader. The transition had to be rapid enough to maintain the narrative momentum, but at the same time, it had to convey the sense of a very long time passing – in fact, about ten whole years of the *pícaro's* life. In this context, argues Willis, the fifth *tratado* is a very deft touch.

One puzzling aspect of Willis's argument, however, is that he does not really address the specific subject matter of the fifth *tratado*, preferring instead to treat it only on stylistic grounds. The content of this episode was controversial enough to warrant its total expurgation in the 1573 edition and subsequent printings of the so-called *Lazarillo castigado*. The revisions for this edition (basically the total omission of the fifth *tratado* as well as one other particularly anticlerical *tratado* suggesting homosexuality, the episode of the *fraile de la Merced*) were undertaken by Juan López de Velasco, the secretary and cosmographer for the Council of the Indies.[10] I will demonstrate how the content of this *tratado*, and not just its style, is integral to the educational formation of the *pícaro* – his acquisition of knowledge – and provides important influences on his future development.

During the first part of the episode, Lazarillo is a childlike, credulous spectator witnessing what he believes to be an authentic demonic possession and exorcism.[11] It is only after he hears the *alguacil* and the *buldero* chuckling to themselves and each other afterward that he realizes he has been taken in by the performance along with the rest of the crowd. The episode opens with a supposed argument (staged, Lazarillo later discovers) between the *buldero* and the *alguacil* over the efficacy of indulgences.[12] The next morning at the church, the *alguacil* denounces the *buldero* before the congregation and proclaims that he is a charlatan. The pardoner listens patiently and kneels calmly in prayer; he then prays out loud for God to strike him down seven *estados* beneath the earth if the accusations are true. But if they are false, he asks God to punish the *alguacil* for trying to prevent people from receiving the grace of the indulgences. At this moment, the *alguacil* drops to the floor on cue and begins acting the part of a demoniac. Here is how the naive narrator Lazarillo tells this part of the story:

Apenas había acabado su oración el devoto señor mío, cuando el negro alguacil cae de su estado, y da tan gran golpe en el suelo, que la iglesia toda hizo resonar, y comenzó a bramar y echar espumajos por la boca y torcerla, y hacer visajes con el gesto, dando de pie y de mano, revolviéndose por aquel suelo a una parte y a otra. El 'estruendo y voces de la gente era tan grande, que no se oían unos a otros. Algunos estaban espantados y temerosos.

Unos decían:

– ¡El Señor le socorra y valga!

Otros:

– ¡Bien se le emplea, pues levantaba tan falso testimonio!

Finalmente, algunos que allí estaban, y a mi parecer no sin harto temor, se llegaron y le trabaron de los brazos, con los cuales daba fuertes puñadas a los que cerca dél estaban. Otros le tiraban por las piernas y tuvieron reciamente, porque no había mula falsa en el mundo que tan recias coces tirase.

Y así le tuvieron un gran rato, porque más de quince hombres estaban sobre él y a todos daba las manos llenas, y si se descuidaban en los hocicos.

(My devout master had hardly finished his prayer, when the black constable falls from his place, and gives such a large blow to the floor, that he made all the church resound, and began to roar and throw out spumes from the mouth and twist it, and make visages with the face, giving with the foot and the hand, revolving himself on that floor to one part and another. The noise and shouts of the people were so great, that they did not hear each other. Some were astonished and fearful.

Some said:

– The Lord succour and aid him!

Others:

– Well is he employed, for he gave such false testimony!

Finally, some who were there, and to my impression not without sufficient fear, came to him and shackled him by the arms, with which he gave strong punches to those who were near him. Others tugged him by the legs and held on roughly, because there was not a false mule in the world who let forth such rough kicks.

And thus they held him a long time, because more than fifteen men were above him and he kept all of their hands full, and if they were not careful [he kicked them] in the nose.)[13]

Here there appear some classic symptoms of demonic possession: falling down, writhing, and foaming at the mouth. The strength of the demoniac – requiring fifteen men to subdue him – is also characteristic.

The assumption of the onlookers, of course, is that the *alguacil* is being punished for speaking disrespectfully of the indulgences and the pardoner who dispenses them. The *buldero* totally ignores the spectacle, pretending to be engrossed in divine ecstasy or rapture as he kneels at the pulpit. He allows the performance to continue until the onlookers beg him to intervene, fearful that the *alguacil* will die if he does not. They ask him not to hold the evil words of the *alguacil* against him, since he has already received punishment for them. The pardoner acquiesces and performs an exorcism upon the demoniac:

Y ansí bajó del púlpito y encomendó aquí muy devotamente suplicasen a nuestro Señor tuviese por bien de perdonar a aquel pecador, y volverle en su salud y sano juicio, y lanzar dél el demonio, si Su Majestad había permitido que por su gran pecado en él entrase.

Todos se hincaron de rodillas, y delante del altar con los clérigos comenzaban a cantar con voz baja una letanía. Y viniendo él con la cruz y agua bendita, después de haber sobre él cantado, el señor mi amo, puestas las manos al cielo ... comienza una oración no menos larga que devota, con la qual hizo llorar a toda la gente ... suplicando a nuestro Señor, pues no quería la muerte del pecador, sino su vida y arrepentimiento, que aquel encaminado por el demonio y persuadido de la muerte y pecado, le quisiese perdonar y dar vida y salud, para que se arrepintiese y confesase sus pecados.

Y esto hecho, mandó traer la bula, y púsosela en la cabeza. Y luego el pecador del alguacil comenzó poco a poco a estar mejor y a tornar en sí, y desque fué bien vuelto en su acuerdo, echóse a los pies del señor comisario, y demandóle perdón y confesó haber dicho aquello por la boca y mandamiento del demonio, lo uno por hacer a él daño y vengarse del enojo, lo otro y más principal, porque el demonio reciba mucha pena del bien, que allí se hiciera en tomar la bula.

(And thus he descended from the pulpit and recommended here very devoutly that they supplicate our Lord that he see fit to pardon that sinner, and to return him to his health and sane judgment, and to cast out from him the demon, if His Majesty had permitted it to enter him through his great sin.

All knelt down on their knees, and before the altar with the clerics began to sing a litany in a low voice. And coming with the cross and holy water, after having sung over him, the gentleman my master, his hands raised to heaven ... begins a prayer no less long than devout, with which he made all the people cry ... supplicating to our Lord, since he did not want the death of the sinner, but his life and repentance, that that one overrun by the demon and persuaded by death and sin, he would wish to pardon and give life and health, so that he repent and confess his sins.

And this done, he ordered the bull brought, and placed it on his head. And then the sinner of a constable began little by little to be better and to come to himself, and after he was well returned to his senses, he threw himself at the feet of the gentleman commissary, and demanded his pardon and confessed to having said that by the mouth and commandment of the demon, the one to do him damage and avenge his annoyance, the other and more principal [reason], so that the demon would receive much pain from the good, that was done there in taking the bull.)[14]

The exorcism is only effected by placing the indulgence on the forehead of the possessed – an effective propaganda technique which results in the sale of many more *bulas*. Some other props and ingredients of a typical exorcism are also present: a cross, holy water, and prayers to cast out the demon.

Although this exorcism is absolutely explicit, it is rarely discussed as such by scholars who write about this work. They most often refer to the obvious hypocrisy of the pardoner without looking at the specific means he uses to deceive the people. The specifics are important, for Lazarillo's future life is symbolized in a significant way in this undeniably strange episode. Like the *alguacil's*, Lazarillo's complicity with a priest (or in his case, an archpriest) to deceive society for personal gain signals an unprecedented moral degradation. Lazarillo's future is typified in the performance of the *alguacil*, who literally twists himself into knots according to the stage directions of a priest. Society will not be able to prove that Lazarillo is a cuckold any more than it can prove that the *alguacil* is a fake. Meanwhile, both the cuckold and the fake demoniac stand to gain in worldly prosperity (while, of course, losing in personal integrity) from this agreed-upon arrangement.[15] Both are the pawns (although Lazarillo is more helpless than the *alguacil*) of powerful, cynical priests who are masterminds of performances designed to deceive society. Perhaps to make the point clearer – and this is a detail almost completely ignored by critics – the anonymous author even makes Lazarillo himself into the apprentice of an *alguacil* at the beginning of the last chapter: 'asenté por hombre de justicia con un alguacil' (I apprenticed myself, being a man of justice, to a constable).[16] Although a passive participant in the spectacle of fake exorcism, he is learning actively as he watches – learning how to become, like the *alguacil*, a convincing performer.[17]

Another often ignored aspect of this episode which makes it integral to the work as a whole is the blatant Erasmianism of the exorcism scene. It is a commonplace of *Lazarillo* criticism that the work bears at least some Erasmian undertones:[18] it criticizes abuses by the clergy, including the sale of indulgences and the maintenance of concubines. Some critics have even suggested the author's anticlerical bias and other Erasmian leanings as one potential reason for his decision to remain anonymous.[19] Thus it is not particularly surprising that the oft-cited Erasmian outlook of the work as a whole would permeate this understudied episode with almost ferocious intensity. Aside from the obvious satire on indulgences,[20] the exorcistic aspect of the episode also echoes the humanist of Rotterdam. Erasmus deals specifically with exorcism in his colloquy 'Exorcism, or the Spectre.' In this biting but quite humorous satire, his attitude toward exorcism is much the same as that of the anonymous author of *La vida de Lazarillo de Tormes*.

The contagious nature of madness is Erasmus's theme in his colloquy 'Exorcism, or the Spectre' (1524). This time, however, the madness does not really trace its source to demonic activity, but rather to human credulity and superstition. In several respects the colloquy resembles the scene in *Lazarillo de Tormes* (1554): the exorcism ritual is a staged event, and the author exploits its theatricality to the fullest. According to legend, Thomas More was believed to have played the part of the mischievous son-in-law in a real-life version of these events.[21] In the literary version, the whole thing begins when Polus starts a rumour about a spectre near a bridge; this vision is taken by the villagers to be a soul in torment because of its pitiful wailings. Polus performs the role of the spectre to test the credulity of Faunus, a superstitious priest. Faunus undertakes the task of exorcism by marking off a circle with crucifixes, holy water, a sacred stole, and a wax Agnus Dei figurine. After repeatedly invoking the relics of the saints, he is terrified by what he takes to be devils with blazing eyes and fiery nostrils on black horses (actually Polus and a friend on black horses with fire torches). Polus also uses a long rope skipping along the ground to trip Faunus, who has been joined by another priest. During each of these incidents Faunus repeats the exorcism ritual, afterward bragging about how effectual it was. Polus then dresses as a devil and rushes toward the circle, claiming that the wretched howling soul belongs to him, but stopping at the edge of the rope as though driven away by the exorcist's power. Finally Polus, again playing the devil, accuses Faunus of fornication and therefore disqualification as an exorcist. Although it was a random guess, it happens to be true. Faunus turns to the other priest for confession and absolution.

Finally the 'tormented soul' sends the priest in search of money it had stolen and hidden on earth. After the priest has made a fool of himself searching for the money and telling anyone who would listen about the spectre, Polus directs the finale of the show by preparing a letter on parchment, supposedly from the soul now in heaven, ordering him to cease his efforts and rejoicing in his success.

Erasmus warns against superstitious credulity as he clearly describes practices and beliefs which had gained wide currency during his time. He is careful not to claim that all supernatural manifestations are charades, since to do so would mean contradicting the numerous gospel accounts of Jesus and the disciples casting out demons. He simply urges caution, discernment, moderation – those Erasmian virtues with which we are so familiar in other contexts. The championing of these virtues, as well as the targeting of clerical hypocrisy in whatever form, have been seen by many critics as threads of Erasmian thought running through *La vida de Lazarillo de Tormes*.

Long viewed as an anomaly by critics who stress Lazarillo's passivity in the episode, this *tratado* nonetheless provides the protagonist with a significant formative experience which will affect him in later years. What is more, the change in perspective of the narration signals an important shift for the *pícaro* toward integration into society: he becomes part of the crowd of onlookers, but he also becomes complicit in the deception being propagated. His outlook is no longer so individualistic, as he realizes the potential benefits of cooperation with the corrupt as a means to mutual gain. The *tratado* thus offers a logical foreshadowing of the resolution of the picaresque tale. As such, it does fit satisfactorily with the work as a whole, both on stylistic grounds and on those of substance. As for the content of the episode, my interpretation of it offers further support for the position that this text is Erasmian in both its general outlook and its choice of subject matter. Although the Erasmianism of the work as a whole is often discussed, the word 'exorcism' is rarely used to label (accurately and undeniably) what is happening in this episode;[22] perhaps it is for this reason that no one has compared Erasmus's colloquy 'Exorcism, or the Spectre' to the fifth tratado of *La vida de Lazarillo de Tormes*.

In the foregoing analysis we have seen how the picaresque hero – one classic figuration of the early modern self as it becomes autonomous – uses the witnessing of a spectacle of demonic possession to further his education in the ways of the world. In this picaresque intrigue of charlatans and gullible spectators, many of the elements of a comical treatment of exorcism are still present. The fraudulent exorcist, the props (including the *bulas*), the acting out of symptoms of possession: all of these are theologemes which also received emphasis in the comic drama. Now we will turn to several satirical genres to see how the phenomenon of exorcism in literature mutates when it is poured through this particular generic filter. Some of the comical theologemes remain prominent, but some of the more serious theologemes also start to prevail. We will see, furthermore, how the ambiguity of demonic possession is exploited to offer the satirical persona – and thus the early modern self who reads the satire – access to supernatural knowledge that is otherwise forbidden.

Another *Pícaro* and Another *Alguacil endemoniado*: Quevedo's *Buscón*, *Sueños*, Satirical Poetry, and *La endemoniada fingida*

Michel Foucault wrote that 'the wisdom of fools ... is a forbidden wisdom.'[23] Only from the mouth of a fool, a *pícaro*, a madman, or a demoniac can this wisdom be spoken.[24] Now we turn both to another *pícaro* and to another *alguacil endemoniado*, alike the brainchildren of the Spanish Baroque poet Francisco de Quevedo.

The picaresque *Vida del buscón Don Pablos* gives us only a foretaste of what we will see in the *Discurso del alguacil endemoniado* by the same author. The picaresque novel includes a snippet of a tale not fully developed in which an old man at an inn starts coughing while eating and thus spits out some of his food. When he curses in reference to Satan, a priest and a student immediately assume that he is exhibiting the symptoms of a demoniac and begin to exorcize him. The farcical vignette is told from the perspective of the young protagonist, Pablos:

> Comenzó a escupir y hacer gestos de asco. Llegamos todos a él, y el cura el primero, diciéndole que qué tenía; empezó a ofrecerse a Satanás, y dejó caer las alforjas; llegóse a él el estudiante, y dijo: 'Arriedro vayas, Satán, cata la cruz.' El otro abrió un breviario, y hiciéronle creer que estaba endemoniado, hasta que él mismo dijo lo que era, y pidió que le dejasen enjuagar la boca con un poco de vino que él traía.

> (He began to spit and to make faces of nausea. We all went to him, and the priest the first, asking him what was wrong; he began to offer himself to Satan, and he let the saddle bags fall; the student approached him, and said: 'Get behind me, Satan, behold the cross.' The other one opened a breviary, and they made him believe that he was demon-possessed, until he himself said what it was, and asked that they let him rinse out his mouth with a little of the wine that he brought.)[25]

Although misunderstood, these symptoms are typical (spitting and gesticulation), as are some props and other components of the exorcistic ritual (the cross, the breviary, and the vulgarization of the Latin '*Vade retro*' [Get thee behind me] formula).

Quevedo repeated this vulgarization of the '*Vade retro*' exorcistic imperative in his poem 'Pintura de la mujer de un abogado, abogada ella del demonio' (Painting of the wife of a lawyer, herself being the advocate of the demon). The poem is a satirical portrait of an old woman whom Quevedo demonizes because of her ugliness. It begins:

> Viejecita, arredro vayas,
> donde sirva, por lo lindo,
> a San Antón esa cara
> de tentación y cochino.

> (Little old woman, get thee behind me,
> where it will serve, for its beauty,
> Saint Anthony – that face
> of temptation and filth.)[26]

Here Quevedo refers to the hagiographical legend, often depicted in paintings from this period, in which demons appeared to Saint Anthony to tempt him into sin.[27] The poet even refers to the woman as a 'sueño de Bosco con tocas,'[28] a painting of Hieronymous Bosch, that infamous painter of demons and kindred spirit of Quevedo's to whom he would refer again in his *Sueños*. Quevedo does not suggest seriously, even for a moment, that the woman is demon-possessed. Rather, he uses demonic possession as a witty metaphor to convey what seems to him to be the supernatural degree of her ugliness. Never one to resist puns and wordplay, Quevedo stretches the grotesque metaphor as far as it will go, describing the woman in the same terms one would use for a demoniac: 'alma en pena con soplillo' (soul in anguish with breath) (l. 18). Here he makes fun of her not only because she is ugly, but also because she is old – so old, in fact, that she is near death, and her face betrays this likelihood:

> no cara, sino Carón,
> el barquero del abismo;
> de la capacha del diablo,
> andadera de espartillo ...

> (not a face, but Charon,
> the shipman of the abyss;
> of the devil's basket,
> cart made of grass ...)   (ll. 37–40)

Quevedo ends this poem with an irreverent invocation of the exorcism ritual, by which he hopes to drive away this demonically ugly woman. Comparing her to a lizard, he goes off to search for a proper exorcist who will remove her not only from his presence but also from the world:

> Mas yo me parto a buscar
> quien conjure basiliscos,
> por si a sacaros del mundo
> pueden valer exorcismos.

> (But I leave to seek
> one who conjures basilisks,
> in case to remove you from the world
> exorcisms can avail.) (ll. 127–32)

Quevedo usually repeated jokes he particularly liked in several different contexts; thus we find a line of another poem, 'Describe operaciones del Tiempo y verifícalas también en las mudanzas de las danzas y bailes' (Describing the operations of Time and verifying them also in the movements of the dances and ballets), in which he refers to another old woman as 'una dueña arriedro vayas' (old maid get thee behind me).[29] This diabolical woman appears yet again in Quevedo's *romance* 'Advertencias de una dueña a un galán pobre' (Warnings of a widow to a poor gallant).[30] The poor young man addresses the older woman in the same way we have heard her described in the other poems:

> bien sé yo que contra ti,
> por ser entre sombra y duende,
> no valen sino conjuros
> del misal y de los prestes.
> Yo traeré quien destas casas,
> con cruz, estola y asperges,
> saque, como los demonios,
> la dueña legión que tienen.

> (well I know that against you,
> for being between shadow and poltergeist,
> do not avail [anything] except conjurings
> of the missal and of the priests.
> I will bring someone who from these houses,
> with cross, stole and sprinklings,
> will remove, like the demons,
> the widow legion they contain.) (ll. 93–100)

He threatens to bring a priest to exorcize her with a cross, stole, missal, holy water, and 'conjuros.' This demonically old, ugly woman is a vaguely defined but insistently recurring figure, a phantom who lurks in the shadows of Quevedo's satirical poetry.[31]

Quevedo's burgeoning curiosity about the exorcism material – as evidenced by his youthful foray into the picaresque genre, as well as his satirical poems – would not attain maturity until his satirical *Discurso del alguacil endemoniado*, which we shall discuss momentarily. It should also be mentioned that there are two further works of doubtful authenticity that have been attributed to him which deal specifically with exorcism – the *romance* 'El exorcista Calabrés' and the *Entremés famoso de la endemoniada fingida y chistes de Bacallao* (Famous interlude of the pretended demoniac and jokes of Bacallao). The first, while of considerable literary and possibly even historical interest, has been discarded definitively by reputable scholars such as James Crosby as a nineteenth-century elaboration of Quevedo's famous *Discurso del alguacil endemoniado*.

While it is unclear who wrote the second work, the *Entremés famoso* is generally considered to date back to the seventeenth century;[32] in other words, if Quevedo did not write it, then one of his fairly close contemporaries did. It is not out of the question that Quevedo did write it, considering the fact that he is known to have written several *entremeses*.[33] In this funny interlude, the married woman Faustina is wooed by an older man who longs to be her paramour. She feigns demonic possession with two goals in mind: she tells the old man that her purpose is to smuggle him (disguised as an exorcist) into her house, while she tells her husband Duarte that her purpose is to punish the would-be suitor for his audacity. The old man and his servant, Bacallao, arrive at midnight armed with all the appropriate props: a priest's cassock and cap, a cauldron, and something resembling a branch of hyssop for sprinkling holy water. The husband and his friend take revenge upon the intruders by dressing up like devils and assaulting them, claiming that Pluto needs more *castratos* in hell. They relent when the clever wife reenters merrily with musicians, and the *entremés* ends with a song about deception as a just punishment for deception.

Personally, I believe Quevedo did write this *entremés*.[34] It is a very erudite specimen of its genre, including references to specific saints associated with exorcism (Hilario, Pedro Mártir, and Longino) and comically macaronic Latin spoken by the old man during the exorcism ritual: 'Dominus vobiscum, arre[ptitie]. / ... Fili Dei. / Et ne nos inducas' (God be with you, raving mad one. / ... Son of God. / And lead us not [into temptation]).[35] The servant also begs, 'Noli me tangere' (Do not touch me; a clear reference to the Vulgate John 20:17, where Jesus speaks to Mary Magdalene immediately after the resurrection)[36] when the husband threatens him with castration. All of this playful erudition – and abuse of erudition – would seem to echo the kinds of jokes Quevedo was fond of making. Perhaps the most convincing argument in favour of Quevedo's authorship is the trademark 'arredro vayas' phrase we have already seen in two works by him. When Duarte's friend Osorio first witnesses Faustina's performance, he is taken in by it and exclaims, 'Demonio es, hacedle cruces, / Espíritu arredro vayas' (It is a demon, make crosses to it, / Spirit get thee behind me).[37] Although variations of this phrase were common in vernacular exorcisms, it is far from unusual to find the exact same variant of it in several different works. I conclude that in Quevedo's mind, this was a tag phrase associated with exorcism, and he normally used it whenever he wrote about this topic. He developed this topic most fully in the *Discurso del alguacil endemoniado*, a work which exemplifies early modern fascination with demonic possession as a form of access to diabolical knowledge.

Alguacil endemoniado or *Demonio alguacilado*?

The setting of the *Discurso del alguacil endemoniado* is the parish church of San Pedro el Real in Madrid. The artistic decision to locate the scene in this particular church bears much resonance because it was named for San Pedro Mártir, the patron saint of the Spanish Inquisition. This detail supports the view that the work is a protest against Inquisitorial censorship. The bell of this specific church was also famous at the time for its power to protect against lightning and to make demons flee. Quevedo made fun of this bell in two other sonnets.[38]

The narrator goes to the church to visit his friend and confessor, a cleric named Calabrés. Some scholars have seen a certain affinity between Calabrés and another (similarly named) unforgettable character, the *licenciado* Cabra of the *Buscón*.[39] The narrator finds Calabrés in the process of exorcizing a possessed *alguacil*. The exorcist is satirized mercilessly in an unforgettably detailed character portrait which is arguably unrivalled in the work of Quevedo:

> clérigo de bonete de tres altos, orillo por ceñidor, puños de Corinto, asomo de camisa por cuello, rosario en mano, disciplina, zapato grande y de ramplón, habla entre penitente y disciplinante, los ojos bajos y los pensamientos tiples, color a partes encendida y a partes quebrada, tardón en la mesa y abreviador en la misa, gran lanzador de diablos, tanto que sustentaba el cuerpo a puros espíritus.

> (cleric of a bonnet three stories high, selvadge for a belt, wristbands of Corinth, sign of a shirt at the neck, rosary in hand, scourge, large and coarse shoe, speech between penitent and flagellator, the lowered eyes and the high thoughts, color partly enflamed and partly broken, who stays at the table and abbreviates the mass, great caster-out of devils, so much that he sustained his body on pure spirits.)[40]

The details all fit the picture of a fraudulent exorcist: the pot belly, the beggar's shoes, and the hat 'three stories high.' All the usual props are also present: the rosary in hand, the disciplinary whip at his side, and the stole used to bind the demoniac. The exorcist uses heretical charms and incantations (*ensalmos*), claims powers of divine revelation and miracles, and is described by Quevedo as a Pharisaical hypocrite ('hipócrita, embeleco vivo, mentira con alma y fábula con voz' [hypocrite, live delusion, lie with a soul and fraud with a voice]).[41] Crosby sees this hypocritical cleric as a descendant of the *buldero* of *Lazarillo de Tormes*.[42] He is 'drunk with *flagelum demonis*,' a reference to Girolamo Menghi's famous exorcism handbook *Flagellum daemonum* but also a clear reference to his beating the (bound) demoniac. It is implied that this greedy priest is paid for his services, something the church also prohibited.

The demon begins speaking and joins in the conversation between narrator and exorcist. The exorcist moves to silence him, but the narrator, 'que había comenzado a gustar de las sutilezas del diablo' (who had begun to like the subtleties of the devil),[43] implores him to allow the demon to continue speaking. The exorcist acquiesces, even though the Church unequivocally condemns this practice. Ilse Nolting-Hauff has called this dialogue, memorably, a 'grotesque interview'[44] with a demon who speaks through the body of the possessed. Technically speaking, there are four entities present – the possessed *alguacil*, the exorcist Calabrés, the narrator, and the demon – but only three of these speak, for the *alguacil* is present only in body, having been taken over completely by the possessing demon. There is a joke to this effect, when the demon complains that the proper term for the fusion of the two entities is *demonio alguacilado* instead of *alguacil endemoniado*. Begging to be expelled, the demon claims to feel degraded by being trapped inside so despicable a human being.

He is, however, constrained in this world by the authority of the exorcist who attempts three times (in the end, successfully) to silence him. Harry Sieber does not see an antagonism between the exorcist and the narrator here, but I believe that he is missing the point.[45] The narrator is the one who urges the demon to speak, asking him questions and rebuking the exorcist for attempting to silence the only source of truth within the narrative. Sieber asserts that 'the narrator abandons his passive role as listener only when his self interest is threatened,'[46] in other words, when the devil starts to malign poets and lovers. I think Sieber misunderstands the larger issues at stake, beyond any petty concerns of self-interest on the part of the narrator; the narrator's piercing intellectual curiosity leads him to probe for forbidden knowledge and ask questions instead of merely listening as the devil volunteers information. The narrator's Faustian curiosity leads us to the main point of this chapter: the exorcism ritual seen as a potential source of knowledge. In this case, the knowledge sought by the early modern man concerns hell and its inhabitants.

'The Experienced Mysteries of Damnation'

The idea of hell was fascinating to the early moderns, although it is increasingly marginalized in today's secular society.[47] Through the ages the conceptualization of hell has changed dramatically with each successive epoch; in a series of possible hells, the baroque version was a particularly horrifying one:

> The great invention of the Baroque hell lay in the restoration of disorder, in the return to an infernal chaos; it made the damned person into a devil *malgré lui*, and turned his neighbour who had fallen beside him into a torturer. Everyone became the involuntary persecutor of the next man, everyone was an insupportable burden to his co-inhabitant. There was enforced cohabitation, overcrowding and intolerable promiscuity ... Probably no other century regarded this world more disconsolately through the eyes of the other world; over no other age did hell exert such an attraction and repulsion, and in so spasmodic and obsessive a fashion as the seventeenth century. The tortured bodies of the underworld were a sinister invitation to massacre and torment in this world. So that it might be avoided, the painful well was depicted in the cruel flagellation of the diseased flesh of the Christian who squirmed along the earth, weighted down by his guilt and goaded by the exorbitant burden of a doubtful eternity.[48]

Catholics in the early modern period were encouraged to spend time imagining how this hell would smell, taste, and feel by St Ignatius Loyola, whose *Spiritual Exercises* became favourite meditations during the Counter-Reformation. His express purposes in the Fifth Exercise, a meditation on hell, were as follows:

> To ask for a deep awareness of the pain suffered by the damned, so that if I should forget the love of the Eternal Lord, at least the fear of punishment will help me to avoid falling into sin.
>
> *First point*: To see in imagination the great fires, and the souls enveloped, as it were, in bodies of fire.
>
> *Second point*: To hear the wailing, the screaming, cries, and blasphemies against Christ our Lorde and all his saints.
>
> *Third point*: To smell the smoke, the brimstone, the corruption, and rottenness.
>
> *Fourth point*: To taste bitter things, as tears, sadness, and remorse of conscience.
>
> *Fifth point*: With the sense of touch to feel how the flames surround and burn souls.[49]

Painters and engravers of the period further exploited the imaginative potential of hell and its horrors. Albrecht Dürer's woodcut *Harrowing of Hell* (1510), Luca Signorelli's frescoes 'Hell' and 'The Damned' (1503), Hieronymous Bosch's

Vienna *Last Judgment* (early 1500s), Pieter Bruegel I's (1528–69) *The Fall of the Rebel Angels*, Pieter Huys's *The Last Judgment* (1554), B. Van Orley's (1488–1541) portrayal of the rich man in hell (found on the back of his tryptich *The Virtue of Patience*), and the school of Pieter Bruegel's *Triumph of Death* (1620), not to mention Michelangelo's *Last Judgment* (1536–41), were all devoted to the depiction of hell, its inhabitants, and its torments.[50]

As could be surmised from this baroque preoccupation with hell,[51] the phenomenon of a demon speaking about hell through the body of a demoniac was common in early modern 'real–life' experience. The English demoniac Thomas Darling claimed to have been taken to hell, and he offered his visitors a lively accounting of its particulars.[52] The 'Surey Demoniack' was possessed by a devil who spoke of hell with piercing insight:

> Yea, so uncommonly did Satan penetrate as into the experienced Misteries of Damnation, as if he were gushing out all *Etnae*'s roaring Floods of blazing Sulfur Rocks, or stirring up the very dregs and bottoms of the fired Brimstone Lake, so as surely might have flasht Lightning into the most closed Eyes of divers Consciences that could possibly be lift up before tormented in this Flame ...[53]

A female demoniac of about the same period was seen by her visitors as a source of supernatural knowledge about hell and specific sinners:

> They did usually put many questions unto her, as sometimes asking what became of any one that was dead, whether they went to Hell or to Heaven, and she would instantly resolve them; and so far as they could guess she answered truly; for those who had been evil livers, she would tell all their faults and misdemeanours ...[54]

Sometimes in these 'real-life' cases, the exorcists or their audiences questioned the permissibility of interrogating the devil. Although the churches of both Spain and England expressly condemned it, some exorcists rationalized the practice casuisitically by emphasizing the knowledge that could be gained from it:

> Some professors questioned the lawfulness of talking to Satan ... [I]t was found unlawful, if it were by way of *Eve*'s curiosity ... But yet on the other hand, it seem'd lawful and useful when manag'd in a right manner ... Or should Satan meet a Man in a Humane Apparition, would it not be natural? Or in some other resemblances, would it not be lawful for a Man to speak to him? If so, Why not in a *Demoniack*, as well as in such other appearances?[55]

Other exorcism manuals warned against fraudulent exorcists who, by questioning the demon, 'have transgressed the bounds of their Authority, and inquire into things that they ought not.'[56] According to these manuals, the prognostications of demoniacs were dangerous; and King James proclaimed 'that since all Prophecies and visiones are nowe ceased, all spirites that appeares in these formes are evill.'[57] These manuals invoked Thomas Aquinas and John Chrysostom to support their case 'that it was unlawful to adjure the Devil, in order to learn something from him, for *Aquinas* from *Saint Chrysostom* assures us, that we ought not to believe the Devil, though he declare nothing but the truth.'[58]

One of the foremost of these demonological manuals to address this question in Spain was Martín Del Río's *Disquisitionum magicarum libri sex*, of which Quevedo is known to have possessed a copy.[59] Del Río specifies which questions to be posed to a devil are 'licit' and 'illicit':

petunt nomen daemonis ... [N]on liceat peter vt socios indicent, vt sciamus cum quibus confligendum: petunt causam ingressus: vt à similibus peccatis alii caueant, & eo vitato vel expiato facilius sanetur energumenus, signum egressionis petunt, vt constet iam vere liberatum aegrum. Mendax quidem est diabolus: sed exorcismi verum inuito extorquent ... Monendi ergo vt abstineant exorcizatos superfluis colloquiis & terminis illis actuum iudiciariorum, quibus iubent daemonem nunc erire ... [H]oc etiam prohibuit ne energumenoru[m] huiusmodi in corporibus loquentes daemones auscultemus ... Moneatur ipse exorcista non minus quam caeteri, nihil curiositatis aut discendi causa daemonem interrogare, aut ab eo exquirere, licet id honestissimum sit & vtile videatur.

(They seek the name of the demon ... It would not be allowed to ask that they name their associates, so that we might know with whom we must fight: they seek a cause for the entry, in order that others might shrink from similar sins, so that with this avoided or expiated, the possessed one might more easily be restored to health. They seek a sign of exit, so that it might then be clear that one who has truly been freed is weak. The devil is indeed deceitful: but exorcisms wring out the truth from an unwilling person ... Having been warned therefore that they keep those who have been exorcized from superfluous conversations and those limits of acts associated with law courts, by which they order the demon to come forth at once ... [t]his indeed has forbidden us to listen to demons speaking in the bodies of those possessed in this way ... Let the exorcist himself, no less than the others, be warned not to ask a demon anything out of curiosity or in order to learn, or to inquire from him, although it seems most excellent and useful.)[60]

Del Río also gives a (rather humorous) example of the potential danger of speaking to a demon illicitly:

Vidi ... in conuentu Coloniensi, fratrem, verbis satis iocosum, sed in gratia expellendi daemones valde famosum. Hic cum in terminis conuentus Coloniensis daemonem in obsesso corpore arctaret: daemon petiuit à fratre locum recedendi: quo gavisus frater ait in ioco. In cloacam meam vadas. Exijt igitur, daemon, & noete cum frater ventre purgare vellet, daemon tam dire eum torsit prope cloacam, vt vitam cum difficultate saluaret.

(I saw in a monastery in Cologne a monk, quite jovial in speech but very famous for his gift of expelling demons. When he restrained a demon in a possessed body within the confines of the monastery in Cologne, the demon asked the monk where he could withdraw to: the monk was amused by this and said in jest, 'Go into my ass.' The demon therefore came forth, and when the monk wanted to purge his stomach at night, the demon wrenched him so violently toward the anus that he was barely able to escape death.)[61]

We see here how Del Río specifically warns against asking questions of the devil and recounts frightening instances of cases where this prohibition was violated.

But even the theologians who warned against these diabolical conversations acknowledged that the devil could be a source of truth. Caspar Peucer wrote in 1553 about the devil's enormous capacity for knowledge:

Daemonum est & fuit magna potentia, astutia, & calliditas incredibilis, sapientia tanta, quanta in nullis alius creaturis praeter sanctos Angelos, perspicacitas acutissima ... in interpretandis notis & signis praecipua, vigilantia summa, artificium struendi technas perniciosissimas fuco speciosissimo incomparabile, malitia infinita, odium erga genus humanum ... Ex vtrisq[ue] coniunctis aestimant argutissime, quae cuiusque sit natura, ad quae vitia feratur ... propendeat, ad quae studia ducatur, qui redundent humores & vincant, qui sint affectus dominaturi quae sit vel consensio futura, vel discrepantia ... quibus regitur & dispensatur corpus humanum: quos morbos, vel naturae imbecillitas partitura, vel quius sponte alias aliis occasionibus sit attracturus, quae pericula impendeant vitae & fortunis, aliaq[ue] his similia.

(Great was the power of demons, unbelievable their astuteness and cleverness, their wisdom was as great as any other creatures except the holy angels, their perspicuity most keen ... outstanding in interpreting marks and signs, very great their vigilance, incomparable their cleverness in constructing the most pernicious devices with the most beautiful pretence, limitless their malice, their hatred toward the human race ... From each and every association they calculate most subtly what the nature of each is, to which vices it is born ... it would incline, to which studies he is led, which humours well up and prevail, what emotions will prevail, what the agreement or disagreement will be ... by which the human body is ruled and managed: what diseases, either natural weakness will engender or on other occasions of its own accord it will otherwise attract, what dangers loom over life and fortune, and other similar things.)[62]

Here we see how knowledgeable demons were able to interpret occult signs and propel human beings toward the vices that most perfectly suited their humours and inclinations. Quevedo, like a select few other early modern minds, was interested in obtaining this demonic knowledge.

The specific Quevedian *Sueño* or *Discurso* in which we are interested is written in dialogue form, somewhat reminiscent of the colloquies of Erasmus.[63] It falls within the traditions of Lucian's *Dialogues of the Dead* and such religious, prophetical works as Hippolytus's *End of the World and Second Coming of Christ*. It also bears some resemblance to Seneca's *Apocolocyntosis*, which Quevedo also owned.[64] Some Renaissance adaptations of these classical works were Justus Lipsius's *Satira Mennipea, Somnium,* and *Lusus in nostri aevi criticos* as well as Juan Luis Vives's *Somnius Vivis.*[65] In his own discourse of the damned, Quevedo satirizes artillerymen, scribes or notaries, gossips, lovers, bakers, astrologers, alchemists, medical doctors, merchants, government officials, fools, tavern-keepers and innkeepers – all in ingenious juxtapositions of certain occupations based on their underlying affinities (for instance, physicians next to executioners).[66] In this sense, his work draws upon late medieval traditions such as the fourteenth-century dances of death (see fig. 4). He also makes fun of the writers of *comedias,* who must be punished in hell for having made queens adulterous, arranged unequal marriages at the ends of their plays, and allowed honourable men to receive blows at the ends of their *entremeses*. He self-consciously satirizes poets by condemning them to an eternity of hearing their rivals' works read aloud. Additionally, he reiterates his oft-repeated attacks against antiquated mythological poetry by having poets who arrive in hell ask to see the mythical figures thought by the Ancients to inhabit this or a similar place. They only accept with great reluctance the admonitions of the demons that such figures never existed.

The type or profession most viciously satirized is obviously that of the *alguacil,* whom Quevedo may have regarded with special rancour because of his own lawsuits over his property, the Torre de Juan Abad, and his various experiences of incarceration.[67] Scholars have speculated that he makes fun of the six orders of demons in Psellus by offering six classes of *alguaciles,* each worse than the last.[68] Quevedo may have owned a copy of Psellus which he annotated: Aureliano Fernández-Guerra claimed to have seen an exemplar in the library of San Isidro with marginalia matching Quevedo's youthful handwriting.[69] In his study of the dispersion of Quevedo's library, Maldonado found a 1615 Psellus in the Biblioteca de San Martín, where many of Quevedo's books came to be located; this date of publication, however, is too late for the composition of the *Discurso del alguacil endemoniado*.[70] But whether we are reading the effects of personal resentment or not, no one is safe from the poisonous pen of Quevedo, who even satirizes the reader who has become infected by reading his demonic works.

The parade of satirical types presented by Quevedo does not appear in a random order. As Gonzalo Díaz Migoyo has demonstrated convincingly, the satire alternates in a masterfully regular rhythm between 'worldly' and 'otherworldly' topics and persons. According to this scheme, poets are 'worldly,' but hell (which is described next) is 'otherworldly'; lovers are 'worldly,' while demons are 'otherworldly.' Likewise, kings, merchants, and judges are 'worldly,' but the allegory of Justice is 'otherworldly'; women are 'worldly,' while the poor are not attached to this world in either a literal or a figurative sense. Díaz Migoyo also sees another underlying structural feature of this work: the description of hell as a place where figures of speech come to life. Quevedo even makes the demon say at one point: 'Todo el infierno es figuras' (all hell is figures).[71] Díaz Migoyo identifies a single common sin among all the condemned, and it is simply this: they have believed in fiction too literally. By this he means that they have either transformed their reality into fiction or else hidden their reality behind fiction:

> Los poetas y enamorados, lectores figurativos del mundo, viven la mentira o error consistente en tomar por sentido del mundo las figuras que ellos mismos inventan ... Los reyes, mercaderes, jueces y mujeres, en cambio, viven en el error de literalizar unas ficciones recibidas. Aquéllos usan las ficciones recibidas para ignorar la realidad de este mundo ... En ambos casos ignoran la relación dialéctica de realidad y ficción ...

> (The poets and lovers, figurative readers of the world, live the lie or consistent error in taking for the sense of the world the figures that they themselves invent ... The kings, merchants, judges and women, in contrast, live in the error of literalizing some received fictions. Those use the received fictions to ignore the reality of this world ... In both cases they ignore the dialectical relation of reality and fiction ...)[72]

In every case, their punishment in hell consists of the literalization of their fictions. Thus the writers of *comedias* are condemned to a place next to procurers and solicitors because all of these people have woven intricate webs of deceit. Scribes and artillerymen are placed side by side because they both fire shots into the world. In this way the damned have become like the demons, who interpret figures of speech about themselves literally.

While I appreciate Díaz Migoyo's proposed structure for the work, I see another structure shaping this *discurso*. In light of my thesis that this work is really about knowledge and the printing of forbidden knowledge, I see a structure of individual questions posed by the narrator, followed by the devil's responses to those specific questions. These responses are followed in turn by the devil's tangential complaints, which serve to assert his illicit control over the dialogue. The narrator asks about poets, the demon answers about poets – and then changes the subject to other satirical types (notaries, tailors, undertakers, bakers, astrologers, alchemists, doctors, merchants, tavern-keepers, and innkeepers). The narrator asks about lovers, the demon answers about lovers (including nuns), and then changes the subject to how demons object to figures of speech and paintings of themselves. The narrator asks about kings, the demon answers about kings, and then changes the subject to Genovese merchants. Up to this point the narrator has maintained some control over the conversation in the sense that he has remained able to steer the demon back toward the topics of most interest to him. He is even able to extract fairly short answers from the talkative demon on the subject of judges. But the narrator begins to lose control over the dialogue when he asks about Justice; the demon launches into a parable about the descent of Truth and Justice to earth.[73] Truth was refused lodging because she was naked, while Justice was turned away because she was rigorous. Crosby notes that Quevedo may have witnessed a recurrent pageant in Valladolid in the years 1601–6 about this parable of Justice on earth.[74] Crosby cites Sepúlveda's *Historia de varios sucesos* for a description of the pageant, in which Avarice found lodging with the Duque de Lerma and Pride, with the Duquesa. The figure of Justice knocked at the door of the palace and was told by the king that only innocence and ignorance resided there.

The demon's story soon becomes a sermon, which he follows with two other sermons[75] on the topics of 'all life is theft' and the sanctity of pious poverty.[76] The content of this *discurso* is as varied as its structure, for this demon is not only a preacher, but also a prophet and political advisor. The *alguacil endemoniado* offers political commentary, just like the English demoniac who predicted a war with Ireland,[77] or the Italian demoniac who predicted that the Turks would invade Rome and the French king would be elected emperor.[78] This demonic prophet speaks knowledgeably, for example, about the Genovese bankers who lent large sums to the king of Spain using the cargo of gold and silver bullion that was expected on ships from America as collateral (for this service they of course charged very high interest rates). Quevedo, through the mouthpiece of his prophet, also offers commentary on the role of a king, drawing from the long 'mirror of princes' tradition.[79] He notes that a king's special temptations are to pride, cruelty, and greed, but to soften this criticism, he blames the *privados* or ministers of the king for influencing him perniciously. In the 1627 edition, Quevedo or an editor inserted a few phrases at this point to praise the Spanish king as an exception to this rule, but in the 1631 edition, these phrases were removed; instead, Quevedo protected himself by inserting the word 'pagan' in his discussion of kings. This distinction automatically excluded the Catholic kings of Spain. In the later edition he also added some obsequious words describing how difficult the jobs of kings and their ministers were; these additions were a jarring contradiction when juxtaposed with the earlier criticisms of these officials within the same text.[80] Quevedo's demonic prophet warns that a bad king, through his sins, can even bring his whole kingdom to damnation. But Quevedo distances himself from this potentially dangerous and subversive subject matter by remaining twice removed from the narrative: he speaks through the demon, who speaks through the *alguacil.*

How does this macabre interview end? Sieber claims that 'only when the devil accuses Calabrés of hypocrisy does the interview come to an end. Calabrés, refusing to hear the truth about himself and others like him, uses his power to silence the devil.'[81] In this respect, Calabrés would not be unlike his 'real-life' counterparts – exorcists who sought to silence the devil as soon as he began revealing their secret sins,

> which discoveries of such secret transactions, made some more circumspect against ill Words, Thoughts, Actions, lest Satan should publish them at these Conferences in vast Assemblies ... Whence the Ministers often blest the Lord ... for that he kept Satan from reporting their past Frailties.[82]

In addition to covering their own sins, however, these ministers who sought to silence the devil were – in Quevedo's mind – committing the much graver sin of refusing to think for themselves and question received orthodoxy. As Gonzalo Díaz Migoyo explains it, the exorcist Calabrés commits the same sin that all the damned in Quevedo's hell have committed: he is an intransigent literalist who defends received values and refuses to doubt. Both he and they

> insistían también en afirmar una verdad unitaria y monolítica, no dialéctica, de la realidad ... [d]e donde se seguiría la arbitrariedad y la contingencia de considerar un orden cualquiera de creencias como autónomamente válido.

> (insisted also in affirming a unitary and monolithic truth, not dialectic, of reality ... from whence would follow the arbitrariness and contingency of considering any order whatsoever of beliefs as automatically valid).[83]

The narrative actually comes to an end in a way that provides subtle closure and highlights the internal logic of the dialogue:

Y si un diablo por sí es malo, mudo es peor que diablo. V. Excelencia lea esto con curiosa atención y no mire a quien lo dijo, que Herodes profetizó, y por la boca de una sierpe de piedra sale un caño de agua, en la quijada de un león hay miel, y el salmo dice que a veces recibimos 'salutem ex inimicis nostris et de manu qui oderunt nos,' etc.

(*And if a devil by himself is bad, a mute is worse than a devil.* Your Excellency, read this with curious attention and do not look at who said it, for Herod prophesied, and from the mouth of a serpent of rock flows a stream of water, and in the jaw of a lion there is honey, and the psalm says that sometimes we receive 'health from our enemies and from the hand of those who have hated us,' etc.)[84]

What Harry Sieber calls these 'riddle-like paradoxes,'[85] spoken directly by the author to the dedicatee (the Conde de Lemos), are in fact parodies of unofficial exorcisms, or *ensalmos*. They have been correctly identified as such by James Crosby, who has found and reproduced a more modern version of these printed charms which were sometimes worn around the neck (see fig. 3).[86] These riddles or *ensalmos* all bear the same message: no knowledge should be forbidden. If Quevedo had been Eve in the garden, he too would have taken a bite of the apple from the tree of the knowledge of good and evil. For Quevedo, even demons (speaking through snakes or demoniacs) can speak the truth. The truth should never be suppressed. In the face of Inquisitorial censorship, this was Quevedo's wish for his world and for all early modern intellectuals who thirsted after forbidden knowledge.

'Da ... al discurso miedo': The Printing of Forbidden Knowledge

At the beginning of the *Discurso del alguacil endemoniado*, Quevedo wrote:

[H]ay tres géneros de hombres en el mundo. Los unos que, por hallarse ignorantes, no escriben, y éstos merecen disculpa por haber callado y alabanza por haberse conocido. Otros, que no comunican lo que saben; a éstos se les ha de tener lástima de la condición y envidia del ingenio ... *Los últimos no escriben de miedo de malas lenguas*; éstos merecen reprehensión, pues si la obra llega a manos de sabios, no saben decir mal de nada ... Esta razón me animó a escribir ... y me permitió *osadía para publicar este discurso*.

(There are three kinds of men in the world. Those who, finding themseves ignorant, do not write, and these deserve pardon for having kept quiet and praise for having known themselves. Others, who do not communicate what they know; for these it is necessary to have pity for their condition and envy for their genius ... *The last ones do not write for fear of evil tongues*; these deserve reprehension, for if the work arrives at the hands of wise men, they do not know how to speak evil of anything ... This reason animated me to write ... and permitted me *bravery to publish this discourse*.[87]

Why did Quevedo need to muster enough *osadía* to publish his *discurso*?

The *Sueños y discursos* have a rather tortured publishing history. These five short works circulated separately in thousands of manuscript copies before they were published together for the first time in 1627.[88] Each individual work (except one) bears a date on the dedicatory note which is generally considered to be the date of composition. For the *Discurso del alguacil endemoniado*, this date is 1607. Quevedo had planned to publish it in 1610, along with two of the other *Sueños*, under the title *Sueños y discursos de verdades descubridoras de abusos, vicios y engaños en todos los oficios y estados o sea el (Sueño del) Juicio final* (Dreams and discourses discovering the abuses, vices and deceptions of all the offices and estates; or, The [Dream of the] Last Judgment). This project was scuttled by the censure of Fray Antolín Montojo – a Dominican whose colleague, Fray Antonio de Santo Domingo, had given his *imprimatur* to the proposed edition two years previously.[89] The first four editions of the *Sueños* were never officially recognized by Quevedo;[90] in fact, he disavowed having had anything to do with them when the Inquisition expressed interest in their contents and ultimately placed them on the Index. In 1631 Quevedo published an authorized edition designed to appease the Inquisitors: it bore the completely different, apparently disingenuous title, *Juguetes de la niñez y travesuras del ingenio* (Toys of childhood and pranks of ingenuity). It included the *Sueños* (in somewhat altered form) as well as six other prose satires, including the *Discurso de todos los diablos* (Discourse of all the devils).[91]

Quevedo made certain changes in this later, authorized edition of 1631, but it is known now that these were not the first changes he had made to the same texts out of fear of the authorities. Only one manuscript preserved what was presumably the first draft of the *Discurso del alguacil endemoniado*, a draft which contained some extremely dangerous attacks against the clergy, the Inquisition, and even the king himself.[92] In it Quevedo satirized the promiscuity of mendicant friars, the feverish intensity of the Inquisition, and the proliferation of heretical sects during the reign of Philip II.[93] And in a gesture of Dantesque boldness, he even condemned King Philip II himself to hell, not mentioning him by name but instead painting an unmistakeable portrait of a king (aided by Cardinal Espinosa) who had assassinated his son and wife.[94] In this version of the *discurso*, the prince and the queen now torture him in hell. The passage from this lost manuscript, quoted in Fernández-Guerra's edition (who quotes from Castellanos's edition), is as follows (the demon is speaking):

Allá tenemos un rey que hace poco llegó de acá, y si no fuera porque su mujer y un hijo que nos mandó antes, le atormentan, arañándole por asesino de sus vidas, lo pasara bien; porque en el tiempo que reinó en el mundo nos llenó el infierno de leña y de diablos ya amaestrados en el oficio. Mozo fué recomendado por él, que enciende el mayor hornillo de un soplo, y que á una vuelta de pala echa á la caldera un centenar de inquisidores. A estos les pesa más por ser del oficio, y nosotros les damos más con que seguir allá el ejercicio que aquí tuvieron.

(There we have a king who a little while ago arrived from here, and if it were not because his wife and a son, that he sent us before, torment him, clawing him as the assassin of their lives, he would get on well; because in the time that he reigned in the world he filled hell for us with firewood and with devils [who were] already masters in the office. There was a servant boy recommended by him, who ignites the largest furnace with a breath, and who at one turn of the spade throws to the cauldron a hundred inquisitors. These it pains more for being of the office, and we give them more with which to continue there the exercise that they had here.)[95]

Ilse Nolting-Hauff postulates that Quevedo himself probably removed this section in later manuscripts and editions, most likely out of political shrewdness.[96]

In 1634 Quevedo wrote a sonnet, 'Venerable túmulo de Don Fadrique de Toledo' (Venerable tomb of Don Fadrique of Toledo) with the ambiguous last words, 'da ... al discurso miedo' (it gives ... fear to discourse).[97] John Elliott interprets these words as conveying 'a sense of the danger of speaking out in the Spain of Olivares.'[98] It is known that the regime kept dossiers on its opponents. Elliott reveals an irony in this situation with a letter written by Fadrique before his death in which he too wishes for free speech:

'Everything here is going in such a way that I dare not be the one to tell you about it ... In Spain we cannot even write ...' The attempt by the Olivares regime to safeguard itself by exercising a tight control over public opinion could hardly fail in the long run to antagonize a man like Quevedo, who had neither the inclination nor the ability to curb his tongue.[99]

The *privados* actually satirized in the *Discurso del alguacil endemoniado* were probably the dukes of Lerma and Uceda, not the count-duke of Olivares. But after he published the *Sueños* and other disturbing works, Quevedo was arrested and imprisoned for the final and longest time, from 1639 to 1643. He had written various books which probably contributed to his arrest: Elliott mentions the roman à clef of the Isla de los Monopantos (a chapter of *La hora de todos y la fortuna con seso*) and the verses addressed to the *Católica, sacra y real majestad* 'which the king had found beneath his napkin.'[100] These works may or may not have been written by Quevedo, but the important thing is that someone at the time thought they were.

Quevedo was not the first author to have been imprisoned for his works. Fray Luis de León was imprisoned by the Inquisition from 1572 to 1576, in part because he had translated the *Song of Songs* into the vernacular despite the prohibition of translations from the Bible other than the Vulgate. Saint Teresa of Ávila was confined to Toledo after her autobiography was denounced to the Inquisition by conservative Carmelites who resisted the reforms she advocated; these enemies tried to have her deported to Latin America but failed in this attempt. Quevedo proudly took his place among such illustrious precursors. As a result of his inimitable *osadía*, he insisted on printing forbidden knowledge and opening a doorway hitherto inaccessible for the early moderns.

The English author Thomas Lodge explains the fascination for the emergent self of the kind of forbidden diabolical knowledge to which Quevedo found himself so attracted in the *Discurso del alguacil endemoniado*: 'So delightfull is the emperie ouer nature, the knowledge of the stars, the commanding of spirits, the manner of exorcisme, that in stéed of forsaking them, men rather earnestlie affect them.'[101] Quevedo's narrator 'affects' or attempts to command spirits out of a curiosity for forbidden knowledge. This was the curiosity the Inquisitors lacked, as do their modern-day successors who favour censorship and the stifling of knowledge:

> Many of his critics, whether orthodox Catholic or otherwise, have proved themselves
> to be of lesser stature than Quevedo ... [T]hey have turned away from Quevedo with
> a feeling of revulsion. What they lack is not primarily vision but courage, courage to
> see, with Quevedo, life as it is really lived, in the bowels of hell.[102]

'*Libido sciendi*'

> Lovers and madmen have such seething brains,
> Such shaping fantasies, that apprehend
> More than cool reason ever comprehends.
> The lunatic, the lover, and the poet
> Are of imagination all compact.
> One sees more devils than vast hell can hold ...
>
> (Shakespeare, *A Midsummer Night's Dream*, 5.1.4–9)

By going where no other author of his time dared to go, Quevedo displayed a courageously (but also perversely) transgressive instinct[103] to violate his society's distinctions between the sacrosanct and the taboo.[104] Instead of simply witnessing the exorcism ceremony, Quevedo as narrator attempted to transform the rite of exorcism (a ceremony designed to expel demons) into a rite of conjuration (a ceremony designed to summon them). Richard Kieckhefer's book *Forbidden Rites* contains an excellent chapter (chapter 6, 'Formulas for Commanding Spirits: Conjurations and Exorcisms') on the formal similarities between the respective rituals for the distinct practices of exorcism and conjuration. Although very different in intent, both ceremonies contain variations on the elements of declaration, address, invocation, and instruction to the demon or demons. As avant-garde iterations of the early modern self, the narrator and Calabrés were 'adventurous inquirers daring to conjure the forces of hell to satisfy their curiosity and their quest of forbidden entertainment.'[105]

The recent theorist who has described most powerfully what I believe to be Quevedo's kind of transgression into the realm of the taboo is Roger Shattuck, in *Forbidden Knowledge: From Prometheus to Pornography*. In this collection of retold stories and myths, followed by an analysis of curiosity (*libido sciendi*) as the 'lust of the soul,' Shattuck explores a phenomenon as old as Pandora's box, Eve's apple, and Faust's bargain:

> Every myth, every tale I have mentioned, deals with an awakening to the dilemma of curiosity about something both attractive and dangerous ... The force of taboo insulates 'the spiritual force' in the object or person from violation and also insulates us – at times not adequately – from its forbidding yet alluring power.[106]

Shattuck borrows the *libido sciendi* motif from St Augustine's Book X of the *Confessions*. He then quotes Thomas Hobbes's repetition of the motif in the sixth chapter of *Leviathan*: 'Desire to know how and why, curiosity ... is a lust of the mind, that by a perseverance of delight in the continual and indefatigable generation of knowledge, exceedeth the short vehemence of carnal pleasure.'[107] Shattuck notes that 'curiosity carries within itself a principle of doubt – doubts about received knowledge and the conventions of the status quo.'[108] He also reminds us that Milton's injunction to Adam through his mouthpiece, the archangel Raphael, was 'Be lowly wise.'[109] This placement of a limit on proper or permissible curiosity – this 'forbidding' – is the originating condition for the generation of forbidden knowlege. Whether the 'forbidders' are the Inquisitorial censors or the exorcist who silences the devil, Quevedo goes against the grain of their admonitions not to seek the knowledge they want to stifle.[110]

While no one has applied Shattuck's work to Quevedo, Gonzalo Díaz Migoyo has offered a reading of this particular *Discurso* which I find to be quite compatible with the theme of 'forbidden knowledge.' He postulates that Quevedo is really reacting to the crisis of European scepticism – in other words, the crisis of what is knowable. As Díaz Migoyo has suggested, the interlocutors of this text (the narrator and the exorcist) are given to us as models representing two possible readings or receptions of the text's message or truth: the one that surpresses forbidden knowledge and the one that seeks it, the one that is closed to doubt and uncertainty and the one that embraces these complexities.[111] As such, the narrator and the exorcist represent divergent possibilities for nascent protomodern selves and trace out options for which directions they might like to develop.

My response to this interpretation is to recall that the demon in Quevedo's *Discurso del alguacil endemoniado* offers one solution to the crisis of the knowable: he is a prophet. While European intellectuals were experiencing a crisis of the knowable, here is a literary character offering a solution through one of the only recourses remaining to a Christian intellectual of the time. The solution is supernatural knowledge, about which there can be both a mystery and a certainty that is impossible for easily available, imperfect, naturally generated knowledge. Quevedo's religious sincerity was quite serious.[112] Like Erasmus, he was perfectly capable of satirizing clerical abuses and still believing with all his heart in the reality of hell. Perhaps he felt his dark, confusing, baroque world shifting around him in such a way that he could be more certain of the other world (i.e., hell) than he could of this one. As someone who loved richly complex allusions and figures of speech, he might also have seen the poetic potential inherent in the 'demon as prophet' figure he had created.

Here my argument becomes necessarily more speculative, but as a closing thought, I believe it is not impossible that the ingenious Quevedo saw in demonic possession an inverse metaphor for poetic furor. Etymologically speaking, poets were considered by early modern literary theorists such as Luís Alfonso de Carvallo to have descended from the prophets:

> Con un propio premio gratificaban a profetas y Poetas los antiguos, que era con una corona de laurel. Tienen también común el nombre porque, *vates* ... igual y comúnmente significa el profeta y al Poeta.

> (With one same prize the ancients gratified the prophets and poets, which was with a crown of laurel. They have also the name in common, because *vates* ... equally and commonly signifies prophet and poet.)[113]

This poetic furor or frenzy is described by Carvallo as that quasi-divine state in which poets become most creative: 'Pues el Poeta cuando está ansí transportado, los afectos de su entendimiento tienen más luz y claridad, por no estar ofuscados con las cosas corporales' (for the poet when he is thus transported, the affects of his understanding have more light and clarity, for not being obfuscated with corporal things).[114] Just as the *alguacil*'s body is taken over by the demon, so the poet's body is taken over by poetic frenzy. And just as the demon has access to knowlege not available to human beings, so the muse brings knowledge to the poet: 'pues de la mano divina gratis es dado, sin que con fuerza humana se pueda adquirir ... [L]a poesía es revelación divina y soberana, y no ciencia adquirida con humana diligencia y arte ...' (for from the divine hand it is freely given, without being able to be acquired with human force ... Poetry is divine and sovereign revelation, and not science acquired with human diligence and art).[115]

We must note here the fundamental ambiguity attributed by early modern writers to the state of demonic possession. If it is in any universe comparable to poetic frenzy, then it must contain more than a germ of something beneficial. Demonic possession is Janus-like in its inextricably connected qualities of threat and enhancement: it can threaten the early modern person's entire order and identity, but it can also offer enhancements such as supernatural wisdom or the ability to speak other languages.

Keeping in mind this Janus-like interpretive model, when we see early modern literary theorists such as Carvallo calling poets 'endiosados' (deified),[116] it is not difficult to imagine Quevedo's perverse *ingenio* fixating upon their diametrical opposite, the 'endiablados' (demonized). Carvallo continues that 'muchos profetas fueron Poetas y muchos Poetas fueron profetas' (many prophets were poets and many poets were prophets) but asks of the current generation of poets in Spain: 'Pero decidme, ¿qué Poetas de su profesión hay que sean profetas?' (But tell me, what poets of their profession are there who are prophets?)[117] Perhaps Quevedo wanted to answer this question: 'I am one.' Aside from his general concerns as a representative early modern self, perhaps Quevedo the humanist wanted to imitate the classical poets who were also prophets.[118] Carvallo ends his section on poetic furor as we shall end our chapter, with a question as to whether forbidden supernatural knowledge (such as prophecy or a picture of hell) is attainable by poets (or demoniacs, as Quevedo wryly calls himself: 'Es más endemoniado el autor que el sujeto' [The author is more demonized than the subject]).[119] Carvallo answers the question – using the literary form of poetry – in the affirmative, but leaves the further question of agency as an unresolved ambiguity:

> Profético furor es un divino
> espíritu, que alguno Dios ha dado,
> con que de lo futuro es adevino
> y pudo el calor ser en tanto grado
> de algún Poeta que a declarar vino
> lo futuro. De que han adevinado

es cierto, si fue acaso gracia o seso,
o lo reveló Dios, Dios sabe aqueso.

(Prophetic furor is a divine
spirit, that God has given someone,
with which he is a diviner of the future
and the heat could be in such degree
of some Poet that he came to declare
the future. That they have divined
is certain, if it was by chance, grace, or sense,
or God revealed it, God knows that.)[120]

Does the poet's knowledge derive from himself or from a supernatural source? With Carvallo, Quevedo, and certain other very brave early modern writers, we can answer (un)certainly: 'Only God (and the demon) knows.'

Romance, the Interlude, and Hagiographical Drama: The Humanization of Possession and Exorcism

The genres of romance and the dramatic interlude contain many of the same theologemes as the genres of comic drama or even the picaresque, with one major difference: they place special emphasis on the theologeme of the lovers' ruse. The genres of romance and the dramatic interlude appeal to 'romantics' both in the sense that they attract the erotic, desiring early modern self and in the more fundamental sense that they attract optimists who 'just want everything to work out right in the end.' Romance is traditionally the genre which involves wish fulfilment or even escapism, the genre for those who yearn for order to be restored. Within this context exorcism serves as a 'magic wand' which can bring discordant elements back into joyful harmony. Especially in the context of romantic love, demonic possession can serve as a metaphor for sexual possession until the two become virtually identical. The frenzy of love madness can appear so similar to the frenzy of demonic possession that metaphor and its referent intermingle until the two conditions seem indistinguishable from one another.

The genre of hagiography, by contrast, gives an honoured place to several theologemes which do not even appear in romance: its features include a serious treatment of the demon's entrance into the body as well as an earnest assessment of the successful exorcism. Exorcism at once serves to test the saint's power over supernatural forces and to enhance the saint's reputation for godliness once the exorcism is completed. Especially in medieval times but also in the early modern period, demonic possession was difficult to distinguish from the ecstasy of mysticism.[1] But early modern selves did care – even passionately so – about trying to distinguish between them. While it was considered most desirable to be possessed by the Holy Spirit, it was often considered extremely undesirable to be inhabited by a demon (unless you were one of those brave souls who, like Quevedo, dared to explore the realm of the demonic with the goal of furthering his own quest for forbidden knowledge). Demonic possession and exorcism were polyvalent categories in the early modern period, as we have seen, but the genre of hagiography interpreted them as fundamentallly serious and unequivocally negative phenomena. Unlike the genres of the romance and the *entremés*, which treat demonic possession and exorcism with a somewhat frivolous attitude, the genre of hagiography never jokes about something as serious as salvation or martyrdom.

How could these seemingly irreconcilable approaches to exorcism coexist without dissonance during a single literary period, let alone within the *oeuvre* of any single author? There are two exorcism scenes in *Los trabajos de Persiles y Sigismunda* (The labours of Persiles and Sigismunda) and *El rufián dichoso* (The fortunate ruffian), for example, which mark the opposite ends of the spectrum of Cervantes's attitudes toward the supernatural. The scene in the *Persiles*, which I shall compare to an interlude by Lope de Vega, has been cited as evidence that 'Cervantes also seems to have marked out the practice [of exorcism], if not as a fraud, at least as a ritual that had already been exhausted – "emptied out" – and therefore one that could be refilled.'[2] Meanwhile, the *Rufián dichoso*, a hagiographical drama which I shall compare to two *comedias de santos* by Calderón and Lope de Vega (yes, the same Lope de Vega who wrote the humorous interlude about exorcism), 'se ha difundido ampliamente ... como obra constatadora del fervor religioso de Cervantes' (has been diffused widely ... as a work attesting to the religious fervour of Cervantes).[3] These two distinct treatments of exorcism within the oeuvres of both Cervantes and Lope de Vega are so violently different that at first glance it is difficult to believe they came from the same period, let alone from the same pen.

In this chapter I will show how it is possible to reconcile these conflicting treatments of, and attitudes toward, exorcism. Early modern authors often showed such apparent cognitive dissonance in their thinking about the supernatural. I will demonstrate that not only do the contrasting views complement one another, but when seen in all their nuanced complexity, they appear as two facets of the same 'humanizing' religious sensibility. By 'humanizing' I do not mean to imply that these authors of romance, the interlude, and the hagiographical drama in any way diminish the mystery of demonic possession or the miracle of exorcism. I do not mean that the experience of possession and exorcism is any less supernatural, only that it is made more approachable to early modern intuition. It is a truism of scholarship on Cervantes, for example, that he humanized the genre of the pastoral in innovative and disturbing ways when he wrote *La Galatea*.[4] In the works we are discussing here, we will see that in much the same way, Cervantes and his contemporaries, through the genres of romance, the interlude, and hagiography, ultimately humanized the ritual of exorcism and its participants as well.

Romance, the Interlude, and the Restoration of Order:
Cervantes' *Persiles* and Lope's *La endemoniada*

Both the exorcism episode of Cervantes' *Persiles* and Lope's comic interlude *La endemoniada* highlight the humorous resolution of a fake spectacle of possession as the restoration of order culminating in the traditional happy ending of marriage. Northrop Frye has described this traditional ending in terms of the romance genre's oscillation between two contrasting worlds:

> The characterization of romance is really a feature of its mental landscape. Its heroes and villains exist primarily to symbolize a contrast between two worlds, one above the level of ordinary experience, the other below it. There is, first, a world associated with happiness, security, and peace; the emphasis is often thrown on childhood or on an 'innocent' or pre-genital period of youth, and the images are those of spring and summer, flowers and sunshine. I shall call this world the idyllic world. The other is a world of exciting adventures, but adventures which involve separation, loneliness, humiliation, pain, and the threat of more pain. I shall call this world the demonic or night world. Because of the powerful polarizing tendency in romance, we are usually carried directly from one to the other ... This means that most romances exhibit a cyclical movement of descent into a night world and a return to the idyllic world, or to some symbol of it like a marriage ...[5]

Let us see how Cervantes and Lope integrate their treatments of exorcism into these conventions of the romance genre as well as one of its miniature versions – in this case, the comic interlude.

The ritual of exorcism is treated comically by Cervantes in *Los trabajos de Persiles y Sigismunda*, a book in which supernatural evil[6] poses a threat to the early modern self in such multifarious and serious forms as werewolves, cannibals, bewitchers,[7] and barbarous gang rapists. It is interesting to speculate that if the exorcism scene had occurred toward the beginning rather than the end of the work, and in the northern rather than the southern clime, it probably would have been altered unrecognizably.[8] It probably would have been staged very seriously, with fiery demons emerging from the mouth of the victim, just as in the exorcism paintings by the northern artist Rubens (see fig. 5). But since it occurs in the south and toward the end of the work, the exorcism scene in the *Persiles* is very funny indeed.

Even though the trajectory of this romance could be seen as a lengthy process by which the various evil forces are exorcized by the good forces in the romance universe, Cervantes was never one to take himself too seriously. While the 'romance writer' side of him[9] probably saw the attraction of romance conventions as 'magical'[10] and powerful enough to chase away evil, Cervantes' attitude toward the specific exorcism in this work is light-hearted and fun-loving without risking irreverence. The Isabela Castrucha episode of Cervantes' *Persiles*, while symbolic of the work's overall pattern of deliverance from demonic bondage, is nonetheless a mischievous wink in the tradition of Greek New Comedy[11] at the credulity of an old uncle who is fooled by his niece's pretended possession.

Isabela convinces the female pilgrims in the group, sitting on the four corners of her bed like the four saints on a printed *ensalmo* or *rescrito* used in exorcisms (see fig. 3), to serve as supporting actresses in the little performance she is staging. Scripting her lover Andrea to play his part, she allows herself to be tied to the bed as her 'demon' declares that only Andrea can exorcize her. The 'demon' also claims that, as was typical with recalcitrant demons, it will give a 'signal' of its imminent departure (in this case, Andrea's arrival). Meanwhile, Isabela's uncle comes in with an entourage of priests bearing 'props' for an exorcism: a cross, hyssop, and holy water. The uncle, in an unorthodox gesture since he is not a priest, pronounces the same words of the exorcism ritual which the hero of *El rufián dichoso* will later use in a more serious context: '¡Ea, demonio maldito, *vade retro, exi foras* ...!' (Hey, cursed demon, get thee behind me, go out ...!)[12] He then announces the arrival of Andrea Marulo. Not playing his part very well, Andrea catches the contagious hysteria and acts like a demoniac himself, shouting words that have more to do with a Spanish *romance* than with a rite of exorcism.[13] The two lovers then declare their subterfuge and their intention to be married. Before the uncle can object, they do marry immediately, with a priest witnessing and pronouncing their union valid. Their freedom from demonic bondage[14] is complete when the uncle dies abruptly, leaving no impediment to their happiness. The episode ends strangely, with a philosophical commentary by the narrator on the mysteries of the natural life cycle.

The ending is not the only philosophical part of the episode. Throughout the scene the lovers both make numerous comments about how being in love is very similar to being possessed by a demon:

> Una legión de demonios tengo en el cuerpo, que lo mismo es tener una onza de amor en el alma.

> (A legion of demons I have in the body, which is the same as having an ounce of love in the soul.)[15]

> Mis amorosos pensamientos son los demonios que me atormentan.

> (My amorous thoughts are the demons who torment me.)[16]

Vayan de aquí fuera los demonios que quisieren estorbar tan sabroso nudo, y no procuren los demonios apartar lo que Dios junta ... [S]in que aquí intervengan trazas, máquinas ni embelecos, dame esa mano de esposo y recíbeme por tuya.

(Let them go out of here, the demons who would want to impede such a delicious union, and let not the demons procure to sever that which God joins ... Without tricks, machines or frauds intervening here, give me that hand of a spouse and receive me for yours.)[17]

This work of Cervantes shows us, in his words, 'quién es el amor, pues hace parecer endemoniados a los amantes' (who is love, who makes lovers appear demon-possessed).[18] Diana de Armas Wilson calls Isabela 'unequivocally the most vocal and desiring woman in the Cervantine canon.' Appearing (as she does) literally lying in bed, bound to her bedposts, she is certainly one of the most openly erotic early modern characters we will encounter. In contrast to Dulcinea and the 'prudish' Sigismunda, she 'frankly equates her demonio – "el que me atormenta" ... – with her libido.'[19] Here we see Cervantes humanizing the experience of demonic possession for all early modern lovers by equating it metaphorically with the experience of being in love.[20]

Cervantes may have taken his cue on this particular form of humanization from his source, Heliodorus, who includes a similar episode of fake possession and exorcism in the Byzantine Greek romance *Aethiopica*. In this episode, Calasiris pretends to exorcize the heroine Chariclea even though both he and his patient acknowledge that she is simply lovesick. The English Renaissance translation of the scene reads as follows (Calasiris recounts his pagan 'exorcism' of Chariclea):

Get you hence, quoth I, and all the rest avoid, and let one set me a three footed stoole here, and a little laurell with fire, and frankincense. And let none come in to trouble me before I call. Caricles willed the same, and it was done. Nowe, having gotten good occasion, I began to play my pagent, as if I had bene upon a stage, and burned frankincense, and mumbled with my lippes, and laide laurell on her, from toppe to toe, and at length when I had drowsily, or olde wiselike gaped, and playde the foole a great while with my selfe, and the Maide, I made an end. Shee, while I was thus doing, wagged her heade oft, and smiled, and tolde me, that I was deceived, and knew not her greefe, Therwith I sate neare her, and saide, My daughter be of good cheere, thou greefe is common and easie to be healed, without doubt ...[21]

In Heliodorus as in Cervantes, the problem is that an elderly father figure (for Isabela, her uncle) has arranged a match for the young woman which is not palatable to her. But in this situation it is somewhat dangerous to assume that

Cervantes humanizes the experience of demonic possession by transferring the category of 'demon' completely to the person of Isabela's uncle. Diana de Armas Wilson demonizes him more than is necessary when she emphasizes his house-keeping metaphors, which she interprets as his efforts to 'rent out' his niece's body.[22] Wilson is clearly not familiar with the scriptural allusion Cervantes is making here through the uncle's words (a reference to Matthew 12:43–5), in which an expelled demon threatens to return to the 'well-swept house' from whence he just came:

> And when an unclean spirit is gone out of a man, he walketh through dry places seeking rest and findeth none. Then he saith: I will return into my house from whence I came out. And coming he findeth it empty, swept and garnished. Then he goeth and taketh with him seven other spirits more wicked than himself: and they enter in and dwell there: and the last state of that man is made worse than the first.[23]

Instead, Wilson's unsympathetic view of the patriarchal uncle makes her interpretation of the ending extremely harsh:

> One may recoil from the virtual 'murder' of a character who seems to be merely the proverbial obstacle. Readers of 'The Captive's Tale' in Don Quixote, part 1, however, will remember that this is not the first 'heavy father' figure that Cervantes has done away with ... Cervantes's rhetorical wordplay invites us to equate Isabela's uncle with her demon, a strategy that decreases the readerly impulse to mourn the dead: he who wished to exorcise her is now exorcised ... Instead of her being sacrificed to a marriage arranged by the Law of the Father, the surrogate father who would have bartered her is snuffed out – exorcised – from the text.[24]

In contrast, Alban Forcione's view of this problematic ending recognizes its somber tone without overly demonizing the abruptly dying uncle.[25] I would speculate that maybe Cervantes caused the uncle to die because he had reservations as a Catholic author about his apparent trivialization of both a sacrament (marriage) and a sacramental (exorcism). By bringing in several sacraments to converge at the end of the chapter (baptism, a more official marriage, and the rites of burial), perhaps he revalidates his commitment to Catholic orthodoxy.[26] Whatever Cervantes' motives were for killing off the uncle at the end – whether or not he intended to humanize the demon by identifying it with the uncle – Frye reminds us that death may be assimilated into the structure of romance through the motif of the life cycle.[27]

Cervantes does humanize the experience of demonic possession for the early modern woman in this episode, but he does not trivialize it. Forcione shows how this incidence of possession repeats the 'cycle of bondage and liberation on which the main plot and most of the episodes are based':

> Isabela passes through the moment of 'near-death,' as she lies tied to her bed, attempting to eat her own flesh, screaming about the demons within her, and addressing the pilgrims as angels from heaven sent to deliver her, to the moment of deliverance, as the devils are cast out and she marries her beloved. Similarly we discover the imaginative linkage of the events of the comic action to the Christian myth in the familiar symbols and motifs – 'ángeles,' 'demonio,' 'Satanás,' 'ligaduras,' the 'cruz' and 'agua bendita,' with which the uncle tries to cure the possessed girl, 'los Evangelios,' which the priests read to the girl, and the movements from death to rebirth and sterility to fertility through marriage.[28]

In other words, Cervantes' humour in this episode appears festive rather than corrosive. He celebrates the comic potential of confusing love madness with demonic possession and humanizes the experience of possession by making it understandable to anyone who has ever been in love.

It is one small step, however, from this gently humorous treatment of exorcism in romance to the farce of the dramatic interlude. Let us now look at this coarser sort of humour generated by a similar kind of exorcistic incident.

It is almost certain that Lope de Vega wrote the *entremés* about exorcism called *La endemoniada*: this short but fascinating work appears along with eleven other *entremeses*, purportedly by Lope, in the 1609 Valladolid edition of Lope's *comedias* as they were compiled by Bernardo Grassa,[29] and Lope's biographer Hugo Rennert believes that he could have written the piece.[30] It is a funny repetition of the 'lovers' ruse' theologeme of the paradigm for literary exorcism which we have already seen appearing in both the comic drama and the romance genres.[31] As in the typical 'lovers' ruse' theologeme, two lovers decide to trick the woman's father into allowing them to be together. She feigns demonic possession, while her suitor poses as an exorcist; the whole situation is parodied within the *entremés* by a servant and a fool who pretends possession too – hoping for preferential treatment – and receives nothing but punishment.

Lope's technique of juxtaposing demonic possession with love madness works particularly well in this experiment. The 'demoniac' female speaks with *double entendre* of the 'demons' (really the symptoms of love madness) which torment her: 'Ladrones, robadores de mi bien, ídosme de aquí, no me atormentéis el alma; dejadme ir á buscar mi contento, que me le tenéis usurpado' (Thieves, robbers of my good, go away from me here, do not torment my soul; let me go to seek my contentment, which you have usurped from me).[32] The young lover, posing as the exorcist, arrives and makes his entrance with a question in macaronic Latin:

'¿Dónde estavit mulier que tenebi demonios en corpore suo?' (Where has the woman been who will have demons in her body?).[33] The exorcist/lover insists that for the cure to be effective, he must remain with the patient for twenty or thirty days. The father acquiesces for the sake of his daughter's health. The *entremés* ends on a comical note with the servant rescuing the fool, who finds himself in trouble after feigning possession in imitation of the young lovers' deception.

The farcical interlude or *entremés* as a marginal and potentially subversive genre[34] in the early modern period is used effectively here as a vehicle for exploiting the enormous subversive potential of the fake performance of possession in the face of authority. The *entremés* genre was a liminal space where competing, marginalized languages and dialects (such as the shepherds' *sayagués* or the *vizcaíno's* nearly incomprehensible corruptions of Spanish) vied for recognition. In this particular *entremés* the contested territory of language appears in the exorcist/lover's use of macaronic Latin. Latin was the language of the exorcists and it served to set them apart as learned and holy.[35] The scurrilous abuse of this linguistic register, ordinarily reserved for the realm of the sacred, exploits the theologeme of polyglossia and mirrors the young lovers' revolt against the established authority of the older generation.

Ultimately, as in the genre of romance, the triumph of the younger generation in the dramatic interlude results in the restoration of order. Demonic possession is understood as love madness in which all early modern couples can participate, and exorcism is humanized into a marriage that most of them can accept. The theologeme of the lovers' ruse is emphasized along with some of the symptoms of possession – in this case, the ones (such as pining, paleness, and acting upon the desires of another) which coincided for the early modern imagination with the symptoms of being in love.

Thus far we have seen humorous treatments of exorcism written by both Cervantes and Lope de Vega. Let us now contrast these two authors' humorous approaches to exorcism with their much more serious views of demonic possession in the hagiographical dramas *El rufián dichoso* (The fortunate ruffian) and *El divino africano* (The divine African) along with Calderón's *Las cadenas del demonio* (The chains of the demon). In doing so we will study three 'humanized' miracles – miracles which 'humanize' the experience of demonic possession and exorcism for the early modern saint in completely different, much more serious ways than the genres of romance and the interlude can accommodate.

Rebirth and Hagiography: Cervantes' *El rufián dichoso*[36]

Shakespeare's King Henry VI prays for the dying bishop of Winchester:

O Thou eternal Mover of the heavens,
Look with a gentle eye upon this wretch!
O, beat away the busy meddling fiend
That lays strong siege unto this wretch's soul,
And from his bosom purge this black despair![37]

This demon of despair, the one that tempts a person who is dying, is the same devil exorcized successfully in the play *El rufián dichoso*.

This play has been maligned by such older critics as Rodolfo Schevill, Adolfo Bonilla, and Francisco Ynduráin,[38] whose condescending view of Cervantes' 'piadosa credulidad' has elicited angry responses from such modern critics as Joaquín Casalduero and Stanislav Zimic.[39] The play is a drama based on a real-life event: the conversion of a ruffian named Cristóbal de Lugo into a holy man named Cristóbal de la Cruz.[40] The first act takes place in the picaresque underground criminal world of Seville, where Lugo, although he lives with the Inquisitor Tello de Sandoval, 'moonlights' as the leader of a gang of *valentones*. First he vows to become a professional thief and then, in a sudden change of heart, a priest. Even his new name is significant, as the cross was the primary tool used in exorcisms; in a moment of wonderful artistic foreshadowing, the ruffian Lugo anticipates both his future name and his role of exorcist: 'mas huyóse de su aspecto, / como el diablo de la cruz' (but he fled from his aspect, / like the devil from the cross).[41] At the very end of Act 1, he defies all demons, confident that he will overcome them, although he does not yet know in what setting:

¡Ea, demonios; por mil modos
a todos os desafío,
y en mi Dios bueno confío
que os he de vencer a todos!

(Hey, demons; by a thousand ways
I defy you all,
and in my good God I trust
that I will conquer you all!)[42]

The second and third acts are set in Mexico, where Lugo (now called Cruz) journeys to fulfil his vow. There he is renowned for his saintliness, while an old ruffian friend of his, now also a cleric, continues to backslide. Cruz is tempted also – by demons appearing as lascivious nymphs – but he does not succumb. Instead he uses the sanctioned words of exorcism, '*Vade retro! Satanás*,'[43] to make them flee.

Early in the second act, Cruz is summoned to the deathbed of a wealthy, dying young woman named Ana de Treviño. When Ana is surprised by death, almost like the figures arrested in motion in the medieval dances of death[44] (the reader should refer again to fig. 4), she despairs of God's mercy and declares that for her, there is no God.[45] Other clergymen have been unable to prevail upon her to receive absolution in the sacrament of confession. Cruz performs a beautifully Cervantine, humanized version of the exorcism ritual by reasoning with Ana and even making a bargain with her. If she will confess her sins, he (like Christ) offers to take them all upon himself and give her all his good works instead. Hesitant at first, Ana requests witnesses to their transaction. It was actually quite typical for exorcisms to take the form of a trial scene, in which the demon was the accused, the Virgin Mary was a lawyer for the prosecution, and God was the judge. Cruz chooses to follow this formula as laid out in the exorcism manuals.[46] Giving her the Virgin Mary and Christ Himself for witnesses, he completes the exchange and is immediately struck with leprosy. Ana's soul is carried off by eleven thousand virgins to heaven.[47]

In the third act, Cruz is elected prior of the monastery after thirteen years of suffering and severe temptation by demons who appear to him in various forms, reminding him of his former criminal life. At one point, his old friend sees the demons as well, in a scene that Alban Forcione calls a baroque masque.[48] Cruz dies shortly thereafter, and the demons discuss the unfairness of the bargain he made years ago. The demons are driven away from the corpse by the rosary hanging from the bier, and his soul too is taken up to heaven. The townspeople almost sack the monastery in an effort to obtain relics of the saint. Casalduero notes a certain symmetry between Act 1 and Act 2, both of which end with the repentance and conversion of a sinner to grace, and between Act 3 and Act 4, both of which end with a soul being transported to Paradise.[49]

The act that is of most interest for us here is the second one, particularly the scene in which the exorcism occurs. Joaquín Casalduero characterizes Ana as possessed when he speaks of the demons that use her voice: 'los demonios ... hablando por boca de la moribunda' (the demons ... speaking through the mouth of the dying woman).[50] And Diana de Armas Wilson identifies Cruz's action at another point in the play as an exorcism: 'Cristóbal de la Cruz ... exorcises some half-dozen screaming demons from an infernal, and highly eroticized, vision with the cry of "*Vade retro*! Satanás."'[51] Without stating explicitly that Cruz exorcizes Ana, Casalduero relates the protagonist's appropriation of the exact words of the exorcism formula to paintings and sculptures of exorcisms from this time period:

No tiene más remedio que exclamar: '*Vade retro*, Satanás,' y los demonios salen gritando. La pintura y el grabado de la época nos han dejado la realidad plástica de semejantes experiencias ... El Gótico ha expresado alegóricamente esta agonía, esa pelea entre ángeles y demonios, el Barroco nos la hace vivir.

(He has no other remedy than to exclaim: 'Get thee behind me, Satan,' and the demons depart, shouting. The painting and the engraving of the epoch have left the plastic reality of similar experiences ... The Gothic has expressed allegorically this agony, that struggle between angels and demons, the baroque makes us live it.)[52]

Ana surely voices this agony when she cries, '¡Ay, que se me arranca el alma! / ¡Desesperada me muero!' (Ay, that my soul is being torn out! / Despairing, I die!).[53] But no one has specifically called Cruz's interaction with Ana an exorcism (albeit a humanized one), although this is clearly what happens in the scene.

We shall see how Cervantes marshals such strategies as diction, poetic metre, and rhetoric to fashion a coherent picture of a 'humanized' exorcism made more accessible to the early modern audience. Casalduero notes that this scene is demarcated within the text by a shift in poetic rhythms: most of the scene where Ana appears is written in *redondillas*, but when Cruz begins to speak to her, he breaks the pattern by speaking in *octavas*. The effect of this change of meter is to emphasize the transition from a conversational tone to a more lofty Italianate style. Cruz's speech to Ana makes use of the *miles Christi* metaphor so common during the Counter-Reformation:

El que, en el palenque puesto,
teme a su contrario, yerra,
y está el que animoso cierra
a la victoria dispuesto.
En el campo estáis, señora;
la guerra será esta tarde ...

(He who, placed in the palisade,
fears his adversary, errs,
and he who animatedly closes in
is disposed to victory.
You are on the battle field, madam;
the war will be this afternoon ...)[54]

Cruz breaks the metrical pattern again, but in a different way, when he addresses himself directly to God ('Cielos, oíd' [Heavens, hear]);[55] for this speech he uses the more formal and elevated *endecasílabos sueltos*. Finally, the successful exorcism, executed almost exclusively through the power of reasoning, is signalled in the text by another shift in poetic verse forms: as soon as Ana assents to the bargain, the *redondillas* change into the more relaxed, soothing form of free hendecasyllables.[56] Later we are told by another character in the play that at this moment, there issued forth from Ana the characteristic shout that, we remember, sometimes signalled the end of an exorcism: 'Alzó al momento un piadoso grito' (She raised at that moment a pious shout).[57]

At this moment, it is even possible to say based on the text that not only the leprosy, but also the demons themselves are transferred from Ana to Cruz. This aspect of the exorcism reminds us that although it may be 'humanized,' it is nonetheless all too real a response to a diabolical incursion into the early modern soul. Real demons are at work here, bearing names like Lucifer and Saquiel and appearing in the shapes of lascivious nymphs and a bear. While the saintly Cruz is clearly not possessed by demons, his human sight is obsessed by their apparitions (the word *obsedere* means 'to attack from without,' as opposed to within). This is not at all unusual in the exorcism manuals. It was a known danger inherent in the ritual that the demons, once expelled, would immediately search for another place to go. The classic example of this transferral was Jesus' exorcism of the demoniac among the tombs and the demons' request to him that he allow them to enter the herd of swine.[58] When he assented, the pigs committed collective suicide by jumping off a cliff. The exorcism manuals warn that the demon, if expelled, will attempt to enter the exorcist or one of the bystanders instead. The exorcists were instructed to guard against this possibility by making sure their hearts were pure before they began the exorcism ritual. Otherwise, their sins would provide the perfect entrance for the demon. Two examples from Richard Baxter, an early modern physician, will suffice. He reported in *The certainty of the worlds of spirits* that wounded exorcists came to him for treatment after they had been attacked by the demons they were trying to expel:

> But this same Exorcist (Priest) that same Year was brought to me, to *Basil*, to be cured, having a pain in his Hip, that he could not walk, and he lodged with us. But when many things were used in Vain, at last he confest to me, that this befell him by the Devil: Whom when he by his Exorcisms, would have cast out of one possest, the Devil then, as he had done oft before, threatned him in these words, in the *German* Tongue [*Psaff ich will dir noch den thou geben dase du mich alses verit eist.*] And at once, thrust him so violently up to the Chimney, that his Hip hurt, hath been in this Case ever since ... [In another case an exorcist] seeing the Demoniack Man pass by in the Street, by the noise of the company, he earnestly prayed to God for him: In the very Moment of his praying, by some invisible Genius, he had suddenly such a Stroke on his Neck, as cast him down on his Face, on the Ground; I think, because that malignant Spirit would not that Men should pray for him that he had possess'd.

He profess'd that he did sensibly perceive something like the Hand of a strong Man strike him ... (98–9, 104)

In the case of Cruz, likewise – although his heart was pure and the demons could not possess him – they could nonetheless obsess him and bring leprosy (a real, not imagined, illness) upon him.

This type of demonic obsession was, unfortunately, the fate of several real-life early modern people who voluntarily took on demonic problems in the same sort of humanized exorcism 'bargain' that Cruz made with Ana. The historical Cristóbal de la Cruz was not the only holy person to have conducted an unusually humane exorcism by taking upon himself the sufferings of another. Various saints, from fourth-century desert monks to late medieval nuns, were said to have taken upon themselves voluntarily the sufferings of someone else – including, if necessary, the possessing demon who was causing those sufferings. The story of a fourth-century monk living in the desert who asked to receive someone else's demon is told in the *Apophthegmata patrum* (transl. Ward):

> An ascetic, having found someone possessed by the devil and unable to fast, and being (as it is written) moved by the love of God, and seeking not his own good but the good of the other, prayed that the devil might pass into himself and that the other might be liberated. God heard his prayer. The ascetic, overwhelmed by the devil, gave himself with redoubled insistence to fasting, prayer, and *ascesis*. At last, because of his charity, God drove the devil away from him after a few days. (61)

The nun Marie of Oignies, whose life was recorded by Jacques de Vitry in a thirteenth-century account (later incorporated into a collection of *Acta sanctorum*),[59] fasted for forty days on behalf of another nun who was possessed by the demon of despair.[60] This demon often caused blasphemy and led to the sin against the Holy Spirit: despair of God's mercy. Marie of Oignies made a Cruz-style bargain with the despairing nun. She fasted in the nun's presence until finally the demon seemed to transfer its efforts to Marie herself, if not through possession, then at least through obsession. She, then, began to see demonic visions as part of 'this vicarious exchange.'[61]

As Barbara Newman explains this 'vicarious suffering,' the '*mulieres sanctae* favored pain as a currency of love's exchange, and in one variant of this privileged therapeutic technique, they actually transferred demons (with their attendant symptoms) from the original victim to her would-be healer.'[62] In another saint's life edited by a Spaniard, the *Vita Idae Nivellensis* in *Quinque prudentes virgines* (1630), Ida of Nivelles healed a demoniac nun in much the same way.[63] The nun was frenetic and blasphemous, hiding from other nuns in shadowy nooks. Ida watched with her for an entire day and night, holding her hand over the nun's mouth so she would not utter blasphemy. Then Ida prayed that she herself might take on her sister's temptation and suffering. For three days Ida lay all but lifeless, oppressed by the demon, while her sister was set free. The 'humanized bargain' model of exorcism can be effective for the restoration of the early modern patient, but the demons involved are no less real, and the consequences of dealing with them are no less serious.

In this literary drama, Cervantes humanizes the conventions of exorcism – without degrading their sanctity or trivializing their mystery – just as he did the conventions of the pastoral in *La Galatea*. He humanizes the exorcism ritual for the early modern by transforming it into a rhetorical bargain. But *La Galatea* is still a pastoral, and this is still an exorcism – in fact, an exorcism with historical corollaries extending into the time period of Cervantes's life and beyond. From 1637 to 1642 Luís de la Concepción performed an exorcism upon an old woman in the Valle de Tena and argued with the demon in formal Latin syllogisms, after the manner of the scholastics.[64] The demon proposed to the exorcist the following syllogism: 'Quidquid in virtute Christi praecipitur, ut fiat, vel dicatur; & ita fit, vel dicitur, verum est: Tu mihi praecepisti, in virtute Christi, ut dicerem nomen meum, & dixi ergo verum est' (Whatever through the merits of Christ is commanded to happen or be said, and so happens or is said, is true; You have commanded me through the merits of Christ that I say my name, and I therefore said [it], [it] is true). When an 'inexperienced' bystander approved the syllogism as self-evident, Luis de la Concepción argued to the contrary. The demon claimed in Latin that the exorcist did not know how to give a response, but the exorcist responded that he knew nothing from his own knowledge and therefore relied on the knowledge of God. The exorcist then proved the demon's argument to be false by stating the following major and minor premises in Latin 'according to the manner of the schools':

Quidquid in virtute Christi praecipitur, ut fiat, vel dicatur; & ita fit, vel dicitur, verum est. Concedo maiorem.
Ego praecepi tibi, in virtute Christi, ut diceres nomen tuum: distingo minorem:
ut diceres nomen tuum, absque damno aliquo, & prae-iudicio cuiuscumque perso-nae Catholicae: concedo minorem.

(Whatever through the merits of Christ is commanded to happen or be said, and so happens or is said, is true. I grant the major [premise].
I command you, through the merits of Christ, to say your name. I distinguish the minor [premise]: that you say your name, without any loss, and prejudice of any Catholic person: I grant the minor [premise].)

By means of this overtly rhetorical exorcism, the demon was defeated and forced to leave the woman forever. The English author Thomas Lodge relates exorcism to rhetoric in much the same way when he gives one of his characters the line: 'My arguments against him were fatall exorcisms.'[65]

It is easy to see how these supernatural feats of exorcism, 'humanized' or 'rhetoricalized' though they are, might lead even saints into the sin of spiritual pride. Cristóbal de la Cruz has been accused by modern critics of exactly this sin. William Stapp argues that in one sense, Cruz has not changed at all from the pridefulness of his former ruffianesque self, Lugo. He is now simply fighting demons instead of Sevillian street gangs. This misinterpretation of the play is dangerous because it does not take into account the exorcistic techniques that were typical at this time. In fact, Stapp misunderstands this scene to the point that he implicates Cervantes in a near-blasphemous privileging of the redemptive powers of the saint over those of God. For him, Ana is 'una pecadora que pone más fe en una de sus criaturas que en Él. En efecto, Cruz baja a Cristo de la categoría de redentor a la de testigo ... de la salvación que efectúa Cruz mismo' (a sinner who puts more faith in one of his creatures than in Him. In effect, Cruz lowers Christ from the category of redeemer to that of witness ... of the salvation which Cruz himself effects).[66] What Stapp does not understand is that what happens here is an exorcism, and Catholic exorcists were called as Christ's ministers to proclaim their authority boldly over the demon. Especially in this humanized version of exorcism, the exorcist relies on the powers of rhetoric and thus must build his own *ethos* to persuade. To do this he draws upon a long tradition, stretching as far back as the rhetorician Gorgias, who believed that the persuasive word acts upon the soul in the way that medicine acts upon the body:

> Just as some medicines eliminate one humor from the body, and other medicines another, and some free from disease while others take away life, so too do some words grieve, others cheer, others frighten, others inflame him who listens to them and others, finally, with effectively malign persuasion poison and bewitch the soul.[67]

Stapp also does not understand that exorcists were always *proud* to gain the victory over the demon: this was out-and-out spiritual warfare. How much more should the exorcist be proud when he, with God's permission, uses his own powers of reasoning to effect the healing process.

Another danger of Stapp's interpretation is that it betrays little understanding of the character of demons, whose primary attribute is wounded pride. It is two dejected but prideful demons in the play who discuss the mysterious relationship of culpability and grace:

¡Que así nos la quitase de las manos!
¡Que así la mies tan sazonada nuestra
la segase la hoz del tabernero!
¡Reniego de mí mismo, y aun reniego!
¡Y que tuviese Dios por bueno y justo
tal cambalache!

(That thus he would snatch her out of our hands!
That thus our so-ripe harvest
would be reaped by the sickle of the tavern-keeper!
I curse myself, and I even blaspheme!
And that God would take as good and just
such a barter!)[68]

These proud demons are complaining about the fact that God would be willing to accept such a humanized, 'bargain' exorcism. They can only be conquered by a confident or even 'proud' exorcist who is sure of his powers to persuade.

It should be pointed out that in the passage just quoted, these characteristically proud – and also characteristically wise – demons are referring to the debate between Jesuits and Dominicans about free will (1582–94), as a result of which Pope Clement VIII imposed silence on the issue. This debate is ultimately the theological ground upon which Cruz bases his humanized exorcism of Ana. For the Thomistic Dominican Domingo Báñez (*Scholastica commentaria*, 1584), God created men with free will but disposes or predestines them 'infallibly' to choose good works.[69] In contrast, for the Jesuit Luis de Molina (*De concordia*, 1588), God gave men complete free will, and they can refuse to do good works, therefore causing a lack of concordance between divine will and human will.[70] Cervantes seems to have confused these opposing positions, or at least avoided taking sides in the debate, for he places a Molinist view of free will in the mouth of a Dominican friar.[71] However, it is characteristically Cervantine to champion the *libre albedrío* of the human soul, and Cervantes could probably not imagine a God who would not give such free will to his creatures. It is this free will that Cruz assures Ana she has – free will to choose God's mercy, even when it seems too late.

In the triumph of this rational free will over the demons' temptations, there is a symmetry between Ana's death and Cruz's, as both of their souls are fought over by demons who hover about and continue to hope for victory. In the demons' words,

Mientras no arroja el postrimero aliento,
bien se puede esperar que en algo tuerza

el peso, puesto en duda el pensamiento:
que a veces puede mucho nuestra fuerza.

(While he does not give forth the last breath,
well can it be hoped that in something will twist
the weight, placed in doubt the thought:
for at times our force can do much.)[72]

Later Lucifer pronounces the efforts of these demons a failure, admitting that the defences of the saintly souls were too strong to overcome:

Aun no puedo llegar siquiera al cuerpo
para vengar en él lo que en el alma
no pude; tales armas le defienden.

(I cannot even arrive at the body
to avenge in it what I could not do
in the soul; such arms defend him.)[73]

The friars Angel and Antonio overhear this demonic conversation at the time of Cruz's death and affirm, 'son los diablos' (they are the devils).[74]

The demons in this drama were very real for Cervantes. When he included them in his play he did not at all break his cardinal rule of literary verisimilitude. Far from it – for in fact, to orthodox Catholics of the baroque age, the demons were more real than the fleeting worldly ephemera around them. The conclusion of this book will explore the larger implications of this acceptance by early modern selves of the supernatural as the legitimate marvellous. For now, let us examine in the rest of this chapter first the debate over the genre of the *comedia de santos*, and then how two other authors writing in this same genre exploited the humanized Christian marvellous to lend verisimilitude to their fictions.

'False Miracles and Apocryphal Things': Cervantes and the Debate over the *Comedia de santos*

There were debates about the nature of this genre – debates which distilled some of the essence of our larger discussion of the early modern self and the supernatural in literature. In the case of the *comedia de santos*, the very genre itself became a laboratory where experiments were conducted to determine how far was 'too far' when it came to the inclusion of supernatural devices such as visions, apotheoses, miracles, and *tramoyas* or theatrical machinery in stage plays (and thus their incursion into literary portrayals of the early modern self). Cervantes himself weighed in on the disadvantages of this genre as it was practised by the less subtle playwrights of his time. He inserted a vitriolic diatribe into the *Quijote* against the *comedias divinas* as they appeared in the *corrales* of his day, full of sensational stage tricks designed to draw a large audience from the ignorant populace. This passage includes the following harangue:

> Pues, ¿qué, si venimos a las comedias divinas? ¡Qué de milagros falsos fingen en ellas, qué de cosas apócrifas y mal entendidas, atribuyendo a un santo los milagros de otro! Y aun en las humanas se atreven a hacer milagros, sin más respeto ni consideración que parecerles que allí estará bien el tal milagro y apariencia, como ellos llaman, para que gente ignorante se admire y venga a la comedia; que todo esto es en perjuicio de la verdad y en menoscabo de las historias, y aun en oprobio de los ingenios españoles; porque los estranjeros, que con mucha puntualidad guardan las leyes de la comedia, nos tienen por bárbaros e ignorantes, viendo los absurdos y disparates de las que hacemos.

> (Then what, if we come to the divine comedies? What false miracles do they pretend in them, what of apocryphal and poorly understood things, attributing to one saint the miracles of another! And even in the human [comedies] they dare to do miracles, without more respect or consideration than its appearing to them that in that place would be good such a miracle or appearance, as they call them, so that the ignorant people will admire and come to the comedy; and all of this is in prejudice of the truth and in detraction from the histories, and even in opprobrium of the Spanish geniuses; because the foreigners, who with much punctuality keep the laws of the comedy, take us for barbarians and ignorant, seeing the absurdities and the foolish things we do.)[75]

These words are stern, but Stanislav Zimic reminds us that Cervantes levels this criticism against the abusers of the genre of the *comedia de santos*, not the genre itself. He, like other critics, also believes that Cervantes wrote *El rufián dichoso* for the express purpose of showing everyone how a responsible *comedia de santos* was to be written.[76]

Unfortunately, Zimic's argument breaks down when he goes through rhetorical contortions to attempt to claim that Cervantes, 'despite all his affirmations' to the contrary, did not intend for supernatural elements in the play to be taken at face value.[77] Jenaro Talens and Nicholas Spadaccini persist in the same obstinate and doomed attempt to second-guess Cervantes, claiming that the author really invited the 'discreet reader' to 'demystify' the play.[78] Cervantes may have humanized the exorcism ritual for the early modern audience, but he never 'demystified' it to the point of trivializing it. In page after page of his *comedia de santos*, Cervantes himself tells us just the opposite, that in fact he did mean for the apparitions, demons, and bodiless souls to be taken seriously, and not just as 'poetic metaphors.' As E.C. Riley reminds us:

> The verisimilitude that he [Cervantes] harps on is not indeed what we understand by the word, but it is perfectly comprehensible ... The marvellous was necessary ... but since this could no longer be conveniently supplied by the old heathen deities, it must be furnished by supernatural agencies recognized among Christians – angels, devils, or beings endowed by God or Satan with extraordinary powers, such as saints, wizards, and fairies.[79]

Likewise Joaquín Casalduero, in a salubrious antidote to the sceptical critics' unwillingness to accept the obvious, reminds us with great sensitivity that Cervantes 'tiene buen cuidado ... de advertirnos que no acepta en la comedia de santos nada más que los hechos verdaderos, preocupación que es la de la Contrarreforma' (takes good care ... to warn us not to accept in the comedy of saints anything more than the true deeds, a preoccupation which is that of the Counter-Reformation).[80] He continues with a responsible summation of the baroque view of the supernatural as it repeats and even amplifies some beliefs of the Gothic era:

> El Barroco, aunque muy alejado ... de la Edad Media, todavía podía aceptar, porque las necesitaba, ciertas formas irracionales de la vida espiritual ... Es el sentido de lucha con los gigantes descomunales del Gótico, y de la victoria. El cristiano no tiene un instante de reposo ... Lucifer ... no es un milagro, es la realidad metafísica de la vida cristiana.

> (The baroque, although very removed ... from the Middle Ages, could still accept, because it needed them, certain irrational forms of spiritual life ... It is the sense of struggle with the monstrous giants of the Gothic, and of the victory. The Christian does not have one moment of repose ... Lucifer ... is not a miracle, he is the metaphysical reality of the Christian life.)[81]

This 'metaphysical reality of the Christian life' was an everyday reality for the early modern subject.

Part of Cervantes' credibility-building technique when he approaches this supernatural subject matter and its relation to the early modern self is the repeated invocation of an authoritative 'source,' which is the history of the saint's life. Cervantes invokes the veracity of this source no fewer than four times in the course of the play, first when he introduces the episode of Ana de Treviño, and again when he introduces the demons (appearing at separate times as lascivious nymphs and a bear named Saquiel).[82] His invocations usually take similar forms:

1) 'Todo esto es verdad de la historia' (All this is truth of history);[83]

2) 'Todo esto de esta máscara y visión fue verdad, que así lo cuenta la historia del santo' (All this of this masque and vision was truth, for thus recounts the story of the saint);[84]

3) 'Todo esto fue así, que no es visión supuesta, apócrifa ni mentirosa' (All this was thus, for it is not a supposed vision, apocryphal or lying);[85]

4) 'Esta visión fue verdadera, que así se cuenta en su historia' (This vision was true, for thus it is told in his history).[86]

This 'source' has been identified tentatively as either the *Historia de la provincia de México* (1596) by Agustín Dávila Padilla (391–461), whom Cervantes may have known personally,[87] or the *Consuelo de penitentes o mesa franca de spirituales manjares* (Comfort of penitents or common table of spiritual nourishments) (1583) by Fray Antonio de San Román, a devotional book which also included some saints' lives.[88] Alternatively, it is known from a 1590 document that Cervantes bought a copy of Hernando del Casal's *Historia general de Santo Domingo y de su orden de predicadores* (1584); he could have used this book in writing his play.[89] Yet another possibility is Juan López's *Historia general de la Orden de Sto. Domingo, y de su Orden de Predicadores* (1563), a choice which I consider seriously because unlike some of the other possible ones, it includes descriptions of miraculous apparitions in the exact forms they take in the play – for example, a demon disguised as a ghostly bear.[90] My favourite choice for Cervantes' 'source,' however, remains Dávila Padilla because his account, by far the longest version of Cruz's life, emphasizes what I have called the 'humanized' or rhetorical aspect of Cruz's bargain with Ana.[91]

Whichever version(s) of the saint's life Cervantes used, it fits with what we know of his character – he read voraciously. It has been assumed that Cervantes was fond of reading devotional books because of an episode in the *Quijote* in which Don Quixote visits a printing press in Barcelona and sees the proof pages being corrected for Fray Felipe de Meneses's *Luz del alma christiana* (Light of the Christian soul). Don Quixote comments on the genre of devotional literature: 'Estos tales libros, aunque hay muchos deste género, son los que se deben imprimir, porque son muchos los pecadores que se usan, y son menester infinitas para tantos desalumbrados' (Books like these, although there are many of this genre, are those that should be printed, because there are many sinners that use them, and an infinite number are needed for so many unenlightened ones).[92] Whether this extrapolation of the author's sentiment may be made from his fiction or not, the specific devotional book *Consuelo de penitentes* was republished in Seville at about the time Cervantes was staying there. Furthermore, the edition bore the printed *aprobación* of his old teacher, Juan López de Hoyos.[93] Given Cervantes's determination to write a responsible and humane *comedia de santos* that would rectify the abuses of contemporaneous popular theatrical productions, it is not surprising that he would turn to these historical chronicles for accurate (as opposed to 'apocryphal') miracles. He was not the only dramatist to do so.

Saint = Exorcist: Calderón's *Las cadenas del demonio* and Lope's *El divino africano*

Both Calderón de la Barca and Lope de Vega wrote *comedias de santos* about exorcism, both of which are worthy of brief consideration here. Like Cervantes, who referred several times to 'la historia del santo' as a source for his play, the religious dramatist Calderón used a hagiographical chronicle as his primary source for *Las cadenas del demonio* (The chains of the demon),[94] one of only two plays in which he explored the *topos* of demonic possession.[95] Alexander Parker has suggested that the chronicle he used was the *Flos sanctorum* of Alonso de Villegas (1594).[96] Although Calderón's play (anomalously among most plays about exorcism) involves a diabolical pact,[97] a brief comparison of his play with that of Cervantes and then that of Lope will be useful because it demonstrates how other suffering saints in stage plays – figures who are the most pious literary figurations of the early modern self – conduct successful 'humanized' exorcisms.

The best way to describe Calderón's *Las cadenas del demonio* is that it is a female version of the imprisoned prince motif in *La vida es sueño*. The princess Irene has been imprisoned by King Polemón of Armenia, her father, because of predictions made that she would bring chaos and destruction to his reign. He intends to choose one of her male cousins as his successor instead. Full of rage and despair, she pledges her soul to the devil, who appears in the form of the pagan god Astarot, in exchange for her liberty. She is rescued and exorcized by San Bartolomé, the apostle/saint (legendarily the first convert to Christianity, fig. 7) who then becomes a martyr on her behalf. The play contains stage directions for terrific supernatural special effects, such as San Bartolomé's multiple flights across the stage. Particularly spectacular as well are the sinking disappearances through trap doors of both the idol's altars and the devil himself as he returns to hell.[98]

The 'chains of the demon' in the title (see fig. 1) refer to the words of the exorcism ritual with which the saint will bind the tongue of the demon: 'Yo con esta cadena, / de fuego, en nombre de Dios, / tengo de ligar tu lengua' (I with this chain, / of fire, in the name of God, / have to tie your tongue).[99] The demon protests that he cannot be cast out of Irene because she gave him permission to enter:

'Della no podràs echarme' (From her you will not be able to cast me out).[100] But the demon wails that he is, in fact, chained by the saint's power:

> No puedo hablar (ay de mí!)
> porque cautiuas, y presas
> con cadena estàn de fuego
> mis acciones, y mis fuerças;
> no me aflijas, no me aflijas,
> Bartolomè ...
>
> (I cannot speak [ay, me!]
> because captured, and prisoners
> with a chain of fire
> are my actions, and my forces;
> do not afflict me, do not afflict me,
> Bartholomew ...)[101]

The saint torments the demon, as the demon torments the princess. Irene exhibits all the classic symptoms of demonic possession:

> Ay infelize de mí!
> dixo, y rendida cayò
> en la tierra, cuyo pasmo,
> cuyo assombro, cuyo horror
> suspenso dexò al amago ...
> Retiraronla, y apenas
> boluiò en sí, quando boluiò
> tan furiosa, que no ay
> lazo, cadena, prision,
> que no rompa, y despedaze
> y con despecho, y furor,
> delirios son quantos dize,
> locuras quanto haze son.
>
> (Oh, unhappy me!
> she said, and faint, she fell
> on the ground, whose amazement,
> whose astonishment, whose horror
> left the nauseous one in suspense ...
> They withdrew her, and she had hardly

returned to herself, when she returned
so furious, that there is not
tie, chain, prison,
that she does not break, and tear to pieces
and with wrath, and furor,
all she says are deliriums,
as many things as she does are crazy.)[102]

Irene's despair sounds very much like Ana's in *El rufián dichoso*: 'Curad otros males, / que tengan remedio, y no / el mío, que no le tiene / mientras que Dios fuere Dios' (Cure other ills, / that have remedy, and not / mine, which does not have it / while God is still God).[103]

San Bartolomé, however, asks God's permission to enter the battle against the demon on her behalf: 'Podrè en tu nombre, Señor, / entrar en esta lid?' (Will I be able in your name, Lord, / to enter into this contest?).[104] Music from heaven sounds, and he hears an answer in the affirmative. He questions further whether the demon will have power enough to win this battle. The heavenly voice responds in the negative. He asks whether he should dare to defy such a dangerous foe. The heavenly voice answers that he may do so with confidence, adding that God will help him. Here, as in *El rufián dichoso*, we see a human being ordained by God for a special mission and given the spiritual confidence (even a sort of pride) to carry it out.

Sharing the 'cruz' motif of *El rufián dichoso*, Bartolomé forces the demoniac princess to look at a cross. The demon howls through her mouth:

Quita, quita,
y no te me acerques, no,
si no quieres que arrancando
pedazos del coraçon
desta infelize muger,
te los tire.

(Leave off, leave off,
and do not come near me, no,
if you do not want me, ripping out
pieces of the heart
of this unhappy woman,
to fling them at you.)[105]

When the demon does not want to allow her to beg for God's mercy, Bartolomé uses a typical exorcistic strategy and casts the devil into the extremity of a single hair of her head:

> En el nombre del Señor,
> te mando, que te retires
> à la extremidad menor
> de vn cabello, y libre dexes
> lengua, alma, discurso, y voz.

> (In the name of the Lord,
> I command you, that you retire
> to the smallest extremity
> of a hair, and that you leave free
> tongue, soul, discourse, and voice.)[106]

After this exorcism, Irene feels as if an asp has been wrested from her breast: 'Siéntome mucho mejor, / que parece que me falta vn áspid del coraçon' (I feel much better, / for it appears that I lack an aspid of the heart).[107] But the exorcism is not complete until the saint has cast out the demon completely. The demon threatens to inhabit a nearby mountain, toppling it and killing all the people below. This is the same danger we saw earlier, in *El rufián dichoso*, that the demon will transfer itself to another nearby habitation. The exorcist specifically forbids the demon to transfer itself to any person, animal, or object nearby:

> Sin hazer daño ninguno
> en desierto, en población,
> en personas, en ganados,
> en mies, en fruto, ni en flor,
> desampara esta criatura.

> (Without doing any damage
> in desert, in population,
> in persons, in flocks,
> in harvests, in fruit, or in flower,
> relinquish this creature.)[108]

After the demon is cast out, he still tries to 'repetir la possession de Irene' (repeat the possession of Irene),[109] but the chains of the exorcist binding him are too strong. This saintly – but still human – exorcist must suffer greatly on behalf of the princess he has exorcized. He dies a martyr's death and returns to the stage on a throne borne by the wings of the seraphim, with the devil in chains at his feet. The exorcism he has performed helps to define him as a saint.

In fact, in medieval canonization proceedings, exorcism became a standard miracle in the repertoire of many candidates being considered for sainthood.[110] The formula 'saint = exorcist' became almost obligatory for any holy person who had truly followed in the footsteps of the apostles. Knowing this, many Golden Age dramatists exploited the aura of sanctity surrounding the figure of the exorcist to make their *comedias de santos* sufficiently laudatory of the virtues of their saints. In doing so, as we have seen, they often drew upon collections of saints' lives or other hagiographical sources such as Counter-Reformation paintings (again see fig. 5, as well as fig. 6) to find specific miracles of exorcism the saints were known to have performed.

Lope de Vega was another one of these Golden Age dramatists. He probably used Pedro de Ribadeneira's *Flos sanctorum* to find specific details of St Augustine's life[111] to help him in the process of writing another *comedia de santos*, *El divino africano* (The divine African).[112] In this play St Augustine performs an exorcism in the third act as one of several miracles presented by the dramatist as 'proof' of his saintliness. The first two acts follow Augustine's autobiography as presented in his *Confessions*, while the last act is drawn from hagiographical accounts published after his death. Along with effecting an erasure of a sin from the devil's ledger, hearing a heavenly voice, appearing in a divine vision, discoursing about the theological mystery of the Trinity, and holding up a pillar of the church together with Saints Ambrose, Gregory, and Jerome, St Augustine performs this exorcism as another saintly miracle.

Lidio and other men bring to him a demoniac woman with her hands bound. She resists violently, with the demon protesting through her that the hands which rebelled against God and erased so many stars (angels) from the sky should not be bound by mere mortal 'dogs.' The demon protests even more vociferously at the sight of Augustine, a detail which would have reinforced the idea of his saintliness to a demonologically informed audience. The woman despairs of her salvation, just as Ana did in *El rufián dichoso*: 'que yo no tengo remedio' (that I do not have remedy).[113]

Augustine, like Cristóbal de la Cruz, begins the exorcism with a rhetorical strategy or reasoning process by asking whether it is possible for the devil to reside in the image and likeness of God (i.e., the body of the woman). The demon responds to this strategy instantly, recognizing what Augustine is trying to accomplish, by asking whether he means to argue with him. Augustine concedes that the demon has access to immense knowledge but proceeds with the exorcism anyway. He asks why he entered the woman, and when the demon replies that her despair gave him entrance, Augustine declares that even despair should have been an insufficient occasion. The saint announces that he will expel the demon: 'yo te le haré dejar' (I will make you leave her).[114] The demon responds by attacking Augustine where he is most vulnerable: his past. He reminds him of his Maniche-ism and his former rebellion against God, and then goes on to specific sins: his 'crazy love' for Africana and his amorous devotion to pagan literature, particularly the story of Dido. Like Cristóbal de la Cruz, who also lived a former life of disso-lution, Augustine argues in turn that his *Confessions* prove his repentance from all of these obsessions.

He then steers the conversation back to the demoniac woman and asks the demon again how he can possess a baptized person. The demon replies that the woman herself has given him leave. The exorcism then commences in earnest:

AGUSTINO: Que le dejes te conviene.
        En virtud de Dios te mando
     que te vayas.
ENDEMONIADA: Agustín,
      no me apremies.
AGUSTINO: ¿A qué fin
     le vienes atormentando?
        Déjale luego, traidor.
ENDEMONIADA: Yo me vengaré de ti.

(AUGUSTINE: That you leave her is convenient for you.
        In virtue of God I command you
   that you leave.
DEMONIAC: Augustine,
     do not constrain me.
AUGUSTINE: To what end
     do you come tormenting her?
        Leave her then, traitor.
DEMONIAC: I will avenge myself of you.)[115]

At this point the demon specifies what his revenge upon Augustine will be by making a prediction of future political events. This symptom of clairvoyance or prophecy in the demoniac is seen here (as elsewhere, particularly in the satirical genre discussed in chapter 2) as a source of diabolical knowledge. The demon prophesies that soon the Goths from Spain will come to Africa and conquer it and that Augustine will die of grief to see his beloved Hippo surrounded by invaders.

Although the exorcism abruptly comes to an end at this point with the cured woman sinking to the ground, the prophecy functions within the play to validate the knowledge of the demon. The Goths do invade Africa just as the demon predicted, and Augustine does die from grief even though the Goths were not intending to kill him or take possession of his city (they make this exception out of reverence for the saint and his holiness). The exorcism in this play has the odd effect of confirming the saint's sainthood while at the same time placing him in fatal jeopardy. If he had never meddled with this demon, he might not have come to this end. Like both the saintly heroes of Cervantes's and Calderón's *comedias de santos*, the hero of this play incurs danger to himself as a result of his contact with a demon through exorcism. But the formula 'saint = exorcist' seems to require that at some point in a saint's life (or, in the case of relics, after his death), he must perform an exorcism to be considered truly holy.

The staging of this exorcism and other miracles in this play has disturbed modern critics such as Marcelino Menéndez Pelayo, who dismissed it as a 'vulgarísima comedia de santos, llena de apariciones y tramoyas' (most vulgar comedy of saints, full of apparitions and theatrical machinery) which employs a 'manera tosca y primitiva de llevar a la escena lo sobrenatural' (coarse and primitive manner of taking the supernatural to the scene).[116] Looking beneath his typical academic aversion to the supernatural in literature, we can nevertheless see that Menéndez Pelayo has certainly put his finger on something here. Why does the *comedia de santos*, a genre devoted to saints and their piety, have to include such messy spectacles as possession and exorcism? Does the formula 'saint= exorcist,' when it is translated into stage directions, end up detracting from the saint's purity or piety instead of confirming or reinforcing it? Is the spectacle of exorcism too grotesque, too *human*, to fit into the idealized portrait of a saint, particularly when (as in the three cases discussed above) the contact with a demon runs the risk of contaminating the pious early modern self and, ultimately, leading to his (earthly) downfall?

I propose that the answer to these questions lies in the humanization of the exorcism ritual. Demonic possession, along with its concomitant ritualistic exorcism, functions in these plays to humanize both the saints and the rituals they perform. It humanizes the saints by engaging them in the messy problems of people's lives and, through the mediation of the demon, even transferring some of those problems – leprosy, martyrdom, or the invasion of Spanish Goths – onto the saints themselves. It humanizes the exorcism ritual by dramatizing it as a rhetorical bargain, where the saints reason with those victimized by the demons and persuade them to trust in God's grace. The net result is related to the way exorcism functions in romance and the interlude because it humanizes the ritual along with the various early modern subjects who participate in it.

Out of these plays also emerges a pattern of an extreme baroque paradox, the sinner/saint. Like Lope's Saint Augustine, Cervantes's hero Cristóbal de la Cruz goes from being the worst of sinners to the best of saints. The oxymoron of the title *El rufián dichoso* is a baroque feat of dexterity in which Cervantes, for example, combines opposite ends of the moral spectrum within a single figure. Just as baroque painters strove to achieve seemingly impossible combinations of light and dark or weightlessness and heaviness within a single work of art (once again, see fig. 5), so these playwrights yoked together the opposing factors of a dichotomy. Baroque antitheses abound in this play and others of its genre:[117] good works/sins, Virgin/prostitute, restoration/loss. Carmelo Lisón Tolosana suggests that these sinner/saint figures represent both superpower and impotency.[118] These early modern figures are chained to a pleasurable and painful humanity, to a radical ambivalence and moral tension. Casalduero attributes our modern (and I would add, postmodern) inability to appreciate these dramas and these dichotomies to the fact that the 'heroism of the absolute' so vital to the Counter-Reformation enterprise has disappeared from our culture.[119] It should be noted, however, that these playwrights take these heroical conventions and modify them as they see fit – namely, to present a more intimate portrait of the hero as a very human figure, not just a saint:

> El rompimiento [de la *comedia de santos*] con la hagiografía ... es ... ideológico. En la narración hagiográfica el santo es un prototipo idealizado con una individualidad inexistente y Cervantes rescata el interés por la vida del personaje, por el individuo.

> (The break [of the comedy of saints] with hagiography ... is ... ideological. In the hagiographical narration the saint is an idealized prototype with a nonexistent individuality and Cervantes rescues the interest in the life of the person, of the individual.)[120]

The other face of heroism is humanity, and surely the humanization of these early modern saints – through their willingness to 'dirty their hands' in the ugly job of exorcism – resonates as loudly today as at any time in literary history.

Perhaps the genres of romance, interlude, and hagiography are not so irreconcilable after all, even within the oeuvre of a conflicted author such as Lope or Cervantes. They illustrate the coexistence of scepticism with belief, but they also bear an affinity to each other through their respective 'humanizations' of the supernatural. They also share another common feature: in all of these genres, demonic possession somehow results in an enhancement of, not a threat to, the early modern self. In the romance and interlude, the experience of being in love or being 'possessed' by the lover enhances the amorous self. In the genre of hagiography, likewise, the ability to cast out demons enhances the aura of saintliness and builds the ethos of the saintly figure.

These three genres' distinct approaches to exorcism and the early modern self, while seeming to conflict, may only be a matter of different emphasis. When certain theologemes of the exorcism ritual (such as the lovers' ruse) are emphasized over others, the result may appear in the form of an entirely separate genre (such as the romance). And when certain figurations of the early modern self (such as the saintly exorcist) are emphasized over others, the result may be the idealization – and concomitant humanization – of this figure in the *comedia de santos*. But in all three of these genres, it is still the humanization of the exorcism ritual and the early modern folk who participate in it that is the focus of intense literary attention; and arguably, it is this humanization of ritual which gives these works their lasting appeal.

Chapter Four

Tragedy As the Absence or Failure of Exorcism

When it appears in tragedy, exorcism fails. Often, however, it is omitted alto-gether. The presence of demonic possession in tragedy without the concomitant presence of exorcism leaves a yawning void, the dismal abyss which is a perennial feature of the tragic landscape. In *King Lear*, the exorcism ritual does appear, but it fails within the text as an effective redemptive process for the early modern self. It does not fail, however, as a metatheatrical metaphor of catharsis. In *A Yorkshire Tragedy*, there is a sort of exorcism, but it also fails as a conductor of the self to ultimate redemption. In the other tragedies discussed in this chapter, exorcism never even appears. Instead, the topos of demonic possession is exploited in three of the plays to create a 'demon as scapegoat' pattern that attempts to explain the inexplicable act of murder. Finally, even the 'demon as scapegoat' pattern fails in *Hamlet*, where demonic possession is only one possible explanation for the pro-tagonist's madness. The Ghost and Hamlet try on the 'masks' of demon and demoniac, but only as part of their endless series of roles to perform.

In these plays I will show a progression of decreasing potency, efficacy, or per-vasiveness of the exorcism ritual for the early modern self. Richard Hornby, in his discussion of tragedies which incorporate rituals and ceremonies, notes:

> Ceremonies fulfilled, whether onstage or in real life, engender feelings in us of har-mony, peace, and happiness; ceremonies unfulfilled, for whatever reason, engender feelings of disorientation, discord, and sadness ... In tragedy ... we can note three significant types of ceremony: the offstage ceremony, the anti-ceremony, and the quasi-ceremony. In all these types, the ceremony is absent in some way, yet also of great importance ... [T]his notion can be expanded to include all the cultural systems or codes within which any kind of symbolic expression occurs. The fact that

we do recognize absence when it occurs is evidence that these cultural systems are indeed there, in the background for us. Indeed the very notion of a tragic, 'broken' ceremony implies that we have a sense of what a proper, completed ceremony should be.[1]

This discussion of the significance of what is not there, 'the presence of absence,' is derived directly from the deconstructive criticism of Jacques Derrida, who in turn draws inspiration from Heidegger on this point.[2] Derrida states: 'Play is the disruption of presence. The presence of an element is always a signifying and substitutive reference inscribed in a system of differences and the movement of a chain. Play is always play of absence and presence.'[3] The importance of absence, however, can also be traced to Ferdinand de Saussure's notion of *langue*, in which the speaker and listener are always relating a particular utterance (*parole*) to the surrounding language (*langue*) as a whole.[4] In Derridian terms, the presence of exorcism in tragedy is experienced as the negative of its absence. Demonic possession resonates through the genre of tragedy, but the self's hope for an ultimate exorcism is forever raised and then dashed to pieces. It is the nature of the tragic experience that exorcism cannot succeed. Nonetheless it lingers in the early modern imagination as a very real and poignant absence.

The Relationship of Satire to Tragedy: Harsnett's *Declaration*

Much of the study that has been done on Shakespeare's use of contemporaneous demonological texts has been limited to *King Lear* and its association with Samuel Harsnett's *A Declaration of Egregious Popish Impostures*.[5] The lively, scandalous content of Shakespeare's favourite treatise on exorcism consists of two priestly accounts and five witnesses' statements concerning the Denham possessions of 1585–6.[6] These accounts focus on a series of exorcisms conducted in and around London by Catholic missionary priests led by William Weston, S.J. The exorcists' rituals involved the chanting of prayers in English and Latin and the use of such 'props' as relics, vestments, oils, water, galbanum, salt, rue, and sack (strong, dry wine). Each successful exorcism resulted in a dispossession, which was called a miracle. The most subjective component of Harsnett's treatise, reaching beyond the descriptions, examinations, and confessions, is his own analysis of the events and personages under scrutiny. He concluded that the exorcisms were frauds and that the Jesuit priests were the real devils.

Complications in assessing Shakespeare's borrowings from Harsnett arise because of Harsnett's sceptical bias (a bias which, it may be noted, several New Historicists have assimilated to their own sceptical position). After reviewing the evidence, a scholar cannot help suspecting that in spite of his ecclesiastical position as domestic chaplain to Richard Bancroft, bishop of London, Samuel Harsnett may not have written an altogether honest report in his vituperative zeal to denounce practices he undoubtedly viewed as absurd and sacrilegious. As an Anglican governing authority, Harsnett did not believe in the authenticity of these demonic possessions, for to do so would have been to acknowledge that some forces in the world were ungovernable.

Shakespeare appropriated both Harsnett's explicit language and his implicit fear confronting the exorcisms for precisely this reason: to create a world out of control, an atmosphere of madness for *King Lear.* What sorts of material did Shakespeare cull from Harsnett's diatribe, and where did he see fit to include echoes of Harsnett in his own writing? The over eighty parallels which Kenneth Muir has traced between *King Lear* and *A Declaration of Egregious Popish Impostures* demonstrate that Harsnett's treatise profoundly affected Shakespeare in the process of composing his tragedy.

The most often discussed examples of attributes or symptoms of madness which Shakespeare derived from the experiences of the demoniacs examined in Harsnett's *Declaration* occur in the performance of Edgar as Poor Tom. The most immediate specific source for Edgar's entire performance of simulated possession as Poor Tom was Harsnett's account of the experience of the first demoniac, Nicholas Marwood. Edgar's contortions to brush off his beggar's lice mimic the vigorous air-grabbing of a demoniac trying to catch demons. A.L. Soens has offered an interpretation of Edgar's lines and probable gestures as a portrayal of a fencing match with a demon, similar to the 'fencing matches' which Harsnett mockingly describes the exorcists as having with devils.[7] Harsnett provided Shakespeare with a source for painful verbal adjectives – 'beaten,' 'scourged,' 'stung,' 'flayed,' 'tortured,' 'scalded,' and 'pierced' – denoting actions which Edgar could perform to demonstrate madness.[8] Another commonly cited appropriation of Harsnett by Edgar in *King Lear* is the series of devils' names that Shakespeare borrowed from the examination of Sara Williams in *A Declaration of Egregious Popish Impostures*:

Declaration	*King Lear*
Fliberdigibet	Flibbertigibbet
Hoberdidance	Hopdance, Hobbididance
Haberdicut	Obidicut
Smolkin	Smolkin (Trayford's devil)
Modu	Modo (Mainy's devil)
Maho	Mahu (Sara's devil)
Killico	Pillicock
Purre	Pur.[9]

Shakespeare borrowed these outrageous names from the *Declaration* for use by the disguised Edgar on the heath in his last words as a demoniac:

Five fiends have been in poor Tom at once: of lust, as Obidicut; Hobbididence, prince of dumbness; Mahu, of stealing; Modo, of murder; Flibbertigibbet, of mopping and mowing, who since possesses chamber-maids and waiting-women.[10]

The 'chamber-maids and waiting-women' refer to Sara Williams, Friswood Williams, and Ann Smith, all demoniacs in Harsnett's *A Declaration of Egregious Popish Impostures*. The 'mopping and mowing' of which Edgar speaks comes from an identical comment by Harsnett on the performance of these women.[11]

In addition to his naming of the devils, Edgar fabricates his disguise of madness with other rantings that allude to or follow the form of episodes of exorcism. These episodes and snatches of episodes, almost like fragments of overheard conversations, do not consist simply of gibberish thrown together to mimic a madman's speech. Far from nonsense, these allusions may be traced to events recounted by Harsnett that lack significance when detached from their context. One such allusion is Edgar's mention of a fiend that 'hath laid knives under his pillow, and halters in his pew.' These apparently random actions described as having been performed by a demon do not make much sense by themselves. They are actually a direct reference to an episode recounted by Friswood Williams in her examination in *A Declaration of Egregious Popish Impostures*:

This examinate further saith that one ... Apothecarie, having brought with him from London to *Denham* on a time a new halter and two blades of knives, did leave the same upon the gallerie floare in her Maisters house. The next morning ... a great search was made in the house to know how the said halter and knife blades came thether ...[12]

This identification of a source for Edgar's words is not incompatible with the traditional assumption that he is listing potential instruments of suicide. Another superficially obscure reference made by Edgar concerns 'a servingman! proud in heart and mind; that curl'd my hair, wore gloves in my cap.'[13] The origin of this reference is the priests' description of Richard Mainy's enactment of the seven deadly sins in the last confession of the *Declaration*: 'Ma:[ster] Mainy ... curled his haire, and used such gestures as Ma: [ster] Edmunds presently affirmed that that spirit was Pride.'[14]

Edgar is not the only character who regularly engages in apparently obscure Harsnettian discourse in *King Lear*. The Fool and Cordelia – both of whose discourse is also tainted with madness at different times, in different ways, and for different reasons[15] – produce an occasional reference to an episode which can be contextualized by consulting Harsnett. The Fool laments in a song 'that such a king should play bo-peep.'[16] An explication of what it meant to 'play bo-peep' in a demonic context may be found in Harsnett's account of a devil who hides in a girl's toenail, '[w]here hee must lye for a skout like the Sentinel in a watch, and suffer every boy to play bo-peepe with his devilship.'[17] The Fool continues a few lines later: 'Thou hast par'd thy wit o' both sides ... Here comes one o' the parings.'[18] This remark to Lear draws upon the same account of the toenail devil: Harsnett wrote of the opportunity to 'pare away the devil lying in the dead of the nayle.'[19] Just as the Fool's discourse derives occasionally from Harsnett, so Cordelia makes one utterance which may be traced to the *Declaration*. Her cry of 'poor perdu!'[20] may have been inspired by the exposed sentinel described by Harsnett.[21] The tainting of the rhetoric of these characters – the ones who are supposed to be less prominent and less mad – by allusions to exorcistic episodes contaminates them with the madness of the major characters. This madness, conceived in demonic terms, spreads like a legion of demons to anyone with whom the protagonists have contact.

A reversal of this contamination process occurs with yet another appropriation technique of Shakespeare: the use of demonic animals, mentioned by Harsnett, with which Shakespeare surrounds his mad protagonists. The contamination of madness occurs in reverse order because, with this technique, Shakespeare uses animals embodying demons to incite his protagonists to a heightened insanity. Lear's mouse originated with a mouse devil in a passage of Harsnett's *Declaration*.[22] The appearance of this demon-associated mouse in *King Lear* suggests an upside-down world in which animals as well as persons have succumbed to a madness that simulates demonic possession. Another possessed animal appearing in both the treatise and the play is a horse. One confession by the demoniac Richard Mainy contains the gentleman's recollection of his supposedly demonic horse: 'It was given forth ... that the horse I rid upon was a devil, and that I had devils attending upon me in liverie coates.'[23] Shakespeare appropriates this demonic animal by giving to his character Edgar a 'bay trotting-horse' that rides over 'four-inch'd bridges.'[24] He also borrows from Harsnett the demonic dogs which Poor Tom tries to drive away with a rhyming spell. Furthermore, in using demonic animals to create an upside-down world, Shakespeare plays upon the facile transition from demonic bestiality to demonic personality. By having a female character such as Goneril make the animal noise 'mew!' within the context he has established of demonic bestiality, Shakespeare associates her with demonic possession and madness;[25] it will be remembered that Lear even calls Goneril a fiend, an epithet which Albany will later repeat.[26]

Women are further associated with demonic possession and madness in this text through a different appropriation technique of Shakespeare: he adds from the Harsnett material new sexual metaphors to his already ample repertoire. The priests whom Harsnett denounced had allegedly hunted devils in possessed women's bodies,[27] and the exorcists had supposedly told Sara Williams that her first menstruation was diabolical because a devil inhabited her vagina.[28] This horrifying treatment of women by the exorcists afforded a rich, sexually charged language for Lear in the mad scene:

> Beneath is all the fiends': there's hell, there's darkness,
> There is the sulphurous pit, burning, scalding,
> Stench, consumption.[29]

Lear is raving about his daughters Regan and Goneril here, for only in the body of a woman is found this 'bottomlesse pit of hell.'[30] With exorcistic terminology, Harsnett offered to Shakespeare an unsurpassed technique for linking femininity and feminine sexuality with madness and evil.

Shakespeare's borrowings are not limited to language, however; they extend to the more concrete features of stage properties, scenery, and specific events as well. In *King Lear* Shakespeare draws upon Harsnett's *Declaration* for physical scenery and props such as the hovel on the heath, Kent's stocks, and the chair and joint-stool in the mock trial. Shakespeare also takes from Harsnett's recurrent storm imagery the idea for the symbolic dramatic event of the storm. This appropria-tion does bear an association with demonology, moreover: King James wrote that demons 'can rayse stormes and tempestes in the aire ... [w]hich likewise is verie easie to be discerned from anie other naturall tempestes that are meteore, in respect of the suddaine and violent raising thereof, together with short induring of the same.'[31] The specific devils who raise tempests are the fourth ones classified by Reginald Scot, the *Aquei* – 'waterie, of the sea' – who raise storms and provoke lust in human beings.[32]

We shall see that with typical demonological connotations, Shakespeare infuses this storm with all the dramatic tension of the spectacle of an exorcism. After Harsnett described an exorcism as a storm, Shakespeare inverted the relationship to invoke the possibility that his storm could be viewed as an exorcism. Thus he appropriated satirical elements for his tragedy without turning his tragedy into a satire.

Exorcism as Neo-Aristotelian Catharsis:[33] *King Lear*

Various associations have been suggested to explain both why Shakespeare would have been interested in reading a treatise on exorcism and how his audience would have responded to his inclusion of exorcistic material. Some New Histori-cists suggest that Shakespeare read the treatise with the intention of pleasing King James I by writing a timely satire on the fraudulent exorcisms (we know from the title page of the first edition that the play was performed at court in Whitehall on St Stephen's Night, 26 December 1606), but this argument is problematic because of King James I's early credulous stance toward demonic possession as expressed in his treatise *Daemonologie*. Scholars agree that intelligent spectators in his audience would have noticed and comprehended Shakespeare's allusions to Harsnett, but how would the audience have interpreted these allusions? New His-toricists such as Stephen Greenblatt, in their conscious decision to blur the boundaries of genre, have emphasized a satirical reading of this material in the tragedy by interpreting Edgar's feigned possession as a parody of the perfor-mances of the demoniacs exorcized by the Jesuits at Denham.

Greenblatt claims that 'by 1600 ... Shakespeare had clearly marked out posses-sion and exorcism as frauds ... When in 1603 Harsnett was whipping exorcism toward the theater, Shakespeare was already at the entrance to the Globe to wel-come it.'[34] Not interested in exploring the consequences of the exorcism material for our understanding of Lear's madness, Greenblatt states unequivocally that 'Lear's madness has no supernatural origin.'[35] The rhetoric of the New Histori-cists is permeated by scepticism and unbelief: 'Demonic possession is *responsibly* marked out for the audience as a theatrical *fraud*, designed to *gull* the *unsuspect-ing*.'[36] Sometimes this New Historicist reading attempts to 'explain away' or gain-say evidence in the text itself; witness the following twisted argument concerning devils, spirits, and prayers:

> When Albany calls Goneril a 'devil' and a 'fiend' (4.2.59, 66), we know that he is not identifying her as a supernatural being – it is impossible, in this play, to witness the eruption of the denizens of hell into the human world – just as we know that Albany's prayer for 'visible spirits' to be sent down by the heavens 'to tame these vild offenses' (4.2.46–7) will be unanswered.[37]

Such a secularized interpretation of *King Lear* proves as strained as it does anach-ronistic: '*King Lear* is haunted by a sense of rituals and beliefs that are no longer efficacious, that have been emptied out ... For all the invocation of the gods in *King Lear*, it is clear that there are no devils.'[38] 'It is clear' only to those New His-toricists who wish it so.

Some recent studies refute antireligious assumptions like these about why Shakespeare chose to appropriate material from Harsnett. Most of these recent critical assessments echo in some way or other the work of the Chicago Critics, whose approach provides a salutary corrective to that of the New Historicists. In one study, F.W. Brownlow offers a different basis for Shakespeare's interest in Harsnett as well as an alternative interpretation of his attitude toward the *Declaration of Egregious Popish Impostures.* He points out that the *Declaration* savagely attacked persons Shakespeare probably knew: the exorcist Robert Dibdale, the son of a Stratford family intimate with the Hathaways; Thomas Cottam, a man feared by the demons of the exorcisms who was the brother of Stratford's (and probably Shakespeare's) schoolmaster from 1579 to 1582; and Edward Arden, who was probably Shakespeare's second cousin.[39] In this assessment, Brownlow does not concur with Greenblatt's view that Shakespeare took only a secular interest in the *Declaration.* Brownlow's criticism of 'Shakespeare and the Exorcists' is a valid one: in it, Greenblatt does not demonstrate enough sensitivity to the spirituality of Jesuit priests or Catholic rituals. Peter Milward notes that Shakespeare's family included some Catholics, and if this information is accurate, such a background might have influenced Shakespeare's approach to the persecution of the Jesuit exorcists.[40] In a similar argument, John L. Murphy theorizes that the hunted Edgar represents the hunted Jesuit exorcists.[41] In perhaps the most recent and influential refutation of Greenblatt, John D. Cox points out that 'it is not clear that the thrust of skepticism is as broad as Greenblatt suggests ... Metatheatrical references are not necessarily a comment on the devil himself, let alone on all religious symbols.'[42]

Varied as their interpretations are, scholars writing against the New Historicists agree on one thing: the main problem with the New Historicists' interpretation is that they ignore the possibility that the playwright's noncynical use of the supernatural might contribute to the overall tragic effect of the drama. An alternative reading of the play, with more respect for the boundaries of genre, would view its inclusion of demonic possession as an effective way for the playwright to manipulate the topos of exorcism as a metaphor for catharsis. By enacting possession by demons, Edgar serves as a surrogate for the devastating madness of King Lear, who also exhibits (unfeigned) symptoms of possession. Edgar's mad discourse 'functions dramatically to trigger, mark, and counterpoint the specific moment of Lear's own break with sanity, which occurs decisively at his emotionally apt but logically groundless identification with Poor Tom.'[43] By watching Lear watching Edgar, the audience achieves catharsis – a concept which is, I will argue, intimately connected with the Renaissance metaphorical meaning of exorcism.

Shakespeare invokes the specific types of pity and fear expressed in the Aristotelian cathartic formula. When Gloucester asks the disguised Edgar, 'Now, good sir, what are you?' he answers:

A most poor man, made tame to fortune's blows,
Who, by the art of known and feeling sorrows,
Am pregnant to good pity.[44]

This passage has been discussed specifically in relation to Aristotle by J.V. Cunningham, who notes that Edgar, the ideal tragic spectator, has attained the capacity for feeling pity.[45] Cordelia, too, will stress the importance of pity: 'Had you not been their father, these white flakes / Did challenge pity of them';[46] 'Therefore great France / My mourning and importun'd tears hath pitied';[47] and (in this instance, her words reported by the Gentleman) 'What, i' th' storm? i' the night? / Let pity not be believ'd!'[48]

More importantly, Lear also experiences the specific emotion of pity at several points in the play, most notably when he meets Poor Tom on the heath: 'I am mightily abus'd. I should e'en die with pity / To see another thus.'[49] Norman Maclean depicts Lear as undergoing catharsis as a result of his new-found pity for Poor Tom – a pity which then extends to his shivering Fool:

> Lear, purging his feelings ... turns to the Fool in new tenderness and in a new role, for the first time considering someone else's feelings before his own ('How dost, my boy? Art cold? ...') ... [I]n the enactment of the enormous moment he (and we) get some kind of emotional release for which undoubtedly there is some clinical term.[50]

The 'clinical term' is, of course, catharsis. I would add that Lear and other characters experience fear as well, and thus complete the Aristotelian cathartic process. Kent remarks to Lear during the thunderous storm that 'man's nature cannot carry / Th'affliction nor the fear.'[51] Edgar reports of his alter ego that 'Poor Tom hath been scar'd out of his good wits.'[52] Lear himself expresses fear of madness: 'I fear I am not in my perfect mind.'[53]

Given these references to pity and fear in this play, it is possible to hypothesize that Shakespeare was invoking the Aristotelian formula explicitly and deliberately. O.B. Hardison, Jr., has argued that Renaissance theories about catharsis 'are self-consciously utilized by Shakespeare,' and Maurice Hunt agrees.[54] Further examples may be adduced, as in *Hamlet*, where Horatio describes the tragic situation as filled with 'woe' and 'wonder' – perhaps Shakespeare's translations of 'pity' and 'fear.'[55] It is possible to demonstrate even further Shakespeare's clear understanding of Aristotelian catharsis by his reference in *Richard II* to the musical catharsis described in Aristotle's *Politics*: 'This music ... have holp mad men to their wits.'[56] Shakespeare, in fact, uses musical catharsis to cure his mad or psychologically disturbed characters in several plays, such as *Pericles*, *The Tempest*, and (not surprisingly) *King Lear.*[57]

But did Shakespeare understand that the catharsis described in Aristotle's *Politics* was the same as that described in his *Poetics*? Again, evidence from the playwright's own work suggests that he did. He seems to have been interested in a non-medical version of catharsis, as we can conclude from King Richard's lines in

Richard II: 'Let's purge this choler without letting blood.'[58] A word search of the Shakespeare corpus reveals an intense interest in concepts of 'purging,' and it is worth noting that the bard uses the word 'purge' most often in the context of emotion, not sin (examples are 'to purge melancholy';[59] 'purge this black despair!';[60] 'purge his fear';[61] 'soul is purg'd from grudging hate';[62] and 'rage / Would not be purg'd.'[63] In fact, Shakespeare identifies the drama itself as one of the ways through which catharsis may be attained. Witness his own metatheatrical explanation of how catharsis works by means of drama in *The Taming of the Shrew*:

> For so your doctors hold it very meet,
> Seeing too much sadness hath congeal'd your blood,
> And melancholy is the nurse of frenzy.
> Therefore they thought it good you hear a play ... [64]

Shakespeare's mention of 'frenzy' and its subsequent cure through drama brings us back full circle to our discussion of catharsis as exorcism.[65]

The most important appropriations of Harsnett's exorcistic material by Shakespeare occur when Lear describes his own madness in terms of demonic possession. In Shakespeare's version, as opposed to *The True Chronicle Historie of King Leir* or other renditions of the story, Lear's 'new and shattering knowledge of the irrational and the demonic forces in himself and in the world around him drives him to the edge of madness.'[66] Josephine Waters Bennett suggests that Lear is possessed,[67] and Herbert Coursen similarly identifies 'Lear's nightmare of insanity' with 'some malign deity.'[68] Another critic sensitive to religious nuance, F.W. Brownlow, comments on the peculiar effectiveness achieved by Shakespeare's appropriation of exorcistic terminology to construct a model of madness for Lear. He observes that each phrase borrowed by a protagonist from the exorcists 'figuratively names and diagnoses an experience of present mental agony and proposes a relationship between psychic disintegration and a principle of evil located "below," both in human nature and the cosmos.'[69]

The prime example of Lear's appropriation of exorcistic discourse is his detached commentary on his own mental degeneration. His cry of 'Darkness and devils!'[70] echoes a passage from Harsnett: 'Resort unto the Oracles of the devil ... and ... conjure up from hel the Prince and power of darknes.'[71] He further addresses his own madness:

> O how this mother swells up toward my heart!
> Hysterica passio, down, thou climbing sorrow,
> Thy element's below.[72]

Lear's introspective lament also finds its source in Harsnett: 'Ma[ster]: *Maynie* had a spice of the *Hysterica passio*, as seems, from his youth; he himselfe termes it the Moother.'[73] Lear's physical motions designated by internal stage directions would have typified the symptoms of possession. His trembling,[74] for example, is a symptom described vividly by Harsnett: 'Instantly began the possessed to tremble, to have horrour, and rage thorough out his whole body.'[75] Lear's fear of whipping[76] recalls the demoniacs' fear of the exorcists' practise of whipping them with a priest's stole,[77] and his tearing of his clothes imitates the garment-rending of demoniacs in their fits. Lear identifies himself with Poor Tom repeatedly, even assuming he also has three daughters, until the king comes to a 'complete identification with a mad beggar';[78] likewise, Poor Tom connects Lear to himself and 'places Lear's mind in the underworld'[79] when he warns him to 'take heed o' th' foul fiend.'[80] Finally, Lear's 'never, never, never, never, never' may resonate with a contemporaneous demoniac's cry that sinners would be deprived of the vision of God 'for ever, for ever, for ever, for ever, for ever.'[81]

The scenes on the heath in Act 3 mimic the formulae, catechetical injunctions, and confessional strategies of Catholic exorcists and demoniacs. When Kent asks at the outset, 'Who's there, besides foul weather?'[82] he sounds like an exorcist interrogating an as-yet-unidentified demon inside a demoniac; and when he asks a few lines later, 'But who is with him?'[83] he echoes the exorcists who inquired which demons were keeping company together inside the possessed. Kent's beckoning of Poor Tom to come forth from the hovel ('Come forth'[84]) parallels the exorcists' beckoning of demons to come forth from inhabited persons. Poor Tom's list of injunctions from the Ten Commandments follows the order of exorcistic rituals which incorporated scriptural imperatives: 'Take heed o' th' foul fiend. Obey thy parents, keep thy word's justice, swear not, commit not with man's sworn spouse, set not thy sweet heart on proud array.'[85] Poor Tom then utilizes a more technical exorcistic term with his 'aroint [avoid or begone] thee, witch, aroint thee!'[86] Until now Poor Tom has played the part of a demoniac, but in the course of this scene he switches roles to play the part of an exorcist; when asked by Lear, 'What is your study?' he answers, 'How to prevent the fiend.'[87]

The trial scene on the heath is especially packed full of exorcistic language and imagery, and in a much more focused way: it is a mock exorcism in which Poor Tom officiates.[88] This scene draws on an ancient tradition in which exorcists staged legal trials where demons (in this case, Shakespeare's 'fiends' Goneril and Regan)[89] were arraigned, indicted, and condemned to perpetual torment.[90] In many ways the mock exorcism serves to exorcize Lear more than it does Poor Tom (who shortly thereafter, incidentally, resumes his old identity as Edgar). Poor Tom instructs Lear to 'Pray, innocent, and beware the foul fiend,'[91] and then attempts to cast out his demons, who appear in the shape of hell-hounds or demonic familiars ('Avaunt, you curs!').[92] Lear's catharsis is probably not complete until, through the musical therapy discussed earlier, he recognizes Cordelia, but the turning point or beginning of his catharsis undoubtedly occurs on the heath as a result of witnessing the pretended demoniac / exorcist.

Perhaps, as Shakespeare writes in the reconciliation scene, Cordelia's tears are the true 'holy water'[93] meant to contrast with the sacramental substance used in the Catholic exorcism ritual. Her name means 'cordial,' or 'heart medicine,' and she is consistently endowed with Christlike attributes by explicit New Testament references in the text.[94] Her rhetoric is strewn with therapeutic adjectives, nouns, and verbs: 'aidant,' 'remediate,' 'restoration,' and 'repair.'[95] Herbert Coursen, emphasizing the baptismal allusions in this scene, explains the reconciliation in spiritual terms, even exorcistic ones: 'Clearly, a new spirit enters Lear in this scene.'[96] Lear then voluntarily undergoes one of the 'litmus tests' administered to former demoniacs: 'Let's see, / I feel this pin prick. Would I were assur'd / Of my condition!'[97] Edgar has previously mentioned this test when describing the demoniacs he plans to imitate: 'Bedlam beggars who, with roaring voices, / Strike in their numb'd and mortified arms / Pins, wooden pricks, nails, sprigs of rosemary.'[98] Lear 'tests' as 'cured' according to the received wisdom of the day, for demoniacs and witches alike were commonly believed to feel only numbness when pierced with sharp objects.

If Cordelia exorcizes Lear, then her action toward her father parallels that of Edgar toward his. Edgar says of his strategy: 'Why I do trifle thus with his despair / Is done to cure it.'[99] As Greenblatt rightly points out,[100] Edgar pretends to have seen a demon depart from Gloucester: 'As I stood here below, methought his eyes / Were two full moons; he had a thousand noses, / Horns welk'd and waved like the [enridged] sea. / It was some fiend ...'[101] Guy Butler labels what happens in this scene correctly: 'Edgar as "doctor" has exorcised suicidal thoughts.'[102] Like this 'psychological miracle' performed upon Edgar's despairing father, Cordelia's treatment of Lear might be an effective (and rationalized) true emotional exorcism. When writing about the supernatural, Shakespeare often juxtaposes the counterfeit to the genuine phenomenon in areas such as prophecy.[103] Here he seems to be contrasting Tom's pretended exorcisms to Edgar's and Cordelia's true ones.

In short, by enacting possession by demons, Edgar serves as a surrogate for the devastating madness of King Lear, who also exhibits (unfeigned) symptoms of possession. By enacting exorcism of demons, Edgar serves as a cathartic healer for Lear[104] in the same way that he will later 'exorcize' his own father and Cordelia will later heal the king. By watching Lear watching Edgar watching Lear, the audience in turn achieves catharsis. Lear experiences a catharsis by purging the emotions of pity and fear on the heath, after which he is able to sleep quietly, and we, watching him, do the same. It is a supreme tribute to Shakespeare's theatrical self-consciousness that he chooses to bring about Lear's catharsis through nothing other than the explicit trope of exorcism, the ultimate catharsis.

Why this relationship of exorcism to catharsis? It is not merely intuitive (both processes signify the expulsion of negative forces), but even necessary, given the history of the word *katharsis* and its Greek religio-purificatory origins as they were understood by Renaissance literary theorists. Antonio Minturno expressed the connection of these ideas when he wrote of 'the untamed fury of the human soul' and then of its soothing in Aristotle's original sacred context.[105] Lorenzo Giacomini's *Sopra la purgazione della tragedia* (1586) explains catharsis as something that happens in the soul or the mind, not the body. Giacomini objects to critics who use the medical metaphor of purgation to describe catharsis because they do not understand that Aristotle removed this metaphor from its original corporeal context and transported it to the spiritual realm: 'è trasportata fuor del proprio soggetto, cioè dal corpo a l'animo' (it is transported away from its own subject, that is from the body to the mind).[106] He describes a negative state of being – which catharsis is designed to cure – in terms of 'many spirits' that trouble the soul:

> E stando lei fissa nel tristo pensiero e ne la trista imaginazione, salgono in alto e vaporano al capo *molta copia di spiriti*, e massimamente a la parte anteriore ove alberga la fantasia, ne la quale si fa una certa agitazione di umore et infiammazione, sì che divenuto più acuto e più salso e mordace ...

> (And [the soul] being fixed in sad thought and in sad imagination, a great abundance of spirits rise up and vaporize to the head, and mostly to the front part, where fantasy resides, in which there is made a certain agitation of humour and inflammation ...)[107]

He later speaks of the need for these 'furious torrents' of spirits[108] to be given 'free exit' through catharsis: 'dare libero esito a furiosi torrenti' (to give free exit to these furious torrents).[109] Another Italian literary critic, Giambattista Guarini, takes the whole discussion of catharsis two steps further into the spiritual realm only partially explored by Giacomini: first into madness, and then into exorcism. He claims that catharsis

> purges melancholy, an emotion so injurious that often it leads a man to grow mad and to inflict death on himself, in the same way as, according to Aristotle's teaching, melody purges the feeling the Greeks call enthusiasm; the Sacred Scriptures in dealing with it say that David, with the harmony of his music, drove away the evil spirits from Saul, the first king of the Hebrews.[110]

Figure 1   Manuscript illumination, *The Devil Chained in the Abyss* (c. 950). From Beatus of Liébana, *Commentary on the Apocalypse* (Morgan Beatus) Pierpont Morgan Library, New York.

Figure 2   Goya, *La lámpara del diablo* (1794). National Gallery, London.

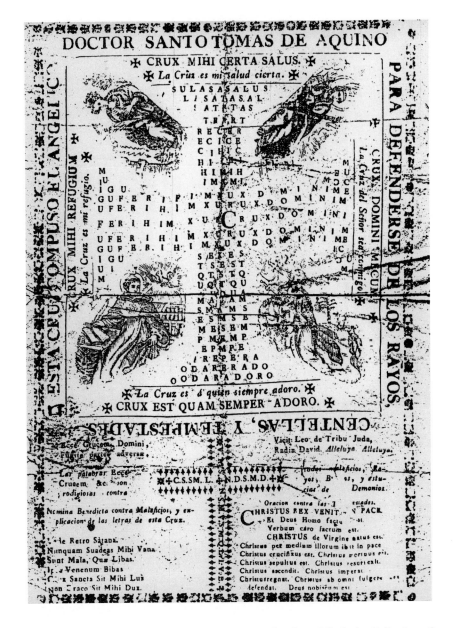

Figure 3 Twentieth-century printed *rescrito* or *ensalmo* from Ribadavia. Collection of James Crosby.

Figure 4   Feyerabend, *Der Prediger-Totentanz* (1806). Historisches Museum, Basel, Barfüsserkirche.

Der Tod zum König.   Der Tod zur Königin.   Der Tod zum Cardinal.   Der Tod zum ...

Der Tod zum Juristen.   Der Tod zum Rathsherrn.   Der Tod zum Chorherrn.   Der Tod zum ...

Der Tod zum Waldbruder.   Der Tod zum Jüngling.   Der Tod zum Wucherer.   Der Tod zur Jun...

Der Tod zum Krämer.   Der Tod zum Blinden.   Der Tod zum Juden.   Der Tod zum ...

Der Tod zum Maler.   Der Tod zu Malers.   Todtentanz   (Ehemalige St. Domenikaner...

Figure 5   Rubens, *Miracles of Saint Ignatius of Loyola* (1619). Kunsthistorisches Museum, Vienna.

Figure 6   Valdés Leal, *Saint Ignatius Exorcizing a Possessed Man* (1660–64). Museo de Bellas Artes, Seville.

Figure 7 *Storie della vita di S. Bartolomeo,* Anonymous artist from the Marches, ca. fifteenth century. By permission of il Ministero per i Beni e le Attività Culturale delle Marche-Urbino.

Paolo Beni makes a similar connection by citing the same story of Saul and David, and he even does so in the context of Aristotle's *Politics* passage and of calming Bacchic revellers.[111] Therefore we see that as it was understood metaphorically in the Renaissance, exorcism was an apt vehicle for the cathartic experience.

Interestingly enough, several of my key points have been anticipated by the New Historicist Stephen Greenblatt: 'the cult of Dionysus out of which the Greek drama evolved was a cult of possession'; 'theater itself is by its nature bound up with possession'; and 'what matters is the theatrical experience, the power of the performance to persuade the audience that it has heard the voices of radical evil and witnessed the violent expulsion of the agents of Darkness.'[112] Unfortunately, however, Greenblatt appears to have backed away from these points to insist that in *King Lear*, exorcism functions primarily as theatrical fraud. The additional evidence I have presented makes it difficult if not impossible to retain this interpretation.

My approach here is different from Greenblatt's in the one fundamental respect that I allow for the possibility of early modern belief in the supernatural, and he does not.[113] Otherwise, we are not that far apart; he himself even admits that 'Shakespeare intensifies as a theatrical experience the need for exorcism, and his demystification of the practice is not identical in its interests to Harsnett's.'[114] But Greenblatt here specifically and anachronistically invokes Brecht's 'alienation effect' to describe what he sees to be happening in the play.[115] What is ironic about this manoeuver is that Brecht understood the catharsis of *King Lear* far better than does Greenblatt.

Berthold Brecht hated the whole notion of catharsis. He saw it as an inward-turning evasion of constructive social action.[116] He found the explicit catharsis-inducing strategies of Shakespearean tragedy (what he calls *Einfühlung*, empathy or total emotional identification as the main basis of performance) to be such anathema that he termed them 'drama for cannibals':

> Through four acts Shakespeare drives the great individual, Lear, Othello, Macbeth, out of all his human connections with family and state out on to the heath, into total isolation, where he must show himself great in his ruin ... The object of the exercise is the great individual experience. Later times will call this drama a drama for cannibals.[117]

Brecht specifically called *Lear* a 'barbaric play.'[118] But it is the cathartic principle operating in *Lear*, the one that Brecht hated and that Greenblatt refuses to see, which helps us to understand the true function of exorcism in the tragedy.

All of this goes to demonstrate that there is an important problem raised by viewing Shakespeare's exorcism in *King Lear* as empty showmanship: if exorcism is nothing more than this, how can we account for the power of this tragedy (to which exorcism is central) to arouse and calm the emotions? In other words, if exorcism is always fraudulent, how can we account for the catharsis in *King Lear*? Without catharsis, tragedy becomes indistinguishable from comedy – and laughter is not the effect that any observer I know has taken away from *King Lear*. In the end, then, Greenblatt's approach prevents him from seeing that Shakespeare could not have invoked Aristotle more explicitly than in his repeated references to pity and fear throughout this play, and that the appropriations from Harsnett's treatise on exorcism guide us to precisely the understanding of catharsis we need in order to make some sense of what remains one of Shakespeare's most enigmatic dramas.

I have brought the discussion of *Lear* to the foreground in this chapter for several reasons: the presence of demonic possession and exorcism in this play is more universally recognized than in any other; various New Historicist analyses of exorcism in this play have received much attention in the scholarly realm; and the alternative interpretive model I propose of 'exorcism as catharsis' can be extended to discussions of other tragedies where exorcism appears. Now it is time to look at some of these other tragedies and see what further nuances the exorcism topos acquires for the early modern playwright when it is adapted to suit the generic purposes of the tragic dramatist.

The Demon As Scapegoat: *A Yorkshire Tragedy*, with a Note on *Othello* and *Macbeth*

Demons were a convenient explanation for why bad things happened to good people in the early modern period. Demonic possession was an effective way for early modern victims to attempt to rationalize tragedy, to find a scapegoat to take the blame for all the sadness and outrage they felt.[119] The literary result was not a weakening of tragic effect, but instead an intensification of the evil aura surrounding the tragic outcome.

When this evil aura was intensified to the extreme, demonic possession became a convenient way for playwrights to explain the actions of villains. A model of a villain's evil madness derived from descriptions of demoniacs could function in various ways. For some characters already disposed to sinful ways of life, the author's decision to make them demonically possessed was nothing more than 'enviar al pecador sus propias inclinaciones secretas. . . [d]e modo que la seducción diabólica no tiene más secreto que pervertir el soliloquio del hombre consigo mismo' (to send to the sinner his own secret inclinations ... in such a way that the diabolical seduction has no more secret than to pervert the soliloquy of the man with himself).[120] This model still functions in a particularly effective manner to explain the actions of contemporary villains because it takes into account the Freudian 'repressed desires' that produce complex illusions.

In this section we will look at three villains – the Husband of *A Yorkshire Tragedy*, Othello, and Macbeth. These are representations of early modern evil-doers whose actions are specifically associated with demonic possession. In each case, we will see how the demon or demonic figure in the play – the devil himself, Iago, or Lady Macbeth – becomes the scapegoat for the villain's evil deeds.

In *A Yorkshire Tragedy*, the villainous Husband stabs his wife and murders two of his children in an apparently senseless explosion of violence.[121] Given to gambling and jealous by nature, he leaves his brother wasting away in debtor's prison without lifting a finger to help him. He squanders his wife's fortune and reduces the family to beggardom. Finally he channels his self-loathing into a blind annihilatory impulse which savagely destroys everything in his path. The only way the anonymous playwright can explain what has happened is through recourse to the scenario of demonic possession.[122] It may be argued that from the perspective of the playwright, any nonsupernatural explanation is entirely insufficient; to support this point, A.C. Cawley cites as evidence the lines from the play: 'Let him [the devil] not rise / To make men act vnnaturall tragedies.'[123] There is no natural explanation for this horrific figuration of the early modern self. Instead it must be explained in demonic terms.

This play was based on recent current events, about which a pamphlet and a ballad were also published.[124] The Husband was modelled on Walter Calverley, and the Wife was Philippa Brooke, of noble family; they lived in Yorkshire, about five miles from Leeds. The two murdered children were William and Walter, buried in Calverley Church, while the surviving son was named Henry. The murders took place in April of 1605. The murderer was examined before Justices John Saville and Thomas Bland on 24 April of that year. He was sentenced to execution and subsequently pressed to death at York on 5 August 1605. His wife later remarried, to Thomas Burton of Leicester. All of this we know from the pamphlet, which has survived.

The interesting difference between the pamphleteer's perspective and that of the playwright is that the playwright entirely invents the explanation of demonic possession. The pamphleteer attributes Calverley's actions to a fit of madness, just as many lawyers invoke the 'insanity defence' in murder cases to this day. But the playwright takes the Husband's madness into a different realm altogether: 'Those whom men call mad / Endanger others; but hee's more then mad.'[125] As A.C. Cawley notes:

> The use in *A Yorkshire Tragedy* of the theme of demonic possession is one of the most remarkable differences between the play and the pamphlet, in which this theme is

not exploited at all. The idea of possession occurs early in the play and becomes more and more insistent until the murder scene is reached. In the end there is no more room for doubt that the Devil has possessed the Husband completely, body, heart, and soul. The Devil gives the Husband's body the power to perform unnatural deeds of strength, and corrupts his heart to the point where he is ready to commit unnatural murder. The moment when his soul is shown to be possessed comes at the climax of the play, just before he stabs his eldest son.[126]

The diagnosis of demonic possession is introduced by the Wife[127] and then repeated by the Gentleman (to the Husband),[128] by the Servant (to the Wife,[129] then to the Husband,[130] then in a soliloquy,[131] and finally again to the Wife[132]), and by the Husband himself.[133]

It should be noted that the playwright's artistic decision to introduce the demonic element was wholly in keeping with the beliefs of his day. Richard Napier, the astrological physician and exorcist whose case histories of some two thousand patients have been studied exhaustively by Michael MacDonald in *Mystical Bedlam*, recorded at least six instances of demonic temptation to murder.[134] These six male and female patients reported being tempted by demons to slaughter their children, parents, or spouses. Thus the 'demonology defence' was probably more convincing then than it would be now. Even some modern critics, however, find the 'demonology defence' to be artistically convincing.[135] For some readers, at least, the demonic possession in this play remains as potent as it ever was for early modern spectators who viewed it on the stage.

What about exorcism? It is tempting to say that there is an exorcism at the end of *A Yorkshire Tragedy.* The Husband even speaks the words: 'Now glides the deuill from mee, / Departes at euery ioynt, heaues vp my nailes.'[136] But there is no exorcism ritual of any kind, and Cawley views the Husband's repentance and 'physical dispossession' as incomplete at best:

> [T]he Husband has no hope of escaping eternal punishment for his crime: his repentance, although it includes acknowledgement of sin and contrition for it, still excludes the trust in God's mercy that is needed to make repentance complete. Like Faustus he believes himself to be damned, and sees no loophole through which his soul can escape to salvation. He is freed from diabolic influence, but his spiritual defeat remains.[137]

Cawley points out that the Husband's language does return to normal (he uses religious words in religious contexts again), and he does express profound remorse for his actions. But he does not undergo a 'spiritual dispossession' or real exorcism, and his soul is clearly damned. Like Ana before her exorcism in *El rufián dichoso*, the

Husband despairs of God's mercy. Cawley contrasts his 'physical dispossession' with 'spiritual dispossession': 'although the Devil has left his body, his soul remains irretrievably lost. The Devil, with valuable assistance from the World and the Flesh, has won again, and his victim is too horribly incriminated to be able to expect or ask for mercy.'[138] Even if we place the question of exorcism aside, Cawley concludes that the Husband's repentance is incomplete.[139]

In summary, we have seen how the anonymous author of *A Yorkshire Tragedy* exploits the motif of demonic possession to attempt an explanation for the inexplicable. The villain's actions simply cannot be rationalized in human terms alone. This playwright responded to this dilemma by attributing agency to a demon – clearly a convenient scapegoat. Even though demonic possession serves to explain or rationalize an otherwise incomprehensible chain of events, there is no exorcism possible for the early modern soul within the theological economy of this tragedy. From a social and literary perspective, perhaps a successful exorcism would have been unacceptable because it would have almost trivialized the deaths of innocent babies. From a theological perspective, a successful exorcism was impossible because the villainous character refused to trust in God's mercy.

This pattern of the demon as scapegoat may be seen in other tragedies as well, especially when a villain is inexplicably evil unless conceived in supernatural terms. This pattern works particularly well in *Othello* and *Macbeth*, where there is actually a demonic figure in the text who incites the villainous murderer to action.

When we read Reginald Scot's statement that 'a damned soule may and dooth take the shape of a blacke moore,'[140] we are immediately reminded of Othello. Othello in turn calls women 'devils being offended.'[141] The most obvious example of the language of demonic possession in the play occurs in Othello's speech over Desdemona's dead body:

This look of thine will hurl my soul from heaven,
And fiends will snatch at it ...
                              ... O cursed, cursed slave!
Whip me, ye devils,
From the possession of this heavenly sight!
Blow me about in winds! roast me in sulphur!
Wash me in steep-down gulfs of liquid fire![142]

His word play on possession is confirmed by Othello's fit on stage.[143] This physical collapse would be explained by modern physicians with an assumption that Othello suffers from epilepsy. But for the Jacobean audience, the two conditions of epilepsy and madness might as well have been one and the same. Epilepsy was called the sacred disease in ancient times, and we still call fits 'seizures' because 'most sixteenth and seventeenth century physicians believed that epileptic attacks were linked to demoniac possession.'[144] Frank Brownlow insists that

> Iago's effect on Othello is implicitly compared in these lines with the phenomena of possession ... Othello suffers a fit which, to a contemporary audience will have looked like a demoniac's seizure ... Not that one intends to make Iago into an allegory ... [I]n the play's imagery [he appears] as the emblem and minister of an evil that, by his agency, possesses his master.[145]

Iago compares himself to a devil: 'Divinity of hell! / When devils will the blackest sins put on, / They do suggest at first with heavenly shows, / As I do now.'[146] As the devilish Iago exerts more and more influence over Othello, he 'foams at mouth; and by and by / Breaks out to savage madness.'[147] A passage from Reginald Scot describes a similar fit:

> And if it be a subterrene diuell, it doth writh and bow the possessed, and speaketh by him, using the spirit of the patient as his instrument ... when *Lucifugus* possesseth a man, he maketh him dumbe, and as it were dead: and these be they that are cast out ... onelie by fasting and praier.[148]

Brownlow has explained the significance of another passage about demonic possession spoken in *Othello* (1604) by relating it to Harsnett's *Declaration*. Othello speaks these lines of Desdemona:

> [Her] name, that was as fresh
> As Dian's visage, is now begrim'd and black
> As mine own face. If there be cords, or knives,
> Poison, or fire, or suffocating streams,
> I'll not endure it. Would I were satisfied![149]

Brownlow's explication reveals that the last part of Othello's suicide list does not fit with the rest: suffocation or drowning would be components of contemporary suicide enumerations, but the phrase 'suffocating streams' makes little sense. Brownlow is convinced that both 'suffocating streams' and the image of Desdemona's blackened name came from Harsnett's *Declaration*. The original context was a description of an exorcistic procedure called (suf)fumigation, in which the demoniac was forced to inhale fumes from brimstone and poisonous herbs. He also notes that like the demoniacs who had suffered the rigours of exorcism at Denham, Othello finally yields to psychic torture.

Thus we see that Othello's murderous deed is subtly blamed on Iago, the devilish Girardian 'scapegoat' in the text. Herbert Coursen affirms of Iago that 'some see him as the Devil.'[150] This villain enlists the 'tribe of hell' to aid him in destroying Othello's marriage to Desdemona, and he mentions 'hell pains' to which he is eerily sensitive.[151] He invokes 'Hell and night' as the inspiration for his plot, and he shouts 'Diablo, ho!' as it begins to succeed.[152] As the end approaches, he appropriately refers to 'the spite of hell, the fiend's arch-mock.'[153] After Iago is captured and brought before him, Othello thrusts his sword at him to see whether he is a spirit and says in the presence of the embassy from Venice: 'I look down towards his feet, but that's a fable. / If that thou be'st a devil, I cannot kill thee.'[154] Othello's murder of Desdemona is made verisimilar only by the supernatural jealousy which overtakes him. This jealousy is instilled in him by Iago, the 'demonic possessor' figure in the text. Othello asks at the end of the play, 'Will you, I pray, demand that demi-devil / Why he hath thus ensnar'd my soul and body?'[155]

Again, there can be no exorcism here. In his fine article 'Othello Possessed: Notes on Shakespeare's Use of Magic and Witchcraft,' David Kaula asserts that 'the final clarification does serve for him [Othello] as a kind of exorcism, but of illusory rather than actual demons.'[156] With this statement, I find myself obliged to disagree. To exorcize Othello would be to trivialize the murder of Desdemona, and Shakespeare is not given to such easy answers for sin's complexities. The demonic Iago may be the catalyst of this tragedy, but there can be no redemption for the villainous Othello who chooses to listen to the counsel of a 'demon.'

A similar situation arises in *Macbeth* when Macbeth listens to Lady Macbeth, one of the most clearly demonic figures in the text, and then commits murder as a result. W. Moelwyn Merchant, in 'His Fiend-Like Queen,' proposes that Lady Macbeth is not only possessed but even becomes the figure of a demon. She specifically calls on 'spirits ... you murth'ring ministers':[157]

> ... Come, you spirits,
> That tend on mortal thoughts, unsex me here,
> And fill me from the crown to the toe topful
> Of direst cruelty![158]

Lady Macbeth also asks the demons to thicken her blood. Critics have called this invocation 'a formal stage in demonic possession – though the implications of that statement are rarely if ever pursued ... [T]he impact of the demonic invocation is reduced, both in critical reading and in our experience in the theatre.'[159] The lines above are not the only clues Shakespeare gives us about her diabolic nature. Lady Macbeth's Doctor speaks thus: 'This disease is beyond my practice;

yet I have known those which have walk'd in their sleep who have died holily in their beds.'[160] The doctor also speaks of 'infected minds'[161] and confirms his diagnosis:

> More needs she the divine than the physician.
> God, God forgive us all! Look after her,
> Remove from her the means of all annoyance
> And still keep eyes upon her ...
> I think, but dare not speak.[162]

The Doctor suggests in this speech that Lady Macbeth is possessed and in need of an exorcist. Two scenes later the Doctor reiterates that 'she is troubled with thick-coming fancies.'[163] Macbeth responds by commenting on the anguish of 'a mind diseased' and asks the doctor to 'cleanse the stuff'd bosom of that perilous stuff.'[164] The demonologists repeat frequently that sleepwalking, such as Lady Macbeth's, is a tell-tale sign of demonic activity, whether it be possession or bewitchment. A source which Shakespeare might have consulted in reference to Lady Macbeth's somnambulism has often been identified as Bright's *Treatise of Melancholie*. But King James writes of somnambulism too: 'where spirites fol-lowes upon certaine persones, and at devers houres troubles them.'[165] Reginald Scot describes male somnambulists in terms that could just as easily apply to Lady Macbeth: 'It is possible that the ... midwife hath not baptised him well, but omitted some part of the sacrament ... [W]ho or whatsoever is newlie exorcised must be rebaptised: as also such as walke or talke in their sleepe.'[166]

Lady Macbeth influences her husband to the point that he manifests textbook symptoms of diabolical inhabitation. We think of her when we read what Regi-nald Scot writes of a witch who makes her husband believe he is mad: 'She maketh him beleeve he is mad or possessed, & that he dooth he knoweth not what.'[167] Macbeth begins to manifest symptoms of possession as soon as she pours the contagious 'spirits' into his ear.[168] Even before she contaminates him, however, Macbeth questions his sanity in front of Banquo: 'Or have we eaten on the insane root / That takes the reason prisoner?'[169]

Like Othello, Macbeth is also epileptic, and he describes himself in a fit as 'cabin'd, cribb'd, confin'd, bound in.'[170] This is a classic description of a demoniac in exorcistic language. Macbeth's visions of the bloody dagger, the armed Head, the bloody Child, and the crowned Child, as well as the episode when he sees Banquo's ghost, would also have registered immediately to a Jacobean audience as diabolical apparitions. Banquo's ghost may have been suggested by Le Loyer's *Treatise of Specters*, the English translation of which appeared in 1605.[171] Thomas Lodge explained that if the demons chose to appear corporally, then all in the room would be able to see them in whatever shape they chose; but 'if according to imagination, [then] they appeare to none but to those to whom the vision appertaineth.'[172] The voices Macbeth hears are also explicable after this fashion because as King James reports, the devil may appear by voice only.[173] Likewise, the other sounds he hears, such as the thunder, may be attributed to demonic agency. The storm in the second act, accompanied by earthquakes, screams of death, and chimneys being blown down, is overtly demonic in nature.

Various lesser characters in the play echo demonological allusions,[174] as when Banquo speaks of the 'instruments of darkness':

oftentimes, to win us to our harm,
The instruments of darkness tell us truths,
Win us with honest trifles, to betray's
In deepest consequence.[175]

Banquo also prays for divine protection against demonic dreams. There are still more allusions to episodes of exorcism in the speeches of minor characters. The Porter plays at being the keeper of hell's gate (i.e., Macbeth's castle) soon after the murder of Duncan: 'Knock, knock. Who's there, in th' other devil's name?'[176] The presence of the demonic in this play also includes introductions of specific devils' names. The song 'Black spirits' has been identified by several scholars as having its unmistakeable source in Reginald Scot. Another song in the play, 'Come away,' draws the names of the demons from Scot: Hoppo, Stadlin, Puckle, and Hellwain.

The most easily identifiable forces of evil in this play are, of course, the Weïrd Sisters. Walter Clyde Curry postulates that 'in essence the Weird Sisters are demons or devils in the form of witches.'[177] Some spells of the Weïrd Sisters may have come from Reginald Scot's excerpts from old conjuring books.[178] Obviously, their prognostications are diabolical; royal dogma proclaimed 'that since all Prophecies and visiones are nowe ceased, all spirites that appeares in these formes are evill.'[179] One line spoken by the Weïrd Sisters is particularly interesting because it demonstrates how Shakespeare used a contemporary leaflet *Newes from Scotland* (1591) or Reginald Scot's account of the same events to obtain a peculiar phrase for his witch. Several scholars have noticed the similarity between the line of the first witch, 'But in a sieve I'll thither sail,'[180] and the wording in the leaflet: 'conuayed into the middest of the sea by all these witches, sayling in their riddles or cives [sieves].'[181] The context of the witch's line, and the immediate cause for the publication of the leaflet, was that in 1589 there was a storm which struck the fleet of Anne of Denmark, James's bride. The tempest sank a boatload of jewels and caused a contrary wind for James's boat, but not for the other ships. According to legend, this incident provoked James to write his *Daemonologie*. Curry observes concerning the Weïrd Sisters that 'having persuaded and otherwise incited Macbeth to sin and crime, the Devil and his angels now employ illusions which lead to his betrayal and final destruction.'[182] He makes the further assessment that 'the whole drama is saturated with the malignant presences of demonic forces; they animate nature and ensnare human souls by means of diabolical persuasion, by hallucination, infernal illusion, and possession.'[183]

Given the demonic presence in this play, it is convenient to rationalize or explain Macbeth's villainous murder of Duncan in terms of our Girardian 'demon as scapegoat.' Macbeth, like Othello, almost becomes a sympathetic figure if we consider that he might not have committed murder had he not listened to the diabolical prophecies of the Weïrd Sisters and the demonic counsel of his wife. As Carol Neely argues, the Weïrd Sisters and Lady Macbeth become scapegoats for the evil in the text:

> The witches and Lady Macbeth, as Peter Stallybrass has argued, are indirectly identified with each other ... by their parallel roles as catalysts to Macbeth's actions. They function as cultural scapegoats for the unnaturalness, disorder, and violence let loose.[184]

But there is a limit to how much blame the scapegoats in the text can absorb. The fact remains that Macbeth, like the Husband of *A Yorkshire Tragedy*, chose to succumb to demonic possession through various sinful choices that he made. Garry Wills sees this choice as explicit:

> As Macbeth moves toward his chosen encounter with the witches, his invocations of darkness become more and more explicit ... We can trace these steps toward his necromantic act as stages in a descent toward hell ... Macbeth will find night empowering as he becomes more and more a creature of the darkness.[185]

He is identified as a devil in the text through the lines of Macduff: 'Not in the legions / Of horrid hell can come a devil more damn'd / In evils to top Macbeth.'[186]

In all three of these plays, we see how exorcism fails in the text. Exorcism cannot wipe away murder, and the playwrights do not even attempt to exploit the exorcism motif in this way. These are truly dramas of the early modern soul's damnation, and as such, they are perhaps examples of true Christian tragedies. Let us look at one final play, *Hamlet*, as an example of a drama where the lack of exorcism is even more total and complete. Demonic possession is no longer a universally satisfying explanation for the protagonist's madness in this play;

instead, it appears as only one of the possible 'masks' he tries on. The Ghost equally defies reduction to demonological terms. The identity of a demon is only one of the roles he plays. We will see in this tragedy the disintegration of the 'demon as scapegoat' pattern and the consequent emphasis on performativity, as the demonic becomes only one of the potential registers or grammars in the language of tragedy.

Tragedy, Possession, and Performativity: *Hamlet*[187]

In reference to the Ghost, Hamlet speaks the lines:

> ... The spirit that I have seen
> May be a [dev'l], and the [dev'l] hath power
> T' assume a pleasing shape, yea, and perhaps,
> Out of my weakness and my melancholy,
> As he is very potent with such spirits,
> Abuses me to damn me ...[188]

The theme of performativity or role playing as employed in *Hamlet* has been emphasized by many critics, but they have limited the meta-performative aspect of the play to discussions of Hamlet, not of the Ghost.[189] If we give the Ghost another role to perform, discourse fragments from demonology found within the play will contribute to its rich texture of multiple layers and levels of interpretation.

Many of these demonological discourse fragments derive from two sources, King James I's *Daemonologie* and Reginald Scot's *Discouerie of Witchcraft*. These demonological resonances in the text suggest an atmosphere of demonic possession. While I do not claim reductively that Hamlet is demonically possessed or that the Ghost is the possessing demon, I do believe there are tantalizing suggestions of this connection as one of their many possible relationships to each other (i. e., father/son, ghost/visionary, tormented spirit/fellow tormented spirit). Just as Hamlet self-consciously tries on many masks in the course of the play, so too the Ghost appears in many different guises and speaks in several ambiguous registers. The demonological register in this play is simply one among many, but it is one which has not been explored sufficiently. Ultimately I will argue that the presence of the language of demonic possession, without the concomitant presence of any form of exorcism, contributes to the overall effect of the tragedy by raising our expectations for the early modern stage character and then leaving them unfulfilled.

'Be thou a spirit of health, or goblin damn'd ...' Hamlet addresses the Ghost, 'O, answer me!.'[190] In the course of the play, the Ghost 'tries on' these identities and many more. The whole scene where the Ghost first appears is illuminated by demonological treatises. The internal stage directions tell us that the Ghost walks away from the watchmen – no surprise, considering that, according to Reginald Scot: 'No man is lord ouer a spirit, to reteine a spirit at his pleasure.'[191] It is also no surprise that the Ghost appears wearing armour, a detail which corresponds to biblical expressions of diabolical strength invoked by Renaissance treatise writers: 'The diuell is called ... a strong armed man ... the most subtill, strong and mightie enimie.'[192] The speculation by Horatio and Marcellus about the Ghost's warlike appearance is given an added facet of meaning by this detail from King James:

> [The devil will appear] in the formes he will oblish him/selfe, to enter in a dead bodie, and there out of to give such answers, *of the event of battels, of maters concerning the estate of commonwelths*, and such like other great questions.[193]

The two men keeping watch in *Hamlet* discuss 'the event of battles' (Denmark's conflict with Fortinbras of Norway) and 'matters concerning the estate of commonwealths': they comment, 'This bodes some strange eruption to our state.'[194] Horatio also asks the Ghost to predict the future estate of the commonwealth: 'If thou art privy to thy country's fate, / Which happily foreknowing may avoid, / O, speak!'[195]

Still further details from demonological treatises illuminate certain other aspects of the play. The Ghost appears at night ('soules appeare oftenest by night')[196] because the demonologically informed Elizabethan audience would expect 'his nightwalkings, his visible appearings.'[197] The Elizabethan template for this sort of experience also mandates that Hamlet warn his friends not to hinder him. The following passage, which describes an exorcism, sounds like the guards, the Ghost, and Hamlet, with their various interactions:

> If the spirit make anie sound of voice, or knocking, at naming of anie one, he is the cousener (the conjuror I would saie) that must have the charge of this conjuration or examination. And these forsooth must be the interrogatories, to wit: Whose soule art thou? Wherefore comest thou? What wouldest thou have? ... This must be done in the night ... There is no feare (they saie) that such a spirit will hurt the conjuror ...[198]

In this context, 'conjuror' is a synonym for 'exorcist.' Horatio is the designated 'exorcist' in this scene because scholars know Latin, the language of exorcism; Marcellus says 'Thou art a scholar, speak to it, Horatio.'[199] He does in fact ask the Ghost these exact questions: 'What art thou that usurp'st this time of night ...? By heaven I charge thee speak!'[200]

It is also not surprising that the Ghost returns to speak with Hamlet, for the spirit described here always 'settes an other tryist, where they may meete againe.'[201] One further detail from the Ghost's return is also present in demonological treatises: the fear that the Ghost might lead Hamlet to fall from a cliff. King James stated explicitly that devils were fond of leading their victims to high places from which they might fall. Reginald Scot wrote in a slightly different context: 'Whatsoever is newlie exorcised must be rebaptised: for (saie they) call them by their names, and presentlie they wake, *or fall if they clime* ...'[202] This piece of religious lore was derived from a common source, the biblical account in Luke 4:9–12, where Jesus is led by Satan to a high peak and tempted to jump off in order to prove that angels will catch him. The corresponding lines of the play are Horatio's: 'What if it tempt you toward the flood, my lord / Or to the dreadfull summit of the cliff.'[203]

Some of the 'Ghost critics' have pointed to the fact that one of the shapes which devils could take on was the form of a dead friend or family member; they argue that this happened in the case of Old Hamlet. King James I believed that the devil, when appearing to men, frequently assumed the form of a person newly dead to possess the soul of one still alive.[204] From Reginald Scot's perspective, a person was especially prone to see apparitions of devils in the shapes of dead friends when he was already melancholy, or susceptible to demonic influence: 'Manie thorough melancholie doo imagine, that they see or heare visions, spirits, ghosts, strange noises ...'[205] King James agreed:

> And finding them in an utter despair ... he prepares the way by feeding them craftely in their humour, and filling them further and further with dispaire, while he finde the time proper to discover himself unto them. At which time ... in likeness of a man, inquires of them, what troubles them: and promiseth them, a suddaine and certaine waie of remedie.[206]

A similar passage from Thomas Lodge's *The Diuel Coniured* illuminates for us the scene in which the Ghost appears to Hamlet, but Gertrude cannot see him:

> They either appear imaginatiuely by mouing humours and blood (and thereby forme certain apparitions) or they appear in assumpted bodies, appropriat to their intents ... and if according to imagination, they appear to none but to those to whom the vision appertaineth: but if in an assumed body, it is by their power, and in that sort are subiect to many mens sights.[207]

It certainly fits the paradigm presented by the demonologists that the younger, suicidal Hamlet should see such an apparition or imagine that he does, for 'they are oftenest seene by them that are readie to die.'[208]

The Ghost's ultimate purpose also fits neatly with certain details of demonology. The demonologists explain the desire for revenge in a way that sounds like the Ghost luring Hamlet: 'Such as ... burnes in a despaire desire of revenge, hee [the devil] allures them by promises, to get their turne satisfied to their hartes contentment.'[209] In afflicting madmen, this type of spirit specializes in 'teaching them waies howe to get themselves revenged.'[210] King James explains this concept in ways that cast light upon *Hamlet*:

> These kindes of spirites, when they appeare in the shaddow of a person newlie dead ... to his friendes ... When they appeare upon that occasion, they are called Wraithes in our language. Amongst the Gentiles the Devill used that much, to make them beleeve that it was some good spirite that appeared to them ... *to discover unto them, the will of the defunct, or what was the way of his slauchter*, as is written in the booke of the histories Prodigious. And this way hee easelie deceived the Gentiles, because they knew not God: And to the same effect is it, that he now appeares in that maner to some ignorant Christians.[211]

As the reader or audience of *Hamlet* will remember, the Ghost 'discovers unto' Hamlet both 'the will of the defunct' and 'the way of his slaughter.' He informs him: 'The serpent that did sting thy father's life / Now wears his crown.'[212] The Ghost then describes the murder in gruesome detail, how the 'leprous distillment' took its effect.

What effect does the Ghost's message have upon Hamlet? Martín Del Río and other demonologists wrote frequently of the danger of learning enough from a demon to be endangered as a result. Del Río wrote about the common ploys of a treacherous devil who leads his listeners to destruction: 'Diffamat innocentes, noce[n]tium occulta crimina reuelat, vt male de illis suspicentur caeteri' (he defames the innocent ones, reveals the hidden crimes of the guilty, in order that the remaining ones [those present at the exorcism] might look with suspicion upon them).[213] In fact, literary critics agree that the Ghost's message is one of the provocative factors in Hamlet's downward spiral into madness. The assertion of his authority over Hamlet – and his ability to manipulate the vulnerable young man – take the form of a boast of the demonic powers to which he has access:

> I could a tale unfold whose lightest word
> Would harrow up thy soul, freeze thy young blood,
> Make thy two eyes like stars start from their spheres,
> Thy knotted and combined locks to part,
> And each particular hair to stand on end,
> Like quills upon the fearful porpentine.[214]

As Hamlet's later madness (sometimes manifested using a 'mask' of the symptoms of possession) demonstrates, the Ghost is capable of engendering all these responses and more.

Gertrude later describes Hamlet's appearance using the language of the exorcists to describe demoniacs:

Forth at your eyes your spirits wildly peep,
And as the sleeping soldiers in th' alarm,
Your bedded hair, like life in excrements,
Start up and stand on end ...[215]

Gertrude's predecessor Queen Geruthe in Shakespeare's source Belleforest speaks specifically of 'démons' and hypothesizes that her husband may already have learned from these demons of Amleth's stabbing of the person spying on them: 'I am greatly afraide that the devils have shewed him what hath past at present between us.'[216] Winfried Schleiner explores the consequences of Belleforest's inclusion of these demons: 'Since he presumably would not adduce the demon theories if he did not think them somehow useful in accounting for Amleth's extraordinary abilities, he is apparently not bothered at all by the implication that his hero is somehow in league with devil-demons, or possessed by them.'[217]

The raving, half-dressed Hamlet also appears to Ophelia in her closet with his garters crossed (a typical feature of demoniacs) 'as if he had been loosed out of hell.'[218] And he wonders aloud, asking who is responsible for the symptoms (classic signs of demonic possession) that he feels:

Who calls me villain, breaks my pate across,
Plucks off my beard and blows it in my face,
Tweaks me by the nose, gives me the lie i' th' throat
As deep as the lungs? Who does me this?[219]

One answer for the confused early modern self may well be, 'a demon.'

It is a commonplace of *Hamlet* criticism that these symptoms should be attributed to melancholy. But in order to grasp more fully the multifaceted nature of Hamlet's madness, let us briefly examine period concepts of melancholy as they are explained in two demonological treatises. King James, in his *Daemonologie*, describes this illness: 'For as the humor of Melancholie in the selfe is blacke, heaule and terrene, so are the symptomes thereof, in any persones that are subject thereunto, leannes, palenes, desires of solitude: and oft they come to the highest degree thereof, mere folie and Manie.'[220] John Draper quotes this passage from King James and then comments, 'Hamlet aptly remarks that melancholy persons are especially predisposed to demonic influences.'[221] Winfried Schleiner concludes that '[m]elancholy as a pathway of the devil into the body, demonic melancholy, is entertained by Hamlet at least temporarily as a real possibility.'[222]

What most other critics seem to ignore is the fact that, for many Elizabethans or Jacobeans, melancholy was actually caused by demons. Reginald Scot explains that the devil 'provoketh the merrie to loosenesse, and the sad to despaire.'[223] King James describes how Satan and his devils produced the symptoms we recognize in the early modern self: 'They can make folkes to becom phrenticque or Maniacque, which likewise is very possible to their master to do, sence they are but naturall sicknesses.'[224] We recognize further symptoms of Hamlet:

> This [melancholy] maketh sufferance of torments, and (as some saie) foresight of things to come ... it maketh men subject to leanenesse, and to the quartane ague. They that are vexed therewith, are destroiers of themselves, stout to suffer injurie, fearefull to offer violence.[225]

This would seem to be the perfect picture of the sickly, suicidal Hamlet. King James proposed, in writing his treatise, to leave 'the reasones refuted of all such as would call it but an imagination and Melancholique [i.e., not diabolical] humor.'[226] He defines the very phenomenon of demonic possession, conversely, as what 'is thought likewise to be but verie melancholicque imaginations of simple raving creatures.'[227]

Therefore we see that even if Hamlet's ailment is 'only' melancholy, our understanding of this early modern illness calls for further nuancing if we would glimpse Hamlet's many faces of madness. Shakespeare probably knew Timothy Bright's *Treatise of Melancholie* (1586), and it probably contributed to his portrayal of Hamlet, yet few scholars have investigated what other intertexts might also lie beneath the melancholy surface of the play. Neglecting to move beyond modern assumptions, they turn to medical instead of demonological treatises.

What are the thematic implications of the appearance of this demonic linguistic register? I would postulate that demonology illuminates not only Hamlet's shifting perspective on the Ghost but also the iterations the Ghost itself performs. Surely 'the growing and often anxious Renaissance awareness of historical multiplicity and of a proliferation of human meaning'[228] could extend to the Ghost as well. In each of their many guises, Hamlet and the Ghost both invite misunderstanding.[229] If Hamlet plays the part of a demoniac at certain moments, the audience will associate him with madness. If the Ghost plays the part of a demon or a damned soul, the audience will catch this nuance. These moments of *anagnorisis* recall Aristotle's 'recognition by dramatic representation' as explained in the *Poetics*.[230] I believe the Ghost appears Catholic one moment, Protestant the next, and pagan or perhaps demonic the third precisely because he, like Hamlet, tries on different identities in the course of the play. If the whole of *Hamlet* is a play in which identity is problematized, then why should not the Ghost play as many roles, try on as many masks as Hamlet himself does?

An awareness of this role playing or performativity opens up critical horizons and prevents reductive readings of the play. If we wish to discuss any one particular reading of the play – for instance, possession/exorcism motifs in relation to Hamlet – we may do so with the proviso that this is only one model for his madness. No one model of early modern madness is supposed to fit all the way; otherwise the play would be reduced to a flatness, a lack of texture, a univocality which is unthinkable for Shakespeare. A nonreductionist view of the intertextuality of demonological treatises and this play only adds more *texture* to a *text* already rich in meaning. It is another tribute to Shakespeare's art that we are taken in by the incessant trying on of different identities by both Hamlet and the Ghost in this play – so much so that critics have, for centuries, partaken of it and attempted to invent pat labels for these polyvalent characters.

Thus we understand the significance of demonology and even demonic possession for this play. But what about exorcism? Although there are various allusions to exorcistic rituals, there is no exorcism scene, nor is there any alleviation whatsoever for Hamlet's tortured soul. Neither can Ophelia find peace: she succumbs to the ultimate despair and commits suicide, a common end for incurable demoniacs and other disturbed individuals in the early modern period. None of the other characters arrives at any state of tranquility or rest from perturbation. It is clear that there is no exorcism in the play, even though its linguistic register has been invoked repeatedly.

The fact that there is no exorcism in this play despite the numerous references to demonic possession results in the literary equivalent of *coitus interruptus*. The conspicuous absence of climax or release was perhaps what T.S. Eliot was 'groping toward' when he complained that this tragedy was one of the worst ever written:

> The only way of expressing emotion in the form of art is by finding an objective correlative; in other words, a set of objects, a situation, a chain of events which shall be the formula of that particular emotion; such that when the external facts, which must terminate in sensory experience, are given, the emotion is immediately evoked ... The artistic 'inevitability' lies in this complete adequacy of the external to the emotion; and this is precisely what is deficient in *Hamlet* ... In the character Hamlet it is the buffoonery of an emotion which can find no outlet ...[231]

Eliot also called the play an 'artistic failure.' There is no 'objective correlative' for Hamlet's madness, only the tantalizing suggestions of demonic possession. There is only an anticipated or yearned-for exorcism which never happens. Hamlet is never able to accept his father's death and his mother's remarriage. He is never able to rid his feverish brain of the injunctions of the Ghost, to accept the new order for family and state. There is a painful emptiness which pervades the ending of the play. The lack – or implicit failure – of exorcism in the play leaves a yawning void where resolution might have been.

Chapter Five

Self-Exorcism and the Rise of the Novel

The novel is the genre which has been most associated with the rise of the autonomous early modern self.[1] In the novel, the early modern self awakens and fully takes on a life of its own, divorced from the hand of its creator. In the novel, the early modern self fashions all the means to reach its own ends. In the novel, the early modern self exorcizes its own demons.

This genre is unique in its treatment of literary exorcism because it sees several theologemes converge to form one. The exorcist is the same figure as the demoniac; in other words, the demoniac exorcizes himself. The purposes of this chapter are first, to demonstrate how the linguistic register of demonic possession and exorcism is employed in *Don Quijote*; second, to explore the uniqueness of Don Quixote's exorcism of himself; third, to show how self-exorcism is paradigmatic of the autonomous action of a novelistic character; and fourth, to draw out the generic implications of the birth of the autonomous character for the rise of the modern novel.

As every reader knows, Don Quixote's mind is a mass of intertextual confusion. However, no one has explored in detail the intertextuality between the *Quijote* and contemporaneous popular manuals of demonology, written in the vernacular and thus providing a register of specifically Spanish terminology being used in the Golden Age to describe the phenomena of apparitions, diabolical pranks, demonic possession, and exorcism.[2] Cervantes utilizes the linguistic register of diabolical mysteries as one of multiple narrative techniques which lend verisimilitude to Don Quixote's madness. Many of the other parodic linguistic registers – medical, psychological, or literary – employed in this masterpiece of heteroglossia to describe the protagonist's madness have been taken into account by critics who have demonstrated the polyvalent richness of this text.[3] This chapter is an attempt to recover for contemporary readers the resonances of yet another of these layers – an additional linguistic register which Cervantes deliberately exploited. This is certainly not the only or necessarily the best model for Don Quixote's madness. It should not in any way displace any of the others. Demonology is not *the* key with which to unlock the mysteries of this text because there is no such facile solution to the problems posed by Cervantes' genius. But demonic vocabularies cannot be ignored when they are employed to this degree. They represent one facet of a characterization so complex that it has defied centuries of attempts to categorize it. Thus the intention here is not to reduce but rather to enhance the rich texture of this hilariously funny, all-encompassing literary experience.

In fact, the similarly all-encompassing proliferation of discourse at this time on many aspects of the supernatural explains Cervantes' narrative recourse to various forms of demonic vocabularies in the text. He does not limit himself to the serious language of demonic possession; indeed he incorporates more humorous diabolical resonances in the adventures, such as the alleged pranks of the trickster *duendes*. In her study of the *Persiles*, Diana De Armas Wilson has claimed that Cervantes adopts a completely sceptical, satirical stance toward exorcism which would coincide with the comic playfulness I discuss in the first part of this chapter.[4] Ironically, the *Persiles* is acknowledged to be a much more serious work than the *Quijote*, but Cervantes treats exorcism more seriously in the *Quijote* than in the *Persiles*. It should not surprise us, however, that Cervantes' reactions to – and appropriations of – the constructed discourses of demonology in general and exorcism in particular would remain polyvalent instead of univocal.

The following assessment of Cervantes' appropriations of demonological discourse in the novel will thus be divided into two sections: one on Cervantes' more playful recourses to demonology within the narrative process, the other on his treatment of the supernatural on a serious (not overtly farcical) level. Again, it should come as no surprise to *cervantistas* that the more playful moments usually occur early in Part I, while the darker side of demonic agency assumes greater power toward the end of Part I and continues in the more somber Part II of the *Quijote*, published ten years later, near the time of Cervantes' death. The polyvalent nature of the demonic undertones in the text makes them powerful enough to be absorbed into the fictions of both comic and tragic events.

Poltergeists and Wizards: Supernatural Pranks in Part I of *Don Quijote*

There are certain texts containing references to some form of demonology which we can be fairly sure Cervantes read.[5] These include both ancient pagan works such as Apuleius's *The Golden Ass* or Heliodorus's *Aethiopica* and contemporary miscellanies such as Antonio de Torquemada's *Jardín de flores curiosas*. I will argue that Cervantes demonstrates a fairly sophisticated knowledge of some of the finer points of specifically Christian demonology, especially points concerning demonic possession and exorcism. This knowledge, in fact, would have been difficult for him to obtain through literary or 'nonspecialist' sources. There is no way to know which specialized works on demonology Cervantes might have read, but it is possible to study some representative demonological sources to see what kinds of information he might have appropriated from them or books like them.

Most works of this genre were comprehensive volumes on witchcraft and superstition, with occasional passages about possession included as components of a supernatural panoply. There were, however, some demonological treatises which gave special emphasis to possession and exorcism. Two of these works that might have been available to Cervantes were Pedro Ciruelo's *Reprobación de supersticiones y hechicerías* (A treatise reproving all superstitions and forms of witchcraft) (1530) or Martín de Castañega's *Tratado muy sotil y bien fundado de las supersticiones y hechicerías y vanos conjuros y abusiones* (Very subtle and well-founded treatise on superstitions and witchcrafts and vain conjurations and abuses) (1529). There were also manuals of exorcism which were published exclusively as guides to casting demons out of possessed persons. A typical example of this kind of text is Benito Remigio Noydens, *Práctica de exorcistas y ministros de la Iglesia. En que con mucha erudición, y singular claridad, se trata de la instrucción de los Exorcismos para lançar, y ahuyentar los demonios, y curar espiritualmente todo género de maleficio, y hechizos* (Practice of exorcists and ministers of the Church. In which with much erudition, and singular clarity, is treated the instruction of Exorcisms for casting out, and making demons flee, and curing spiritually every kind of malefice, and bewitchments) (1660). Although written later than some of its counterparts, this particular treatise was a vernacular one composed exclusively for exorcists. This representative work, while published after the *Quijote*, nonetheless provides anecdotes of episodes occurring during the lifetime of Cervantes. It also incorporates elements from many earlier Latin manuals of exorcism.

In light of these contemporaneous texts, let us turn to several humorous adventures throughout the novel which allude to the devil, a perpetrator capable of both humorous tricks and deadly torment. Don Quixote and Sancho often interpret naturally explicable situations by viewing them through the lens of belief in the supernatural. The first pertinent occurrence of the word 'diablo' appears in the mouth of Sancho immediately after he is introduced in the novel. Sancho warns Don Quixote, 'Mire que digo que mire bien lo que hace, no sea el diablo que le engañe' (Look! I say that you should look well what you do, that it not be the devil who deceives you).[6] Just prior to these words of Sancho, Don Quixote, like a demoniac, has attacked something sacred, something related to the church: he has charged against Benedictine monks in the company of travellers, but not against any other members of the party. Michael Hasbrouck makes a meaningful observation on this point, that it is particularly curious for Don Quixote to attack monks on mules instead of the nonreligious figures on horseback, who probably would have reminded him of the knights errant of the romances of chivalry.[7] Perhaps the friars' habits have also reminded him of the world of chivalric romance, where monks often appear in processional scenes or make mysterious magical speeches. Another factor here might just be that the *frailes*, who are mounted on slow and plodding mules, seem easier targets for the fury of the knight errant. The situation is further complicated when Don Quixote imagines that the *frailes* with the carriage are enchanters with captive princesses and demands the release of the 'prisoners' immediately; he addresses the supposed enchanters as 'gente endiablada' (bedevilled people).[8] The women of the company, in turn, flee from him, 'haciéndose más cruces que si llevaran al diablo a las espaldas' (crossing themselves more times than if they carried the devil at their backs).[9]

This adventure and similar ones – that of the famous windmills, for instance – are triggered by misperceptions or hallucinations on the part of the knight errant. The visions or hallucinations of Don Quixote are also explicable to the characters within the text as (among other possibilities, of course) demonic apparitions. Cervantes, the champion of perspectivistic truth, wants his readers to hear multiple parodies at the same time: for instance, simultaneous parodies of chivalric romance and popular religious beliefs. Popular belief in demonic apparitions was common among clergymen as well as laypeople, as we see from the cleric Noydens's description of these apparitions:

> Algunas vezes suelen los demonios, saliendo de los cuerpos de los Energúmenos, mostrarse, y aparecer en figura espantosa de varios animales, y otras cosas terribles, aunque no sean vistos de los circunstantes ... estas apariciones pueden ser solamente imaginarias, por mover el demonio la sangre, y los humores del hombre, y formar alguna imagen, que le representa, y ésta por ser visión imaginaria, solo aparece a quien se haze la visión.

> (Sometimes the demons, leaving the bodies of the Energumens, are accustomed to show themselves, and appear in the frightening shape of various animals, and other terrible things, although they not be seen by the bystanders ... These apparitions can only be imaginary, through the demon's moving the blood, and the humours of the man, and forming some image, that represents him, and this – because it is an imaginary vision – only appears to him to which the vision is made.)[10]

These diabolical hallucinations could take various forms because demons commonly appeared to those whom they were about to possess.[11] Thus Don Quixote specifically conjures Doña Rodríguez, operating on the assumption that she is some sort of diabolical vision or soul from purgatory and using elaborately formulaic language in the style of the exorcists to confront this 'phantasm': 'Conjúrote, fantasma, o lo que eres, que me digas quién eres, y que me digas qué es lo que de mí quieres. Si eres alma en pena, dímelo' (I conjure you, phantasm, or whatever you are, that you tell me who you are, and that you tell me what you want of me. If you are a soul in torment, tell me so).[12] Don Quixote's assumption here and elsewhere in the text is not unfounded. A common argument invoked by the demonologists was that the devil had taken the form of a snake in the Garden of Eden and thus could take any shape he chose. Noydens's observations offer us a parallel explanation of the *rebaños* episode[13] which corresponds to the hallucination of Don Quixote that a flock of sheep is really an army dressed for battle:

El demonio tal vez entra en los cuerpos de los animales brutos ... no ... para atormentar a ellos, sino para hazer daño al hombre en sus bienes, y haziendas, ò para engañarle, y armarle algún peligro, como le armó a nuestros primeros Padres en la Serpiente.

(the demon perhaps enters into the bodies of the brute animals ... not ... to torment them, but to do damage to the man in his goods, or estates, or to deceive him, and cause him some danger, as he did to our first parents in the serpent).[14]

Later Noydens provides an example of a demon that entered a *papagayo* (parrot), another animal,[15] for the purpose of deceiving one of the popes. Perhaps Cervantes parodies this type of superstitious episode along with his parody of epic literary conventions in the adventure of the *rebaños* and, again, with the herd of six hundred pigs.[16] Incidentally, Hasbrouck makes an attempt to relate this latter episode to the biblical account of the legion of devils cast into a herd of swine in Luke 8:27–33.[17] Be that as it may, according to a story related by Martín del Río,[18] devils may also appear in the shapes of military armies.[19] This detail would explain why Don Quixote imagines that flocks of animals turn into armies that he must fight (he, of course, infers that an enchanter has made this transformation).[20]

Many of the other comical-mysterious adventures are suggested within the text as the intervention of poltergeists (*los duendes*), the demons who specialize in practical jokes. Given the superstitious agrarian atmosphere, the novel's characters undoubtedly believe in the possibility of intervention by these tricksters. One text which forms a part of Don Quixote's library is the *Jardín de flores curiosas* (Garden of curious flowers) (1570) of Antonio de Torquemada. This book contains descriptions of the poltergeists in Salamanca,[21] supernatural beings who also figured prominently in the pamphlet literature of the time.[22] Noydens also describes these notorious demons:

> La experiencia enseña, que ay otros demonios, que sin espantar, ni fatigar a los hombres (porque Dios no se lo permite, ni les da mano para ello) son caseros, familiares, y tratables, ocupándose en jugar con las personas, y hazerles burlas ridículas. A estos llamamos comunmente trasgos, ò duendes.

> (Experience teaches that there are other demons who, without frightening or fatiguing men [because God does not allow it, nor does he give them a hand for it] are domestic, familiar, and approachable, occupying themselves in playing with people, and playing ridiculous jokes on them. These we commonly call poltergeists, or 'duendes.')[23]

Sancho does not understand what has happened after the adventure in the inn with Maritornes, and thus he alludes to demonic intervention: '¿Qué tengo de dormir, pesia a mí – respondió Sancho, lleno de pesadumbre y de despecho – , que no parece sino que todos los diablos han andado conmigo esta noche?' ('What [desire] do I have for sleeping, to my dismay,' responded Sancho, full of heaviness and despair, 'for it does not appear but that all the devils have walked with me this night?').[24] Sancho's question in the inn does not appear strange in light of the fact that Noydens's treatise contains a reference to a demon who 'se manifestò en forma humana, vestido de rústico' (manifested itself in human form, dressed as a rustic).[25] The peasant atmosphere of the inn is conducive to belief systems containing these apparitions of *duendes*, trickster demons from superstitious folklore.

These trickster demons and similar figures recur often in the text. We recall that Don Quixote tries to explain the disappearance of his library by means of the intervention of an enchanter or wizard whom he names Frestón.[26] It is interesting to note that when Don Quixote invents a specific action for the enchanter Frestón, this action is presented with dramatic irony: Don Quixote believes that the enchanter has robbed him of his library, but the readers know that the books have been lost in a bonfire lit by his own friends. The insinuation is that Frestón is not the only identification for the enchanter. This is not necessarily his correct name, just as this was not an action of his. But a splendid piece of demonic lore explains Don Quixote's attempt to seek a name for his enchanter: an animistic theory held that knowledge of a devil's name gave an exorcist control over him.[27]

Perhaps Don Quixote's attribution of agency to the enchanter is no accident.[28] Perhaps readers of the text are supposed to hear yet another level of parody when he and other characters in the novel make diabolical associations, most of them quite playful, in connection with the stolen library. For one thing, the library contained many books of chivalry, which were attacked by moralists as diabolical products.[29] But Don Quixote's books may bear more overt diabolical resonance. Let us consider for a moment that it was common 'knowledge' during the Golden Age that some demoniacs had called their affliction upon themselves by reading aloud from conjuring books. In these diabolical conjurations, prayers intermingled with superstitious formulae until the average listener could not tell the difference. One man in Deza examined by the Inquisition of Toledo in 1600, Román Ramírez, recited entire books from memory.[30] Perhaps readers of the text are supposed to wonder whether Don Quixote's books, burned by his friends, did contain devilish material, by means of which he might have invoked evil spirits unintentionally. Such a speculation (and it is one) only adds to the comedy of the unwitting knight in his unusual predicament. The priest swears in reference to the books, 'Encomendados a Satanás y a Barrabás sean tales libros' ('Let such books be commended to Satan and Barrabas')[31] and later speaks of 'las endiabladas y revueltas razones' (the diabolical and doubled-over arguments) they contain.[32] Books could potentially be very dangerous: on 10 December 1564 one offender was punished by the Inquisition of Murcia for using a conjuring book.[33] A 1583 Index of prohibited books totally banned such

libros, tratados, cedulas, memoriales, receptas, y nominas, para inuocar demonios, por qualquier via, y manera, ora sea por nigromancia, hydromancia, pyromancia, aeromancia, onomancia, chiromancia, y geomancia, ora por escriptos, y papeles de arte magica, hechizerias, bruxerias, agueros, encantamentos, conjuros, cercos, characteres, sellos, sortijas, y figuras.

(books, treatises, deeds, memorials, recipes, and catalogues, for invoking demons, by whatever way, and manner, whether it be by necromancy, hydromancy, pyromancy, aeromancy, onomancy, chiromancy, and geomancy, or by writings, and papers of magic art, spells, witchcrafts, omens, enchantments, conjurings, circles, characters, seals, rings, and figures.)[34]

Demonologists were also aware of the dangers their investigations posed for their own safety; there was always the possibility that they might call up a demon without intending to. The Englishman Reginald Scot reports that the Frenchman Jean Bodin was worried about these occupational hazards: 'and yet *J. Bodin* confesseth, that he is afraid to read such conjurations as *John Wierus* reciteth, least (belike) the divell would come up, and scratch him with his fowle long nailes.'[35]

At least one of the authors featured in Don Quixote's library, Jorge de Montemayor, appeared in the Índice de Valdés of 17 August 1559 'in that which touches upon devotion and Christian things.'[36] Is it not possible that Don Quixote poisoned his brain with magical formulae as well as 'la razón de la sinrazón' (the reason of the unreason)[37] of the chivalric romances? This theory is supported by the fact that the bonfire of his library is a parody of the Inquisitorial *auto de fe*. Books (as well as people) were burned by the Inquisition because of heretical or diabolical content.[38] Don Quixote's niece confirms that the contents of the books might be diabolical when she mimics the exorcism ritual by bringing hyssop and holy water to the barber and the priest, asking them to bless the room of the library so that a demon (invoked by the books to be burned) will not come back to haunt her: 'Tome vuestra merced ... rocíe este aposento, no esté algún encantador de los muchos que tienen estos libros, y nos encanten, en pena de las que les queremos dar echándolos del mundo' (Take this [branch of hyssop], your honour ... sprinkle this chamber [with holy water], so that there will not remain some enchanter of the many these books contain, who would enchant us, in penalty of the pains we want to give them in banishing them from the world).[39] The edition by Francisco Rico and Joaquín Forradellas notes concerning this passage that these 'pains' refer to 'las penas del infierno al que han de volver tras el exorcismo' (the pains of hell to which they must return after the exorcism).[40] The note in this edition continues:

> En el *Exorcismus domus a Daemonio vexatae*, según el Ritual Toledano, se asperjaba con agua bendita en tres momentos ... La *conjuratio* del rito del exorcismo es la siguiente: 'Adiuro te, serpens antique, per iudicem vivorum et mortuorum, per factorem mundi, qui habet potestatem mittere te in gehennam, ut ab hac domo festinus discedas. Ipse tibi imperat, maledicte diabole, qui ventis ac mari et tempestatibus imperavit. Ipse tibi imperat, qui de supernis coelorum in inferiora terrae te demergi praecepit. Ipse tibi imperat, qui te retrorsum abire praecepit.'

> (In the *Exorcism of the house vexed by a Demon*, according to the Ritual of Toledo, holy water was aspergated in three moments ... The conjuration of the rite of exorcism is the following: 'I adjure you, ancient serpent, by the judge of the living and the dead, by the maker of the world, who has the power to send you to Gehenna, that you depart from this house quickly. The same One, cursed devil, who ruled over the winds and the sea and the tempests, rules over you. The same One who ordered that you be plunged from the heights of heaven to the depths of the earth, rules over you. The same One who ordered you to go back again rules over you.')[41]

The state of possession which could result from reading conjuring books matches Don Quixote's confused state exactly. It has been a commonplace of *Quijote* scholarship that the texts he appropriates provide the raw material for his peculiar strain of madness. For example, after being inside the Cave of Montesinos, Don Quixote reports that he encountered two imprisoned knights who remain there under enchantment by Merlin – whom he recognizes to be, according to the *libros de caballerías*, the son of the devil.[42] This linkage of the chivalric romances with demonic power and occult activities provides an even firmer foundation for the inclusion of the diabolical linguistic register as a complement to the chivalric one in the recognized canon of Cervantine intertexts.

Mysterious Caves and Flying Horses: Diabolical Humour in Part II of *Don Quijote*

The comic episodes involving demonic intertextuality are not limited to the first part of the novel. They appear in the second part as well, offering further coherence to the sequel. These episodes include the encounter with the *Cortes de la Muerte*, where the Wagon of Death is driven by the Devil himself (on this fictive literalization of metaphor, Ruth El Saffar comments that 'the Devil-driven wagon portrays Don Quixote's state well').[43] A similar sort of humour is generated when the dukes arrange, for their own entertainment, a comic performance by a devil figure who gives an order to disenchant Dulcinea. Still another parodic use of the demonic occurs when Sancho, as governor of the *Ínsula*, hears the petition of the *labrador engañador*, who claims specifically that his son is possessed by a demon: 'mi hijo es endemoniado, y no hay día que tres o cuatro veces no le atormenten los malignos espíritus; y de haber caído una vez en el fuego, tiene el rostro arrugado ... se aporrea y se da de puñadas él mismo a sí mismo' (my son is a demoniac, and there is not a day that three or four times he is not tormented by the malign spirits; and from having fallen once into the fire, he has a scarred face ... he beats himself and mauls himself).[44]

Some of these comic episodes bear serious undertones. For example, in the adventure of the Cave of Montesinos, Juan Bautista Avalle-Arce believes the descent into the cave is a symbolic journey into hell.[45] Henry Sullivan offers a different interpretation of the cave episode as a descent into purgatory to atone for sins.[46] Perhaps not incidentally, Cervantes returns to the cave as a locus of popular superstition and/or demonic activity in his *entremés* about the cave of Salamanca.[47] Don Quixote's adventure in the cave of Montesinos could also be seen in a different light: consider that the demonologist Del Río relates stories of treasure demons who guard their hordes in caverns.[48] One Spanish conjuror named Marquina was prosecuted on 10 December 1564 by the Inquisition in Murcia for invoking these demons by means of conjuring books and speaking to them when they arrived; one of his clients was Diego de Heredia, of Bárboles.[49] The demons were supposed to aid in finding buried treasure, and when it was not uncovered, their response was, 'no era cumplido el tiempo del encanto' (the time of the enchantment was not completed).[50] All that the treasure hunters found were coal and ashes. The phrasing of the demons' response – typically present in stories told by conjurors before the Inquisition – reminds us of the plight of Don Quixote as he tries to find his treasure, Dulcinea, whose time of enchantment is not completed either.

There is no question that Cervantes appropriates certain specific details from demonological treatises to infuse authenticity into his comic fiction in Part II. In the episode of Clavileño, for example, flying through the air is a sure sign of demonic activity.[51] The explicit reference to Eugenio Torralba alludes to a spectacular rumour, a supposed demonic possession, which enjoyed tremendous popularity in Spain for a long time after it occurred.[52] The medical doctor Eugenio Torralba was tried by the Inquisition from 1528 to 1531 because of his dalliances with the devil. He confessed to having witnessed the sack of Rome in 1527 after allegedly having been carried through the air on a cane from Valladolid in record time. He was condemned in 1531 but then set free.[53] Here Cervantes recasts his fascination with diabolical phenomena and human belief in light of the more sceptical, satirical stance he sometimes takes toward these matters. This stance is echoed in some passages of the *Quijote* where he pokes fun at popular beliefs.

In passages of the *Quijote* as well as in certain parts of the *Persiles*, several of his *Novelas ejemplares*,[54] and in particular in the *Rufián dichoso*, Cervantes takes a radically different position regarding the supernatural, treating as the neo-Aristotelian 'legitimate marvellous' the phenomena of demonic possession, the witches' Sabbat, and even werewolves. Alban Forcione has urged critics not to detract from the complexity of Cervantes' genius by reducing his posture toward the supernatural to simple scepticism or satire:

> The examination of these various contexts in his works would indicate, then, that Cervantes was a writer whose fiction was plainly influenced in a significant way by the pervasive religious culture of his age and a writer who understood quite well the formal conventions, the spirit, and the possibilities for creative use of the various literary forms that gave expression and support to that culture. Just what Cervantes's most private attitudes and authentic beliefs in religious matters were will probably remain forever a secret, but, if the variety of positions toward religion encompassed by his fiction, some undoubtedly motivated more by the demands of literary genre than by personal convictions, is any indication, it is likely that they were extremely complex and that they may well have been troubled and unstable.[55]

What most modern critics have failed to realize, living as they do in an age of disbelief, is that the fascination of Cervantes with demonology, especially exorcism, does not stop with satire. Don Quixote fictionalizes his life to the extent that, in one sense at least, his beliefs convert themselves into realities. Thus it is worth asking whether he believes himself to be possessed, for if he does, the allusions to demonic agency in the text suddenly assume a much more sinister face. Here is the darker side of the comical Don Quixote, the consequence of his dabbling in diabolical adventures.

Lucid Intervals and a Wise Enchanter: Demonic Possession in *Don Quijote*

The exorcist Benito Remigio Noydens explains symptomatic occurrences that should arouse suspicion that someone is possessed: 'mudança repentina de vida, como aver sido hombre agradable, y ser aora agreste, y furioso' (a sudden change of life, as in having been an agreeable man, and now being aggressive and furious).[56] Don Quixote, in his transformation from poor *hidalgo* to knight errant, becomes the classic example of a person who experiences a 'mudança repentina de vida.' When a soul is inhabited by a demon, the victim's comportment and appearance change in a drastic manner (see fig. 6): he or she speaks with the voice of the devil and, at times, assumes a personality distinct from his or her own. But at other times, the demoniac experiences what are specifically called 'lucid intervals' by Golden Age exorcists: 'Para esto mandará el Exorcista al demonio, que no le ponga obstáculo, y que le dexe con sus lúzidos intervalos' (For this the exorcist will command the demon, that he not place an obstacle, and that he leave him [the demoniac] with his lucid intervals).[57] Lucid intervals – any *cervantista* will recognize this phrase as a focus of generations of Cervantes scholarship. Another treatise writer explains the belief that in the case of a demoniac, 'algunas veces le venían algunos intervalos y espacios breves de alguna devoción, que poco duraban, y en tal tiempo de aquella devoción (que era espíritu de Dios) profetizó y anduvo elevado en espíritu entre los profetas, y no cuando el demonio lo atormentaba' (sometimes there came to him some intervals and short spaces of some devotion that lasted briefly, and in the time of that devotion [that was the spirit of God] he prophesied and walked elevated in spirit among the prophets, and not when the demon tormented him).[58] This capability for quasi-prophetic utterance appears in Don Quixote's speech on the Golden Age as well as his pronouncement on Arms and Letters.

According to the exorcists, the possession of a person's soul by a demon also manifested itself by certain other specific symptoms, among which the feeling of being pursued was especially significant. The possessed person always tried to escape from the demon who would return to attack him. In the course of his adventures, Don Quixote expresses a growing awareness that something or someone is pursuing him. At the beginning his perception is limited to a notion that his 'enemy' attacks him and follows him wherever he goes. But who is it? The Golden Age lexicographer Sebastián de Covarrubias Orozco, like Noydens, uses the word 'encantador' as a synonym for bewitcher, necromancer, or devilish magus.[59] Within the *Quijote*, a bewitcher who acts as a vehicle for the Satan of Catholic exorcistic doctrine appears as one implicit identity for the 'sabio encantador' (wise enchanter) who pursues Don Quixote.[60] As was mentioned above, even the familiar *magus* of the chivalric romance was often accorded demonic agency, as was the case with Merlin, believed to have been fathered by the devil. It is hard not to think immediately of Don Quixote's fantasy that a diabolical enchanter pursues him when we find the following uses of the word 'enchanter' in Noydens's exorcism manual:

[S]e vale el Exorcista de la industria de otros demonios ... como lo hazen los encantadores.

(The exorcist avails himself of the industry of other demons ... just as the *enchanters* do.)

[Así son l]os que están enfermos por ... encantos del demonio.

([Thus are] they who are sick by ... *enchantments* of the demon.)

Suele el demonio, quando le aprietan con los Exorcismos, dezir, que no puede salir del Energúmeno, por estar en él ligado por los conjuros de algún encantado[r].

(The demon is accustomed, when they constrain him with the exorcisms, to say, that he cannot leave the energumen, because he is tied to him by the conjurements of some *enchanter*.)[61]

Noydens also uses 'encanto' as a synonym for possession.[62]

These relationships are solidified further by the fact that Cervantes' enchanter is narratively linked to the chronicler Cide Hamete Benengeli and thus to the stereotypes surrounding alleged Moorish use of black magic. E.C. Riley relates the chronicler Cide Hamete Benengeli to the enchanter:

The Knight invents an enchanter-chronicler and proceeds to believe in him ... Although the specific idea of Benengeli evidently arrived belatedly to Cervantes (he is not mentioned until chapter 9 and only attains his full stature in Part II), an unknown Benengeli certainly existed in the Knight's mind from the moment he first set out on his adventures.[63]

In an especially interesting argument for our purposes, Riley goes on to connect this Moorish enchanter-chronicler to the diabolical art of necromancy:

> The marabouts or holy men of Algiers ... were commonly designated 'Cide,' venerated as scholars, and credited with necromantic skill. Benengeli shares this title and these distinctions with them. As a sorcerer, he is privileged to know the smallest thoughts and most trivial feelings of his characters ... Chroniclers cannot know the secret thoughts of their subjects – unless, of course, they happen also to be magicians.[64]

Ruth El Saffar echoes Riley's connection of the chronicler with the enchanter, citing as evidence a passage from Part I, chapter 17, in which Sancho asks whether the enchanted Moor is coming back to give them more punishment, if there is any ink left in the inkwell.[65]

What are the potentially pernicious effects of evil enchanters? According to the exorcist Noydens, the demoniac experiences 'un desaslossiego [*sic*] extraordinario, de manera, que el enfermo no puede estar quieto, busca lugares lobregos, y apartados' (an extraordinary disturbance, in such a manner, that the sick person cannot be quiet, but seeks dark and distant places).[66] As Henry Sullivan notes,[67] Don Quixote exemplifies this behaviour when he practises penitence in various episodes,[68] although it should be added that in the Sierra Morena he parodies the conventions of sentimental romance by tearing off his clothes and performing somersaults. Sancho, who does not like the idea of penitence very much, complains that this awful place is like purgatory; Don Quixote responds: 'Mejor hicieras de llamarle infierno, y aún peor, si hay cosa que lo sea' (You would have done better to call it hell, and even worse, if there is such a thing).[69] The reaction of Sancho is immediate; it is the church's pronouncement over the souls of the dead: '*quien ha infierno ... nula es retencio*, según he oído decir' (Whoever has hell ... there is no holding back, as I have heard it said).[70] This formula sparks Don Quixote's interest, and he asks what it means. In a significant reply, Sancho says: '*Retencio* es ... que quien está en el infierno nunca sale dél, ni puede. Lo cual será al revés en vuestra merced' (*retencio* is ... that whoever is in hell never leaves it, nor can he. The which will be the reverse in your honour).[71] What reversal does Sancho have in mind? Perhaps he means that instead of Don Quixote's never leaving hell, hell itself (or the demons thereof) will never leave him.

It should be emphasized that Don Quixote does not simply remain passive in his struggle with the demons he perceives. Penitence carries great significance in both the *Quijote* and the exorcism manuals, and the Sierra Morena exchanges remind us of demonologists' accounts of how the exorcist fasts with the demoniac or prays with him late into the night. For example, Noydens cites Matthew 17:20 concerning the relationship between penitence and demonic possession: 'Este género de demonio no se lança, sino por medio de la oración, y ayuno' (This type of demon is not cast out, except by means of prayer and fasting).[72] According to this manual, the exorcist 'tendrá particular cuydado de ... no llegar a hazer los *exorcismos* sin averse prevenido con el ayuno, ò otras obras de satisfación, y penitencia' (will take particular care not to ... arrive to do the *exorcisms* without first having fortified himself with fasting, and other works of satisfaction, and penitence) because 'estos requisitos de la Oración, y ayuno conducen grandemente para la expulsión a todo género de demonio' (these requisites of prayer and fasting conduct greatly toward the expulsion of every kind of demon).[73] We should note, however, that there is no exorcist present with Don Quixote. Instead, he himself performs these required rituals while literally 'performing' the role of Beltenebros in the Sierra Morena. We will see later how this incipient self-exorcism is significant. For now it is enough to note that the demonic vocabulary is reconciled here with the linguistic register of the sentimental romance, just as it harmonizes more frequently in the text with the register of the romance of chivalry.

It is also important to observe how penitence has failed, both in these texts and in this scene which reflects their conflation. For both Cervantes and Noydens, a more rigorous process is required to cure the disturbed individual. During this era, exorcism was conceived in terms of a battle:

> La primera, y principal armadura, de que se ha de armar el Exorcista, es una viva, é indubitable fé, y confiança en Dios ... y pisar, no solamente al León más bravo sino tambien al Dragón, aunque venga del Infierno.

> (The first, and principal armour, with which the exorcist has to arm himself, is a vivid and undoubtable faith, and confidence in God ... and [his purpose is] to trample, not only on the bravest lion but also on the dragon, even though it come from hell.)[74]

One exorcistic treatise even begins with the famous Latin citation from the *Aeneid* of Virgil: 'Arma virumque cano' (I sing of arms and the man).[75] It may seem strange to cite this pagan verse at the beginning of an ecclesiastical manual, but the military model of exorcism was a response to the military model of possession: the Latin term *obsessio* had long been used to refer both to demonic possession and to military seiges.[76] The cleric continues the metaphor with the phrases 'lid, y contienda' and 'sangrienta batalla' ('contest, and struggle' and 'bloody battle'). The author refers to Saint Paul's spiritual armour[77] in another extension of the military analogy: 'Es la guerra en lo espiritual, y contra enemigos más poderosos' (It is war in the spiritual realm, and against more powerful enemies).[78] He then describes los Ministros de la Iglesia, a quien toca de oficio tomar las armas, para rendir, y vencerlos: y como no han de guerrear con armas de fuego, y sangre, sino con las de la Iglesia, las han de sacar de su armería ...

(the ministers of the church, whose office it is to take up arms, to destroy, and vanquish them: and how they do not have to fight with arms of fire, and blood, but with those of the church, which they have to take out of their armory ...)[79]

This reliance by exorcists on chivalric terminology to describe or explain supernatural phenomena became more and more common: the exorcist 'se arma para la pelea espiritual' (arms himself for the spiritual battle) with a 'cuchillo ... riguroso' (rigorous knife) against the 'enemigo ... de Dios' (enemy ... of God).[80] Noydens also writes warnings for the exorcist with the purpose of helping him to 'alcança[r] más presto la victoria' (achieve more quickly the victory) over the 'común enemigo' (common enemy).[81] He explains to the exorcists 'con què confiança pueden pelear con el demonio': 'debe el Exorcista no desmayar, y no mostrar señales de desconfiança en su contienda' (with what confidence they can fight with the demon: the exorcist should not faint, and not show signs of lack of confidence in his contest).[82] An exorcism which is considered to be successful is called a 'conquista' (conquest),[83] and the question of honour presents itself here in an explicitly chivalric metaphor. The purpose of the exorcist is that the victim 'cobra tanto animo para resistir a sus enemigos, que no podràn dél llevar triunfo, ni honra ninguna' (recover enough spirit to resist his enemies, who will not be able to take from him any triumph or honour).[84]

What is his history, from the perspective of Don Quixote, except a series of battles designed to test his chivalric honour? Even the participants in the battles described by each of these authors, respectively, appear to be similar. The battle against a lion is highlighted as a significant parodic event when Don Quixote acquires another knightly name, 'el Caballero de los Leones' (the Knight of the Lions).[85] It is no accident that the devil had been compared to a roaring lion in the Bible.[86] In a similar manner, the author of this ecclesiastical treatise cites Saint Bernard when composing a catalogue of names of the enemy demons, including the terms 'Bestia fiera,' 'Dragón infernal,' 'ladrón,' and 'robador' ('fierce beast,' 'infernal dragon,' 'thief,' and 'robber'). The priest writes here in all seriousness; he alludes in another place to a specific demon in the form of an 'espantoso Dragón, que se hundió en el mar Bermexo' (frightening Dragon, who drowned himself in the Red Sea).[87] In addition to the adventure of the not-so-vicious lion, Don Quixote encounters the majority of these other figures in the course of his journeys.

Don Quixote's battles with those he encounters become more violent later on in Part I. During the adventure of the encounter with the priests (notice another clash with the sacred) who are accompanying the dead body on the litter, 'Don Quijote los apaleó a todos y les hizo dejar el sitio, mal de su grado, porque todos pensaron que aquél no era hombre, sino diablo del infierno que les salía a quitar el cuerpo muerto que en la litera llevaban' (Don Quixote beat them all and made them leave the place, much to their displeasure, because all of them thought that he was not a man, but a devil of hell who had come forth to steal the dead body that they carried on the litter).[88] In passages such as this one the narrator suggests, by means of the perspectives of other characters within the story, a connection between Don Quixote and the devil. We will see how they begin to isolate and polarize him. They begin to call him 'el diablo' (the devil). The priest 'determinaba de no pasar adelante, aunque a don Quijote se le llevase el diablo' (determined not to pass further, even though the devil take Don Quixote).[89] The innkeeper refers to 'don Quijote, o don diablo' (Don Quixote, or Don Devil).[90] Even the faithful Sancho must ask when Don Quixote attacks the *disciplinantes* at the end of Part I: '¿Qué demonios lleva en el pecho, que le incitan a ir contra nuestra fe católica?' (What demons does he carry in his chest, that incite him to go against our Catholic faith?).[91]

One explanation for this marginalization or even persecution of Don Quixote as a malevolent force might be his physical appearance, which contains indicatory signs of demonic possession. As Noydens clarifies: 'Es pues señal conocida, que uno està hechizado, quando al enfermo se le ha trocado el color natural en pardo, y color de cedro, y tiene los ojos apretados, los humores secos, y al parecer todos sus miembros ligados' (It is thus a recognized sign, that one is bewitched, when the sick person's natural colour has been traded for brown, and the colour of cedar, and he has his eyes shut tightly, and his humours dry, and all his members apparently constrained).[92] Much has been written about the dry humours of Don Quixote. It is generally recognized that Cervantes read and used Huarte de San Juan's *Examen de ingenios*, but even this 'medical' treatise specifically attributes some forms of madness to demonic agency, stating that Satan takes advantage of the humours and uses physical ailments to his victim's spiritual detriment.[93] The old *hidalgo* is so sick with these ailments at several points in the novel that he cannot rise out of bed. Noydens also refers to the demoniac as a sick person,[94] and the symptoms of this sickness conform to those which Don Quixote manifests:

Suele el demonio en tiempo de los Exorcismos causar en el Energúmeno algunos accidentes; de suerte, que parece, que le maltrata, y que le aflige con una inflamación, ò hinchazón en la garganta, o cabeza, &c.[;] y es ardid suyo, para obligar al Exorcista, que no passe adelante con el conjuro.

(The demon is accustomed, at the time of the exorcisms, to cause in the energumen some accidents; of a sort, that it appears, that he mistreats him, and afflicts him with an inflammation, or a lump in the throat, or head, etc.; and it is his scheme, to obligate the exorcist, that he not pass forward with the conjuring [exorcism]).[95]

Castañega also affirms that 'el demonio más atormenta a quien la ... complexión corporal le es contraria y desfavoresce' (the demon torments more the one whose corporal complexion is contrary and unfavourable).[96] He reiterates: 'Muchas veces la enfermedad corporal (como la que habemos dicho) es disposición para que el demonio tenga más entrada para atormentar aquel cuerpo, así mal dispuesto y enfermo' (Many times the corporal infirmity [like the one we have described] is a predisposition so that the demon will have more entry to torment that body, thus ill disposed and sick).[97]

As the end of the first part of his history draws near, Don Quixote begins to suspect that the devil and his demons might have had a hand in his torment: with demonic possession lies one explanation for his adventures (or mis-adventures). The knight errant considers the inn, the site of several misadventures, to be a bad place where demons live: '¿No os dije yo, señores, que este castillo era encantado, y que alguna región [he means *legión*] de demonios debe de habitar en él?' (Did I not tell you, gentlemen, that this castle was enchanted, and that some region [he means legion] of demons must inhabit it?).[98] Suspicious also of the prophetic monkey of Maese Pedro, Don Quixote ascertains that the animal 'nos hace creer que tiene el diablo en el cuerpo' (makes us believe he has a devil in his body) that its master must be 'en concierto con el demonio' (in concert with the demon), and that to the devil, the monkey 'le dará su alma, que es lo que este universal enemigo pretende' (will give his soul, which is what this universal enemy seeks).[99] After an argument with a goat herder, Don Quixote engages in a fist fight with him, which the goat herder wins easily. The only way Don Quixote can explain his defeat is to address his opponent as, 'hermano demonio, que no es posible que dejes de serlo, pues has tenido valor y fuerzas para sujetar las mías' (brother demon, for it is not possible that you are not one, for you have had the valour and strength to subjugate my powers).[100] It was commonly believed in the Renaissance that demons gave to the human beings they possessed the gift of unnatural strength, and that this strength was a sign of possession. King James I of England refers to 'the incredible strength of the possessed creature, which will farre exceede the strength of six of the wightest and wodest of any other men that are not so troubled.'[101] Pedro Ciruelo, another Spanish treatise writer, affirms that spirits, good and bad, are by nature superior to men, and so they possess more natural power and strength than the strongest man.[102]

A little later Don Quixote realizes the import of his supernatural infirmity and gravely discusses the theme of possession in undeniably explicit terms. A prisoner in the cage, he believes that the priest, the barber, and the other characters are demons who are taking him away: 'Son todos demonios que han tomado cuerpos fantásticos para venir a hacer esto y a ponerme en este estado' (They are all demons who have taken fantastic bodies to come to do this and to put me in this state).[103] The humour of the scene is heightened by Sancho's running commentary on the inverisimilitude of his master's assessment of the situation; he objects that if the captors were demons, they would smell like sulfur. A rhetorical question from Noydens reminds us of this scene in the novel:

> Què harèmos con la persona endemoniada, que haze maravillas, y le haze pedazos? ... la encierran, y si fuere menester la aten, como se suele hazer con los locos, porque no acaezca el refrán común, *un loco haze ciento,* como ha acaecido muchas vezes por curar estas enfermedades.

> (What shall we do with a demoniac person, who does marvels, and tears himself to pieces? ... enclose him, and if it be necessary tie him up, as is usually done with the crazy ones, so that the common proverb not be fulfilled, one crazy person makes a hundred, as has happened many times to cure these infirmities.)[104]

With his characteristic credulity, Don Quixote describes to Sancho the special abilities of demons 'porque te hago saber que los diablos saben mucho ... Y la razón es que como ellos, dondequiera que están, traen el infierno consigo, y no pueden recebir género de alivio alguno de sus tormentos' (because I would have you know that the devils know much ... and the reason is that they, wherever they are, bring hell with them, and they cannot receive any manner of alleviation from their torments).[105]

It seems that until his death, Don Quixote cannot receive alleviation from his torments either. But it appears that he does complete a process through which he identifies one source of these torments: the devil is one enemy who pursues him. This idea tortures him, and it appears that his belief in his own possession continues to grow. At the end of his life he is still fighting off demons, as on the night of San Juan in Barcelona.

The *Noche de San Juan* was a festival explicitly connected to exorcism in the popular imagination. Even before Christian times, a version of this festival had been celebrated by pagans, replete with bonfires, to drive away evil spirits. This eve of the feast day of Saint John the Baptist (24 June) was celebrated at the time of the summer solstice, or 23 June. The special elements of this celebration were fire and water. Fireworks and *hogueras*, or bonfires, were commonly lit, and people sang and danced around them. The bonfires were probably a residue of the pagan solstice celebrations; originally, they may have formed part of a practice of worship in a cult of the sun. But the bonfires came to have special resonance within the Catholic context of exorcism, as one folklorist explains: 'El fuego también destruye lo malo, lo dañino y se prenden fuego para exorcizar lo perverso y rechazar al mal' (The fire also destroys that which is evil, that which is damaging, and they [the people who light the *hogueras*] use fire to exorcize that which is perverse and to repel evil).[106] She reiterates that the purpose of the bonfires was 'purificar, quemar o destruir las influencias dañinas de brujas, demonios y monstruos ... En tiempos de hechiceros y brujas, el hombre destruía los hechizos con fuego' (to purify, burn or destroy the damaging influences of witches, demons and monsters ... In the times of bewitchers and witches, man used to destroy the charms with fire).[107] This night was also considered particularly favourable to miracles, and often young people would leap over the bonfires or walk barefoot over hot coals to prove the ardour of their faith.

On this traditionally exorcistic night, at the party in Barcelona, some women approach Don Quixote with the desire to dance with him. In a hilarious yet poignant appropriation of the exorcists' discourse, Don Quixote shouts the exact words of the official exorcism ritual of the church: '*¡Fugite, partes adversae!*' (Flee, adverse parties!)[108] Here Cervantes deliberately engages in double-edged parody of the most elaborate nature. This night was also traditionally associated with some degree of sexual licence and promiscuity. Dances, masks, and special altars set up in honour of Saint John the Baptist gave young people the excuse (or disguise) to go out late at night and mingle together. For young women, the act of dancing around the bonfire was also believed to lead to marriage within a year.[109] Therefore, on one level, the words are a funny refusal by Don Quixote of the women's advances, but on another level, the allusion to exorcistic ritual is a richly complex assertion of novelistic autonomy.

Cervantes' placement of these words in the mouth of Don Quixote suggests a radically new appropriation of exorcistic procedure. Close attention to the original ritualistic context from which these words were transposed will reveal that something about this exorcism scene presents an extreme departure from the norm. For the words Don Quixote uses are normally spoken by the priest as he raises the cross of Christ for the purpose of expelling the demon from the demoniac by its power: 'Ecce crucem Domini, fugite, partes adversae' (Behold the cross of God; flee, adverse parties).[110] There is absolutely no ritualistic context in which the demoniac would speak these words for himself.

It should not surprise careful readers of Cervantes' *Persiles* and *El rufián dichoso* to see this author once again approaching orthodox ritual from a refreshingly humanizing perspective. After wrenching these words from their original context of regulatory dogma, he places them in the mouth of a character who can use them as irreverently as he chooses. The words are no longer regulatory, but irregular; no longer ritualistic, but novelistic. In fact, the more dogmatic their original context, the more disruptive their transposition. By giving these words to Don Quixote instead of to a priest, Cervantes grants to his character the opportunity to make a declaration of independence. Don Quixote is, in effect, exorcizing himself. Only an understanding of the magnitude of this innovation will allow us to grasp the ramifications of Cervantes' technique for the subsequent development of the novelistic genre.

The Paradox of Self-Exorcism

Don Quixote's self-exorcism literally makes literary history. It would have been easy for Cervantes to provide his protagonist with an appropriate exorcist when he needed one. In fact, two prime candidates were already present in the text: remember that Don Quixote's two friends from his village, who pursue him, burn his books, and try to restore his sanity, are the priest and the barber. These two friends are the two figures in Spanish Golden Age society who were called in most frequently to deal with cases of possession.[111] Since these characters were already part of the story, it would have been easy to have one or both of them exorcize Don Quixote. If Cervantes had wanted to satirize exorcism, he could have written a tremendously funny scene with the *cura* and *barbero* as the parodied exorcists. The fact that he did not, and that he chose instead to have his protagonist exorcize himself, must be significant.[112] This conscious choice on the part of the artist merits close attention.

This is not the only sacrament Don Quixote has performed upon himself. At the very beginning of his story, he also baptizes himself (and since baptism included a rite of exorcism, this is his first self-exorcism). Marthe Robert calls Don Quixote 'both priest and poet' when he baptizes Rocinante,[113] but she pays even more attention to his self-baptism:

> He baptizes without the sanction of any authority; indeed, he performs his own baptism, which is, properly speaking, a heresy according to his faith ... By introducing the ceremony of baptism into his book, Don Quixote not only commits an anachronism, he appropriates a privilege that refers to the right of an ancient and anonymous authority and is not transferable to an individual.[114]

Laypeople were ordinarily only permitted to baptize in case of emergency. But Don Quixote, without the excuse of an emergency, transfers this right to himself, as well as the right to perform his own exorcism.[115] He performs more of the rituals of exorcism in the Sierra Morena, as was mentioned earlier in this chapter, and then clearly exorcizes himself on the *Noche de San Juan* in Barcelona.

In doing so, he is about sixty years ahead of his time. In all my research with Spanish and English exorcism manuals, I have found only one prescriptive non-fictional text which offers the option of self-exorcism.[116] However, I am aware of some similar attitudes, if not practices, in Spanish southern Italy of this time period or slightly later. By attitudes I mean the willingness of ecclesiastical officials to allow or even encourage the people to perform certain 'self-help' religious rituals. David Gentilcore mentions, for instance, that in southern Italy 'the Church also advocated "self-help" remedial forms, of which the rosary is the most interesting example.'[117] Gentilcore also quotes Giralomo Menghi in describing some other 'sacramentals' which were at least partially performed upon one's self, usually after certain objects or substances used for the rituals had been blessed by a priest. Some examples of 'sacramentals' are 'the continuous invocation of saints, that is, reciting litanies; sprinkling oneself with holy water; taking exorcised salt through the mouth; carrying a blessed candle on one's person on Candlemas day; or a blessed palm or olive branch on Palm Sunday.'[118] Gentilcore explains concerning 'sacramentals' that 'in terms of the sacred system, they were in many ways analogous to the popular healing rituals in providing a means of order and psychological security through access to sacred power.'[119] But saying a rosary, carrying a candle, or sprinkling oneself with holy water are very different matters from exorcizing one's self. In any form, self-exorcism seems almost counterintuitive; how is it possible for a possessed person to muster the psychological or liturgical resources to perform self-purification through the expulsion of demons?

The unique text discussed in the following pages does not account for this apparent paradox. The only explanation I can see is that the form of self-exorcism differs radically from normal exorcisms: it resembles a meditation more than an exorcism. Perhaps this is where the comparison with Gentilcore's rosaries becomes more meaningful. But the fact remains that the gulf separating simple rosary prayers from something so radical as self-exorcism remains virtually unbridgeable, and no amount of comparison with other forms of religious devotion can remove the element of sheer surprise from any reading of this text. The text is not rigid, but fluid; not normative, but liberating. Unlike some other works of devotional piety, this book actively encourages self-awareness.

This text is quite rare, but since it is unique only in this one feature, it is relatively easy to describe succinctly. The manual bears the following title, all of which is important:

Iugum ferreum Luciferi, seu exorcismi terribiles, contra malignos spiritus possidentes corpora humana, & ad quaevis maleficia depellenda, & ad quascumque infestationes Daemonum deprimendas. Quatuor primi ex Evangelijs collecti, & *vna deprecatio vulgaris, pro ignaris, & mulieribus, vt possint semetipsos praeservare, & liberare Deo auxiliante, si non habuerint Sacerdotem.* Coeteri vero, ex varijs Authoribus compositi; cum doctrinis probatissimis.

(The fiery yoke of Lucifer, or terrible exorcisms, against evil spirits possessing human bodies, both for expelling whatever has been wickedly done, and for apprehending whatever infestations the devils have caused. The first four taken from the Gospels, *along with prayer in the vernacular for women and the unlettered, so that with God's help they might be able to preserve and free themselves, if they do not have a priest at hand.* The remainder brought together from various authors, whose learning is beyond reproach.)[120]

On the same title page, the author is identified as a Franciscan 'evangelistic preacher': 'Authore Patre Fratre Didaco Gómez Lodosa, dictionis Ecclesiae, Ordinis Minorum Regularis Observantiae Seraphici Sancti Patris nostri Francisci Praedicatore Evangelico, & huius almae Provinciae Valentiae filio' (The author is Father Brother Diego Gómez Lodosa, under church authority, of the Order of the [Friars] Minor of the Regular Observance, evangelical preacher of our seraphic holy father Francis, and son of this dear province of Valencia). Was this remarkable man the original self-help guru? Or was he just a prophet ahead of his time?

What is remarkable here is that within a standard exorcism manual designed to be used by priests, a section appears which is designated for the use of lay people who want to perform self-exorcism. Gómez Lodosa specifies women and the 'ignorant' as the potential users of this text. He addresses them directly and tells them when they should self-exorcize: 'Hermano, ò hermana ... quando te sentiràs en alguna enfermedad, ò melancolia, ò en el alma, ò en el cuerpo' (Brother or sister, when you feel yourself in some infirmity, or melancholy, either in the soul, or in the body).[121] He recommends that they go to a medical doctor first, then to a priest; if a priest is not available, then the important thing is that the ritual be performed anyway, either by the patient or by a friend: 'Y si no puedes tener Sacerdote que te la lea; te la podràs leer tu mismo, y si no sabes leer; te la haràs leer de qualquier persona devota' (And if you cannot have a priest who will read it to you, you will be able to read it yourself, and if you do not know how to read, you will have it read by any devout person whatsoever).[122] He coaches them on what to respond to doubting physicians who do not believe theirs is a supernatural illness,[123] and even offers pharmaceutical advice right alongside the spiritual counsel: be sure to throw out expired prescription drugs once a year or have a doctor ascertain their potency.[124] He also gives an insider's warning about other exorcists: if they ever try to make you drink something, refuse it (for it is probably sulfur).[125]

After these words of general advice, the exorcism follows. Unlike typical exorcisms, it is basically a meditation which uses a biblical passage from the Latin Vulgate, the Passion according to St John (all verses of chapters 18 and 19),[126] and provides a vernacular prayer after each verse of the Latin Scripture. The following is an example of one of these prayers:

> Señor mio dulcissimo Iesu Christo ... os ruego, y suplico, como pobre *siervo, ò sierva vuestra*, que si este mi cuerpo ò alma fuesse molestada, ò vexada de espiritus inmundos, ò de qualesquiera mal del Demonio, y tambien de qualesquiera mal natural, os ruego mi buen Iesus, que sea apagado deste mi cuerpo, todo calor, toda frialdad, todo ardor, toda peste, y toda la virtud de los adversarios infernales, todos los exercicios del Demonio, todos los incursos, todas las fantasmas del enemigo, todos los enredos, imaginaciones fabricadas por arte Diabolica, sean destruidas, y desplantadas, y quitadas, deste mi cuerpo, y alma ...

> (My sweetest Lord Jesus Christ ... I beg you, I supplicate you, as your poor [*male or female*] servant, that if this my body or soul be molested, or vexed by filthy spirits, or by whatever ailment of the Demon, and also by whatever natural ailment, I beg you my good Jesus, that there be exterminated from my body, all heat, all cold, all ardour, all pestilence, and all the virtue of the infernal adversaries, all the exercises of the Demon, all the incursions, all the phantasms of the enemy, all the traps, imaginations fabricated by diabolical art, be destroyed, and uprooted, and removed, from this my body, and soul ...)[127]

Note once again the gender-inclusive language. This prayer is fairly typical of one that a priest would ordinarily pray over a patient in the course of an exorcism, the only exception being that here there is no priest present. Thus the pronouns all deviate from the standard form of an exorcism by reverting to first person instead of second or third person.

The self-exorcism makes further provision for liberation from an enchanter or bewitcher, such as the one who plagues Don Quixote: 'O bendito Christo ... os ruego, que libreis este mi cuerpo, y esta mi alma de todos los echizos del Demonio arriba dichos, quitando las fuerças a los echizeros, ò echizeras, que por arte del Demonio maltratassen este mi cuerpo' (O blessed Christ ... I beg you, that you liberate this my body, and this my soul from all the aforesaid bewitchments of the Demon, removing the forces of the enchanters, or enchantresses, who by the art of the Demon mistreat this my body).[128] The patient is urged to insert his or her own name into the self-exorcism in the form of an announcement: 'Mi nombre Señor mio Iesu Christo es: N. siervo vuestro' (My name, Jesus my Lord, is: [name], your servant).[129] This is an especially interesting detail, considering the importance of naming, especially self-naming, in the *Quijote*. The patient is also (almost novelistically) encouraged to create his own attributes and to boast of his own righteousness in comparison to the evil deeds of the enchanters.[130] The liberating effect of this treatise is astounding: the author declares that every day is Easter for the true faithful, just as every person is his or her own exorcist.[131]

This is not even a manual written entirely in the vernacular, although by this time there were many of those. It retains the more ethos-building Latin as the language of choice for the part of the book designed to be used by priests, but it reverts to Spanish for the one section devoted to self-exorcism by laypeople. Gómez Lodosa is somewhat apologetic on this score: he urges the reader to pay no attention to the poverty of the Castilian language, as long as it was written with devotion: 'No atie[n]das à la retorica del lenguaje Castellano; porque mi fin no ha sido mas, que ponerlo con devoción' (Do not pay attention to the rhetoric of the Castilian language; because my end has not been more than to put it down with devotion).[132]

Ostensibly, this treatise was written primarily for the devout in rural areas who did not have regular access to a priest. But Gómez Lodosa also seems to allow for the possibility that some of the devout may feel more comfortable exorcizing themselves, and he even commits the potential treason of offering this self-help option to those who have been disappointed by the failures of official exorcists.

Self-Exorcism and the Rise of the Autonomous Novelistic Character

Was the ritual of self-exorcism sanctioned by Gómez Lodosa being practised before he codified it and committed it to paper? If so, could Cervantes have heard about it? Or was the novelist simply anticipating this innovation in the way that he anticipated so many others? We will probably never know. But one thing is certain: with self-baptism, self-exorcism, and similar gestures of emancipation, Don Quixote issues a declaration of independence for all future novelistic characters. Stephen Gilman describes this revolution in precisely these terms:

> a tacit declaration of independence, of which the first article is a guarantee of free speech ... Freedom of speech has as its inevitable corollary freedom of choice ... the gift of liberating Don Quijote and Sancho both from the narrative control of the author and, little by little, from the tyranny of their own roles.[133]

E.C. Riley further describes Don Quixote's autonomy: 'Don Quixote is ... an artist in his own peculiar way ... Consciously living a book and acting for a sage enchanter to record, he is in a sense the author of his own biography ... Don Quixote must improvise to meet the situations life offers him.'[134] Likewise, Ruth

El Saffar calls Don Quixote 'fiercely assertive of his freedom and autonomy,' citing as examples the facts that

> he creates his own name, plans his own career, and even projects the book which will be written about him ... [B]oth the narrator and the character are shown creating themselves out of a rejection of a past which is to be totally effaced.[135]

For the early modern subject, self-exorcism is an important aspect of this effacement.

Critics agree that Cervantes not only created his own autonomous characters, but also opened the door for the first time for future novelists to do the same. Thus it is that Michel Foucault called the *Quijote* 'the first modern work of literature.'[136] Stephen Gilman reminds us that 'it is a commonplace of Cervantine criticism to explain how the author of the *Quijote* was the first to create – or contrive – what are called autonomous characters.'[137] In *The Theory of the Novel*, Georg Lukács writes of the *Quijote* as the 'first great battle of interiority' for the early modern self and singles out the character's 'concrete autonomous life' and 'abstract self-dependence' as essential to the novel as a genre.[138]

The classic essay on the topic of novelistic autonomy is Joseph Gillet's 'The Autonomous Character in Spanish and European Literature.' In it Gillet describes Cervantes' honoured place in the history of the autonomous character which he then traces through Carlyle, Kierkegaard, Galdós, and Unamuno:[139]

> Up to now the autonomous character has been traced as far back as Cervantes. Cervantes created two worlds, never clearly separated, and some of his amphibious characters are equally at home in either of them. They often casually cross the fluctuating line between imagination and reality ... Don Quixote as well as Sancho speak critically of their book and of themselves in the book ... [T]he fictional character is suddenly transformed into one of reality, in which they are masters of their fates. That is what Cervantes had in mind when he said that Don Quixote knew how to act, while he, the author, only knew how to write, and why Cervantes disclaimed being the father of Don Quixote, and was content with being his stepfather ... Most of the elements of the theme we are discussing may already be found in some measure in Cervantes: the author who speaks to his characters, the characters who criticize their author and fear he may not understand them, citizens all of a shifting double world, in which they can claim both a literary life and a real one.[140]

Who knows whether even Cervantes himself was aware of what he was doing when he created autonomous characters in Part I? Some scholars certainly think that a writer so aware of contemporary literary debates could not remain unaware of his own innovations.[141] Some even claim that he left such indications of this awareness as the ambiguity of the very title of the work: 'In Cervantes's ironical equation of the name with the book itself ... Cervantes presents us not with a story but with a living person.'[142] As has been mentioned, he also presents himself as the stepfather, not the father, of his own book. And he further presents himself as a painter who does not know what he is painting. Gillet explains this *topos*:

> In Spain there is an anecdote, of which I find a trace as early as 1548. A certain 'pintor de Orbaneja,' when asked what he was painting, answered: *lo que saliere*, whatever happens to come. Or as they say in Andalusia: 'Si sale con barbas, San Antón, si no, la Purísima Concepción.' Lope de Vega, Calderón, Sor Juana de la Cruz, felt a deeper meaning in this jest and applied it to their technique.[143]

The novelist Henry James, probably unaware of its Renaissance precedents, offers a modern adaptation of this principle: 'A character is interesting as it comes out, and by the process and duration of that emergence.'[144]

At any rate, by Part II Cervantes certainly was aware of what he had done, in particular because of Alonso Fernández de Avellaneda's sequel[145] and its presentation of other potential lives for his characters: 'the game of autonomy and self-determination ... is the point of departure of Part II.'[146] At the beginning of Part II, Cervantes' characters want their author to portray them favourably; they think their author is an ignorant chatterer and that he interpolated too many stories in Part I.[147] They come alive in startling ways throughout Part II: they

> now can be themselves in any way they choose – and their behavior as a result often seems to come as a surprise, as when the translator judges Sancho's speech to his wife to be apocryphal, or when Cide Hamete puzzles over the truth or falsehood of Don Quijote's adventures in the Cave of Montesinos.[148]

They also insist on controlling details of the fiction in spite of, and in contradiction to, the author's intentions. Cervantes had planned to send his characters to the jousts at Zaragoza, but when Don Quixote learns that Avellaneda's character, his 'unidentifiable rival,' did do exactly that, he determines to go to Barcelona instead. One can only speculate that perhaps Avellaneda's very bad sequel did in fact change the course of literary history by acting as midwife in the birth of the autonomous character and thus, the modern novel.[149]

In the other chapters of this book I have used Renaissance literary criticism whenever possible to elucidate definitions of various genres, but Cervantes' nascent novel with its autonomous character has been viewed in hindsight as an innovation so radical that it took literary critics several generations to catch up. Even today critics speak of the 'basic incompatibility between the novel and a poetics'[150] and the 'extraordinary difficulty inherent in formulating a theory of the novel.'[151] E.C. Riley asserts that 'in the sixteenth and early seventeenth centuries there was, strictly speaking, no theory of the novel.'[152] This should come as little surprise, considering that 'before Cervantes wrote this book, there was no novel.'[153] Gilman offers a particularly touching analogy for how the novel was born in the process of Cervantes' writing: 'It took just ten chapters of profoundly "happy" gestation, and then all of a sudden the newborn, as yet unnamed, and seemingly miraculous infant uttered its first tentative cry.'[154] And Gilman thinks Cervantes did realize the magnitude of what he had just done: 'Cervantes knew that he had created a strange, buoyant, life-giving book that Renaissance critical theory could not possibly account for.'[155]

Conclusion: Liturgy in Literature, or Early Modern Literary Theory and the Christian Legitimate Marvellous

Scholars from Burckhardt to the Marxists, cultural materialists, and New Historicists have wanted to remove God from the early modern period. Jacob Burckhardt described what occurred in the Renaissance as

> the dissolution of the most essential dogmas of Christianity. The notion of sin and salvation must have almost entirely evaporated. We must not be misled by the effects of the great preachers of repentance or by the epidemic revivals ... The passive and contemplative form of Christianity, with its constant reference to a higher world beyond the grave, could no longer control these men.[1]

Burckhardt, a friend and intellectual kindred spirit of Nietzsche's, painted a picture of the early modern self which bears a not-so-curious resemblance to the Nietzschean *Übermensch*.[2] Likewise, the Marxist Georg Lukács describes the Renaissance as 'the time when the Christian God began to forsake the world.'[3] Similarly, the cultural materialist Jonathan Dollimore makes the bald statement: 'Of one thing we can be fairly certain: in the Renaissance God was in trouble ... the humanist might say "the desertion of God by man for man."'[4] In the same way, the semiotician Algirdas Greimas has called the sixteenth century 'the period when the Western world was definitely desacralized.'[5] Following the lead of these formidable intellectuals, many New Historicists such as Stephen Greenblatt want to see early modern selves as like ourselves in the early twenty-first century, buffeted about by political and social forces and 'energies'[6] so strong that individual talent, let alone individual worship, is inconceivable.

But God refuses to be removed entirely from the early modern world, as the literature of the period in all its eloquent specificity demonstrates. This book challenges the above assumptions about this period by demonstrating the beliefs of some early modern selves in God, angels, and – yes – demons. Satan and his demons are the inevitable counterpoint to God and his holy forces, and it is a sad testament to the prevalence (or aftermath) of deconstruction that we feel uncomfortable with the starkness of this dichotomy. A 'third term,' if there were one, would somehow soften the harshness of this binomial world view. But early moderns were not deconstructionists, and for many of them there was no aporia. God vs Satan, angels vs demons, light vs darkness – such was still the structure of their universe. This continuation of elements and antitheses that many postmodern scholars have preferred to associate with medieval writers may stretch our fixed notions of periodicity and blur the boundaries between categories which deny the fluidity of history. On this point I agree with the cultural materialist Jonathan Dollimore:

> History is not a unilinear development; on the contrary, at any historical moment 'there will be found contradictions and liaisons, dominant and subordinate elements, declining or ascending energies ...' The residual is not to be confused with the 'archaic' (elements of past culture which survive but are obsolete nevertheless); it denotes past experiences, meanings and values which have been formed in the past, which cannot be expressed in terms of the dominant culture and may even be in opposition to it, yet are still active ... [I]t is wrong to represent the (emergent) Marlovian atheist repudiating (dominant) religious orthodoxy from a position of atheistic independence and modernity.[7]

The atheistic position of which he speaks is evidenced not only by many scholars of early modern England but also by some scholars of Golden Age and baroque Spain. For example, Víctor García de la Concha makes the erroneous assumption about religious faith that 'hay que concluir que en la España medieval, renacentista, barroca y hasta en la España del XVIII – recuérdese a Feijóo – no creía casi nadie' (it must be concluded that in medieval, Renaissance, baroque Spain and even in the Spain of the eighteenth century – remember Feijóo – almost no one believed).[8] Similarly, Gonzalo Díaz Migoyo has attempted to 'de-demonize' Quevedo's *Alguacil endemoniado* by claiming that all that is really demonic about the *alguacil* is his human error:

> Por su maldad el hombre puede dejar de ser hombre ... para convertirse en un anti-hombre o demonio ... Doble ficción, como se ve, respecto de la existencia del demonio: primero, porque es nuestra mentira la que crea al demonio como chivo expiatorio y, segundo, porque se le atribuye, hipostasiándola, aquella parte de nosotros mismos que preferimos considerar mentira.

(By his evil man can stop being man ... to convert himself into an anti-man or demon ... Double fiction, as is seen, with respect to the existence of the demon: first, because it is our lie which creates the demon as an expiatory scapegoat and second, because it attributes to him, by hypostasis, that part of ourselves that we prefer to consider a lie).[9]

This is a blatantly ahistorical, anachronistic attempt to secularize a piece of litera- ture which clearly arose from a context of religious belief.[10]

Atheistic or secularizing assumptions have become so pervasive in academia that they even colour supposedly neutral, unbiased reference works such as ency- clopedias of poetics.[11] An entry on 'myth criticism' in one such work includes off- handedly the cognitively dissonant phrase, 'real though nonexistent entities such as demons or divinities.'[12] Such unreflective atheistic – or ademonic – assump- tions, inexcusable as they are in any field of literary inquiry, are especially danger- ous when applied to early modern literature. Demons and exorcisms were all too real and existent to many people living in this age, and as Douglas Biow reminds us, 'a given period's conception as to what constitutes history in turn underpins the representation of the marvelous.'[13]

Actually, historians are sometimes more sensitive to religious belief than liter- ary critics. For example, Stuart Clark insists (against historians of a more atheistic disposition)[14] in his recent lengthy study *Thinking with Demons*:

A striking example [of irresponsible scholarly assumptions] is D.P. Walker's argu- ment that what we ought to be doing in cases of possession from the sixteenth and seventeenth centuries is discovering what actually happened. For him this excludes the possibility that demoniacs were actually possessed. The undoubted fact that this is not an explanation likely to appeal to a modern audience is his reason for siding with the other two available in the period itself. 'Historians,' he urges, 'should not ask their readers to accept supernatural phenomena.' The realism implicit in this rec- ommendation is, no doubt, still seductive. It reassures the observer of exotic behav- iour in the past that it can be described in ways that satisfy his or her own expectations of what can and cannot happen. Its limitations are none the less funda- mental. The view that we cannot understand the actions and beliefs of others with- out accepting them as true and valid ourselves preempts the history of cultures with models of reality different from ours. It cannot even begin to account for the activity of the anthropologist. In the case of possession (and much else concerning demonism and witchcraft) our task cannot, therefore, be to trace the relationship between what was said about it and what it 'actually' amounted to – as if the two can be successfully matched up or shown to be at odds. At the very least we are obliged to take up a relativist position with regard to what could count as real.[15]

This diatribe comes from a well-respected historian who is writing for other historians. How much more do his words apply to the field of literature, where our mission lies more with interpretive than with ontological questions? Without a basic respect for the religion of the past, we can never hope to appreciate its literature.

Much (if not all) of the literature of the early modern period was influenced in some way or other by poetics treatises and their prescriptions about the use of the Christian legitimate marvellous. Whether early modern writers followed these prescriptions, reacted against them, or modified their adherence to them – to fashion literary figurations of the early modern self in increasingly creative ways within increasingly hybrid genres – these poetical manuals were too pervasive to be ignored. I will first consider 'Longinus,' Petronius, and Aristotle, and then I will focus on Renaissance adaptations of the literary theories of these classical authors. In the process I will look at Tasso (without whom any discussion of the Christian legitimate marvellous in this time period would be meaningless) and his contemporaries, including those in England and Spain. I will conclude this study of exorcism in the literature of these two countries by showing how each genre in turn responded to the incorporation of exorcism as a manifestation of the legitimate marvellous.

As we shall see shortly, Aristotle was more restrained than some advocates of the marvellous in antiquity. For example, 'Longinus' and Petronius both recommended the inclusion in poetry of generous doses of the marvellous without much attention to verisimilitude. The influence of Aristotle was much more prevalent than that of 'Longinus' or Petronius, but these were the two other main critics from antiquity who were revived in sixteenth- and seventeenth-century discussions of the legitimate marvellous. Let us look first at these two figures to see how moderate Aristotle was in comparison.

'Longinus,' in *On the Sublime*, described human nature's passion for the supernatural in ways that were later appropriated to justify the inclusion of the legitimate marvellous in poetry:

> She [nature] therefore from the first breathed into our hearts an unconquerable passion for whatever is great and more divine than ourselves. Thus within the scope of human enterprise there lie such powers of contemplation and thought that even the whole universe cannot satisfy them, but our ideas often pass beyond the limits that enring us ... Also we expect a statue to resemble a man, but in literature, as I said before, we look for something greater than human.[16]

Petronius, likewise, was later seen to have made a plea for the Homeric *deus ex machina* and for supernatural excitement as opposed to the historical dullness of

Lucan's *Civil Wars*. He supposedly voiced this exhortation through the old poet
Eumolpus in the *Satyricon*:

> Non enim res gestae versibus comprehendendae sunt quod longe melius historici
> faciunt: sed, per ambages, deorumque ministeria, praecipitandus est liber spiritus, ut
> potius furentis animi vaticinatio appareat, quam religiosae orationis, sub testibus,
> fides.

> (For it is not historical fact that has to be handled in the poem – historians do this far
> better. No, the unfettered inspiration must be sent soaring from the catapult of wit
> through dark messages and divine interventions and stories, so that it gives the
> impression of prophetic ravings rather than the accuracy of a solemn speech before
> witnesses.)[17]

Petronius may in fact have been satirizing Eumolpus here; furthermore, he is not
always even thought of as a literary critic. But baroque theorists later appropriated his words in their poetics treatises to support the inclusion of extreme supernaturalism.

Unlike 'Longinus' and Petronius, Aristotle insisted that the marvellous should
only be included in poetry if it is tempered by verisimilitude. Nonetheless, he
advocated its inclusion because he saw the marvellous as central to the poetic
project:

> Now then, it is necessary in tragedy to create the marvelous, but the epic admits, even
> more, of the irrational, on which the marvelous especially depends ... The marvelous
> is pleasant, and the proof of this is that everyone embellishes the stories he tells as if
> he were adding something pleasant to his narration ... The use of impossible proba-
> bilities is preferable to that of unpersuasive possibilities ... The irrational must be jus-
> tified in regard to what men say and also on the grounds that it is, sometimes, not at
> all irrational. For it is reasonable that some things occur contrary to reason.[18]

We shall see how these words from the *Poetics* became famous as they were appropriated, along with the passages from 'Longinus' and Petronius, to justify the
inclusion of the marvellous in humanistic imitations of (and reactions to) the
classics in the sixteenth and seventeenth centuries.

Some Italian Renaissance and baroque literary theorists favoured 'Longinus' and
Petronius over Aristotle. For example, Francesco Patrizi does not insist on verisimilitude as a necessary component of the marvellous. Instead, in one of the most
anti-Aristotelian stances of his day, he lists twelve sources of the marvellous: ignorance, fable, novelty, paradox, augmentation, change from the usual, the extranat-

ural, the divine, great utility, the very exact, the unexpected, and the sudden.[19] He also posits a separate cognitive faculty of 'marvelling' which is located in the soul.

But 'Longinus' and Petronius were more pervasive in their influence on English than on Italian baroque poetics. They became the basis of seventeenth-century English defences of 'heroic' drama by John Dryden and Abraham Cowley. In his essay 'Of Heroic Plays,' Dryden quotes Petronius directly:

> it is Petronius Arbiter, the most elegant, and one of the most judicious authors of the Latin tongue; who, after he had given many admirable rules for the structure and beauties of an epic poem, concludes all in these following words:-
> *Non enim res gestae versibus comprehendendae sunt ...*
> In which sentence ... it is thought he taxes Lucan, who followed too much the truth of history ... Lucan used not much the help of his heathen deities: there was neither the ministry of the gods, nor the precipitation of the soul, nor the fury of a prophet ... The oracle of Appius, and the witchcraft of Erictho, will somewhat atone for him ... For my part, I am of opinion, that neither Homer, Virgil, Statius, Ariosto, Tasso, nor our English Spencer, could have formed their poems half so beautiful, without those gods and spirits, and those enthusiastic parts of poetry, which compose the most noble parts of all their writings. And I will ask any man who loves heroic poetry ... if the ghost of *Polydorus* in Virgil, the *Enchanted Wood* in Tasso, and the *Bower of Bliss* in Spencer ... could have been omitted, without taking from their works some of the greatest beauties in them. And if any man object the improbabilities of a spirit appearing, or of a palace raised by magic; I boldly answer him, that an heroic poet is not tied to a bare representation of what is true, or exceeding probable; but that he may let himself loose to visionary objects, and to the representation of such things as depending not on sense, and therefore not to be comprehended by knowledge, may give him a freer scope for imagination. 'Tis enough that, in all ages and religions, the greatest part of mankind have believed the power of magic, and that there are spirits and spectres which have appeared. This, I say, is foundation enough for poetry; and I dare further affirm, that the whole doctrine of separated beings, whether those spirits are incorporeal substances (which Mr. Hobbs, with some reason, thinks to imply a contradiction), or that they are a thinner or more aèrial sort of bodies (as some of the Fathers have conjectured), may better be explicated by poets than by philosophers or divines.[20]

Dryden repeats these same sentiments in his 'Apology for Heroic Poetry and Poetic License,' where he cites 'Longinus' repeatedly and gives even more examples from English Renaissance literature:

> And poets may be allowed the like liberty for describing things which really exist not,

if they are founded on popular belief. Of this nature are fairies, pigmies, and the extraordinary effects of magic; for 'tis still an imitation, though of other men's fancies: and thus are Shakespeare's *Tempest*, his *Midsummer Night's Dream*, and Ben Johnson's *Masque of Witches* to be defended. For immaterial substances, we are authorized by Scripture in their description: and herein the text accommodates itself to vulgar apprehension, in giving angels the likeness of beautiful young men. Thus, after the pagan divinity, has Homer drawn his gods with human faces: and thus we have notions of things above us, by describing them like other beings more within our knowledge.[21]

Abraham Cowley had anticipated Dryden's invocation of the authority of the scriptures as a source for knowledge about the supernatural. In fact, he went one step further than Dryden in championing the stories of scripture as the primary source material for Christian poets:

> Why will not the actions of *Sampson* afford as plentiful matter as the *Labors* of *Hercules*? why is not *Jeptha's Daughter* as *good a woman* as *Iphigenia*, and the friendship of *David* and *Jonathan* more worthy celebration then that of *Theseus* and *Perithous*? Does not the passage of *Moses* and the *Israelites* into the *Holy Land* yield incomparably more Poetical variety then the voyages of *Ulysses* or *Aeneas*? Are the obsolete threadbare tales of *Thebes* and *Troy* half so stored with great, heroical, and supernatural actions (since *Verse* will needs *finde* or *make* such) as the wars of *Joshua*, of the *Judges*, of *David*, and many others? Can all the *Transformations* of the *Gods* give such copious hints to flourish and expatiate on as the true *Miracles of Christ*, or of his *Prophets* and *Apostles*? ... All the *Books* of the *Bible* are either already most admirable and exalted pieces of Poesie, or are the best *Materials* in the world for it.[22]

These baroque manifestoes by Dryden and Cowley, based as they are on a strange mixture of Petronius, 'Longinus,' and Holy Scripture, represent a fascinating if short-lived bias toward anti-Aristotelianism which was concentrated primarily in England at this time.

In the rest of Europe, however, particularly in Italy and Spain, far and away the most influential theories about the marvellous to be received by the early modern period from antiquity were those of the moderate Aristotle. The neo-Aristotelians insisted on the inclusion of the marvellous only if it was tempered by the principle of verisimilitude. For example, Jacopo Mazzoni argued for the reconciliation of these apparently contradictory elements:

> But perhaps it is possible to doubt whether this credible marvellous can be found in company with the truth ... I answer that we find some true things more marvellous

than the false, not merely in natural things ... but also in human history ... [T]he true can sometimes be consistent with the marvellous! ... [P]oetry always seeks for a marvellous subject, as Aristotle has testified in many places in his *Poetics* ... Poetics is directed to the credible marvellous.[23]

Mazzoni lists thirty-four ways to make the marvellous credible.[24] Interest in the marvellous in Italy at this time was so intense that Giovanni Talentoni could deliver a lecture in 1597 to the Milanese Academy of the Inquieti exclusively on the topic of the marvellous.[25] Neo-Aristotelian interest in the marvellous was not limited to Italy alone. In Spain, Juan de la Cueva insisted that poetry 'ha de ser nuevo en la invención y raro, / en la historia admirable, y prodigioso / en la fábula ...' (has to be new and rare in invention, / admirable in history, and prodigious / in the fable ...) but requires that the poet must 'saber fingilla de tal arte / que sea verisímil' (know how to pretend it in such a way / that it be verisimilar).[26] Likewise, Alonso López Pinciano describes poems that do not include the marvellous as 'cold dreams': 'los poemas que no traen admiración, no mueuen cosa alguna, y son como sueños fríos ... La poética musa, entre otros ornamentos y arreos que tiene, el principal es el milagro y maravilla' (the poems that do not bring admiration, do not move anything, and are like cold dreams ... The poetic muse, among other ornaments and decorations that she has, the principal one is the miracle and marvel).[27]

Establishing the early modern literary context of the neo-Aristotelian debate over the general concept of the legitimate marvellous is not enough by itself to explain the recurrence of demonic possession and exorcism in the literature of the time. Instead we must make the leap from the broader concept of the legitimate marvellous to that of the specifically Christian legitimate marvellous to encompass these supernatural elements or theologemes in our structuralist paradigm of literary exorcism. The neo-Aristotelians discussed the Christian legitimate marvellous specifically and in great detail.

It is not difficult to make the connection between the passage on the marvellous from Aristotle's *Poetics* and medieval Christianity. James Cunningham knits the two together very clearly:

The effect of wonder will be a familiar notion to any Christian since it is frequently noted in the New Testament as the effect of the words and works of Christ:
And the disciples were astonished at his words ...   [Mt. 13.54]

And straightway the damsel arose and walked, for she was of the age of twelve years. And they were astonished with a great astonishment.   [Mk. 5.42]

Wonder, of course, is the natural effect of miracles, real or apparent. St. Augustine

makes the point in the text which furnishes the standard definition for medieval theology: 'I call a miracle anything great and difficult or unusual that happens beyond
the expectation or ability of the man who wonders at it' (*De Utilitate Credendi*,
16.34). And St. Thomas, in turn, integrates the Augustinian definition with the
Aristotelian. In the *Summa* he takes up the question, 'Whether everything that God
does outside of the natural order is miraculous?' He cites an authoritative text from
St. Augustine: 'When God does anything contrary to the course and custom of
nature as we know it, we call it a miracle.' For the term is indeed derived from the
word for wonder, and wonder arises whenever an effect is manifest and its cause hidden, as Aristotle says in the *Metaphysics*. Consequently, what is wonderful to one
man may not be wonderful to another, but a miracle is fully wonderful since it has a
cause absolutely hidden from all, namely, God. (*ST* 1. 105.7)[28]

But ultimately this explanation only goes as far as St Augustine and medieval
poetics.

Baxter Hathaway explains how Renaissance critics, without relying on the conflation of Augustine with Aristotle in the Middle Ages, nonetheless found a way
to accommodate the Christian legitimate marvellous within their humanistic
'rediscovery' of Aristotle's *Poetics*: 'Aristotle's claim that the verisimilar can be
based upon common opinion provided a loophole for including within poems
marvels and miracles of supernatural origin provided that these could conform to
the religious beliefs of the populace.'[29] Within this framework, James Mirollo
explains that the neo-Aristotelian Christian marvellous was possible for both
Catholic and Protestant literary critics.[30]

These neo-Aristotelian critics began their discussion of the Christian legitimate
marvellous by relating it to the marvellous religious elements included in the
pagan poetry of revered classical authors. Invoking the examples of Homer and
Virgil, López Pinciano asserted:

Supuesto que el poeta deue guardar verisimilitud en todo, la deue guardar también
en la religión, ley y seta que en aquel tiempo y en aquella región se vsaua ... Assí que,
conforme a aquellos tiempos, Homero, Virgilio y los demás prosiguieron muy bien
su imitación, y en ella la verisimilitud, la qual agora en nuestros tie[m]pos se guar-
dará siguie[n]do nuestra religión en los poemas.

(Supposing that the poet should keep verisimilitude in all, he should keep it also in
the religion, law and sect that in that time and in that region was used ... So that,
conforming to those times, Homer, Virgil and the rest continued very well their imitation, and in it the verisimilitude, which now in our times will be kept following
our religion in the poems.)[31]

Likewise, Giovanni Pigna advocated moderate use of the Christian marvellous instead of any inclusion of classical mythology.[32] Giraldi Cinthio, approaching the Christian marvellous from the perspective of decorum, recommended substituting the powers of magicians and infernal beings for the previously invoked powers of the pagan gods.[33] Antonio Minturno, a bishop and delegate to the Council of Trent, also advocated the use of the Christian marvellous instead of any elements of the pagan marvellous:

> Antiquity had its gods, celestial as well as infernal and earthly; the modern age has its angels and the saints in Heaven and only one God. The former had oracles and sibyls, the latter necromancers and magicians; the former enchantresses, of which were Circe and Calypso, the latter fairies. In the former Iris and Mercury were the messengers of Jove; in the latter some of the angels are sent out by God.[34]

The Spaniard Francisco Cascales echoes Minturno almost word for word:

> Si la antigua poesía tenía dioses celestiales, infernales y terrenos, la moderna tiene ángeles, sanctos del cielo y a Dios; y en la tierra, religiosos y hermitaños. Tenía aquélla oráculos y sibilas, ésta, negrománticos y hechizeras; aquélla, encantadoras, quales fueron Circe, Medea y Calipso, ésta, las Parcas; en aquélla eran mensageros de Iúpiter Mercurio y Iris, y en ésta los ángeles traen las embaxadas de Dios.
>
> (If the ancient poetry had celestial, infernal and terrestrial gods, the modern [poetry] has angels, saints of heaven and God; and on earth, the religious and hermits. This [poetry] had oracles and sybils, necromancers and sorceresses; that [poetry], enchantresses, which were Circe, Medea and Calypso, this [poetry], the Fates; in that [poetry] Mercury and Iris were the messengers of Jupiter, and in this [poetry] the angels bring the embassies of God).[35]

This often-repeated conflation of the pagan gods of antiquity with Renaissance angels and demons was one of the most formidable arguments in early modern poetics for the inclusion of the Christian legitimate marvellous.[36]

The most vocal advocate of the Christian legitimate marvellous was undoubtedly Torquato Tasso. Stimulated by a lively debate over the marvellous elements of his own epic poem, *Gerusalemme liberata* – versus what he saw to be the less justifiable marvellous elements of Ariosto's *Orlando furioso* – Tasso wrote the most important Renaissance theoretical manifesto pertaining to the Christian legitimate marvellous. In his *Discorsi del poema eroico*, he expounded at length on his understanding of this crucial neo-Aristotelian concept:

> But though I hold the epic poet to a perpetual obligation to keep to the truth, I do

not therefore exclude the other quality, that is, the marvelous; rather I hold that the same action can be both marvellous and true. I believe there are many modes of joining these discordant qualities ... Some actions which greatly exceed the power of men the poet attributes to God, to his angels, to devils, or to those to whom God or the devils have conceded this power, such as the saints, magicians, and fairies. These actions, if they are considered of themselves, appear marvellous; in fact they are called miracles in ordinary speech. If one regards the virtue and power of the doer, these same things will be judged true to life, because the men of the present age drank in this opinion with their milk when they were in their swaddling clothes and were confirmed in it by the teachers of our holy faith, namely that God and his ministers, and by his permission the demons and the magicians, are able to do wondrous things exceeding the force of nature; by reading and observation they seem every day to get new instances; therefore not merely what they believe is possible but what they think has often happened and can happen many times again will not seem beyond the limits of verisimilitude, just as the ancients who lived in the error of their vain religion saw no improbability in the miracles that not the poets alone but the historians as well fabled of their gods. But if learned men give us little credit, the opinion of the multitude is enough for the poet in this as in many other things ...[37]

Here Tasso specifically grounded his justification for the inclusion of the legitimate marvellous in the foundation of popular belief. For Tasso, verisimilitude was all a question of what we today might call reader response. If some early modern readers believed in certain supernatural phenomena – for the purposes of this study, we might give the examples of demonic possession and exorcism – then those supernatural phenomena were verisimilar by default. The opinion of 'learned men' did not matter in the conception of this (in one sense, at least) great populist poet.

Defenders of Tasso (as previously of Dante) repeated these sentiments ad nauseam in the sixteenth century. Tommaso Campanella defended both of these poets on the grounds that religion is truth, and any violation of religion in poetry is unacceptable. Campanella praised Tasso and Dante for their legitimate inclusion of prophecies, angels, saints' miracles, and the diabolical enchantments of the devil and his instruments.[38] Orazio Lombardelli believed that true but improbable fables were good subjects for poetry and listed four categories of these fables: natural facts that are difficult to believe; facts brought about by diabolical arts, such as dead men speaking or sudden storms in the middle of the day; saints' miracles, such as resurrection of the dead and walking through fire; and the miracles of God himself.[39]

These distinctions among types of miracles could stray into the territory of the heretical. There were some contemporaries of Tasso who were more worried about heresy than others. Giovambattista Strozzi the Younger actually believed that ortho-dox Christians could employ elements of pagan fables as long as they were writing nonreligious poems; if they were writing religious poems, they should use angels and other supernatural beings instead.[40] In contrast, Bellisario Bulgarini warned against the use of superstitious beliefs by poets unless they made it clear that these beliefs should be held in contempt by orthodox Christians.[41] Campanella said the same, perhaps as a result of his serious conflicts with the church.[42] Tasso himself was literally driven insane by the fear that his work might be heretical.[43]

This same fear caused the authors of many sixteenth- and seventeenth-century epics to stay exclusively with Christian subject matter. In Italy, there were Marco Girolamo Vida's *Christiad* and Marino's *La strage degl' innocenti*. In France, between 1635 and 1675, there were many similar literary experiments, usually accompanied by theoretical justifications of Christian poetry or heroic poetry with a Christian theme. Hathaway mentions Jean de la Taille's *Art de tragédie* (1572), written as a preface to his play *Saül le furieux*, and Book III of Boileau's *Art poétique*. Other explicitly Christian French works from this time period (roughly the baroque or Counter-Reformation) include Chapelain's *La pucelle d'Orléans*, Le Moyne's *Saint-Louis*, Saint-Amant's *Moyse sauvé*, Godeau's *Saint-Paul*, Scudéry's *Alaric*, Desmarets de Saint-Sorlin's *Clovis*, *Marie-Madeleine* and *Esther*, Mambrun's *Constantius*, Les Fargues's *David*, Le Brun's *Ignatiade*, Coras's *Samson*, *David*, *Jonas*, and *Josué*, Le Laboureur's *Charlemagne*, Carol de Sainte-Garde's *Childebrand*, L'Abbé's *Eustachiuz*, and Corneille's *Polyeucte*.[44] In England, likewise, Milton and Cowley wrote Christian epics, *Paradise Lost*, *Samson Ago-nistes*, and the *Davideis*. For these imitators of Tasso, it was important to establish that the marvellous was not peripheral to the serious action of the literary work. Tasso's creations of the enchantments of Armida and Ismen, the enchanted wood, and Armida's magical palace had not been mere embellishments but rather inte-gral parts of his Christian epic.[45] Milton's creations of Samson's superhuman strength or the feats in battle of angels and demons were, likewise, not useless decoration but rather the main attributes and actions of his protagonists.[46]

But Tasso and Milton were writing epics, as were most of their baroque imita-tors. The next question to occupy Renaissance and baroque literary critics was: could it be argued that the marvellous had less of a place in other genres than in the epic? In response to this question, early modern literary theorists said, 'no.' Bartolomeo Maranta, for example, believed that *admiratio* must be produced by all poets at all times.[47] Giason Denores, likewise, included the element of the marvellous in all definitions of all genres, even comedy.[48] Francesco Robortello specifically addressed the issue of how the different genres should respond to the inclusion of marvellous elements – or more precisely, how the poet should adapt his use of the marvellous to fit the conventions of different genres.

This issue is of great interest for us here because the chapters of this book have been divided according to genre. They have been differentiated according to the different ways in which each genre incorporates theologemes from our paradigm of literary exorcism. Robortello posited that while, for him, the marvellous is in conflict with the credible, the marvellous must still be used in all the literary genres, but in varying amounts. He recommended that the marvellous be kept to a minimum in comedy, where he said credibility is most essential. He wrote that in narrative (vs dramatic) genres, credibility is less important; more marvellous elements may therefore be included. He addressed directly the genre of tragedy, moreover, and gave a number of specific devices the tragic poet can use to reconcile the marvellous with the credible.[49]

The genres explored in this study of exorcism and subjectivity in literature were the comedy, picaresque, satirical poetry, satire, romance, interlude, hagiography, tragedy, and novel. Let us look at each of these genres or groups of genres in turn, drawing from both early modern and modern literary criticism to understand how the genres differ from one another in their incorporation of the legitimate marvellous.

The reader will remember that I explained exorcism in comedy, particularly such plays as Middleton's *The Phoenix* and Zamora's *El hechizado por fuerza*, as a metaphor for the purificatory act of exorcizing the body politic. Curiously (or perhaps not), it is in the context of purification or catharsis that a Renaissance literary theorist also discusses specifically the question of how the legitimate marvellous is assimilated into the genre of comedy. Antonio Riccoboni theorizes that when we watch a ridiculous deception pertaining to the marvellous in a comedy, we (the audience) are then purged of that same kind of deception. According to Riccoboni, comedy

> debet esse admirabilis, ut per ridiculam deceptionem inducat huiusmodi deceptionis purgationem. Admiratio enim rerum malarum et turpium, quae in comoediis irridentur ac vituperantur, docet spectatores ne in illas incurrant. Nam quemadmodum tragoedia movet admirationem in rebus miserabilibus et metuendis, sic comoedia in turpibus et irridendis.

> (should be admirable, so that it might induce purgation of this sort of deception. Indeed, admiration of bad and torpid things, which in comedies are laughed at and vituperated, leads spectators not to run into them. For as tragedy moves admiration in things that are miserable and to be feared, so comedy [moves admiration] in things that are torpid and laughable.)[50]

In other words, by seeing the wicked marvellous enacted on stage, we are purged

of that same sort of wickedness. My description of exorcism in comedy as a metaphor for the exorcism of the body politic thus can lay claim to illustrious Renaissance critical precursors.

For the genres of the picaresque, satirical poetry, and satire, I emphasized the
marvellous experience of demonic possession (even when feigned) as a source of
knowledge. As I discovered in my study of the *Lazarillo de Tormes* and Quevedo's
Alguacil endemoniado, this knowledge is often 'off limits' or forbidden to the
inquirer who would seek after it. Mary Douglas's study *Purity and Danger: An
Analysis of the Concepts of Pollution and Taboo* is one of the theoretical works
which, along with Roger Shattuck's more recent *Forbidden Knowledge*, informed
my study of the picaresque and satire in the second chapter.

The third chapter on romance, the interlude, and hagiography shows how the
Christian legitimate marvellous could be 'humanized' in the Renaissance to make
possible its inclusion in apparently irreconcilable genres. The playful treatment of
the exorcism motif that we witnessed in Cervantes' *Persiles* and Lope's *La endemoniada* emphasized the theologeme of the joyful exploitation of the exorcism ritual
by young lovers as a means toward marriage and the restoration of order. In seeming contrast, Cervantes' *El rufián dichoso* and Lope's *El divino africano*, along with
Calderón's *Las cadenas del demonio*, incorporate the exorcism ritual into the very
different and much more serious genre of the hagiographical drama. The cognitive act or theologeme of salvation is accomplished in this genre by a humanized
version of the exorcism ritual in which all the crashing thunder of the Christian
legitimate marvellous (in the case of *El rufián dichoso*, for example: eleven thousand virgins attending, angels singing, and demons disguised as nymphs and
bears) is unleashed in the service of a humane rhetorical bargain by which the
saints exchange their good works for the sins of demoniacs. This chapter shows
the rather surprising way in which the Christian marvellous is sometimes assimilated (in this case, by two of the same authors) to both fanciful and 'serious' or
didactic ends.

The fourth chapter, on tragedy, shows successful exorcism to be incompatible
with the tragic experience. The inevitability of failure for exorcism in the context
of tragedy produces three possible permutations of the topos of demonic possession. The first of these is exorcism as a metaphor for neo-Aristotelian catharsis, as
we saw in *King Lear*. For this particular adaptation of the Christian legitimate
marvellous, there is ample critical theorization from Renaissance poetics treatises.
The neo-Aristotelian Lodovico Castelvetro saw the marvellous as a significant
part of the genre of tragedy, specifically as it relates to catharsis:

And because these things are terrible and excite compassion chiefly by means of the
marvellous, it is not well to omit speaking of the marvelous, which generates and

increases terror and compassion, in order that there may be full knowledge of terror and compassion as principal parts of the action or of the fable of the tragedy.[51]

Additionally, the Christian legitimate marvellous in general (and exorcism in particular) may function within tragedy as a means of providing a scapegoat. We saw in *A Yorkshire Tragedy, Othello,* and *Macbeth* how the demon may become a scapegoat to explain the murder by the protagonist of another (innocent) principal character. This permutation of the Christian marvellous in tragedy was also anticipated by Renaissance theoreticians. For example, Castelvetro divides the marvellous into three types:

> as it can be found in animals without reason and things without sensation, in men who do something horrible deliberately and as a result of a plan, and in men who involuntarily do something horrible as the result of an accident ... In the instance of men who do something horrible against their will, the marvelous, by furnishing them a cause for their acts in ways in which they believe it could not be given, receives a second distinction.[52]

In some tragedies where demonic possession appears, the demon acts as a scapegoat for the evil actions (Castelvetro's 'cause for their acts') of the mad protagonists. The third permutation of the Christian legitimate marvellous in tragedy is simply an extension of this one, a situation – such as in *Hamlet* – where no scapegoat is possible. The demonic mask is one of many which are 'tried on' by the Ghost and then discarded in an attempt to make sense of the evil that permeates the play. In all of these three possible permutations, the bleakness of demonic possession with no possible exorcism is one of the desolate features of the tragic landscape.

Finally, the fifth chapter on the novel interprets self-exorcism as the most appropriate assimilation of the exorcism motif for this unique genre born in the early modern period. The novel, unlike any other genre, boasts of an autonomous protagonist; and like no other work examined in this book, *Don Quijote* exemplifies a protagonist who conducts his own exorcism. In the *Quijote*, we see how the struggle between priestly mediation and direct worship, between exorcism by a priest and self-exorcism, is finally decided in favour of the autonomous individual – in the autonomous genre which emerged during the early modern period.

Exorcism and its texts, be they of whatever genre, are powerful testaments to the beliefs of some early modern writers in the real existence of angels and demons. Exorcism and its texts suggest that it is impossible for responsible literary critics to remove God completely from the early modern period. Some early modern scholars, especially some New Historicists, have almost tried to perform a sort of exorcism ritual upon the texts they study, to divest them of any annoying demons or otherwise controversial or unpopular elements. Living as they do in a postmodern, disenchanted world,[53] they refuse to acknowledge that some early modern authors could have lived in a world that was still very much enchanted.

This 'modern' disenchantment is more recent than is often assumed; miracles continued to be viewed as a pleasurable or wondrous part of human experience even by some Enlightenment thinkers. One of these was the philosopher David Hume:

> The passion of surprise and wonder, arising from miracles, being an agreeable emotion, gives a sensible tendency towards the belief of those events, from which it is derived. And this goes so far, that even those who cannot enjoy this pleasure immediately, nor can believe those miraculous events, of which they are informed, yet love to partake of the satisfaction at second-hand or by rebound, and place a pride and delight in exciting the admiration of others.[54]

Stephen Greenblatt, in an entire book about early modern conceptions of the marvellous as they shaped Europeans' views of the 'New' World Encounter, devotes only two pages to Renaissance literary theory and then comes to the inexplicable conclusion that 'the aesthetic theory of the marvellous sidesteps the miraculous but does not altogether resolve questions of credibility.'[55] The fact that he does not pay much attention to literary theories of the Christian legitimate marvellous here should not surprise us, considering the unwillingness of many New Historicists in other contexts to view phenomena such as exorcism as legitimate Christian marvels in the early modern period.

Besides exorcism, the category of the Christian legitimate marvellous in this time period is large enough to encompass many other 'marvels' and supernatural or paranormal phenomena. Studies similar to this one could be done to find the component theologemes of paradigms for witchcraft, prophecy, apparitions, or even astrology in literature. These paradigms form the basis for narrative or literary accounts which then – and this is an explicitly New Historicist lesson, for which I am indebted – influence historical accounts of the same phenomena: 'Wondrous accounts are part of a symbiotic process in which culture shapes narrative accounts and these accounts, in turn, affect experiential reports.'[56] It is only after this symbiosis is understood, using the tools of structuralism, that the real potential of the New Historicist project will be fulfilled. A dialogue between structuralism and New Historicism may produce a third term which will prove both synchronic enough to establish paradigms for supernatural phenomena in literature and diachronic enough to historicize their component theologemes fully.

Epilogue: Problematizing the Category of 'Demonic Possession'

Early modern selves being penetrated by demons: this has been the theme of our study of exorcism in literature. This literature depicts many different figurations of the early modern self: there were kings and saints, but also *pícaros* and murderers. Demonic possession is a great leveller because all of these figures can suffer this affliction. In fact, in light of recent challenges to the premise that runs from Burckhardt to Greenblatt of the nascent unitary self in the early modern period,[1] this field of demonic possession may be one of the only areas left where it is still possible to speak seriously of '*the* early modern self.' Obviously there were many iterations of the early modern self, but all of them could potentially become targets of demonic activity. The symptoms and circumstances of demonic possession were relatively stable categories in the early modern period, although each particular case bore unique nuances. These categories were stable enough for us, four hundred years later, to be able to recognize demonic possession when it appears in early modern literature. And they were stable enough to allow us to trace a set of theologemes which, despite some fascinating deviations, remains relatively accurate as a tool for analysing the phenomenon of demonic possession in literature of this time period. Or so it has seemed.

Where does demonic possession come from in this period, and where does it go? The obvious ancestor of the baroque era is the Middle Ages, when demons peeked out from the leering gargoyles of many a cathedral. After the end of the early modern period, when Neoclassical sceptics abjured acknowledgment of most things supernatural, it was probably not until the Gothic novel or the eerie gleamings of magical realism that demons would once again take centre stage in the theatre of world literature.

In the prologue I promised to address some related phenomena such as melancholy, ecstasy, enthusiasm, and poetic frenzy, and it is here (briefly) that I shall attempt to do so. The purpose of doing this will be to demonstrate the pervasiveness of multiple forms of spiritual 'transport' and the ambiguous appeal – an uneasy combination of attraction and repulsion – which these states could exert upon the early modern imagination.

The state of consciousness normally associated with demonic possession is also recognizable within several other, quite distinct paradigms or systems of belief. The self-styled 'retrospective anthropologist' Clarke Garrett has identified several paradigms through which these 'levels of consciousness that differ from everyday reality' may be viewed:

> When spirit possession takes place during sleep or an ecstatic trance, we call it a vision. When a god (or God) speaks through the mouth of an entranced individual, we call it prophecy. When a god, an ancestor, or a bad spirit takes control of the body of a person, producing behavior that can be bizarre, dramatic, or both, we have a variety of names, one of which is hysteria.[2]

Several generations earlier, R.A. Knox had come to essentially the same conclusion – namely, that these distinct but related phenomena could look so much alike to the spectator that, in some cases, their definition was primarily a matter of interpretation:

> How to explain these phenomena – Camisard child-prophecy, or Jansenist convulsions, or Methodist swoonings, or Irvingite glossolaly – is a question that need not detain us. What is important is that they are all part of a definite type of spirituality, one which cannot be happy unless it is seeing results. Heart-work, Wesley called it; the emotions must be stirred to their depths, at frequent intervals, by unaccountable feelings ...[3]

The purpose of this epilogue will be to show how demonic possession – up until now considered, within this study, to be a relatively stable phenomenon – could closely resemble, or at times be interpreted as, the related phenomena of melancholy, ecstasy, enthusiasm, and poetic furor. These phenomena will then be evaluated to determine (or at least approximate) their degrees of resonance for early modern selves.

The cognitive leap from demonic possession to melancholy is a very small one indeed. Melancholy was thought to be caused directly by the devil and used by him as a preparatory stage before or leading up to demonic possession. The minister, academic, and amateur physician Robert Burton invokes the medieval proverb that 'melancholy is the devil's bath': 'this humour of Melancholy is called the

Devil's Bath; the Devil, spying his opportunity of such humours, drives them many times to despair, fury, rage, &c., mingling himself amongst these humours.'[4] Likewise, Timothy Bright attributes melancholy at least in part to demonic activity.[5] King James I writes that demons use the humour of despair to bring people under their power: 'And finding them in an utter despair ... he [the devil] prepares the way by feeding them craftely in their humour, and filling them further and further with despair.'[6] Reginald Scot, likewise, explains that the devil 'provoketh the merrie to loosenesse, and the sad to despaire.'[7] Gaspare Marcucci wrote a chapter entitled 'Whether Melancholy Can Come from a Daemon' and explained that the ancients had viewed the *bacchantes*, sibyls, and *vates* as being in the grip of melancholy caused by *daimones*.[8]

Why did the state of melancholy resonate in a special way for early moderns? First of all, as is noted in the classic study *Saturn and Melancholy*, this state of mind was particularly associated with heightened self-awareness.[9] Likewise, melancholy was newly valorized by the Neoplatonists as the originating condition from which genius was born. Writers of the period such as Michel de Montaigne affected melancholy because they considered themselves (and wanted others to view them as) geniuses.[10] M.A. Screech defines the word 'genius' as it was understood during the early modern period:

> Geniuses are the men or women whose souls at least partially detach themselves from the restraints and pollution of their bodies; while in this state they may be influenced by good spirits or glimpse divine Truth and Beauty. More sinister, such people can also be possessed by evil spirits. Or they may be mad. Christianity came to limit spiritual possession to diabolical forces, though Platonic doctrines – which do not so limit them – proved very resilient; belief in good daemons was widespread during the Renaissance in the highest intellectual circles.[11]

Melancholy was thus a double-edged sword: it could lead to depraved insanity, or it could lead to the highest intellectual accomplishments. As Screech explains so elegantly, 'fear of madness went hand in hand with hopes of genius.'[12] Winfried Schleiner clarifies why melancholics were believed to be more likely to possess great genius: 'Some of the gifts traditionally attributed to melancholics in the pseudo-Aristotelian and Ficinean tradition, for instance the gift of divination, were commonly explained as the result of the higher penetrability of their bodies to the subtlest spiritus and astral influences.'[13] It was frequently remembered in this period that Democritus had believed that no great minds existed without the inspiration of some *furor*.[14] Thus we see how the category of 'melancholy' was akin to demonic possession and how it bore both negative and positive valences for early modern selves.

Ecstasy and enthusiasm were two other such polyvalent categories which were related to demonic possession in the early modern period. M.A. Screech explains how the term 'ecstasy' became an umbrella for many different experiences of the early modern self:

> Not all ecstasies were high, spiritual ones ... Ecstasies of various sorts were a common experience. Drunkenness was a form of ecstasy; so was falling in love; so were sexual climaxes; so was bravery on the field of battle; so was scholarly devotion to selfless inquiries; so was poetic inspiration; so were the revelations which made Socrates, say, and Hippocrates the authorities they are; so too were several kinds of madness, which share some spiritual powers with genius itself. 'Ecstasy' covered them all.[15]

While only sometimes distinguished from rapture per se,[16] ecstasy was a term often associated with mystics[17] and easily confused with demonic possession – a condition which, it was believed, God could also use to purify and refine his saints. Fernando Cervantes notes: 'Diabolical possessions were frequently a sign of divine favour and mercy. There were countless ways in which God could make use of a possession in order to "purge" a favourite soul in preparation for the mystical union.'[18]

Mystics were not the only subjects for whom ecstasy was significant. Why was ecstasy particularly resonant for the early modern self? Screech demonstrates that large areas of early modern knowledge relied on ecstasy for their relevance and viability:

> Montaigne had to come to terms with religious ecstasy, and with many other kinds as well. Huge claims to infallible knowledge depended on their reality: no discipline taught in school or university was without its authorities, who were often venerated sages from remote antiquity. Many maintained that these authorities were inspired geniuses, specially gifted men to whom wisdom or knowledge had been unveiled during ecstasies.[19]

Ecstasy in some form came to be an experience which was advocated even by such a renowned humanist as Erasmus himself.[20]

The closely related term 'enthusiasm' was normally used in more pejorative contexts. Michael Heyd explores the nuances of the ideologies connected to this word:

> The term itself became a standard label by which to designate individuals or groups who allegedly claimed to have direct divine inspiration, whether millenarians, radical sectarians or various prophesiers, as well as alchemists, 'empirics' and some contem-

plative philosophers. In the Catholic camp, the confrontation with enthusiasm was less prevalent ... since mystical experience, miracles, and spiritualist tendencies were more easily incorporated within mainstream orthodoxy. In the Protestant camp, in contrast, such claims presented a real challenge to the religious order ...[21]

Various treatises were written in the early modern and Enlightenment periods against enthusiasm; two worthy of note are Meric Casaubon's *A Treatise Concerning Enthusiasm* and Henry More's *Enthusiasmus Triumphatus*. Enthusiasts were seen by their opponents as 'shortcut artists' who sought quick and easy access to absolute truth. There were Protestants, Socinians, atheists, alchemists, philosophers, experimental scientists, and radicals who were all called 'enthusiasts.' Such people were often caricatured as being somehow prone to a sort of spiritual falling sickness: they fell down on the ground and either grew still and numb or shook and 'quaked' like the Quakers. During their raptures, they experienced convulsions and started shouting. Like Francisco de Quevedo, they attempted access to forbidden knowledge which other people did not have.

This 'access to knowledge' theme could generate accusations of enthusiasm against some highly visible – and highly unlikely – suspects. Because he did not trust the information revealed to him by his physical senses, the philosopher René Descartes was accused of being an enthusiast.[22] Clearly, like so many other supernatural or paranormal phenomena we have been discussing, enthusiasm had both a negative and a positive side. The negative view of enthusiasm saw its adherents as heretics who privileged their own divine revelations over the received authority of scripture. But in its positive version, enthusiasm could imply being open to the guidance of the Holy Spirit and practising New Testament spiritual gifts such as prophecy.

The mention of prophecy brings us to the final related phenomenon considered here, that of poetic frenzy. This supernatural concept, unlike the others discussed in previous pages, bears almost uniformly positive connotations during the early modern period. It will be remembered from the second chapter that etymologically, poets were considered by early modern literary theorists such as Luís Alfonso de Carvallo to have descended from the prophets.[23] Baroque theorists were only repeating a long tradition reaching back through antiquity to the Middle Ages. Ernst Robert Curtius gives a brief history of the connection between poet and prophet: 'In Homer the poet is the "divine singer," the Romans call him *vates*, "soothsayer." But all prophecy is linked to rhythmical speech; hence *vates* can be said of the poet.'[24] Socrates was commonly believed to have lain for long periods in a trancelike state while receiving inspiration from his *daimon*. This tradition perpetuated by Plato in the *Phaedrus* was resurrected by the Neoplatonists such as Marsilio Ficino.[25] Particularly when coupled with the influence of Jewish mysticism and the *kabbala*, it was absorbed into the erudite hermeticism of 'natural,' beneficial, or 'white' magic.[26] But poetic frenzy was not only a 'magical' phenomenon in the view of early modern humanists. Such venerated authorities as Aristotle,[27] Cicero,[28] and Seneca[29] had also made reference to the poet's necessary insanity, and their early modern successors 'substituted supernaturalism for the difficult task of explaining the creative process.'[30] The romantics would later seize upon this notion in their efforts to exalt the creative Self, and it is indeed only with romanticism that we find a concern with self-fashioning as intense as that evidenced by early modern selves.

Melancholy, ecstasy, enthusiasm, poetic frenzy: to this list of phenomena related to diabolical possession could be added epilepsy,[31] tarantism,[32] ventriloquism, stigmatism,[33] and even asthma.[34] As Michael MacDonald shows in *Mystical Bedlam*, the astrological physician Richard Napier employed both exorcism and necromantic divination to try to separate his bewitched patients from those who were mentally disturbed.[35] Marsilio Ficino, the Neoplatonist who practised a form of cabbalistical magic, admitted to having cast out bad Saturnian demons 'by astrological means' in 1494–5.[36] The boundaries between these categories of affliction and cure could become very blurry indeed.

Many more illustrations of this principle could be adduced, but the examples discussed or alluded to in these brief concluding pages should prove sufficient to make the point that demonic possession was *not* always the stable category we have assumed it to be for the purposes of this study. Let the reader make no mistake: this is not a palinode. But it is important to problematize sufficiently the theologemes and categories we have been working with in this study. Ultimately I believe that the model developed in this study makes it clear that there *is* a difference between demonic possession and melancholy, demonic possession and ecstasy, demonic possession and enthusiasm, or demonic possession and poetic frenzy. But the boundaries between these phenomena could become blurred. It should not be forgotten that the Apostles were confused for drunkards,[37] and even Jesus himself was accused of being diabolically possessed.[38] In fact, since the devil was the ape of God, it was believed that he intentionally constructed the experience of demonic possession to resemble closely the rapture, ecstasy, and visions of the mystics. Here the example of Hamlet may be applicable to all instances of demonic possession in all literary genres. Just as the Ghost appears Catholic, Protestant, devilish, or dead at various moments in the play, so too every demonic possession in literature could appear to some early modern readers or spectators as melancholy, epilepsy, or enthusiasm instead.

Only when the structuralist paradigm has been sufficiently problematized and historicized will it satisfy our craving for a *real* New Historicism. Just as there was no single early modern self, so there was no single experience of demonic posses-

sion and exorcism. But the recognition of this complexity is no excuse for not trying to analyse literature about demonic possession *as literature* with all of its
'marvellous' genres and theologemes. Early modern selves could be remarkably
vulnerable, remarkably open to demonic penetration. Perhaps we, as critics,
ought to learn from them to be more open to seeing supernaturally influenced or
genuinely religious figurations of the early modern self.

Notes

Preface

1 See Burckhardt's *The Civilization of the Renaissance in Italy*, especially Part 2, 'The Development of the Individual.' Greenblatt's seminal study *Renaissance Self-Fashioning* received both a laudatory reassessment and a potent critique at the twentieth-anniversary session organized by David Kastan at the 2000 Modern Language Association convention. For another still-memorable treatment of this topic, see Greene, 'The Flexibility of the Self in Renaissance Literature.'

2 'The author, in medieval times, was little accounted of. The great bulk of narrative poetry remains anonymous' (Chaytor, *From Script to Print*, 139). See also Spearing, *Medieval to Renaissance in English Poetry*, 5. A nuanced challenge to this view, with emphasis on the different medieval concept of what an *auctor* was, may be found in Minnis, *Medieval Theory of Authorship*.

3 This argument has been made most forcefully by Eisenstein in *The Printing Press As an Agent of Change*, 320–1. See also Woodmansee, 'The Genius and the Copyright'; and Rose, 'The Author as Proprietor.' Many of the theoretical underpinnings of this popular new field of criticism may be found in Foucault, 'What Is an Author?'

For a critique of the birth of capitalistic private property, see Marx, *Capital*, 788. The Marxist scholar N. Scott Arnold confirms the link between capitalism and a new emphasis on the individual: 'Only under capitalism is the *individual* (as opposed to some group to which the individual belongs) the focus of nonaltruistic behavior. The explanandum under discussion is not selfish, egoistic behavior per se, but its ubiquity' (*Marx's Radical Critique of Capitalist Society*, 60).

4 On this concept, as well as Renaissance humanism's glorification of man, see Kris-

teller's and Randall's introduction to *The Renaissance Philosophy of Man*, 19. See also in particular Pico della Mirandola's 'Oration on the Dignity of Man'. I believe, with the late Valerio Valeri, that postmodern attempts to reject the notion of the unitary self and the 'rejection of humanism' which they imply are ultimately misguided (Janet Hoskins, introduction to Valerio Valeri, *The Forest of Taboos: Morality, Hunting, and Identity among the Huaulu of the Moluccas* [Madison: University of Wisconsin Press, 2000], xvii–xviii).

5 On Montaigne's 'decision to write about himself, to make himself the central subject of a constantly expanding book,' see Screech, *Montaigne and Melancholy*, 6. On self-fashioning in Machiavelli, see Rebhorn, *Foxes and Lions*, 27. On the ways in which Elizabeth manipulated her public image through official portraits to preserve a picture of herself as eternally youthful, virginal, and powerful, see Frye, *Elizabeth I*; and Haigh, *Elizabeth I*.

6 Caciola, 'Discerning Spirits,' 16.

7 Ibid., 323.

8 Ibid., 42.

9 Maggi, *Satan's Rhetoric*, 8.

10 Krämer and Sprenger, *Malleus maleficarum*, 124–5.

11 Maggi, *Satan's Rhetoric*, 12.

12 Caciola, 'Discerning Spirits,' 246.

13 Skulsky, 'Cannibals vs. Demons in *Volpone*,' 303.

14 Caciola, 'Discerning Spirits,' 248–9.

15 This phrase is Caciola's, but in this specific demonic context, she draws upon more general studies of the body in this period such as Barker's *The Tremulous Private Body*.

16 Recognizing this ambiguity of the early modern self's response to demonic penetration follows a warning made by Stephen Greenblatt in *Renaissance Self-Fashioning*: 'There is no such thing as a single "history of the self" in the sixteenth century' (8). However, it would seem to problematize one of Greenblatt's ten 'governing conditions' for self-fashioning, namely that 'self-fashioning is achieved in relation to something perceived as alien, strange, or hostile. This threatening Other – heretic, savage, witch, adulteress, traitor, Antichrist – must be discovered or invented in order to be attacked and destroyed' (9). If people in the early modern period sometimes saw demons as enhancements to the self which they might even invite, then they were not uniformly condemning demons as something unwelcome and malign.

For a Spanish revival of the Platonic notion of poetic frenzy, see Carvallo, *Cisne de Apolo*, 359. For later appropriation by the Romantics of ancient Greek and Renaissance ideas about *daimones* and poetic creativity, see Burwick, *Poetic Madness and the Romantic Imagination*.

17 On the magic and Neoplatonism of Ficino and Campanella, see Walker, *Spiritual*

and Demonic Magic from Ficino to Campanella. For Bruno's views on the salubrious effects of some types of possession or 'furor,' see his 'De gli eroici furori.'

18 Curry, 'The Demonic Metaphysics of *Macbeth*,' 401–2.

19 For an account of the condemnation of enthusiasm as it was manifested by early modern Quakers and other religious dissidents, see Heyd's *'Be Sober and Reasonable.'*

20 This 'positive' view of melancholy (and thus of the *daemones* who cause it), first studied by Klibansky, Panofsky, and Saxl in *Saturn and Melancholy,* has since been elaborated by Winfried Schleiner in *Melancholy, Genius, and Utopia in the Renaissance.*

21 Schleiner, *Melancholy, Genius, and Utopia in the Renaissance,* 206.

22 Spalding, *Elizabethan Demonology,* 63–4.

23 Quoted in Thomas, *Religion and the Decline of Magic,* 479.

24 Ibid.

25 See Kamen, *The Spanish Inquisition.*

26 See Roth, *The Spanish Inquisition,* 201.

27 Gentilcore, *From Bishop to Witch,* 13.

28 On the epic genre's obligation to include epideictic rhetoric, see Vickers, 'Epideictic and Epic in the Renaissance'; Hardison, Jr., *The Enduring Monument*; and Kallendorf, *In Praise of Aeneas.*

29 For critics who have seen Satan as the true hero of Milton's epic, see Shelley ('A Defence of Poetry,' 512) and Dryden, about whom A.J.A. Waldock wrote that 'Dryden thought the Devil was Milton's hero' (*Paradise Lost and Its Critics,* 1). A more modern partial repetition of this view which emphasizes Satan's 'agony of ruined greatness' may be found in Empson, *Milton's God,* 69.

30 For this interpretation I am indebted to Kristine Haugen.

31 The formal similarities between exorcisms and conjurations have been studied by Richard Kieckhefer in chapter 6 of *Forbidden Rites.* However, I find his conclusions drawn from the inarguable formal similarities between exorcism and conjuration to be overstated. In fact, a close reading of Kieckhefer reveals his admission that the two phenomena are not in fact identical: 'Necromancers use the same formulas with very different intent. Orthodox exorcists and necromancers both use the terms "exorcise," "conjure," and "adjure" interchangeably … The difference, of course, is that while the orthodox exorcist is struggling to dispel demons, the necromancer is trying to allure and use them for his ends' (*Magic in the Middle Ages,* 166).

32 Kieckhefer, *Magic in the Middle Ages,* 153.

33 Marcellus says, 'Thou art a scholar, speak to it, Horatio' (*Hamlet,* 1.1.42). This and all subsequent references are to the *Riverside Shakespeare,* 1974, ed. G. Blakemore Evans. For a similar situation, see Quevedo, *Vida del buscón Don Pablos,* 89.

34 'Literature is not rigidly determined by the literary theory contemporaneous with it'

(Minnis, *Medieval Theory of Authorship*, 7). See also Minnis's chapter 5, 'Literary Theory and Literary Practice,' 160–210.

Introduction

1 Halpern, *The Poetics of Primitive Accumulation*, 2–3.
2 Ricoeur, 'The Critique of Religion,' 214–15.
3 Scot, *The Discouerie of Witchcraft*, 461–2. This and all subsequent references are to the 1584 edition, unless otherwise noted.
4 Ibid., 479.
5 Cox, *The Devil and the Sacred in English Drama*, 125.
6 Deacon and Walker, *Dialogicall Discourses of Spirits and Divels*, 18.
7 The traditional scholarly view has been that Reginald Scot's *Discouerie of Witchcraft* was ordered burned by the public hangman upon King James's accession to the throne. Contemporary evidence for this view is found in Gisbert Voet, *Selectarum disputationum theologicarum* ... (Utrecht: Joannes à Waesberge, 1659), 564. There is not, however, any other contemporary evidence to support this claim. On this debate see Estes, 'Reginald Scot and his *Discoverie of Witchcraft*,' 455 n. 44 (Estes cites Voet). See also Anglo, 'Reginald Scot's *Discoverie of Witchcraft*.'
8 Scot, *The Discouerie of Witchraft*, 489.
9 Mexico, Archivo General de la Nación, Inq., 523.3, fol. 340r, quoted in Cervantes, *The Devil in the New World*, 122.
10 Stephens, *Demon Lovers*, 341.
11 Quoted in Clark, *Thinking with Demons*, 306.
12 Cox, *The Devil and the Sacred in English Drama*, 156.
13 Ibid., 126.
14 Jameson, *The Prison House of Language*, 127.
15 Brad Gregory, a scholar of early modern martyrdom, also criticizes new cultural historians who work from atheistic or areligious assumptions (*Salvation at Stake*, 352–3).
16 Linda Woodbridge and Edward Berry, eds., *True Rites and Maimed Rites: Ritual and Anti-Ritual in Shakespeare and His Age* (Urbana: University of Illinois Press, 1992), 2, 19.
17 Most of my historical research, involving some eighty historical cases of actual exorcisms, will be published as a separate book-length study. Until then the work is available in the appendices to my dissertation, 'Exorcism and Its Texts: Demonic Possession in Early Modern Literature of England and Spain' (Princeton University, 2000).
18 Scholes, *Structuralism in Literature*, 158.
19 Barthes, 'The Structuralist Activity,' 157.
20 Frederic Jameson, 'Metacommentary,' *PMLA* 86 (1971): 9–18, p. 12.
21 Barthes, 'The Structuralist Activity,' 163.
22 Eliade, *The Sacred and the Profane*, 106–7. See also Eliade's *The Myth of the Eternal Return*, 35.

23 Ricoeur, *The Symbolism of Evil,* 5.

24 Lévi-Strauss, 'The Structural Study of Myth.' This essay first appeared in *Journal of American Folklore* 68.270 (1955): 428–44.

25 Ibid., 294.

26 Ibid., 312.

27 Ibid., 313.

28 Ibid., 307.

29 Ibid., 293–4.

30 Greimas, 'Comparative Mythology,' 4.

31 Lévi-Strauss, 'The Science of the Concrete,' 143. The concept of *bricolage* has been problematized by Jacques Derrida, who objects that 'as soon as we cease to believe in such an engineer [a *bricoleur*] and in a discourse which breaks with the received historical discourse, and as soon as we admit that every finite discourse is bound by a certain bricolage and that the engineer and the scientist are also species of bricoleurs, then the very idea of bricolage is menaced and the difference in which it took on its meaning breaks down' ('Structure, Sign and Play in the Discourse of the Human Sciences,' *Writing and Difference,* 285). Derrida does, however, attempt to 'rediscover the mythopoetical virtue of *bricolage*' (286).

32 Lévi-Strauss, 'The Science of the Concrete,' 146.

33 Ibid., 145.

34 Barthes, 'The Structuralist Activity,' 161–2.

35 See Propp, 'Study of the Wondertale.'

36 Ibid., 77.

37 Ibid., 79.

38 Propp defines a 'function' as 'the action of the character from the point of view of its significance for the progress of the narrative' (ibid., 74).

39 Propp, 'Fairy Tale Transformations,' 95.

40 Propp, as summarized by Robert Scholes in the section 'The Mythographers,' 63–4.

41 Propp, 'Fairy Tale Transformations,' 102. The other character types, or as Propp prefers, 'spheres of action,' are as follows:

(1) the villain
(2) the donor (provider)
(3) the helper
(4) the princess (a sought-for person) and her father
(5) the dispatcher
(6) the hero (seeker or victim)
(7) the false hero (Propp, as summarized by Scholes, 'The Mythographers,' 65).

42 Propp, 'Fairy Tale Transformations,' 102.

43 Ibid., 103.

44 Ibid., 102–9. Propp defines 'confessional substitution' thus: 'Current religion is also

capable of suppressing old forms, replacing them with new ones. Here we are involved with instances in which the devil functions as a winged messenger, or an angel is the donor of the magical tool, or an act of penance replaces the performance of a difficult task (the donor tests the hero). Certain legends are basically fairy tales in which all elements have undergone supporting substitutions. Christianity, Islam, and Buddhism are reflected in the fairy tales of the corresponding peoples' (ibid., 106).

45 Propp, 'Study of the Wondertale,' 77.
46 Clark, *Thinking with Demons*, 413.

1. Demoniacs in the Drama

1 Kantorowicz, *The King's Two Bodies: A Study in Medieval Political Theology.*
2 Bandello, *Novelle*, 2:44. Bandello lived from 1485 to 1562. The basic story line of this novella appears in altered form (involving different protagonists) in the Chronicle of Desclot, the *Crónica sarracina* of Pedro del Corral, the *Guerras civiles* of Ginés Pérez de Hita, and the *Historia de la Reyna Sebilla* (Seville, 1532). For a discussion of all of these chronicles, see Menéndez Pelayo's introduction to his edition of *La duquesa de la rosa*, xxv.
3 Juan de Timoneda, *El Patrañuelo* (Valencia: Joan Mey, 1567), ed. Federico Ruiz Morcuende (Madrid: Espasa-Calpe, 1973), 66–76.
4 This cloth was probably a small piece of fabric used to cover a jar of preserves (these cloths are still used today).
5 *La duquesa de la rosa*, 89. Emphasis mine.
6 Ibid.
7 Ibid., 90.
8 Gregory the Great, *Dialogues*, 18.
9 See M.M. Bakhtin, 'Images of the Material Bodily Lower Stratum,' chapter 6 of *Rabelais and His World*, 368–436.
10 Middleton, *A Game at Chess*, 5.3.105–7.
11 Dinzelbacher, *Heilige oder Hexen?* See especially the section 'Dämonische Gravidität' under the heading 'Schwangerschaft' (189–91).
12 *Richard III*, 1.3.227–9.
13 *3. Henry VI*, 5.6.51–2.
14 Latham, '*The Tempest* and King James's *Daemonologie*.'
15 Caciola, 'Discerning Spirits,' 14.
16 Greenblatt, 'Shakespeare and the Exorcists,' 111.
17 [Darrell], *A Briefe Apologie Proving the Possession of William Sommers*. These symptoms are repeated throughout the text.
18 Deacon and Walker, *Dialogicall Discourses of Spirits and Divels*, 4.
19 Scot, *The Discouerie of Witchcraft*, 128.

20 Maggi, *Satan's Rhetoric*, 117.

21 See Kittredge, 'King James I and *The Devil is an Ass.*'

22 Jonson, *The Devil is an Ass*, 5.3.124–7.

23 Ibid., 5.3.100–3.

24 Ibid., 5.3.1–8.

25 See Notestein, *A History of Witchcraft in England*, 92, but some scholars differentiate between Jonson's satire of *fraudulent* demoniacs and exorcists and what could have been a more pervasive satire of all demonic possession and exorcism (Reed, *The Occult on the Tudor and Stuart Stage*, 217–18).

26 See Evans, 'Contemporary Contexts of Jonson's *The Devil is an Ass*,' 162–3.

27 John Darrell addressed Popham directly in Darrell, Balmford, and Schilders, *The Triall of Maist. Dorrell.* See Sanders, 'A Parody of Lord Chief Justice Popham in *The Devil is an Ass*,' 529.

28 These two judges were associates of Coke. They were involved in the trial and execution of nine Leicestershire women in the case of John Smith (see note 21, above). Leah Marcus echoes Kittredge when she discusses these connections in *The Politics of Mirth*, 91–105.

29 Proponents of this view point to Jonson's 1618 complaint to Drummond about 'a play of his, upon which he was accused, The Divell is ane Ass ... The King desired him to conceal it' (*Jonson's Conversations with Drummond* [1619], ed. David Laing [London: Shakespeare Society, 1842], 28; cited in Kittredge, 'King James I and *The Devil is an Ass*,' 208). Kittredge speculates about the meaning of Jonson's complaint (208–9).

30 Kittredge offers this interpretation in connection with his theory that Jonson was writing in response to King James's recent involvement in the John Smith case ('King James I and *The Devil is an Ass*,' 208–9). For some qualifications to this view, see Marcus, *The Politics of Mirth*, 103. She explains that King James's involvement in the Overbury affair actually showed to what extent he still believed in demonic activity, so that any efforts to render Jonson's play an unqualified 'compliment' remain problematic. She also notes that the 1631 printed version of the play was not Jonson's original text (now lost), but a revised one (104). Marcus also believes, as I do, that the possession scene was not inserted at the end but was central to the play's conception from the beginning.

31 Cox, *The Devil and the Sacred in English Drama*, 158.

32 Reed, *Bedlam on the Jacobean Stage*, 120.

33 A fuller discussion of the material in this section appears in Hilaire Kallendorf, 'Exorcism and the Interstices of Language: Ruggle's *Ignoramus* and the Demonization of Renaissance English Neo-Latin,' in *Acta Conventus Neo-Latini Cantabrigiensis: Proceedings of the Eleventh International Congress of Neo-Latin Studies*, ed. Rhoda Schnur, 303–10, Medieval and Renaissance Texts and Studies, vol. 259 (Tempe, AZ: MRTS, 2003).

34 Scot, *The Discouerie of Witchcraft*, 496.

35 *Troilus and Cressida*, 4.4.90–1.
36 *Gammer Gurton's Needle*, 1.2.25–6.
37 Ibid., 3.4.18.
38 Ibid., 2.1.25.
39 Ibid., 1.2.18. On the effectiveness of the use of the demonic possession motif in this play, see Reed, *The Occult on the Tudor and Stuart Stage*, 213.
40 Marston, *The Malcontent*, 1.3.30–1.
41 See Clubb, *Giambattista della Porta: Dramatist*, 284.
42 Alan H. Nelson, ed., *Cambridge*, Records of Early English Drama (Toronto: University of Toronto Press, 1989), 1:542.
43 *The Letters of John Chamberlain*, ed. Norman Egbert McClure (Philadelphia: American Philosophical Society, 1939), 1:597–8.
44 For a full explanation of the legal satire in the play, see Tucker, '*Ignoramus* and Seventeenth-Century Satire of the Law.' Tucker has also prepared the facsimile edition of a manuscript of the play (Hildesheim: Georg Olms, 1987).
45 Two of the ballads were *Ignoramus, an excellent new song: to the tune of, Lay by your pleading, law lies a bleeding* (London, 1681) and *The Ignoramus ballad: to the tune of, Let Oliver now be forgotten* ([London?]: For N. T., 1681).
46 Ruggle, *Ignoramus*, Act 4, Scene 11, pp. 111, 112, 113.
47 Codrington, trans., *Ignoramus*, Act 4, Scene 11, sigs P4v, Q1r, Q2r.
48 In fact Hudibras is haunted by the astrologer Sidrophel's friends who dress up as fiends to thrash him and force him to confess his sins. As part of the dialogue on religious controversy running throughout the poem, the Voice explains exorcism to Hudibras during this thrashing scene. It says that devils enter Catholics more easily because they emphasize demonic activity by practising rituals such as exorcism:

> [The devil] [s]urprises none, but those wh' have Priests,
> To turn him out, and Exorcists,
> Supply'd with Spiritual Provision,
> And Magaz'nes of Ammunition:
> With Crosses, Relicks, Crucifixes,
> Beads, Pictures, Rosaries and Pixes:
> The Tools of working out Salvation,
> By meer Mechanick Operation.
> With Holy Water, like a Sluce,
> To overflow all Avenues.
> But those, wh' are utterly unarm'd,
> T'oppose his Entrance if he storm'd,
> He never offers to surprise ...   (Part III, Canto I, lines 1491–1503, pp. 230–1).

One scholar has referred to this scene as an 'exorcism' of Hudibras (see Van Gundy,

'*Ignoramus*,' 83). The scene may not constitute any sort of proper exorcism, particularly in view of the fact that Sidrophel's friends play the parts of both demons and exorcists, but the language of exorcism is obviously incorporated into the text.

49 George Steiner examines both the negative and the positive valences of the 'seemingly anarchic multiplicity of mutually non-communicating tongues' in *After Babel*, xiii.

50 For the seminal discussion of the sign, the signifier, and the signified, see Saussure, *Course in General Linguistics*, 65–78.

51 See Greenblatt, *Renaissance Self-Fashioning*.

52 Lodge, *The Diuel Coniured*, 24.

53 For a discussion of this Christianized fable (in which the fox becomes a type of the devil) as it appears in medieval bestiaries, Chaucer's 'Nun's Priest's Tale,' Renaissance English translations of Aesop, and Spenser's *Shepherd's Calendar*, see Hallett, 'The Satanic Nature of Volpone,' 41–3.

54 As we saw with *Ignoramus*, the fact that Voltore is a lawyer and is accused of being demon possessed merely echoes one of the commonplaces of seventeenth-century English satire of the law. See Tucker, '*Ignoramus* and Seventeenth-Century Satire of the Law,' 319.

55 *Volpone*, 5.10.10, 34.

56 Ibid., 5.10.49–50.

57 Ibid., 5.12.8–10. Corvino refers to the etymological distinction made in this period between possession and obsession, or torment from within versus torment from without.

58 Ibid., 5.12.21–35.

59 Yamada, '*Volpone* and *The Devil is an Ass*,' 204.

60 Brockbank, Introduction to his edition of *Volpone*, xxvi.

61 The play was first performed by Shakespeare's company, the King's Men, in 1605, presumably at the Globe (see Tulip, 'The Intertextualities of Ben Jonson's *Volpone*,' 27). The first Quarto of *Volpone* was published in 1607.

62 Tulip, 'The Contexts of *Volpone*,' 77, 82–3.

63 *Volpone*, 5.12.101–2.

64 Tulip, 'The Contexts of *Volpone*,' 80.

65 *All's Well That Ends Well*, 5.3.304–5. Stephen Greenblatt concludes from this line that 'by 1600, then, Shakespeare had clearly marked out possession and exorcism as frauds, so much so that in *All's Well That Ends Well* a few years later he could casually use the term exorcist as a synonym for illusion monger' ('Shakespeare and the Exorcists,' 115). I believe it is stretching the evidence to make this conclusion based on a single line out of context. Shakespeare was clearly familiar with the deceptive or counterfeit version of the exorcist figure, but he was also familiar with the genuine exorcist figure from which the counterfeit was derived.

66 These critics include the following: Greenblatt, 'Shakespeare and the Exorcists';

Hamilton, '*Twelfth Night*: The Errors of Exorcism,' in *Shakespeare and the Politics of Protestant England*, 86–110; and Schleiner, 'The Feste-Malvolio Scene in *Twelfth Night*.' For a fuller statement of Schleiner's views on this play, see his *Melancholy, Genius, and Utopia in the Renaissance*, 264–73.

67 Kernan, *Shakespeare, the King's Playwright*, 17.

68 Schleiner suggests that Feste refers to Festus, a biblical judge – a comparison used by John Darrell to appeal to Lord Chief Justice Popham ('The Feste-Malvolio Scene in *Twelfth Night*,' 54). See Darrell, Balmford, and Schilders, *The Triall of Maist. Dorrell*, 4.

69 Hamilton believes that Malvolio's letter to Olivia bears the resonance of Darrell's and other exorcists' letters from prison (*Shakespeare and the Politics of Protestant England*, 101).

70 Greenblatt, 'Shakespeare and the Exorcists,' 115. *Twelfth Night* does take a position of mockery and scepticism, but many other scholars have seen the play as more problematic than the simple satire Greenblatt would make of it. See Barber, *Shakespeare's Festive Comedy*, 255, and Reed, *The Occult on the Tudor and Stuart Stage*, 216.

71 *Twelfth Night*, 2.3.146. On the question of Malvolio's Puritanism, see Simmons, 'A Source for Shakespeare's Malvolio.' He argues that Malvolio's whimsical interpretation of the planted letter refers to the alleged excesses of the Puritans' exegesis of scripture. He also sees Malvolio's desire to marry Olivia as a threat to overturn the foundation of order in the household; this threat might then reflect Anabaptist aspirations to overturn established social hierarchies (186).

72 *Twelfth Night*, 3.4.84–6, 91. Donna Hamilton speculates about the potential sources for these lines, and suggests two: Harsnett's *Declaration* and Darrell's *Detection* (*Shakespeare and the Politics of Protestant England*, 98). But the word 'Legion,' derived from the biblical account in Luke 8:27–33, is so common in exorcistic lore that it would be difficult to trace a specific source.

73 *Twelfth Night*, 3.4.102. For this allusion, Hamilton proposes several possible sources, the Darrell books as well as Deacon and Walker (*Shakespeare and the Politics of Protestant England*, 98). Again, however, it would be impossible to identify a specific textual parallel; I have seen many other references to the same indicator of possession in other contemporaneous pamphlets. A variation on this procedure was to place a patient's urine over a fire to see whether it foamed; if it did not, then the patient was assumed to be bewitched (Midelfort, *Mad Princes of Renaissance Germany*, 108).

74 I do not agree with Winfried Schleiner that the only significance here is an infraction of the Puritan dress code ('The Feste-Malvolio Scene in *Twelfth Night*,' 50).

75 Briggs, *Pale Hecate's Team*, 75. The references to Pythagoras are meant to refer to this uncovering of potentially unnatural knowledge.

76 *Twelfth Night*, 4.2.113–14.

77 Schleiner speculates in 'The Feste-Malvolio Scene in *Twelfth Night*' that Sir Topas's

name is a corruption of 'topaz,' a stone which, according to Reginald Scot, healed
lunatics. See Scot, *The Discouerie of Witchcraft*, 294. Schleiner further speculates that
Sir Topas might have reminded some playgoers of Sir Tophas of Lyly's *Endimion*, a
character who has been seen to represent the Puritan Stephen Gosson, author of *The
School of Abuse* and arch-foe of the theatre (Schleiner, *Melancholy, Genius, and Utopia*,
270–1).

78 *Twelfth Night*, 4.2.5–6.
79 Ibid., 4.2.19.
80 Darrell, *True Narration*, 10.
81 *Twelfth Night*, 4.2.96–7. The words also appear in Harsnett's *Discovery*, George
   More's (John Darrell's assistant's) treatise, and the Marprelate tracts; they are part of a
   continuing cultural dialogue, a fragment of a discourse, 'an idiom widely used in
   English religious polemical writing to discredit someone's religious position' (Hamilton, *Shakespeare and the Politics of Protestant England*, 100–1). See, for example,
   Harsnett, *Discovery*, and More, *A True Discourse*, 9.
82 *Twelfth Night*, 4.2.25–6.
83 Ibid., 4.2.31–3.
84 Schleiner, *Melancholy, Genius, and Utopia*, 272.
85 *Twelfth Night*, 4.2.120–2.
86 Hamilton, *Shakespeare and the Politics of Protestant England*, 101.
87 See Grazzini, *Teatro di Grazzini*, 590–2.
88 Weyer, *De praestigiis daemonum* (1563).
89 Clark, Introduction to his edition of *The Bugbears*, 85.
90 *The Bugbears*, 3.3.100–103.
91 Ibid., 5.2.22–3.
92 Ibid., 5.2.120–7.
93 Ibid., 5.8.16–17.
94 Ibid., 3.3.112–25.
95 Clark, ed., *The Bugbears*, 82.
96 Ibid., 88.
97 *As You Like It*, 3.2.400–2.
98 *Romeo and Juliet*, 1.2.54–6.
99 *The Bugbears*, 5.2.34.
100 Hobbes, *Leviathan*, 77–80.
101 On Shakespeare's adaptation of Plautus, see Miola, *Shakespeare and Classical
    Comedy.*
102 Hamilton, '*The Comedy of Errors*: The Parody of Errors and Heresies,' in *Shakespeare
    and the Politics of Protestant England*, 59–85.
103 Greenblatt, 'Shakespeare and the Exorcists,' 115.
104 Briggs, *Pale Hecate's Team*, 72–3.

105 *The Comedy of Errors*, 4.4.47–8.

106 Ibid., 4.4.54–7.

107 Ibid., 4.4.58.

108 Ibid., 4.4.107.

109 Ibid., 4.4.92–4.

110 Ibid., 5.1.242–51.

111 Reed, *The Occult on the Tudor and Stuart Stage*, 214–15.

112 *The Comedy of Errors*, 4.3.48.

113 See Newman, 'Possessed by the Spirit.'

114 *The Comedy of Errors*, 5.1.39–41.

115 Ibid., 5.1.102–5.

116 Briggs, *Pale Hecate's Team*, 73.

117 Reed, *The Occult on the Tudor and Stuart Stage*, 214.

118 Ibid., 215.

119 Hamilton, *Shakespeare and the Politics of Protestant England*, 79–80.

120 On Shakespeare's attitude toward the nonconformists in *Twelfth Night*, see Simmons, 'A Source for Shakespeare's Malvolio.'

121 Maggi, *Satan's Rhetoric*, 119.

122 For a discussion of this procedure of 'blowing as a sign of exorcism and cleansing,' see Hill, 'When God Blew Satan Out of Heaven,' 133.

123 M'Clintock and Strong, 'Exorcism, Exorcist,' 417.

124 Scot, *The Discouerie of Witchcraft*, 440.

125 Ibid., 447.

126 Ibid., 441.

127 'This expression occurs in [Shakespeare's] "Sonnet cxliv," and evidently with the meaning here explained; only the bad angel is supposed to fire out the good one' (Spalding, *Elizabethan Demonology*, 80n).

128 Ibid., 80; taken from Harsnett and others.

129 *Los menemnos*, Scena 12, p. 97.

130 Ibid., Scena 13, p. 98.

131 Ibid.

132 Ibid.

133 For one scholar concerned with 'the extension of time across the body' and other issues of subjectivity, see Smith, *Discerning the Subject*. For a study of the body in Spanish literature of the time period we are discussing, see Read, *Visions in Exile*.

134 Violence inflicted on the body is discussed in 'The Body of the Condemned,' the first section of part 1, 'Torture,' in Foucault, *Discipline and Punish*.

135 He adds that they are mistaken because the only remedy is prayer (Lodge, *The Diuel Coniured*, 25). The fish liver passage appears in Tobias 6:19, in which the angel

Raphael instructs Tobias: 'And on that night (Tobias's wedding night) lay the liver of the fish on the fire, and the devil shall be driven away' (Douay Bible).

136 This character has been seen as a type of Queen Elizabeth. See Munns, '"The Golden Days of Queen Elizabeth."'

137 The name Smerk may refer to Marvell's Mr Smirk in his condemnation of the archbishop of Canterbury (Marvell, *Mr. Smirke*). On this connection see Slagle, 'Thomas Shadwell's Censored Comedy,' 59.

138 This play contains a couple of glancing allusions to demonic possession and exorcism, as in Doughty's line, 'Had I a sonne to serve mee so, I would conure a divell out of him' (1.1.300–1), or the soldier's remark, 'That spight of all these Rats, Cats, Wezells, Witches / Or Dogges, or Divels, Shall so coniure them / I'le quiet my possession' (2.1.809–11). For Shadwell's reliance on this earlier play, see Berry, 'The Globe Bewitched and *El Hombre Fiel*,' 223.

139 Shadwell, *The Lancashire-Witches, and Tegue o Divelly the Irish Priest*, 36.

140 The censor was Charles Killigrew, Master of the Revels, who first licensed the play without much alteration but then, a month before the first performance, censored the passages because powerful persons found them offensive. These powerful persons later hired mercenaries to hiss at the performance. Some of the censored passages having to do with 'superstition' may be read as an indirect commentary on what many believed to be the 'superstition' of the divine right of kings. For a discussion of the play's censorship, and of Shadwell's possible debt to Hobbes's *Leviathan*, see Slagle, 'Thomas Shadwell's Censored Comedy.'

141 The clerics are so connected to the witches in the play's imagery that at one point, the Catholic priest has sex with a witch. Slagle explains: 'Both religious men are afraid of the witches and, because of their superstition and absurdity, form a parallel to the witches, who provide yet another plot and emphasize not so much the religious conflict as the similarities between the Catholic and Protestant priests. One obvious connection is between the witches' ritual and the high-church Anglican and Catholic ritual abhorred by the Whigs' (Slagle, 'Thomas Shadwell's Censored Comedy,' 60). Slagle alludes to the fact that witches' Sabbats were often obscene parodies of the Catholic mass.

142 See Slagle, 'Thomas Shadwell's Censored Comedy,' 55.

143 Munns, '"The Golden Days of Queen Elizabeth,"' 199. Marsden, however, claims that 'the witches are seen only by the irrational (or politically suspect) characters' ('Ideology, Sex, and Satire,' 53).

144 Armistead, 'Occultism in Restoration Drama,' 62.

145 The play also contains a male devil in the shape of a goat who appears briefly in Act 2 to lead the witches. He is merely a figurehead, however, and remains unimportant for the play's action.

   For another example of a dramatic work about witches that nonetheless also contains an element of exorcism, see Moreto, *Entremés de las brujas*. In this interlude, the only element of exorcism is a brief sprinkling with holy water.

146 Shadwell, *The Lancashire-Witches*, Act 4, lines 263, 271–89, 294, pp. 144–5.

147 For this notion of presence, see Jacques Derrida, 'Structure, Sign and Play in the Discourse of the Human Sciences,' in *Writing and Difference*, 292.

148 Vélez de Guevara, Rojas Zorrilla, and Mira de Amescua, *El pleyto que tuvo el diablo con el cura de Madrilejos*. All quotations are from this *suelta*. The play was first printed with the slightly different title, *El pleito que puso al diablo el cura de Madrilejos* (The lawsuit that the priest of Madrilejos brought against the devil) in the *Flor de las mejores doze comedias de los mayores ingenios de España* (Madrid, 1652). It was reprinted in Lisbon in 1653 and then appeared many times thereafter as a *comedia suelta*.

149 This dating, based on an internal reference to the forbidding of *copetes* (which occurred in Spain in 1639), is the approximation of Spencer and Schevill (*The Dramatic Works of Luís Vélez de Guevara*, 339).

150 (N.p.: n.p., 1608). In the near future I intend to pursue this topic at greater length.

151 Some scholars have felt that this act also bears some touches, at least, from the pen of Mira de Amescua. See Anibal, 'Voces del cielo – A Note on Mira de Amescua,' 63–4.

152 *El pleyto que tuvo el diablo con el cura de Madrilejos*, 29.

153 For a discussion of exorcism in terms of a formal *quaestio*, see Wilson, 'The Histrionics of Exorcism: Isabela Castrucha,' 232.

154 *El pleyto que tuvo el diablo con el cura de Madrilejos*, 29.

155 The following lines are spoken about Latin in the Spanish play:

> CURA: [A]dora a la Trinidad,
>   y di en Latin que la adoras.
> ROSELA: Do adorationem Saçtissimae
>   Triadiae.
>
> (PRIEST: Adore the Trinity,
>   And say in Latin that you adore it.
> ROSELA: I give adoration to the Most Holy Trinity.)
>   (*El pleyto que tuvo el diablo con el cura de Madrilejos*, 30).

156 Scot, *The Discouerie of Witchcraft*, 442.

157 See Nischan, 'The Exorcism Controversy and Baptism in the Late Reformation.'

158 James VI of Scotland and I of England, *Daemonologie*, 63.

159 See, for example, his *El diablo cojuelo* (1641). This work is about a devil who is crippled after his fall from heaven. His clever observations about human society make great satire – but note that it is human beings, not demons, who are being satirized.

160 Christian, *Local Religion in Sixteenth-Century Spain*, 30.

161 Cox, *The Devil and the Sacred in English Drama*, 2, emphasis mine.

162 The phrases in this sentence refer to two rich scholarly studies: Kernan, *Shakespeare, the King's Playwright*, and Mullaney, 'Apprehending Subjects.'

163 This phrase refers to Pye, '*Macbeth* and the Politics of Rapture,' in *The Regal Phantasm*. This study shows how King James I would have seen in *Macbeth* allusions to himself and his notorious investigations of alleged demoniacs in 'rapture.'

164 I intend to explore the historical context of the play and the many exorcisms performed upon King Carlos II in the Alcázar Real, elsewhere in the near future.

165 Dowling, 'La farsa al servicio del naciente siglo de las luces,' 2:275.

166 Caro Baroja affirms that the play was performed before Carlos II, a conclusion he reached only belatedly: 'En algún sitio se indicaba que la comedia se representó ante el mismo Carlos II, lo cual se ha desmentido, también alguna vez, así como que fuera burla del pobre rey. Me parecía poco probable, dado la vago de la referencia, que un joven, empleado en varios organismos del Estado, se atreviera a poner en solfa lo que se decía y repetía en Madrid respecto a hechizos, que llegaban al corazón de palacio y minaban la salud del rey; dichos sobre los que incluso especulaban en sus despachos, los embajadores de las grandes potencias. Pero parece que no hay lugar a dudas ... Ahora no tengo ya porque dudar de que Zamora, a los treinta y tantos años, compuso su obra mejor ... antes de que el asunto de los hechizos llegara al punto más crítico: dos antes de que muriera el rey ... Acaso se compuso con la intención de alegrar y despejar a la par el apocado ánimo real; pero también, produjo un efecto contraproducente y se vió una intención satírica que daría lugar a la opinión luego repetida de que era una burla de la situación del mismo rey. Que sufriera "enmiendas" puede ser debido a esto ... pero nadie se ha preocupado de averiguar por qué ... El caso es que Zamora cobra más relieve, si cabe, con el advenimiento de Felipe V, del que fue un partidario ardiente y en su reinado tuvieron el éxito mayor esta y otras obras concebidas con intención parecida ...' (In some place it was indicated that the comedy was represented before Charles II himself, which has been belied, also some time, as if it were a joke about the poor king. It appeared to me not very probable, given the vagueness of the reference, that a young man, employed in the various organisms of the state, would dare to arrange artfully what was being said and repeated in Madrid with respect to bewitchments, that they arrived at the heart of the palace and sapped the health of the king; sayings about which even the ambassadors of the great powers speculated in their dispatches. But it appears that there is no room for doubt ... Now I have no reason to doubt that Zamora, at thirty-something years old, composed his best work ... before the matter of the bewitchments arrived at the most critical point: two [years] before the king died ... Perhaps it was composed with the intention of cheering and relieving at the same level the diminished royal spirit; but also, it produced a counterproduc-

tive effect[,] and there was seen a satirical intention that would give place to the opinion later repeated that it was a joke about the situation of the king himself. That it suffered 'emendations' could be owed to this ... but no one has preoccupied himself to verify why ... The case is that Zamora recovers more relief, if it fits, with the coming to power of Philip V, of whom he was an ardent partisan[,] and in his reign this and other works, conceived with a similar intention, succeeded ...) (Caro Baroja, *Teatro popular y magia*, 141–2).

167 See Bakhtin, 'Popular-Festive Forms and Images in Rabelais,' chapter 3 in *Rabelais and His World*, and Bristol, *Carnival and Theater.*

168 *El hechizado por fuerza*, 1.785–6. Claudio describes himself as 'hecho un armario de huesos, / con reumatismo y tos' (made a cabinet of bones, / with rheumatism and cough) (3.181–2).

169 The lengthy lists of symptoms appear in the play in 3.295–335.

170 *El hechizado por fuerza*, 3.898.

171 Ibid., 2.769–72.

172 Caro Baroja, *Teatro popular y magia*, 153–4. He adds, 'Los detalles que el criado Picatoste da a Don Claudio en la escena primera del acto segundo, acerca de las artes de Lucigüela, son como un compendio de las creencias que quería satirizar Zamora' (The details that the servant Picatoste gives to Don Claudio in the first scene of the second act, about the arts of Lucigüela, are like a compendium of the beliefs that Zamora wanted to satirize) (144–5).

173 Ibid., 146.

174 'El rey gozaría de la farsa que presenciaba sin verse a sí mismo representado en ese papel' (The king would enjoy the farce that he witnessed without seeing himself represented in that role) (introduction to Ebersole's editon of the play, 13).

175 Dowling, 'La farsa al servicio,' 280.

176 Bristol, *Carnival and Theater*, 185 and 183. Bristol borrows this Latin phrase from Kantorowicz, *The King's Two Bodies*. He borrows the term 'uncrowning' from the following discussion in Bakhtin: 'He [the king] is abused and beaten when the time of his reign is over, just as the carnival dummy of winter or of the dying year is mocked, beaten, torn to pieces, burned, or drowned even in our time ... It is the king's uncrowning' (*Rabelais and His World*, 197). For a discussion of how such rituals as uncrowning look forward to future reigns, see 256.

177 Bristol, *Carnival and Theatre*, 184–5.

178 Ibid., 185.

179 *Carnestolendas* was celebrated three Carnival days before Ash Wednesday.

180 Dowling, 'La farsa al servicio,' 275. The *suelta* bears the shelf mark (*signatura*) T/6366.

181 Ibid., 281.

182 The painting depicts the scene in which Don Claudio speaks the lines:

Lámpara descomunal,
cuyo reflejo civil
me va a moco de candil
chupando el óleo vital ...

(Extraordinary lamp,
whose civil reflection
goes to me like the drippings of a candle
sucking the vital oil ...) (2.757–60).

Goya sold his painting, titled *La lámpara descomunal*, to the dukes of Osuna for their recreation house, El Capricho, on the outskirts of Madrid near the village of Barajas (Dowling, 'La farsa al servicio,' 283). The painting has since been renamed *La lámpara del diablo*.

183 This transition to the Enlightenment's rejection of superstition by such intellectuals as Benito Gerónimo Feijóo y Montenegro has been analysed by Richard Herr in *The Eighteenth-Century Revolution in Spain*, especially the third chapter, 'The Enlightenment Enters Spain,' 37–85.

184 Bawcutt, 'Middleton's *The Phoenix* as a Royal Play,' 287. It was also performed publicly by the Children of Paul's before the first quarto was published in 1607. The title page of this first quarto reads 'as it hath beene sundrye times Acted by the Children of Paules, And presented before his Maiestie' (Williamson, '*The Phoenix*,' 183).

185 On this connection, see Davidson, '*The Phoenix*: Middleton's Didactic Comedy,' 122n8.

186 See Dodson, 'King James and *The Phoenix* – Again,' 434.

187 Raleigh was executed in 1618 as a result of these charges, although the evidence found against him was inconclusive. William Power suggests that Proditor's fate of banishment was Middleton's only dramatic solution to his political quandary of how to represent Raleigh onstage ('*The Phoenix*, Raleigh, and King James,' 60).

188 Dessen, 'Middleton's *The Phoenix* and the Allegorical Tradition,' 293.

189 On this point, see Kistner and Kistner, '*The Family of Love* and *The Phoenix*,' 188.

190 The plot device of the ruler in disguise was also utilized in Shakespeare's *Measure for Measure*, Marston's *The Malcontent* and *The Fawn*, Sharpham's *The Fleire* (1606), and Day's *Law Tricke* (1604) and *Humour Out of Breath* (1607–8) (Brooks, introduction to his edition of *The Phoenix*, 69). For a New Historicist discussion of the 'ruler in disguise' plot device, see Dollimore, 'Transgression and Surveillance in *Measure for Measure*.' For an aggressively anti-New Historicist reading of the same plot device, see Kamps, 'Ruling Fantasies and the Fantasies of Rule.'

191 *The Phoenix*, 5.1.273–341.

192   On the tradition of demon-possessed lawyers on the English stage, see Tucker, '*Igno-ramus* and Seventeenth-Century Satire of the Law.'

193   Jonson, *The Poetaster* (1602), 5.3. The passage from Spenser reads thus:

[Mother Error] spewed out of her filthy maw
A floud of poyson horrible and blacke,
Full of great lumpes of flesh and gobbets raw,
Which stunck so vildly, that it forst [Redcrosse] slacke
His grasping hold, and from her turne him backe:
Her vomit full of bookes and papers was,
With loathly frogs and toades, which eyes did lacke ...
(*The Faerie Queene*, Book I, Canto I, 20.1–7)

194   Greenblatt, 'Loudun and London,' 340, 344.

195   See Greenblatt, 'Towards a Poetics of Culture.' See also Montrose, 'Professing the Renaissance.'

196   Frye, 'Literature as Therapy,' 30. See also Barber, *Shakespeare's Festive Comedy.*

197   Mahood, '*A Midsummer Night's Dream* as Exorcism.'

198   On exorcism as a public baroque spectacle, see Weber, 'L'exorcisme à la fin du XVIe siècle.'

199   Bettelheim, *The Uses of Enchantment*, 7.

2. Possessed *Pícaros* and Satanic Satire

1   The distinction between the two genres is well articulated by Scholes and Kellogg (*The Nature of Narrative*, 74). For an article which makes convincing connections between the two genres, and in particular between the *Lazarillo* and the satirical genre, see Parr, 'La estructura satírica del *Lazarillo*.'

2   For this definition of satire I am indebted to Lía Schwartz Lerner's article 'Golden Age Satire: Transformations of Genre,' 271.

3   One clear exception to this trend is Harry Sieber's Derridian reading of the episode in *Language and Society in* La vida de Lazarillo de Tormes, 59–73.

4   For a sense of the more typical recurrence in other episodes of the active first-person pronouns used by the protagonist, see Jauss, 'Ursprung und Bedeutung der Ich-Form im *Lazarillo de Tormes*.'

5   It has been suggested that one possible source for the plot of the episode is Masuccio Salernitano's *Il Novellino*. In it Fra Girolano, the figure equivalent to the pardoner of the *Lazarillo*, dupes the congregation into believing that a relic he holds is the arm of Judas. He uses the relic to 'heal' his accomplice, who has fallen down half dead (Cisneros, *El* Lazarillo de Tormes, 191). Fernando Lázaro Carreter also thinks it significant for this episode that the first Spanish translator of Apuleius, López de Cortegana, transformed the Syrian priests into *bulderos* (*'Lazarillo de Tormes' en la*

picaresca, 160). The clerical tricksters of semipopular works such as the *Speculum cer-retanorum* and the various texts of the *Liber vagatorum* tradition may also have influenced this episode (Sieber, *Language and Society in* La vida de Lazarillo de Tormes, 63). There is one particular episode in a Flemish *Liber vagatorum* which bears a striking resemblance to this one (García de la Concha, 'La intención religiosa del *Lazarillo*,' 269).

6 Willis, 'Lazarillo and the Pardoner,' 275. García de la Concha also sees some continuity between this master of Lazarillo and two of his previous masters, the blind man and the squire ('La intención religiosa del *Lazarillo*,' 258).

7 For the importance of the triptych pattern for the organization of the work as a whole, see García de la Concha, 'La estructura ternaria del *Lazarillo de Tormes*.'

8 For a discussion of this dishonourable situation and the irony of Lázaro's position as town crier, see Vilanova, 'Lázaro de Tormes, pregonero de su propia deshonra.' Stephen Gilman describes Lazarillo's end as a spiritual death ('The Death of Lazarillo de Tormes,' 153).

9 Gethin Hughes also voices the need for a transition here ('"Lazarillo de Tormes": The Fifth "Tratado"'). García de la Concha had previously made the same point ('La intención religiosa del *Lazarillo*,' 259).

10 The new edition, *Lazarillo de Tormes castigado*, first appeared in Bartolomé de Torres Naharro's *Propaladia* (Madrid, 1573). Versions of the text as it was revised by López de Velasco were reprinted in at least 1586, 1599, 1603, 1632, 1664, and 1769. I have seen the 1769 edition, which appeared (like several of the others) as an appendix to an entertaining courtesy manual, Lucás Gracián Dantisco's *Galateo español* (Valencia: Benito Monfort, 1769).

11 Feigned demonic possession was a common problem in the early modern period. For an exposé of fake possession in France at this time, see Pithoys, *La descovvertvure des faux possedez*. The problem was current in Spain as well, especially among the *beatas* who would feign ecstasy or possession to gain a reputation for holiness or to attract attention. For a study of these women which specifically invokes the literary motif of the picaresque heroine, see Huerga, 'La picaresca de las beatas,' and Imirizaldu, *Monjas y beatas embaucadoras*.

12 Strictly speaking, there is a fine distinction between bulls and indulgences. Sieber explains it in Derridian terms: 'The bull as a piece of paper is the sign; the indulgence, the signified. In buying the bull, the pardoner will argue (as did the Church), one simultaneously acquires its power (indulgence)' (*Language and Society in* La vida de Lazarillo de Tormes, 60). Sieber further explains that a bull cost two *reales*, that bulls became more valuable than money in the economy of the time, that the presses used for printing them were heavily guarded, and that the efficacy of a stolen bull supposedly evaporated (63–4). The bulls could be purchased on a forty-day credit, with the town council responsible for collecting the money later; the pardoners were paid on

commission, and they were so unscrupulous in convincing poor people to buy them that some had their property confiscated in lieu of payment (64–6). Sieber cites one extensive article as his primary source for this information: José Goñi Gaztambide, 'Los cuestores en España y la regalía de indulgencias,' *Hispania sacra* 2 (1949): 3–45, 285–310.

13 *La vida de Lazarillo de Tormes*, Tratado V, 49–50.

14 Ibid., 51.

15 I.M. Lewis describes this economic aspect of the experience of demonic possession in relation to the types of characters who populate picaresque fiction: 'Clearly, in this context, possession works to help the interests of the weak and downtrodden who have otherwise few effective means to press their claims for attention and respect' (*Ecstatic Religion*, 32–3).

16 *La vida de Lazarillo de Tormes*, 56. Sieber compares Lazarillo instead to the pardoner: 'Lázaro ... playing the role of a metaphoric *buldero* ... succeeds in "selling" ... his autobiography' (*Language and Society in* La vida de Lazarillo de Tormes, 62). I think this interpretation is less convincing than a comparison of Lazarillo to the *alguacil*.

17 García de la Concha comments on the attention with which Lazarillo watches and learns from the specific gestures of both the *alguacil* and the *buldero* ('La intención religiosa del *Lazarillo*,' 258).

18 For an Erasmian interpretation, see O'Reilly, 'The Erasmianism of *Lazarillo de Tormes*.' For a scholar who questions the Erasmian view, see Hanrahan, '*Lazarillo de Tormes*: Erasmian Satire or Protestant Reform?'

   The best account of the diffusion of Erasmus's ideas in Golden Age Spain is still found in Bataillon, *Erasmo y España*. Bataillon considered the *Lazarillo* explicitly in its Erasmian context, although he believed that the text showed the literary influence of Erasmus without necessarily demonstrating Erasmian spirituality (*Novedad y fecundidad del* Lazarillo de Tormes, 17).

19 García de la Concha, in 'La intención religiosa del *Lazarillo*,' summarizes the controversy among various scholars about the reasons for the anonymity of the author of the *Lazarillo* (243). He then provides a more balanced view of the religious aspects of the work, not attempting to reduce the author's allegiance to strict Erasmianism, illuminism, or crypto-Judaism.

20 Erasmus makes fun of popular credulity in the efficacy of indulgences (*Praise of Folly*, 114).

21 See Thompson, 'Erasmus, More, and the Conjuration of Spirits.'

22 One exception to this is Sieber, who does use the word 'exorcism' but does not explain it at all (*Language and Society in* La vida de Lazarillo de Tormes, 70).

23 Foucault, *Madness and Civilization*, 22.

24 See Kaiser, *Praisers of Folly*, 296.

25 Quevedo, *Vida del buscón Don Pablos*, 89.

26 Quevedo, *Poesía original completa*, poem #748, ll. 1–4, pp. 898–901. The poem is dated by Blecua, the editor, to after 1610.

27 There are multiple pictorial depictions of this legend. Seven of them, all bearing the title *The Temptation of St Anthony*, are to be found in the Musées Royaux des Beaux-Arts de Belgique in Brussels. They were painted by David Teniers II (1610–90), an anonymous painter of the South-Netherlandish School (first quarter of the sixteenth century), Hieronymous Bosch (early 1500s), Aertgen van Leyden (1498–1564), the Master of the Armoire de Sacristie de Kaufbeuren, École de Souabe (fl. 1480–90), Pieter Huys of Antwerp (1545–81), and Cornelis Massys, also of Antwerp (1531–62).

28 Line 71. Quevedo probably saw Bosch's paintings hanging in the Escorial. Today various versions of Bosch's *The Temptations of St Anthony* hang there in the prior's lower cell, including one by Bosch's school and another copy made in the monastery. Various other original paintings by Bosch remain in the same room, including *The Ascent to Calvary*, *The Hay Cart*, and *The Crown of Thorns*.

29 Poem #757, l. 40, pp. 932–7. The poem begins with the line, 'Lindo gusto tiene el Tiempo.' This poem is dated by Blecua to after 1613.

30 This poem, #713, begins with the line, 'Una picaza de estrado.'

31 Quevedo's references to exorcism in his poetry are not limited to the satirical poems. He also used the language of demonic possession to characterize Orlando's madness in his adaptation of Ariosto's *Orlando furioso*. In his 'Poema heroico de las necedades y locuras de Orlando el enamorado,' Quevedo begins the poem with references to both Orlando and Ferragut as being demonically possessed:

> Canto los disparates, las locuras,
> los furores de Orlando enamorado,
> cuando el seso y razón le dejó a escuras
> el dios enjerto en diablo y en pecado;
> y las desventuradas aventuras
> de Ferragut, guerrero endemoniado ...
>
> (I sing the foolish deeds, the crazy things,
> the furies of Orlando in love,
> when the sense and the reason left him in the dark
> the god grafted onto devil and sin;
> and the unfortunate adventures
> of Ferragut, demoniac warrior ...)   (Canto 1, ll. 1–6)

Later in the same poem he makes reference to the 'endiablado mago impío' (bedeviled impious magician) (l. 963) and to 'demonios que van con espigones / huyendo de reliquias, conjurados ...' (demons that go with irritation / fleeing from relics, conjured ...) (Canto 2, ll. 353–4).

32 See Buendia, 'Índice de obras apócrifas,' 1367. Buendia mentions another possible

author, Félix Persio Bertizo, but notes that this might be a pseudonym. The *entremés* was first published in the 1706 Lisbon edition of the *Comedias portuguezas, Feytas pelo excellente Poeta Simaon Machado.*

33 For example, *El caballero de la Tenaza, La venta, El marido fantasma, El hospital de los mal casados,* and *Los refranes del viejo celoso.* See Asensio, *Itinerario del entremés.* For a study of selected *entremeses* by Quevedo, see Mancini, *Gli entremeses nell'arte di Quevedo.* Mancini does not, however, discuss the *Entremés famoso de la endemoniada fingida y chistes de Bacallao.*

34 Fernández-Guerra also thought the *entremés* was Quevedo's. He did not, however, attribute the *romance* 'El exorcista Calabrés' to Quevedo. Instead he listed it under 'Obras apócrifas' in his inventory. See his edition of Quevedo's *Obras,* Biblioteca de autores españoles, vol. 23 (Madrid: Atlas, 1946), xc–xci.

35 *Entremés famoso de la endemoniada fingida y chistes de Bacallao,* 506.

36 Ibid., 507.

37 Ibid., 503.

38 These sonnets begin with the lines, 'Conozcan los monarcas a Velilla' and 'O el viento, sabidor de lo futuro' (Blecua ed., #568, p. 550 and #92, p. 73). See Quevedo, *Sueños y discursos,* 2:1040.

39 Nolting-Hauff, *Visión, sátira y agudeza,* 249.

40 Francisco de Quevedo y Villegas, *Discurso del alguacil endemoniado,* in *Sueños y discursos* (1 vol.), 158–60. All quotations from the *Discurso del alguacil endemoniado* are taken from this edition unless noted otherwise.

41 Ibid., 160.

42 See Quevedo, *Sueños y discursos,* 2:1055.

43 *Discurso del alguacil endemoniado,* 164.

44 Nolting-Hauff, *Visión, sátira y agudeza,* 85.

45 Sieber, 'The Narrators in Quevedo's *Sueños,*' 106.

46 Ibid.

47 Piero Camporesi echoes this lament in *The Fear of Hell,* vi.

48 Ibid., 8, 28.

49 Loyola, *Spiritual Exercises,* 59.

50 Signorelli's frescoes are two in a series depicting *The Last Judgment* in the Cappella della Madonna di S. Brizio in the Cathedral of Orvieto. Bosch's *Last Judgment* is in the Kunsthistorisches Museum, Vienna. Bruegel's *The Fall of the Rebel Angels* is in the Musées Royaux des Beaux-Arts de Belgique in Brussels. Huys's *The Last Judgment* is in the same museum, as is Van Orley's portrayal of the rich man in hell, found on the back of his tryptich *The Virtue of Patience.* The school of Bruegel's *Triumph of Death* is in the Kunstmuseum in Basel. Michelangelo's masterpiece is in the Sistine Chapel in Rome.

51 For another view of baroque conceptions of hell, see Walker, *The Decline of Hell.*

52 See Sharpe, *Instruments of Darkness*, 199. Sharpe cites Bee, *The Most Wonderfull and True Storie of a Certain Witch named Alse Gooderige of Stapen Hill*, 31.

53 Jollie, *The Surey Demoniack*, 15.

54 Blagrave, *Blagraves Astrological Practice of Physick*, 122.

55 Jollie, *The Surey Demoniack*, 23–4.

56 Taylor, *The devil turn'd casuist*, 4.

57 James VI of Scotland and I of England, *Daemonologie*, 62.

58 Taylor, *The devil turn'd casuist*, 5. Taylor quotes Aquinas: '*Salutiferum nobis dogma datur, ne credamus Daemonibus, quantumcunque denuntient veritatem*' (This salutary dogma is given to us, that we not believe Demons, even so much as they pronounce truth).

59 Del Río's manual appears in an inventory of books formerly owned by Quevedo. See Martinengo, *La astrología en la obra de Quevedo*, 17, 173–4.

60 Del Río, *Disquisitionum magicarum libri sex* (1612 ed.), 1028, 1052. I am much indebted to Craig Kallendorf for help with translating this rather barbaric Latin as well as that in the two following passages.

61 Ibid., 993.

62 Peucer, *Commentarius de praecipuis divinationum generibus*, 23, 45.

63 See Nolting-Hauff, *Visión, sátira y agudeza*, 21. But Nolting-Hauff warns that the *Discurso del alguacil endemoniado* is anything but Erasmian in content; in fact, it is just the opposite (21, 142n88). Far from taking the exorcism ritual seriously enough to see it as a potential source of knowledge (as Quevedo did with the 'tendencia fundamental seria' in this work [Nolting-Hauff, 159]), Erasmus satirized the exorcism ritual in his colloquy 'Exorcism, or the Spectre.' As for the form of Quevedo's work, Nolting-Hauff makes the interesting point that the technical aspects of this narrative anticipate the fantastical stories of romantics such as Hoffmann or the prose poetry of Bertrand and Baudelaire (87). In this way as in so many others, Quevedo was ahead of his time.

64 Maldonado, 'Algunos datos sobre la composición y dispersión de la biblioteca de Quevedo.'

65 Lía Schwartz Lerner explains the process by which these classical works were adapted in 'Golden Age Satire,' 272–5.

66 Celina Cortázar sees these juxtapositions as an affirmation by Quevedo of the power of language – including complicated, conceptist language – to create reality ('El infierno en la obra de Quevedo,' 201). For a further assessment of the deformative powers of conceptism and the cognitive couplings of the baroque emblem, see Pring-Mill, 'Some Techniques of Representation in the *Sueños* and the *Criticón*.'

67 See Cortázar, 'El infierno en la obra de Quevedo,' 200. For the injustices committed by *alguaciles* of this time period, see Quevedo, *Sueños y discursos*, 2:1036.

68 Crosby believes the parody may be of the seven orders of clerics (hostiary, lector, exor-

cist, acolyte, subdeacon, deacon, and priest) or of the six ways witches have of injuring humanity, according to the *Malleus maleficarum*. See Quevedo, *Sueños y discursos*, 2:1033–4. These explanations may be too complicated, however; it is possible that Quevedo is simply satirizing the *alguaciles* without reference to demons, clerics, or witches.

69   See his edition of Quevedo's works, Biblioteca de autores españoles, vol. 23, 302nb.

70   For this piece of book history, see Quevedo, *Sueños y discursos*, 2:1035.

71   *Discurso del alguacil endemoniado*, 173.

72   Díaz Migoyo, 'Desendemoniando *El aguacil endemoniado*,' 60.

73   *Discurso del alguacil endemoniado*, 177–8.

74   See Quevedo, *Sueños y discursos*, 2:1097.

75   Not all of the demon's commentary sounds like a sermon, however: if one reads carefully, it becomes apparent that Quevedo condemned to his hell only those women who were sexually frustrated. Those who had satisfied their desires on earth had repented and gone to heaven. One contemporaneous reader wrote in the margin of his manuscript next to this passage that if these sexually unsatiated women would only come to Salamanca, they would be satisfied. See Crosby, 'Al margen de los manuscritos de los *Sueños*,' 375.

76   Quevedo's praise of the virtuous poor bears strong neo-Stoical, particularly neo-Senecan, overtones. For a study of Quevedo and neo-Stoicism, see Ettinghausen, *Francisco de Quevedo and the Neostoic Movement*.

77   'He also told them what distress *Ireland* was then in, and *England* must pay the Piper ... notwithstanding its present security' (Jollie, *The Surey Demoniack*, 47).

78   Niccoli, *Prophecy and People in Renaissance Italy*, 168–70.

79   For summaries of several Spanish treatises in this tradition, see Truman, *Spanish Treatises*.

80   See Nolting-Hauff, *Visión, sátira y agudeza*, 193.

81   Sieber, 'The Narrators in Quevedo's *Sueños*,' 107.

82   Jollie, *The Surey Demoniack*, 12.

83   Díaz Migoyo, 'Desendemoniando *El aguacil endemoniado*,' 67.

84   *Discurso del alguacil endemoniado*, 184. Emphasis mine.

85   Sieber, 'The Narrators in Quevedo's *Sueños*,' 108. These paradoxes also remind us of emblem books of the time. See Ciocchini, 'Quevedo y la construcción de imágenes emblemáticas.'

86   *Sueños y discursos*, 2:1042. The fact that there are four riddles or pronouncements is significant, according to Crosby, because of the four evangelists or saints printed on the four corners of the *ensalmos*. Crosby explains that *ensalmos* or '*rescritos*' printed on sheets of paper were placed around the necks of demoniacs or even animals. They are mentioned as far back as the fourth century (John Chrysostom) and into the thirteenth century (Thomas Aquinas). An interesting variation on the typical *ensalmo* was

an exorcism or passage from scripture written upon a consecrated host, or Eucharistic wafer (Erik Midelfort, *Mad Princes of Renaissance Germany*, 108).

87 *Discurso del alguacil endemoniado*, 157. Emphasis mine.

88 Although they were originally separate works, they have generated little critical attention in isolation. For the one of interest to us here, the *Discurso del alguacil endemoniado*, one scholar has lamented that 'no tengamos estudios minuciosos sobre ella' (we do not have detailed studies about it) (Gómez-Quintero, 'La crítica social en *El aguacil endemoniado*, de Quevedo,' 89).

The estimate of thousands is from Ilse Nolting-Hauff (*Visión, sátira y agudeza*, 10), the scholar who has written the longest and most well-respected book-length study of the *Sueños*. She explains that although he wrote the works separately, Quevedo soon came to see them as part of a cycle (16). Nolting-Hauff, despite her insistence on the independence of the works from one another, does see some important relationships among them. For example, the *Discurso del alguacil endemoniado*, in its place within the cycle as the second work after the *Sueño del juicio final*, repeats some of the same satirical 'types' mentioned in the first *Sueño* but explores them in greater detail (21).

For the responses of contemporaneous readers as recorded in the margins of these manuscripts, see Crosby, 'Al margen de los manuscritos de los *Sueños*.'

89 Two other censors, Fray Diego Niseno and Bartolomé de la Fuente, are also thought to have been involved with the Inquisition's condemnation of the *Sueños* (Nolting-Hauff, *Visión, sátira y agudeza*, 45).

90 The three 1627 editions were published independently in Barcelona and Zaragoza, while the 1628 edition appeared in Valencia.

91 This work appeared under the title *El entremetido, la dueña y el soplón*. For one modern edition, see Quevedo y Villegas, *Discurso de todos los diablos o infierno enmendado*. For a discussion of several of Quevedo's other works dealing with hell, see Schwartz, 'Figuras del Orco y el infierno interior en Quevedo.'

92 This manuscript, now lost, was used by Basilio Sebastián Castellanos to prepare his edition of 1840. Castellanos cites it as a privately held manuscript owned by José Muso y Valiente. Castellanos, 'Notas' to his edición of Quevedo's *Obras*, 5 vols in 3 (Madrid: Imprenta de Mellado, 1840–5), 388.

93 For Quevedo's interest elsewhere in heretical sects, see Piero, 'Algunas fuentes de Quevedo.'

94 In presenting his satire in this manner, Quevedo was (for once) writing according to the guidelines of the precepts contained in the treatises on poetry. Pinciano had argued for the anonymity of butts of satire: 'Las leyes justas moderaron esta demasía y ordenaron que ningún cómico traxesse a la acción nombre particular de hombre alguno por los escándolos que dello resultauan' (The just laws moderated this excess and ordered that no comic bring to the action the particular name of any man because of the scan-

dals that would result from it) (López Pinciano, *Philosophia antigua poética,* 3:15).

Cascales had also judged that the goal of satire was to 'corregir vicios y costumbres malas, notando a unas y otras personas dignas de reprehensión con dissimulados nombres' (correct vices and bad customs, noting some and other persons worthy of reprehension with dissimulated names) (Cascales, *Tablas poéticas,* 180), with emphasis on the omission or modification of specific names.

95 Fernández-Guerra's edition, Biblioteca de Autores Españoles, vol. 23, 305–6n4.
96 Nolting-Hauff, *Visión, sátira y agudeza,* 194.
97 *Poesía original completa,* Poem #264, pp. 288–9.
98 Elliott, 'Quevedo and the Count-Duke of Olivares,' 204.
99 Ibid., 204.
100 Ibid., 207–8.
101 Lodge, *The Diuel Coniured,* 14.
102 Read, *Visions in Exile,* 83.
103 See the study by Stallybrass and White on *The Politics and Poetics of Transgression.* For a specific study of Quevedo's transgression into the realms of the grotesque and the visceral, see Huergo, 'Bajo el peso de la ley.'
104 Mary Douglas has analysed these concepts fruitfully in *Purity and Danger.* Sieber employs the concept of taboo to describe Quevedo's work ('The Narrators in Quevedo's *Sueños,*' 115).
105 Kieckhefer, *Forbidden Rites,* 127.
106 Shattuck, *Forbidden Knowledge,* 44, 30.
107 Quoted in ibid., 46.
108 Ibid., 165.
109 *Paradise Lost* VIII.173 (quoted in Shattuck, *Forbidden Knowledge,* 76).
110 It will be remembered, however, that Quevedo's fear of the censors and/or the government actually did prompt his removal of certain passages criticizing King Philip II and promoting heretical doctrine.
111 Díaz Migoyo, 'Desendemoniando *El aguacil endemoniado,*' 65.
112 On Quevedo's Christian humanism, see López Poza, 'Quevedo, humanista cristiano'; and Kallendorf and Kallendorf, 'Conversations with the Dead.'
113 Carvallo, *Cisne de Apolo,* 370.
114 Ibid., 359.
115 Ibid., 361.
116 Ibid., 362.
117 Ibid., 368–9.
118 For a discussion of the *poeta theologus* tradition as it was understood at approximately this time, see Craig Kallendorf, 'From Virgil to Vida.' One important *proviso* to this theory is that Quevedo could have seen himself as an ideal prophet or bearer of truth at the same time as he satirized false prophets of his day. For commentary on these

false prophets, see Gómez-Quintero, 'La crítica social en *El aguacil endemoniado*,' 92. For the most outstanding account of one of these contemporaneous prophet figures, see Kagan, *Lucrecia's Dreams*.

119 *Discurso del alguacil endemoniado*, 153.

120 Carvallo, *Cisne de Apolo*, 370.

3. Romance, the Interlude, and Hagiographical Drama

1 See Weber, 'Between Ecstasy and Exorcism.'

2 Wilson, 'The Histrionics of Exorcism,' 224. This critic is of course borrowing Stephen Greenblatt's phrase about 'rituals emptied out.' See Greenblatt, 'Shakespeare and the Exorcists,' 126.

3 Stapp, 'Dichoso por confiado,' 413.

4 Avalle-Arce, '*La Galatea*,' 630.

5 Frye, *The Secular Scripture*, 53–4.

6 See Harrison, 'Milagros, astrología y racionalización de la magia.'

7 See Cruz Casado, 'Auristela hechizada.' See also Díez Fernández and Aguirre de Cárcer, 'Contexto histórico y tratamiento literario de la "hechicería" morisca y judía en el *Persiles*'; and Andrés, 'Erotismo brujeril y hechicería urbana en *Los trabajos de Persiles y Sigismunda*.'

8 I refer to Alban Forcione's persuasive argument that the movement of the story goes from north to south, from darkness to light. See *Cervantes' Christian Romance*, 109.

9 See El Saffar, 'The Truth of the Matter.' She offers a useful contrast between the definitions of 'escapist' and 'quest' romance (240), and it is obviously the latter which Cervantes set out to write according to the model of Heliodorus.

10 See Jameson, 'Magical Narratives.' He deconstructs Frye's discussion of romance as well as Vladimir Propp's work on the wondertale in a clearly Nietzschean/Marxist view of romance (110, 115).

11 I do not mean to imply here that Cervantes had any direct access to New Comedy. His work simply carries on some aspects of the New Comic tradition when seen from the perspective of a theorist of genres such as Frye (*The Secular Scripture*, 71).

12 Cervantes, *Los trabajos de Persiles y Sigismunda*, 409.

13 Carlos Romero cites a *romance* appearing in Pérez de Hita's *Guerras civiles de Granada* (I, ch. 6):

> Afuera, afuera, afuera,
> aparta, aparta, aparta,
> que entra el valeroso Muza
> caballero de unas cañas ...
>
> (Away, away, away,
> apart, apart, apart,

for the valorous Muza enters
knight of some reed spears ...)

(*Introduzione al 'Persiles' di Miguel de Cervantes*, 170).

14 This term, of course, is Frye's, and I believe his brief discussion of true demonic possession is useful for understanding any sort of ordeal which the protagonists of a romance
must pass through: 'It is logical for it to begin its series of adventures with some kind
of break in consciousness ... the collapse of the rightful order in the mind and the sep-
aration of consciousness from the proper rhythm of action ... It is really an obliteration
of memory, and in another type of story it could be the result of a curse or demonic
possession' (*The Secular Scripture*, 103). Frye emphasizes that what is important from
the perspective of genre is not an actual demonic possession and exorcism, but a ritualized ordeal, followed by an exorcism, rescue, or escape (113).

15 *Persiles*, 407.

16 Ibid.

17 Ibid., 410.

18 Ibid., 407.

19 Wilson, 'The Histrionics of Exorcism,' 225. She also notes that the demonic becomes
eroticized, especially in dreams or visions, in other Cervantine works, such as *El rufián
dichoso*. To this list could be added *El viejo celoso* and *El celoso extremeño*.

20 In the Spanish Baroque period the word 'posesión' was understood to mean both the
sexual and the demonic kinds of possession and as such, was siezed upon by satirical
writers as the perfect opportunity for obscene puns.

21 Heliodorus, *Aethiopica*, 1587 English translation by Underdowne, Book 4, p. 102. For
a Golden Age Spanish version see the 1615 translation by Fernando de Mena.

22 Wilson, 'The Histrionics of Exorcism,' 232.

23 Quoted from the Douay Bible.

24 Wilson, 'The Histrionics of Exorcism,' 235, 237.

25 Forcione, *Cervantes' Christian Romance*, 141. For a critic who disagrees with Forcione,
see Williamsen, *Co(s)mic Chaos*, 123–4. I think Williamsen misreads Forcione here,
for he does see the humour of this story (*Cervantes' Christian Romance*, 139). Ruth El
Saffar acknowledges that the uncle's death sounds a discordant note at the end of the
story but attributes this discordancy simply to 'narrative distance' (*Beyond Fiction*,
160). Joaquín Casalduero makes an interesting point about this ending for the story
when he views the uncle's death as a reminder that death is always present in life
through sin (*Sentido y forma*, 197).

26 On questions of orthodoxy and heterodoxy in the *Persiles*, see Alonso, 'Ortodoxia y
heterodoxia en *Los trabajos de Persiles y Sigismunda*.'

27 Frye, *The Secular Scripture*, 80.

28 Forcione, *Cervantes' Christian Romance*, 139.

29 Vega Carpio, *Entremés duodécimo de la endemoniada*, in *Las comedias del famoso poeta Lope de Vega Carpio*.

30 Rennert, *The Spanish Stage*, 288. Rennert has examined the 1609 Valladolid edition and lists the twelve *entremeses* it contains. He notes Lope's admission that he wrote *entremeses* as it appears in the *Arte nuevo de hacer comedias* (288). Rennert goes on to address the question of Lope's conventional disavowals of authorship for minor works (289). It would be interesting to analyse the *entremés* of *La endemoniada* according to the criteria of orthography, rhyme, versification, vocabulary, grammar, and style, as was done with some doubtful plays of Lope by Augusto A. Portuondo in *Diez comedias atribuidas a Lope de Vega*. But until this can be done it is best to rely on the learned opinion of scholars such as Rennert and Eugenio Asensio, author of *Itinerario del entremés*, who simply notes empirically that the 1605 Valencia edition of Lope's *Comedias* contains five *entremeses* (of which one is in verse), while the 1612 Barcelona edition of the third part of his *Comedias* contains three in verse, and the 1617 seventh part of the *Comedias* contains two in prose. The 1609 Valladolid edition contains one verse *entremés* (the same as in the 1605 edition) and eleven prose *entremeses*, including *La endemoniada*.

31 See chapter 1, 'Demoniacs in the Drama,' for other instances of this treatment in a similar dramatic venue, particularly in the comedy *The Bugbears*.

32 Vega Carpio, *Entremés duodécimo: de la endemoniada*, in *Colección de entremeses*, 146.

33 Ibid.

34 See Asensio, *Itinerario del entremés*, 251–2.

35 Sometimes, though, even priests spoke macaronic Latin. Erasmus derided the bad Latin of priests who were not well educated: 'They insist that it detracts from the grandeur of sacred writing if they're obliged to obey the rules of grammar' (*Praise of Folly*, 27:130).

36 On the relationship of this play to an *ars moriendi* manual written by the exorcist Francisco Blasco de Lanuza, see Hilaire Kallendorf, 'Cervantes's Democratization of Demonic Possession: *El rufián dichoso*, Blasco de Lanuza, and the Death-Bed of Every Christian' in *Bulletin of the Comediantes* (invited contribution for special anniversary issue), forthcoming.

37 William Shakespeare, *2. Henry VI*, *The Riverside Shakespeare*, ed. G. Blakemore Evans (Boston: Houghton Mifflin, 1974), 3.3.19–23.

38 Rodolfo Schevill and Adolfo Bonilla, Introducción, in *Obras de Cervantes: Comedias y entremeses*, vol. 6 (Madrid: Gráficas Reunidas, 1922), 126; Francisco Ynduráin, 'Estudio preliminar' to his edition of *Obras dramáticas de Cervantes*, Biblioteca de Autores Españoles, vol. 156 (Madrid: Atlas, 1962), XXXV; Sánchez, 'Conexiones temáticas,' 127.

39 See Casalduero, *Sentido y forma del teatro de Cervantes*, 104; and Zimic, 'La caridad "jamás imaginada" de Cristóbal de Lugo,' 125–6.

40 Alberto Sánchez describes Lugo as fitting within a broader category of 'ruffianesque' or 'monstrous' characters in Golden Age drama, the 'hombres de fiera condición' such as Calderón's bandits ('Conexiones temáticas,' 123).

41 *El rufián dichoso*, 1, ll. 89–90.

42 Ibid., 1, ll. 1202–5.

43 Ibid., 2, l. 1812.

44 This idea is Casalduero's (*Sentido y forma del teatro de Cervantes*, 117).

45 '¡ ... [P]ara mí no hay Dios!' (*El rufián dichoso*, 2, l. 1951).

46 On the formula of an exorcism acted out as a trial scene, see Wilson, 'The Histrionics of Exorcism,' 232, and Clark, *Thinking with Demons*, 579. For an example of this formula see Ciruelo, *A treatise reproving all superstitions and forms of witchcraft*, 267.

47 The text does not specify, but presumably these are the eleven thousand virgins of St Ursula mentioned in one of Cervantes' probable sources: Dávila Padilla, *Historia de la fundación y discurso de la provincia de Santiago de México*, chapter 27.

48 Forcione, 'Cervantes's Secularized Miracle,' 325.

49 Casalduero, *Sentido y forma del teatro de Cervantes*, 122.

50 Ibid., 119.

51 Wilson, 'The Histrionics of Exorcism,' 231.

52 Casalduero, *Sentido y forma del teatro de Cervantes*, 118–19.

53 *El rufián dichoso*, 2, ll. 2016–17.

54 Ibid., ll. 1996–2003.

55 Ibid., l. 2115.

56 'Sí, acepto, padre' (Yes, I accept, father) (*El rufián dichoso*, 2, l. 2157). For this discussion of poetic rhythms see Casalduero, *Sentido y forma del teatro de Cervantes*, 118 and 121.

57 *El rufián dichoso*, 3, l. 2197.

58 Mark 5:1–19.

59 Jacques de Vitry, *Vita Mariae Oigniacensis*, in *Acta sanctorum*, 5 June (Paris, 1867), 542–72; cited in Newman, 'Possessed by the Spirit,' 733, 740–1.

60 The chronicler compares this case to a similar one involving a despairing monk and asserts that although neither one displays the symptoms of classic demonic possession, they should undoubtedly be categorized as possessed by this particular demon of despair.

61 Newman, 'Possessed by the Spirit,' 741. For more accounts of female visionaries in both mystical and demonic contexts, see Dinzelbacher, *Heilige oder Hexen?* 207–8.

62 Newman, 'Possessed by the Spirit,' 742.

63 Chrysostom Henríquez, ed., *Vita Idae Nivellensis. Quinque prudentes virgines* (Antwerp, 1630); cited in Newman, 'Possessed by the Spirit,' 733, 742–3. Ida of Nivelles was a Cistercian of La Ramée who died at age 32, probably of consumption.

64 Concepción, *Práctica de conjurar*, 18–21.
65 Lodge, *The Diuel Coniured*, 13.
66 Stapp, 'Dichoso por confiado,' 441.
67 *Eulogy of Helen*, 14, quoted in Laín Entralgo, *The Therapy of the Word in Classical Antiquity*, 93.
68 *El rufián dichoso*, 2, ll. 2267–70.
69 See Canavaggio, 'La conversión del rufián dichoso,' 11.
70 Ibid.
71 Ibid., 17.
72 *El rufián dichoso*, 3, ll. 2680–3.
73 Ibid., ll. 2818–20.
74 Ibid., l. 2824.
75 Cervantes, *El ingenioso hidalgo Don Quijote de la Mancha*, Part I, ch. 48, pp. 570–1.
76 Zimic, 'La caridad,' 130.
77 Ibid., 132.
78 Cervantes, *El rufián dichoso*, ed. Talens and Spadaccini, 66–7.
79 Riley, *Cervantes's Theory of the Novel*, 179, 191. See also Riley, '"Romance" y novela en Cervantes.'
80 Casalduero, *Sentido y forma del teatro de Cervantes*, 105. Casalduero makes these remarks concerning the demons who appear as nymphs and bears.
81 Ibid., 124–5.
82 Saquiel is also the name of the familiar demon of the historical personage Eugenio Torralba (about whom Cervantes wrote in the Clavileño episode of the *Quijote*). This episode (Book 2, ch. 48) of the *Quijote* is only one of several Golden Age adaptations of Torralba's story. Canavaggio cites two others, by Zapata (*Carlo famoso*, 28–32) and Lope de Vega (*Las pobrezas de Reinaldos*, Act 3). See *Cervantès dramaturge*, 86. The alternative spelling for the demon's name is Zaquiel.
83 *El rufián dichoso*, 2, ll. 1640–5.
84 Ibid., ll. 1740–5.
85 Ibid., ll. 1760–80.
86 Ibid., ll. 2265–70.
87 Dávila Padilla returned to Spain from the New World in 1596. He knew Francisco de Sandoval y Rojas, a relative of Cervantes' patron, Cardinal Sandoval y Rojas. Furthermore, Dávila Padilla served on the commission charged by Philip III in 1600 with examining the question of whether the theatres in Madrid should reopen (the commission approved the reopening). See Canavaggio, *Cervantès dramaturge*, 46–82. Canavaggio also mentions another potential source for Cervantes, the *Historia eclesiástica de nuestros tiempos* (1611) by Alonso Fernández, which also contained a summary of the life of Cristóbal de la Cruz (47).
88 This book was reprinted in 1585. Canavaggio suggests that this book may have

been the source of Dávila Padilla's work (*Cervantès dramaturge*, 47). See San Román, *Consuelo de penitentes*, reprinted in Canavaggio, 'Para la génesis del *Rufián dichoso*.'

89 Luís Astrana Marín, *Vida ejemplar y heróica de Miguel de Cervantes Saavedra* (Madrid: Instituto Editorial Reus, 1948–58), 4:461–4.

90 López, 'De la vida marauillosa del santo fray Christoual de la Cruz,' reprinted in *Los rufianes de Cervantes: 'El rufián dichoso' y 'El rufián viudo,'* ed. Joaquín Hazañas y la Rua (Seville: Imprenta de Izquierdo, 1906), 66.

91 Chapter 22 of Dávila Padilla's account bears the title 'De las vivas razones con que el varon de Dios persuadia la virtud de la obediencia.' This rhetorical emphasis is continued when, in the most personalized version of this hagiographical account to be written, Cruz tells Ana of his own dissolute past: 'El bendito padre le refirió los descuydos de su vida seglar; y como por la divina misericordia avia mudado la vida desde que fue clerigo' (The blessed father related to her the careless errors of his secular life, and how by divine mercy he has changed his life since he was a cleric) (Dávila Padilla, *Historia de la fundación*, 427). In this account, Ana is explicitly possessed by a demon before she agrees to Cruz's proposal: 'Hablaua Dios en aquella muger, en quien antes hablaua el demonio' (God spoke in that woman, in whom before used to speak the demon) (428). Once again, in describing the bargain Dávila Padilla emphasizes its rhetorical aspect: 'Aqui hazia el empleo de su buena Rethorica, loa[n]do la caridad, humildad, ò abstinencia q[ue] en otros aduertia' (Here he employed his good rhetoric, praising the charity, humility, or abstinence that he noticed in others) (437).

92 Cervantes, *El ingenioso hidalgo Don Quijote de la Mancha*, II, 520. This incident is discussed in Bataillon, *Erasmo y España*, 778.

93 Canavaggio, *Cervantès dramaturge*, 47. López de Hoyos died on 28 June 1583, but he had approved the book before he died. The text of the *aprobación* is reprinted in full in Canavaggio, 'Para la génesis del *Rufián dichoso*,' 465.

94 Although A.A. Parker does not totally accept the attribution of this play to Calderón (*The Theology of the Devil in the Drama of Calderón*, 12), Margaret Greer clearly does (*The Play of Power*, 133). Parker notes that the devil appears in forty-seven of Calderón's *autos sacramentales* (3).

95 The other play is *La margarita preciosa*, only the last act of which was written by Calderón; the first act was written by Juan de Zavaleta, and the second was written by Jerónimo Cáncer. See the edition (without line numbers) by Hartzenbusch. In scene 8 of Act 3 of this play, Flora becomes possessed with 'una rabia, un furor, / Una cólera, una ira, / Que por la vista y la voz / Está exhalando del pecho / Pedazos del corazón' (a raving, a furor, / A choler, an ire, / That by the sight and the voice / Is exhaling from the chest / Pieces of the heart) (532). At first it appears that Flora is simply manifesting once again the symptoms of jealousy, the emotion she has harboured toward Margarita since the beginning of the play for being the object of affection of a man Flora herself loves madly. But Margarita immediately suspects demonic possession and asks 'Quien

habla en ti' (Who speaks in you) (532). The episode is very strange and may even qualify as an exorcism performed by a saintly woman – in this case, Margarita, an early Christian persecuted for her faith by pagans. Margarita performs the exorcism, if it is one, by reciting the creed of her faith. In this sense the exorcism is a rhetorical bargain similar to the one performed by Cristóbal de la Cruz in *El rufián dichoso*. The demon speaking through Flora responds to the recitation of the *Credo* with:

No prosigas; calla, calla;
Que á tanta luz deslumbrado,
Que á tanto esplendor rendido,
A tanto abismo vencido
Y á tanta verdad postrado,
Confieso que me has dejado
Temblando ...
    Y pues nada ¡ay triste!
A ti ni á esa cruz resiste,
Del uno y del otro huyendo,
Por el aire iré diciendo
Venciste, mujer, venciste.

(Do not continue; hush, hush;
For at so much light bedazzled,
For at so much splendor yielded,
To such an abyss conquered,
And to so much truth prostrated,
I confess that you have left me
Trembling ...
    And then nothing, oh sad one!
Resists you or that cross,
Fleeing from the one and from the other,
Through the air I will go saying
You won, woman, you won.)   (533)

The demon alludes to a cross, perhaps a prop used by Margarita on the stage. The play ends with the spiritually victorious Margarita nonetheless martyred for her faith. Her bloody, beheaded body is brutally displayed for the audience to see. This play comes as close as any I have read to being an example of the much discussed, elusively paradoxical 'Christian tragedy' in Spain. I am indebted to Cilveti's study, *El demonio en el teatro de Calderón*, for bringing this play to my attention and assuring me that Calderón does not explore demonic possession in any of his other works (149).

96 Parker, *The Theology of the Devil*, 12.
97 Another more well-known play of Calderón's which explores the theme of the dia-

bolical pact in greater theological detail is *El mágico prodigioso*. This play may have been inspired by Mira de Amescua's *El esclavo del demonio*.

98   These special effects have been discussed by Caro Baroja in *Teatro popular y magia*, 73.

99   Calderón, *Las cadenas del demonio*, 213.

100   Ibid., 227.

101   Ibid., 213–14.

102   Ibid., 228. It is worth noting that in this passage, these symptoms of demonic possession are narrated rather than performed onstage; it is clear from internal stage directions, however, that similar symptoms were performed at other points in the play.

103   Ibid., 230.

104   Ibid.

105   Ibid., 231.

106   Ibid.

107   Ibid.

108   Ibid., 231–2.

109   Ibid., 236.

110   See Caciola, 'Discerning Spirits,' 279. See especially graph 5.2, 'Total number of lines in accounts of exorcisms performed by saints, by century' in chapter 5, 'Exorcism from Spectacle to Ritual.'

111   Ribadeneyra, *The lives of the saints*. See 'The Life of Saint Augustine,' which is the entry for 28 August. In the last paragraph of this account, Ribadeneyra notes vaguely, without further elaboration, that some exorcisms were attributed to the saint. For the speculation that Lope used this source, see Case, 'Metatheater and World View in Lope's *El divino africano*,' 132.

112   This play, labelled a tragicomedy by Lope, was first published in the *Décimaoctava parte* of his *Comedias* in 1623. It was first brought to my attention through Checca's 'The Role of the Devil in Golden Age Drama,' 127–9.

113   *El divino africano*, 356.

114   Ibid., 357.

115   Ibid.

116   Menéndez Pelayo, 'Observaciones preliminares' to his edition of Vega, *El divino africano*, lxxiii.

117   The creative use of this topos is not, however, confined to the baroque period. Jean-Paul Sartre would later adapt Cervantes' *El rufián dichoso* in his *Le Diable et le bon Dieu*, another work whose protagonist, Goetz, exemplifies the extremity of rebellion against God.

118   Lisón Tolosana describes this baroque topos by pointing to the human-divine duality of man, always between good and evil, at the same time saint and sinner. In his view,

baroque demonic possession is the poetic expression of this necessary cohabitation, the synthetic fusion of these two interpretive extremes (*La España mental I*, 89).

119 Casalduero, *Sentido y forma del teatro de Cervantes*, 106–7.

120 Varas, 'El *Rufián dichoso*,' 11.

4. Tragedy As the Absence or Failure of Exorcism

1 Hornby, *Drama, Metadrama, and Perception*, 55, 58.

2 On the assessment that Derrida derives much of his critique of the 'repressive' logic of presence from Heidegger, see Alan Bass's introduction to his translation of Derrida, *Writing and Difference*, xi, and Gayatri Chakravorty Spivak, translator's preface to her corrected edition of Derrida, *Of Grammatology*, lxxxvii. I am indebted to Richard Hornby for making these connections to the thought of Derrida and Saussure in the context of tragedy.

3 Derrida, 'Structure, Sign and Play in the Discourse of the Human Sciences,' in *Writing and Difference*, 292.

4 Saussure, *Course in General Linguistics*, chapter 1, 'Nature of the Linguistic Sign,' of Part I, 'General Principles,' 65–70.

5 On Shakespeare's use of Harsnett, see Stevenson, 'Shakespeare's Interest in Harsnett's *Declaration*'; Muir, 'Appendix 7: Samuel Harsnett and *King Lear*'; Muir, 'Samuel Harsnett and *King Lear*.' Muir repeats these connections in *The Sources of Shakespeare's Plays*. Since Muir's work, other studies have revisited the issue: Milward, 'Shakespeare and Elizabethan Exorcism'; and Salingar, '*King Lear*, Montaigne, and Harsnett.'

6 On the possessions, see Pollen, 'Supposed Cases of Diabolical Possession in 1585–86.'

7 Soens, '*King Lear* III.iv.62–5.'

8 These past participles appear on pp. 283, 289, 292, 274, 244, 256, and 287 of Brownlow's edition of Harsnett's *Declaration*.

9 Shakespeare, *King Lear*, especially 3.4, 3.6, and 4.1.

10 Ibid., 4.1.58–63.

11 Harsnett, *Declaration*, 308.

12 *King Lear*, 3.4.54–5; Harsnett, *Declaration*, 368.

13 *King Lear*, 3.4.85–6.

14 Harsnett, *Declaration*, 410.

15 Carol Neely describes the tainting of discourse with madness: 'Shakespeare, prefiguring Foucault's analysis, dramatizes madness primarily through a peculiar language ... Shakespeare's language of madness is characterized by fragmentation, obsession, and repetition, and most importantly by what I will call "quotation," which might instead be called "bracketing" or "italicization." The mad are "beside themselves"; their discourse is not their own' ('"Documents in Madness,"' 323).

16 *King Lear*, 1.4.177.
17 Harsnett, *Declaration*, 251.
18 *King Lear*, 1.4.187–8.
19 Harsnett, *Declaration*, 251.
20 *King Lear*, 4.7.34.
21 Harsnett, *Declaration*, 251.
22 Ibid., 255.
23 Ibid., 400.
24 *King Lear*, 3.4.56–7.
25 Ibid., 4.2.68.
26 Ibid., 1.4.259, 4.2.59–66.
27 Harsnett, *Declaration*, 261.
28 Ibid., 297, 350, 357.
29 *King Lear*, 4.6.127–9.
30 Harsnett, *Declaration*, 250.
31 James VI of Scotland and I of England, *Daemonologie*, 46.
32 Scot, *The Discouerie of Witchcraft*, 495.
33 For a fuller treatment of these issues, see the article by Hilaire and Craig Kallendorf, 'Catharsis As Exorcism: Aristotle, Shakespeare, and Religio-Poetic Liminality' (forthcoming).
34 Greenblatt, 'Shakespeare and the Exorcists,' in *Shakespearean Negotiations*, 115. A shorter version of this essay had been published previously as 'Shakespeare and the Exorcists,' in *Shakespeare and the Question of Theory*, ed. Patricia Parker and Geoffrey Hartman (New York: Methuen, 1985), 163–87. A shorter version of the same article is '*King Lear* and Harsnett's "Devil Fiction."' Another critic who voices an interpretation of *King Lear* which is as secular as Greenblatt's is Carol Neely, who concludes that in this play 'the Church's attempt to outlaw exorcism is furthered' ('"Documents in Madness,"' 333).
35 Greenblatt, 'Shakespeare and the Exorcists,' in *Shakespearean Negotiations*, 119. All citations are to this version of the essay. He further concludes that 'its cure comes at the hands not of an exorcist but of a doctor' (119). While a doctor does treat Lear, it is not clear that he 'cures' him; furthermore, Greenblatt ignores the fact that medicine and religion were still inextricably intertwined during this period. On this point, there are multiple essays in Grell and Cunningham, *Religio Medici*.
36 Greenblatt, 'Shakespeare and the Exorcists,' 119, emphasis mine.
37 Ibid., 123.
38 Ibid., 119.
39 Brownlow, *Shakespeare, Harsnett, and the Devils of Denham*, 109.
40 See Milward, *Shakespeare's Religious Background*.

41 Murphy, *Darkness and Devils*. For a useful corrective to this approach, see Brownlow, Review of *Darkness and Devils*.

42 Cox, *The Devil and the Sacred in English Drama*, 162, 155.

43 Neely, '"Documents in Madness,"' 333.

44 *King Lear*, 4.6.221–3.

45 Cunningham, *Woe or Wonder*, 22.

46 *King Lear*, 4.7.29–30.

47 Ibid., 4.4.25–6.

48 Ibid., 4.3.28–9.

49 Ibid., 4.7.52–3.

50 Maclean, 'Episode, Scene, Speech, and Word,' 106–7.

51 *King Lear*, 3.2.48–9.

52 Ibid., 4.1.57.

53 Ibid., 4.7.62.

54 Hardison, Jr., 'Three Types of Renaissance Catharsis,' 3; Hunt, 'Shakespeare's Tragic Homeopathy,' 83.

55 'What is it you would see? / If aught of woe or wonder, cease your search' (*Hamlet*, 5.2.362–3). It is from these lines, of course, that Cunningham devised the title for his book *Woe or Wonder*.

56 *Richard II*, 5.5.61–2. This view of musical catharsis was first set forth in Aristotle, *Politics* 1341b32–1342a15.

57 Hoeniger, *Medicine and Shakespeare in the English Renaissance*, 261–9.

58 *Richard II*, 1.1.153.

59 *Winter's Tale*, 4.4.763.

60 *2 Henry VI*, 3.3.23.

61 *3 Henry VI*, 5.6.88.

62 *Richard III*, 2.1.9.

63 *Antony and Cleopatra*, 4.14.123–4.

64 *The Taming of the Shrew*, Induction (preceding Act 1), 2.131–4.

65 The mention of 'fury' in a similar context appears in the epilogue of one of Shakespeare's source plays, the anonymous *Timon*: 'I feele throughout / A sodeine change my fury doth abate, / My hearte growes milde & laies aside its hate ...' (*Timon*, ed. G.R. Proudfoot, Malone Society Reprints [Oxford: Oxford University Press, 1978], ll. 2620–2.)

66 Sewall, *The Vision of Tragedy*, 75.

67 Bennett, 'The Storm Within,' 148.

68 Coursen, *Christian Ritual and the World of Shakespeare's Tragedies*, 268.

69 Brownlow, *Shakespeare, Harsnett, and the Devils of Denham*, 120.

70 *King Lear*, 1.4.252.

71 Harsnett, *Declaration*, 333.
72 *King Lear*, 2.4.56–8.
73 Harsnett, *Declaration*, 223. The other source more often cited is Jorden, *A Briefe Discourse of a Disease Called the Suffocation of the Mother.*
74 *King Lear*, 3.2.51.
75 Harsnett, *Declaration*, 255.
76 *King Lear*, 3.2.53.
77 Harsnett, *Declaration*, 273.
78 Maclean, 'Episode, Scene, Speech, and Word,' 109.
79 Ibid., 105.
80 *King Lear*, 3.4.80.
81 Ibid., 5.3.309; Michaelis, *The Admirable Historie of the Possession and Conversion of a Penitent Woman*, 21.
82 *King Lear*, 3.1.1.
83 Ibid., 3.1.15.
84 Ibid., 3.4.45.
85 Ibid., 3.4.80–3.
86 Ibid., 3.4.12.4.
87 Ibid., 3.4.158–9.
88 Ibid., 3.6.
89 They are labelled such in 4.2.59–60, 66.
90 Clark, *Thinking with Demons*, 579; Wilson, 'The Histrionics of Exorcism: Isabela Castrucha,' 232. For a contemporaneous example of an exorcism staged as a trial, see Ciruelo, *A treatise reproving all superstitions and forms of witchcraft*, 267.
91 *King Lear*, 3.6.7–8.
92 Ibid., 3.6.64–5.
93 Ibid., 4.3.30.
94 Coursen, *Christian Ritual and the World of Shakespeare's Tragedies*, 240.
95 *King Lear*, 4.4.17; 4.7.25, 27.
96 Coursen, *Christian Ritual and the World of Shakespeare's Tragedies*, 293. Until 1552 the baptismal ceremony in England contained an exorcism (baptismal exorcism appears, for example, in the First Prayer Book of 1549). See Nischan, 'The Exorcism Controversy and Baptism in the Late Reformation.' Even after exorcism was deleted from the baptismal ceremony, many believers continued to affirm that a baby who cried during baptism was releasing the devil through its mouth.
97 *King Lear*, 4.7.54–6.
98 Ibid., 2.3.14–16.
99 Ibid., 4.6.33–4.
100 Greenblatt, 'Shakespeare and the Exorcists,' 118.
101 *King Lear*, 4.6.69–72.

102 Butler, 'Jacobean Psychiatry,' 20.

103 Matei Chesnoiu, *William Shakespeare*, 157, 162.

104 England, 'Shakespeare as a Renaissance Therapist.' See also chapter 7 of Schleiner, *Melancholy, Genius, and Utopia in the Renaissance*, for a fuller discussion of Edgar's role in curing Gloucester as well as the language of 'curing' which appears in *Hamlet* and *Timon of Athens*.

105 Minturno, *L'arte poetica*, 290.

106 Giacomini, *Sopra la purgazione*, 354–5.

107 Ibid., 358, emphasis mine.

108 These 'spirits' should not be understood as demons per se, but rather as corporeal spirits which demons could use. Tommaso Campanella uses the term *'spirito corporeo'* in this sense (*Opere di Giordano Bruno e di Tommaso Campanella*, 1056). Winfried Schleiner calls these spirits the *'spiritus animales'* that travel between the body and the soul or mediate between the body and the mind (*Melancholy, Genius, and Utopia in the Renaissance*, 48, 245). He asserts that belief in these spirits was a medical commonplace and that melancholy was often explained by means of the devil's use of these spirits (245).

109 Giacomini, *Sopra la purgazione*, 368.

110 Guarini, *The Compendium of Tragicomic Poetry*, 514. Guarini refers to 1 Samuel 18:10.

111 Paolo Beni, *In Aristotelis poeticam commentarii* (Padua, 1613), 194–212, cited in Hathaway, *The Age of Criticism*, 286.

112 Greenblatt, 'Shakespeare and the Exorcists,' 114; Greenblatt, '*King Lear*,' 241.

113 I do not necessarily claim that Shakespeare himself believed in exorcism and other supernatural phenomena, merely that many members of his audience did, and that he wrote with their beliefs in mind.

114 Greenblatt, 'Shakespeare and the Exorcists,' 126.

115 Greenblatt overtly tries to make the play Brechtian: 'This "emptying out" resembles Brecht's "alienation effect"' (ibid., 126).

116 Bertold Brecht, 'Conversation about being Forced into Empathy,' in *Brecht on Theatre: The Development of an Aesthetic*, ed. and trans. John Willett (New York: Hill and Wang, 1964), 270–1.

117 'Ein Drama für Menschenfresser' (149). Berthold Brecht, Cologne radio discussion, 15 April 1928, in Brecht, *Gesammelte Werke*, ed. Elisabeth Hauptmann, vol. 15 (Frankfurt: Suhrkamp, 1967). See also Heinemann, 'How Brecht Read Shakespeare,' 214, 205.

118 Berthold Brecht, *Messingkauf Dialogues*, trans. John Willett (London: Methuen, 1977), 62; quoted in Heinemann, ibid., 216.

119 I refer, of course, to the concept of the scapegoat as elucidated by Girard in *The Scapegoat*.

120 Molho, '"El sagaz perturbador del género humano,"' 30.

121 This one-act play of some 800 lines was divided into ten scenes by an editor named Malone in 1780. The first quarto was published in 1608, and the second quarto appeared in 1619.

122 Throughout its critical history, the most popular candidate for authorship of this play has been Shakespeare. A reasonable guess may be made that he wrote at least some lines of *A Yorkshire Tragedy.*

123 Cawley, '*A Yorkshire Tragedy* and *Two Most Vnnaturall and Bloodie Murthers,*' 116. Cawley cites *A Yorkshire Tragedy,* 10.22–3.

124 The events are recounted in John Stow's *Chronicles* of 1607. This is a relatively late account of the episode. Two months after the murder (but two months before Calverley's trial and execution) a pamphlet describing the murder was entered in the Stationers' Register (12 June 1605). The pamphlet, now surviving in two copies, was titled *A booke called Twoo vnnaturall Murthers, the one practised by master COVERLEY a Yorkshire gent vppon his wife and happened on his children the 23 of Aprilis 1605.* Soon thereafter, on 3 July 1605, a lost ballad titled *A ballad of Lamentable Murther Donne in Yorkshire by a gent vppon 2 of his owne Children sore woundinge his Wyfe and Nurse* was entered in the Stationers' Register. Finally, another item (also now lost) titled *The Araignement Condempnacon and Execucon of Master CAVERLY at Yorke in Auguste 1605* was entered in the Stationers' Register on 24 August 1605. For all of the following, see Cawley, *English Domestic Drama: A Yorkshire Tragedy,* 2. The pamphlet is reprinted as an appendix to Cawley's edition of *A Yorkshire Tragedy,* as is an account of Walter Calverley's examination before the justices.

125 *A Yorkshire Tragedy,* 2.107–8.

126 Cawley, *English Domestic Drama: A Yorkshire Tragedy,* 12.

127 The Wife says her husband behaves 'as if some vexed spirit Had got his form vpon him' (2.38–9).

128 'Thou and the deuill has deceaued the world' (2.146).

129 'I should thinke the deuill himselfe kept open house in him' (3.25–6).

130 'Were you the Deuil, I would hold you, sir' (5.35); 'Nay, then, the Deuil wrastles, I am throwne' (5.40).

131   Ha's so bruizd me with his diuelish waight,
       And torne my flesh with his bloud-hasty spurre.
       A man before of easie constitution
       Till now hells power supplied, to his soules wrong.
       Oh, how damnation can make weake men strong.   (7.2–6)

132 'We strugled, but a fowler strength then his / Ore threw me with his armes' (7.28–9).

133 'Oh, twas the enemy my eyes so bleard' (10.46). A.C. Cawley had amassed previously all of these quotations referring to demonic possession. Cawley here relates the Hus-

band's symptoms of demonic possession, including his unnatural strength, to passages in King James I's *Daemonologie*, Reginald Scot's *Discouerie of Witchcraft*, John Darrell's *A True Narration of the Strange and Grevous Vexation by the Devil of seven Persons in Lancashire, and William Somers of Nottingham*, and George Gifford's *A Dialogue Concerning Witches and Witchcraft*.

134 MacDonald, *Mystical Bedlam*, 202.
135 Cawley, *English Domestic Drama:* A Yorkshire Tragedy, 14.
136 *A Yorkshire Tragedy*, 10.18–19.
137 Cawley, '*A Yorkshire Tragedy* and *Two Most Vnnaturall and Bloodie Murthers*,' 116.
138 Cawley, *English Domestic Drama:* A Yorkshire Tragedy, 13.
139 '*A Yorkshire Tragedy* and *Two Most Vnnaturall and Bloodie Murthers*,' 118.
140 Scot, *Discouerie of Witchcraft*, 535.
141 *Othello*, 2.1.111.
142 Ibid., 5.2.274–80.
143 Ibid., 4.1.50–60.
144 Kail, *The Medical Mind of Shakespeare*, 87.
145 Brownlow, 'Samuel Harsnett and the Meaning of Othello's "Suffocating Streams,"' 112–13.
146 *Othello*, 2.3.350–3.
147 Ibid., 4.1.54–5.
148 Scot, *Discouerie of Witchcraft*, 496. Scot alludes to Matthew 17:20 on exorcism by fasting and prayer.
149 *Othello*, 3.3.386–90. Brownlow complains that most commentators pass over this speech and notes that it does not appear in the First Quarto. One wonders whether these lines about Desdemona's name are meant to call attention to its component parts, one of which is 'demon.'
150 Coursen, *Christian Ritual*, 177. But Coursen also warns that 'to make Iago a devil is to diminish Othello's role in his own fall' (178).
151 *Othello*, 1.3.357 and 1.1.154. Coursen believes these 'hell pains' to be reminiscent of the perpetual agony of Marlowe's Mephisto (*Christian Ritual*, 177).
152 *Othello*, 1.3.403 and 2.3.161.
153 Ibid., 4.1.70.
154 Ibid., 5.2.286–7.
155 Ibid., 5.2.301–2.
156 Kaula, 'Othello Possessed,' 114.
157 *Macbeth*, 1.5.40, 48.
158 Ibid., 1.5.40–3.
159 Merchant, 'His Fiend-Like Queen,' 75.
160 *Macbeth*, 5.1.59–61.
161 Ibid., 5.1.72.

162 Ibid., 5.1.74–9.

163 Ibid., 5.3.38.

164 Ibid., 5.3.40, 44.

165 James VI of Scotland and I of England, *Daemonologie*, 57.

166 Scot, *Discouerie of Witchcraft*, 442.

167 Ibid., 76.

168 *Macbeth*, 1.5.26.

169 Ibid., 1.3.84–5.

170 Ibid., 3.4.23.

171 See Muir, *The Sources of Shakespeare's Plays*, 216. Critics have assented that 'Banquo's Ghost is here certainly a devilish illusion' (Bullough, *Narrative and Dramatic Sources of Shakespeare*, 465).

172 Lodge, *The Diuel Coniured*, 16–17.

173 James VI of Scotland and I of England, *Daemonologie*, 20.

174 For a discussion of King James's *Daemonologie* as a source for some of these allusions, see Jack, 'Macbeth, King James, and the Bible.'

175 *Macbeth*, 1.3.123–6.

176 Ibid., 2.3.7–8. These remarks refer to Henry Garnet, who was executed for treason in the Gunpowder Plot (Kaula, *Shakespeare and the Archpriest Controversy: A Study of Some New Sources* [The Hague: Mouton, 1975], 84).

177 Curry, 'The Demonic Metaphysics of *Macbeth*,' 400.

178 Scot, *Discouerie of Witchcraft*, 47–62.

179 James VI of Scotland and I of England, *Daemonologie*, 62.

180 *Macbeth*, 1.3.8.

181 Quoted in Henry R.D. Anders, *Shakespeare's Books* (New York: AMS Press, 1965), 114–15.

182 Curry, 'The Demonic Metaphysics of *Macbeth*,' 420.

183 Ibid., 425.

184 Neely, '"Documents in Madness,"' 328. She cites Peter Stallybrass, 'Macbeth and Witchcraft,' in *Focus on Macbeth*, ed. John Russell Brown (London: Routledge, 1982), 189–209.

185 Wills, *Witches and Jesuits*, 56–7.

186 *Macbeth*, 4.3.55–7.

187 For a more extended version of this section, see my article 'Intertextual Madness in *Hamlet*.'

188 *Hamlet*, 2.2.598–603. See notes in *Riverside Shakespeare*, 1190, concerning the variations on the word [dev'l] in the earliest editions: the Third and Fourth Quartos read 'a diuell ... a diuell,' while the First Folio reads 'the Diuell ... Diuel'; the First Quarto, similarly, reads 'the Diuell.'

189 See, for example, Rosenberg, *The Masks of Hamlet*.

190 *Hamlet*, 1.4.40–5.
191 Scot, *Discouerie of Witchcraft*, 516.
192 Ibid., 539. The biblical allusion here may be to Luke 11:21–2.
193 James VI of Scotland and I of England, *Daemonologie*, 20. Emphasis mine.
194 *Hamlet*, 1.1.69.
195 Ibid., 1.1.133–5.
196 Scot, *Discouerie of Witchcraft*, 535.
197 Ibid., 540.
198 Ibid., 434.
199 *Hamlet*, 1.1.42.
200 Ibid., 1.1.46–9.
201 James VI of Scotland and I of England, *Daemonologie*, 33.
202 Scot, *Discouerie of Witchcraft*, 442.
203 *Hamlet*, 1.4.69–70.
204 James VI of Scotland and I of England, *Daemonologie*, 60.
205 Scot, *Discouerie of Witchcraft*, 461.
206 James VI of Scotland and I of England, *Daemonologie*, 32–3.
207 Lodge, *The Diuel Coniured*, 16–17.
208 Scot, *Discouerie of Witchcraft*, 535.
209 James VI of Scotland and I of England, *Daemonologie*, 32.
210 Ibid., 34.
211 Ibid., 60–1 (emphasis mine).
212 *Hamlet*, 1.5.39–40.
213 Del Río, *Disquisitionum magicarum libri sex* (1612 ed.), 1052.
214 *Hamlet*, 1.5.15–20.
215 Ibid., 3.4.119–22.
216 Belleforest, as quoted in Schleiner, *Melancholy, Genius, and Utopia*, 239.
217 Ibid., 238.
218 *Hamlet*, 2.1.80.
219 Ibid., 2.2.572–5.
220 James VI of Scotland and I of England, *Daemonologie*, 30.
221 Draper, *The Humors and Shakespeare's Characters*, 64–5. See also Kail, *The Medical Mind of Shakespeare*, and Hoeniger, *Medicine and Shakespeare in the English Renaissance*. A similar study which also includes mention of *Daemonologie* as pertinent to the *milieu* of Shakespeare is Irving Edgar, *Shakespeare, Medicine and Psychiatry*. For a study of melancholy/madness among Prince Hamlet's historical counterparts in Germany during this time period, see Midelfort, *Mad Princes of Renaissance Germany*, especially Part II, 'The Age of the Melancholy Prince.'
222 Schleiner, *Melancholy, Genius, and Utopia*, 308.
223 Scot, *Discouerie of Witchcraft*, 508.

224 James VI of Scotland and I of England, *Daemonologie*, 47.
225 Scot, *Discouerie of Witchcraft*, 58.
226 James VI of Scotland and I of England, *Daemonologie*, 27.
227 Ibid., 28.
228 David Quint, *Origin and Originality in Renaissance Literature: Versions of the Source* (New Haven: Yale University Press, 1983), 23.
229 See Levin, *The Question of Hamlet*, 120.
230 Aristotle, *Poetics*, chapter 16, pp. 27–9.
231 Eliot, 'Hamlet and His Problems,' 765–6.

5. Self-Exorcism and the Rise of the Novel

1 See Weiger, *The Individuated Self*, 3. However, there were other genres at this time which also proved hospitable to the emerging autonomous self, as is demonstrated by Ian Watt in *Myths of Modern Individualism*.
2 Many scholars have published studies on related topics such as superstition or witchcraft in the *Quijote* or other works of Cervantes: Maldonado de Guevara, 'La renuncia a la magia en el *Quijote* y en el *Fausto*'; Castro, 'Cervantes y la Inquisición'; Arco y Garay, 'Cervantes y las supersticiones'; Rodríguez Marín, 'Las supersticiones del *Quijote*'; Caro Baroja, 'El *Quijote* y la concepción mágica del mundo'; Molho, '"El sagaz perturbador del género humano"'; Harrison, 'Magic in the Spanish Golden Age.' Salvador Muñoz Iglesias has written an excellent study of religious elements in the *Quijote*, including demonology, in *Lo religioso en el 'Quijote.'* Most recently Steven Nadler, adopting an exclusively philosophical approach, compares the evil enchanter in the *Quijote* to Descartes's demon, the 'deceptor potentissimus et malignus' of the *Meditations on First Philosophy* ('Descartes's Demon and the Madness of Don Quixote,' 42, 41). Michael D. Hasbrouck has noticed (in a brief article entitled 'Posesión demoníaca, locura y exorcismo en el *Quijote*') Cervantes' allusions to general exorcistic formulas, Biblical episodes, and diabolical places and objects.
3 For the term 'heteroglossia' I refer of course to Bakhtin, 'Discourse in the Novel,' 324.
4 Wilson, 'The Histrionics of Exorcism.'
5 For the best treatment of Cervantes' probable reading list, see Cotarelo Valledor, *Cervantes lector.*
6 Cervantes, *El ingenioso hidalgo Don Quijote de la Mancha*, ed. Murillo, I:133. All quotations are from this edition unless otherwise noted.
7 Hasbrouck, 'Posesíon demoníaca,' 121.
8 *Don Quijote*, I:134.
9 Ibid.

10 Noydens, *Practica de exorcistas*, 71. All references are to the 1688 edition unless stated otherwise.

11 Ibid., 9.

12 *Don Quijote*, II:397.

13 Ibid., II:218.

14 Noydens, *Practica de exorcistas*, 103–4.

15 Ibid., 104. English corollaries to Noydens's examples may be found in the case histories of Richard Napier's patients, who were haunted by spirits appearing in the forms of dogs, cats, mice, bees, weasels, and horses. See MacDonald, *Mystical Bedlam*, 203.

16 *Don Quijote*, II:553.

17 Hasbrouck, 'Posesión demoníaca,' 126.

18 Del Río, *Disquisitionum magicarum libri sex* (1599), book 2, trans. Jesús Moya as *La magia demoníaca*, 534.

19 For a wonderful discussion of ghostly apparitions of armies in Italy during this time, see chapter 3 ('Apparitions as Signs: The Kings of the Dead on the Battleground of Agnadello') of Niccoli, *Prophecy and People in Renaissance Italy*. As Niccoli notes, Ludwig Lavater's *De spectris, lemuribus … variisque praesagitationibus* (1570), published in England as *Of Ghostes and Spirites Walking by Nyght*, trans. R. H[arrison] (London: H. Benneyman for R. Watkyns, 1572), was a source for later discussions of military apparitions (63). Winfried Schleiner quotes Lavater as recalling the character Ajax from classical antiquity, who legendarily drew his sword and set upon herds of swine because, in his madness, he believed them to be Greek armies (Lavater, 13, quoted in Schleiner, *Melancholy, Genius, and Utopia*, 161).

20 Niccoli also discusses the metamorphoses of animal herds into armies and armies into animal herds. She cites a four-page pamphlet, *Littera de le maravigliose battaglie* (Villachiara, 1517), in which the vision of phantom combatants ends with 'an innumerable quantity of pigs' (*Prophecy and People in Renaissance Italy*, 74). She then quotes a witness's account of a vision of 'several thousand black and white sheep' followed by the apparition of 'an infinite number of armed men on foot and on horseback, and many with readied lances' (74).

21 Torquemada, *Jardín*, 708–9.

22 See *Aqui se contiene un caso nueuo que trata de como vn estudiante se fingio duende en vn meson*.

23 Noydens, *Practica de exorcistas*, 254.

24 *Don Quijote*, I:207.

25 Noydens, *Practica de exorcistas*, 256.

26 *Don Quijote*, I:130.

27 Robbins, *The Encyclopedia of Witchcraft and Demonology*, 128. Joseph Kaster explains

this theory in relation to Egyptian rituals, but it applies to Jewish and Christian ones as well (Joseph Kaster, trans. and ed., *The Wings of the Falcon* [New York: Holt, Rinehart and Winston, 1968], 60). The Assyrians and the Babylonians held similar beliefs; see Laín Entralgo, *The Therapy of the Word in Classical Antiquity,* 27.

28 José Antonio Maravall writes of Don Quixote's serious fascination with enchanters and positions him well within the mainstream of European religious belief at this time (*Utopia and Counterutopia in the 'Quixote,'* 119).

29 For a full discussion of the contents of Don Quixote's library, see Baker, *La biblioteca de Don Quijote,* especially 'Los libros de Don Quijote,' 99–105, and 'Taxonomía y economía de una biblioteca ficticia,' 106–34.

30 Del Río, *Disquisitionum magicarum libri sex* (1720 ed.), 233.

31 *Don Quijote,* I:107.

32 Ibid., I:112.

33 Menéndez Pelayo, *Historia de los heterodoxos españoles,* 4:375.

34 *Index et catalogus librorum prohibitorum, mandato Illustris,* 4; reprinted in De Bujanda, *Index de l'inquisition espagnole 1583, 1584,* 884. Thanks to Paul Grendler for help with finding this Index.

35 Scot, *The Discouerie of Witchcraft,* 443.

36 The full entry in the Index reads: 'Obras de George de Monte mayor, en lo que toca a deuocion y cosas Christianas' (*Cathalogus librorum, qui prohibentur mandato Illustrissimi & Reuerend. D. D. Ferdinandi De Valdes Hispalensis Archiepiscopi, Inquisitoris Generalis Hispaniae* [Catalogue of books, which are prohibited by the order of the Most Illustrious and Most Reverend Doctor Don Ferdinand de Valdes of the Archepiscopacy of Spain, the Inquisitor General of Spain] [Valladolid: Sebastián Martínez, 1559], 46; reprinted in De Bujanda, *Index de l'inquisition espagnole 1551, 1554, 1559,* 513–14, 631, 676, 686). Inquisitor General Fernando Valdés, archbishop of Seville, issued this Index in Valladolid. Thanks to Paul Grendler for his help with locating this specific index.

37 *Don Quijote,* I:72.

38 The burnings had begun in the late fifteenth century and continued into Cervantes' lifetime. In 1560, for example, King Philip II (1527–98) ordered an *auto de fe* to impress his new bride Isabel de Valois; in it, several people were burned alive. For an *auto de fe* ordered by Carlos V in Valladolid in a previous year, the spectators ranged from the highest to the lowest members of society: 'altas dignidades eclesiásticas, nobles de rancio abolengo, altos funcionarios del Estado, sacerdotes, frailes y monjas, mezclados con menestrales, artesanos, sirvientes y gente menuda del pueblo' (high ecclesiastical dignitaries, nobles of ancient ancestry, high functionaries of the State, priests, friars and nuns, mixed with workmen, artisans, servants, and insignificant people of the populace) (Olmos García, 'La Inquisición,' 40). On 8 March 1600, Philip III attended an *auto de fe* in Toledo, accompanied by his courtiers and their ladies.

One person was burned, while thirty penitents were placed on display (ibid., 72). One of these spectacles was cancelled in 1604 in Triana, to the disappointment of 500 spectators (participants in a parade) who had awaited the arrival of the prisoners. In the same year, on 7 November, a second similar celebration was cancelled even though it had been publicized in all the usual ways. That year did mark a temporary suspension of the *autos* by order of the king for political reasons. But they resumed again: for details on the 1610 Logroño event, see Johnson, 'Of Witches and Bitches.' Further *autos* were staged in Granada and Toledo in 1615, the year in which the second volume of the *Quijote* was published.

39 *Don Quijote*, I:109.
40 Cervantes, *Don Quijote*, ed. Rico and Forradellas, I:77.
41 Ibid., II:282.
42 Torquemada alludes to this popular belief: 'lo que de Merlín se cuenta, que fue engendrado de un demonio' (what is told of Merlin, that he was engendered by a demon) (*Jardín*, 692).
43 El Saffar, *Beyond Fiction*, 95.
44 *Don Quijote*, II:394.
45 Avalle-Arce, 'Don Quijote, o la vida como obra de arte.'
46 Sullivan, 'The Beyond in the Here-and-Now.'
47 Cervantes, *La cueva de Salamanca* (1615), 237–55.
48 Del Río, *Disquisiciones mágicas*, trans. Moya, 294.
49 Diego de Heredia was a friend of Antonio Pérez, Spain's secretary for Portuguese affairs under Philip II. Pedro Gonzalo de Castel accused him of having in his house books of necromancy written in Arabic. Diego de Heredia had harboured the *morisco* conjuror Marquina in his house so that his guest could show him how to use the books. At the suggestion of Marquina, Diego went in the middle of the night to seek buried treasure in a hermitage called Matamala. Marquina began to conjure with the books, and there was a great thundering sound. Diego heard Marquina speaking with devils. Diego complained that they had found no buried treasure, and the devils replied through Marquina that the time of enchantment was not yet completed (Menéndez Pelayo, *Historia de lo heterodoxos españoles*, 4:375–6).
50 Proceso de D. Diego de Heredia, MS 85 of the Bibliothèque Nationale in Paris, the Llorente collection, quoted in Menéndez Pelayo, ibid., 376.
51 *Don Quijote*, II:344.
52 Ibid., II:350.
53 See *Don Quijote*, ed. Cortázar, Lerner, et al., 2:710n13. See also Avalle-Arce, *Enciclopedia cervantina*, 465.
54 The *novela ejemplar* most deeply concerned with the supernatural is *El coloquio de los perros*. For an unsurpassed analysis of the witch Cañizares as an embodiment of pure evil, see Alban Forcione's *Cervantes and the Mystery of Lawlessness*. He establishes in this

book that Cervantes did explore phenomena such as witchcraft and demonic possession seriously (71).

55 Forcione, 'Cervantes's Secularized Miracle,' 351.

56 Noydens, *Practica de exorcistas*, 16.

57 Ibid., 74.

58 Castañega, *Tratado*, 143.

59 Covarrubias defines 'encantadores' as: 'Maléficos, hechiceros, magos, nigrománticos; aunque estos nombres son diferentes y por diferentes razones se confunden unos con otros. Verás al padre Martín del Río en sus Disquisiciones mágicas, donde difusamente trata desta gente perdida y endiablada' (Maleficent ones, bewitchers, magicians, necromancers; although these names are different and for different reasons they are confused with one another. You will consult Father Martín del Río in his Magical Disquisitions, where he treats diffusely of this lost and bedevilled people) (*Tesoro de la lengua castellana o española*, 467).

60 As Steven Nadler demonstrates, Don Quixote attributes agency to the enchanter primarily in the following chapters in the first and second parts: I:7, I:8, I:18, I:25, II:10, II:32, and 'Descartes's Demon and The Madness of Don Quixote,' 48–53. For an excellent analysis of the theme of enchantment as it appears over one hundred times in the *Quijote*, see Richard Predmore, 'La función del encantamiento en el mundo del *Quijote*,' especially 66 and 71. Nadler ultimately concludes, as I do, that one face of the enchanter is demonic.

61 Noydens, *Practica de exorcistas*, 45, 89, and 246.

62 Ibid., 7.

63 Riley, *Cervantes's Theory of the Novel*, 209.

64 Ibid., 211.

65 El Saffar, *Novel to Romance*, 2. Stephen Gilman repeats the 'creator-enchanter' commonplace as well (*The Novel According to Cervantes*, 99).

66 Noydens, *Practica de exorcistas*, 17.

67 Sullivan, 'The Beyond in the Here-and-Now,' 65.

68 *Don Quijote*, I:299.

69 Ibid., I:310.

70 Ibid. Italics in original.

71 Ibid.

72 Noydens, *Practica de exorcistas*, 5.

73 Ibid., 5–6, 49.

74 Ibid., 2.

75 Ibid., 1.

76 Caciola, 'Discerning Spirits,' 74.

77 Ephesians 6:11,13.

78 Noydens, *Practica de exorcistas*, 2.

79 Ibid.
80 Ibid., 81, 83, 142.
81 Ibid., 3, 184.
82 Ibid., 21, 47.
83 Ibid., 22.
84 Ibid., 82.
85 *Don Quijote*, II:161.
86 2 Timothy 4:17, 1 Peter 5:8.
87 Noydens, *Practica de exorcistas*, 53.
88 *Don Quijote*, I:232.
89 Ibid., I:328.
90 Ibid., I:438.
91 Ibid., I:599.
92 Noydens, *Practica de exorcistas*, 90.
93 For a discussion of the medical details used by Cervantes as a model for Don Quix-
    ote's madness, see Comfort's review of a book by Rafael Salillas on Huarte de San
    Juan's *Examen de ingenios* (*Un gran inspirador de Cervantes*) as well as Heiple, 'Renais-
    sance Medical Psychology in *Don Quijote*.' See also Granjel, *La medicina española del
    siglo XVII*, for general information on Spanish medicine in the Golden Age, a field of
    study which too often ignores the connection with the supernatural frequently made
    even by medical doctors of the time. Many mental disorders and some physical ones,
    such as epilepsy, were considered to be either possession itself or at least the work of a
    demon (Amezúa, prologue to Castañega, *Tratado*, xiv). One treatise writer of the
    time, Castañega, laments that even natural diseases were attributed to supernatural
    causes (*Tratado*, 145).
94 Noydens, *Practica de exorcistas*, 169.
95 Ibid., 206.
96 Castañega, *Tratado*, 147.
97 Ibid., 146.
98 *Don Quijote*, I:544.
99 Ibid., I:237.
100 Ibid., I:598.
101 James VI of Scotland and I of England, *Daemonologie*, 70.
102 Ciruelo, *Treatise*, 267.
103 *Don Quijote*, I:558.
104 Noydens, *Practica de exorcistas*, 56.
105 *Don Quijote*, I:558.
106 Passafari, 'El dominio del fuego y la Noche de San Juan,' 141.
107 Ibid., 141–2.
108 *Don Quijote*, II:513.

109 Passafari, 'El dominio del fuego y la Noche de San Juan,' 142. In Golden Age Spain, this festival and its concomitant romantic intrigue were made famous through a *comedia* by Lope de Vega bearing the title *La noche de San Juan*.

110 In his edition, Murillo includes a footnote on this phrase: 'En los oficios de la Invención [*sic*] y Exaltación de la santa Cruz y en los exorcismos de la Iglesia se lee: *Ecce crucem Domini, fugite, partes adversae*' (In the offices of the elevation and exaltation of the holy Cross and in the exorcisms of the church is read: *Behold the cross of God; flee, adverse parties*) (*Don Quijote*, II:513). See also Avalle-Arce's *Enciclopedia cervantina* (205). Schevill and Bonilla in their edition offer a more specific identification for the phrase: 'Exorcismo que se halla en el oficio: *Proprium S. S. Hispanorum*, 7 y 8, *Exorcismus, Breviarium Romanum*, mayo 3, sept. 14 ... durante el ceremonial del exorcismo el sacerdote pone ambos manos en la cabeza del endemoniado (energúmeno) y dice: "Ecce crucem Domini; fugite, partes adversae, vicit leo de tribu Juda"' (Exorcism which is found in the office: *Proprium S. S. Hispanorum*, 7 and 8, *Exorcismus, Breviarium Romanum*, May 3, September 14 ... during the ceremony of exorcism the priest places both hands on the head of the demoniac [energumen] and says: 'Behold the cross of God; flee, adverse parties, the lion of the tribe of Judah has conquered') (*Don Quijote*, ed. Schevill and Bonilla, 4:447). Vicente Gaos in his edition gives essentially the same the same note (*Don Quijote*, ed. Gaos, 2:879n148a).

111 The barber performed most of the medical tasks for any given village. Winfried Schleiner has commented on the recurrent 'curing' episodes in this text and the efforts by Don Quixote's friends to restore his sanity (*Melancholy, Genius, and Utopia*, 158–9).

112 Schleiner, unaware of Don Quixote's self-exorcism, speculates about the apparent lack of a clear choice for who 'cures' the protagonist in this scenario (ibid., 161, 168).

113 Robert, *The Old and the New*, 130.

114 Ibid., 132–3. José Antonio Maravall also comments on the significance of the baptism as a sacrament and its role in the *renovatio interioris hominis* (*Utopia and Counterutopia*, 114). He fails, however, to account for Don Quixote's radical audacity in baptizing himself.

115 Even George Mariscal, who sees the sacraments in Part II of the novel as serving merely to position the decreasingly autonomous protagonist within a wider community of believers, affirms that here 'religion ... becomes the only practice through which such a[n] [ethical] subject might be constructed' (*Contradictory Subjects*, 204).

116 For a fictional text which contains a sort of self-exorcism, see my discussion of *La margarita preciosa* on p. 238n95.

117 Gentilcore, *From Bishop to Witch*, 7. On popular religion in southern Italy at this time, see also Ginzburg, 'Folklore, magia, religione.'

118 Gentilcore, *From Bishop to Witch*, 95; he translates from Girolamo Menghi's *Flagellum daemonum* (1577). Gentilcore also mentions tarantism as a form of self-exorcism

in which frantic dancing enables people 'ritually to express and come to terms with "crises of existence"' (11).

119 Ibid., 95.

120 The author is Diego Gómez Lodosa. Emphasis mine.

121 Gómez Lodosa, *Iugum ferreum Luciferi*, 138.

122 Ibid., 139.

123 Ibid.

124 Ibid., 140.

125 Ibid.

126 I know of at least one other fragment of an exorcism manual to make use of this same Passion according to St John. It was published in Barcelona (ca. 1508) by Joan Rosembach, a printer who specialized in liturgical printing. This untitled fragment is described in Norton, *A Descriptive Catalogue of Printing in Spain and Portugal*, (Cambridge: Cambridge University Press, 1978), 43.

127 Gómez Lodosa, *Iugum ferreum Luciferi*, 140–1. Emphasis mine.

128 Ibid., 142.

129 Ibid., 143.

130 Ibid., 152.

131 Ibid., 153.

132 Ibid., 160.

133 Gilman, *The Novel According to Cervantes*, 120–1.

134 Riley, *Cervantes's Theory of the Novel*, 37–8.

135 El Saffar, *Novel to Romance*, 2–3.

136 Foucault, *The Order of Things*, 48.

137 Gilman, *The Novel According to Cervantes*, 122. Harry Levin agrees ('The Example of Cervantes,' in *Contexts of Criticism* [New York: Atheneum, 1963], 79).

138 Lukács, *The Theory of the Novel*, 104, 75.

139 Gillet, 'The Autonomous Character,' 182.

140 Ibid., 179–80. See also Reed, '*Don Quixote*: The Birth, Rise and Death of the Novel,' 271.

141 As Alban Forcione demonstrates forcefully in 'Cervantes and the Classical Aesthetic: *Don Quixote*' (in *Cervantes, Aristotle and the* Persiles, 91–155), Cervantes was acutely aware of Renaissance literary theory and self-consciously followed the precepts of the Neo-Aristotelians.

142 Gilman, *The Novel According to Cervantes*, 46.

143 Gillet, 'The Autonomous Character,' 184.

144 James, 'Emergence of Character,' 63.

145 Avellaneda, *El ingenioso hidalgo Don Quijote de la Mancha*.

146 Gilman, *The Novel According to Cervantes*, 56. As Joseph Gillet points out, Cervantes was not the only famous author to have created characters so autonomous that his

work was continued by someone else in a sequel ('The Autonomous Character,' 181); Boccaccio's *Elegia di Madonna Fiammetta*, for example, was also continued by Juan de Flores in *Grimalte y Gradissa* (1480–5). But I might add that Cervantes' situation was different in that he had the advantage over Boccaccio, in the new age of printing technology, of being able to read and respond immediately to an apocryphal sequel. Cervantes, unlike Boccaccio, seems to have realized that his characters had become autonomous. He was then able to manipulate and play with this fact in Part II. See Kawin, *The Mind of the Novel*, 20.

147 On this point see Reed's '*Don Quixote*: The Birth, Rise and Death of the Novel,' 271.
148 Gilman, *The Novel According to Cervantes*, 124.
149 As Riley observes, if Avellaneda had not existed, Cervantes would have had to invent him (*Cervantes's Theory of the Novel*, 214).
150 Reed, *An Exemplary History of the Novel*, 7. Reed notes that critics such as Ortega y Gasset, Lukács, and Bakhtin have all defined the novel in opposition to the epic (20).
151 Bakhtin, 'Epic and Novel,' 4.
152 Riley, *Cervantes's Theory of the Novel*, 1.
153 Thornton Wilder as quoted in Gilman, *The Novel According to Cervantes*, 17. Walter Reed calls the *Quijote* 'the original' novel (*An Exemplary History*, 7), while Bakhtin calls it 'the classic and purest model of the novel as genre' ('Epic and Novel,' 324). Ortega y Gasset writes that it is 'the first novel in point of time and in merit'; he goes on to make his famous statement that 'every novel bears *Quixote* within it like an inner filigree' (*Meditations on Quixote*, 111, 162).
154 Gilman, *The Novel According to Cervantes*, 70.
155 Ibid., 115.

Conclusion: Liturgy in Literature, or Early Modern Literary Theory and the Christian Legitimate Marvellous

1 Burckhardt, *The Civilization of the Renaissance in Italy*, 2:514. Burckhardt did admit, however, that the modern scientific or sceptical spirit he championed 'shows itself but little in literature' of the Renaissance (2:512).
2 Cantor, *Inventing the Middle Ages*, 182.
3 Lukács, *The Theory of the Novel*, 103. At least this scholar acknowledges that religion was not entirely dead in the Renaissance; Lukács's view, though too pessimistic for my taste, still allows for genuine (albeit dying) faith (104).
4 Dollimore, *Radical Tragedy*, xxix.
5 Greimas, *On Meaning*, 216.
6 See Stephen Greenblatt, *Shakespearean Negotiations*. Mark Edmundson offers a potent critique of this aspect of Greenblatt's work (*Literature Against Philosophy*, 191), as does Douglas Bruster (*Quoting Shakespeare*, 90–3).

7 Dollimore, *Radical Tragedy,* 7–8. He quotes E.P. Thompson's *The Poverty of Theory.*

8 García de la Concha, 'La intención religiosa del *Lazarillo,*' 268. He mentions Feijóo, who was a famous sceptic of a period slightly later than ours (1676–1764). See Feijóo y Montenegro, *Teatro crítico universal.*

9 Díaz Migoyo, 'Desendemoniando *El aguacil endemoniado,*' 58.

10 On Quevedo's Christian humanism, see López Poza, 'Quevedo, humanista cristiano'; Kallendorf and Kallendorf, 'Conversations with the Dead.'

11 The academy was not always so inhospitable to religion. Such scholars as C.S. Lewis, W.K. Wimsatt, and G. Wilson Knight demonstrated a sensitivity to things spiritual which has been abandoned by many of their successors. See the following examples of their work: Lewis, *The Discarded Image;* Wimsatt, 'Poetry and Christian Thinking'; and Knight, *The Christian Renaissance.* There have been, however, some modern critics who have continued this scholarly tradition of respect for religion and elements of the supernatural. See, for instance, Ricoeur, *Figuring the Sacred.*

12 Vickery, 'Myth Criticism,' 811.

13 Biow, Mirabile Dictu: *Representations of the Marvelous,* 1. For evidence of early modern belief in the existence of demons, see, for example, Baxter, *The certainty of the worlds of spirits and, consequently, of the immortality of souls: of the malice and misery of the devils and the damned: and of the blessedness of the justified, fully evinced by the unquestionable histories of apparitions, operations, witchcrafts, voices &c. Written, as an addition to many other treatises for the conviction of Sadduces and infidels ...* 'Sadduc[e]es' in this period were those who did not believe in the reality of spirits.

14 A prominent example of a scholar writing recently with this bias is Stephens, *Demon Lovers.* He twists the evidence to the point of sounding like a conspiracy theorist: 'The texts of witchcraft theory must be considered as complete wholes, driven by motivations that are probably *not* obvious. Just because they *claimed* that they believed something or that they never doubted something else does not oblige us to take their word for it ... The less one believed in the verifiable presence of the Devil, the more exaggerated claims one made for his being everywhere, at all times, in all forms' (10, 102). This perspective exemplifies what Paul Ricoeur terms the 'hermeneutics of suspicion' ('The Critique of Religion,' 214–15). A useful corrective to this approach is that of Armando Maggi, in *Satan's Rhetoric.* Maggi states that his book is founded on 'a "credulous" suspension of disbelief, on the basic assumption that, in order to make sense of such an obsolete and "insane" intellectual system, we must endeavour to let it lay out its essential premises and obsessive goals without superimposing our "enlightened" beliefs on what those demonology books *really* meant to say' (3).

15 Clark, *Thinking with Demons,* 396. He cites Walker, *Unclean Spirits,* 15. See also Daston, 'Marvelous Facts and Miraculous Evidence in Early Modern Europe.'

16 'Longinus,' *On the Sublime,* 225, 229.

17 Petronius, *The Satyricon,* section 118, p. 128.

18 Aristotle, *Poetics*, 44, 45, 50.

19 Francesco Patrizi, *Della poetica di Francesco Patrici*. *La deca ammirabile* (MS Parma, Bibl. Palatina, Pal. 408), fol. 57 (cited in Weinberg, *A History of Literary Criticism in the Italian Renaissance*, 2:774). The most important recent resurrection of Patrizi has been effected by Peter Platt in *Reason Diminished*.

20 Dryden, 'Of Heroic Plays, an Essay,' 152–3.

21 Dryden, 'The Author's Apology for Heroic Poetry and Poetic License,' 187.

22 Cowley, 'Preface to *Poems*,' 329.

23 Mazzoni, *On the Defense of the Comedy of Dante*, 371, 388.

24 Jacopo Mazzoni, *Della difesa della 'Commedia' di Dante*, 2 vols (Cesena: Bartolomeus Raverius, 1688), 1:594–5 (cited in Hathaway, *Marvels and Commonplaces*, 77).

25 Talentoni categorizes *admiratio* as a passion of the soul and describes how it is produced by conjunctions of the animate and inanimate, rational and irrational, actions accomplished by chance and actions accomplished by intent. He also discusses the pleasurable effects of *admiratio*. See Giovanni Talentoni, *Discorso ... sopra la maraviglia ...* (Milan: Francesco Paganello, 1597); cited in Weinberg, *A History of Literary Criticism in the Italian Renaissance*, 1:238–9.

26 Cueva, *Ejemplar poético*, 124.

27 López Pinciano, *Philosophia antigua poética*, 2:56.

28 Cunningham, *Woe or Wonder*, 78.

29 Hathaway, *Marvels and Commonplaces*, 58.

30 Mirollo, 'The Aesthetics of the Marvelous,' 63.

31 López Pinciano, *Philosophia antigua poética*, 65–6.

32 Giovanni Battista Pigna, *I romanzi* (Venice: Vincenzo Valgrisi, 1554), 40–1 (cited in Weinberg, *History of Literary Criticism in the Italian Renaissance*, 1:274).

33 Giovambattista Giraldi Cinthio, *Discorso intorno al comporre de i romanzi* (Venice: Gabriele Giolito de Ferrari et Fratelli, 1554), 69–70 (cited in Hathaway, *Marvels and Commonplaces*, 136).

34 Minturno, *L'arte poetica*, 31 (quoted in Hathaway, *Marvels and Commonplaces*, 137).

35 Cascales, *Tablas poéticas*, 155–6.

36 The philosopher Bertrand Russell would later speculate that this conflation was even more literal for the medieval Church Fathers than it was for these Renaissance literary theorists: 'It must be understood that, in the writings of the Fathers, "demons" mean heathen deities, who were supposed to be enraged by the progress of Christianity. The early Christians by no means denied the existence of the Olympian gods, but supposed them servants of Satan – a view which Milton adopted in "Paradise Lost"' ('Demonology and Medicine,' 83).

37 Tasso, *Discourses on the Heroic Poem*, Gilbert 480–1. For Tasso's reiterations of these points in his private correspondence, see his *Le lettere di Torquato Tasso*, vol. 1, letters 30, 42, 43, 45–8, 60, 63, and 75.

38 Campanella, 'XVII: La religione nel poema.'

39 Orazio Lombardelli, *Discorso intorno ai contrasti che si fanno sopra la Gerusalemme liberata de Torquato Tasso* (Ferrara: G. Vassalini, 1586); cited in Hathaway, *Marvels and Commonplaces*, 126.

40 Giovambattista Strozzi the Younger, *Discorso se sia bene a poeti servirsi delle fauole delli antichi* (read before the Accademia Fiorentina, 1588), in *Orazioni et altre prose* (Rome: Lodouico Grignani, 1635); cited in Hathaway, *Marvels and Commonplaces*, 146–7, and also in Weinberg, *History of Literary Criticism in the Italian Renaissance*, 2:1150.

41 Bellisario Bulgarini, *Repliche alle risposte del Sig. Orazio Capponi* (Siena: L. Bonetti, 1585), 44–62; cited in Hathaway, *Marvels and Commonplaces*, 140–1. Hathaway explains Bulgarini's position on the use of the unorthodox Christian marvellous (ibid.).

42 Hathaway, *Marvels and Commonplaces*, 147.

43 See Leo, 'Staunen und Wunder,' 103. Actually, as Stuart Clark has shown, Tasso's work was later seen as so orthodox that he was even appropriated by the demonologists as further evidence for their position ('Tasso and the Literature of Witchcraft,' 7). See further Sozzi, 'Il magismo nel Tasso.' Additionally, see Baldassarri, 'Inferno' e 'cielo.'

44 See Hathaway, *Marvels and Commonplaces*, 148.

45 See Treip, *Allegorical Poetics and the Epic*, 83. Thomas Roche had made this point emphatically before ('Tasso's Enchanted Woods,' 50, 55).

46 Treip, *Allegorical Poetics and the Epic*, 84.

47 Bartolomeo Maranta, *Bartholomaei Marantae Venusini, Lvcvllianarvm qvaestionvm libri qvinqve* (Basel: Mense Martio, 1564), 88, 133 (cited in Weinberg, *History of Literary Criticism in the Italian Renaissance*, 1:492).

48 Giason Denores, *Poetica nella qual si tratta secondo l'opinion d'Aristotile della tragedia, del poema heroico, & della comedia* (Padua: Paulo Meietto, 1588), 2–3 (cited in Weinberg, *History of Literary Criticism in the Italian Renaissance*, 2:787).

49 For the above discussion, see Francesco Robortello, *In librum Aristotelis de arte poetica explicationes* (Florence: Lorencio Torrentini, 1548), 87, 328, 45, and 121 (cited in Weinberg, *History of Literary Criticism in the Italian Renaissance*, 1:397–8).

50 Antonio Riccoboni, *De re comica ex Aristotelis doctrina* (1579), in *Trattati di poetica e retorica del Cinquecento*, ed. Weinberg, 3:265–6.

51 Castelvetro, *The Poetics of Aristotle Translated and Annotated*, 328.

52 Ibid., 338–9.

53 I refer to Gauchet, *The Disenchantment of the World*. Gauchet in turn borrows the term from Max Weber.

54 Hume, 'Of Miracles,' 117.

55 Greenblatt, *Marvelous Possessions*, 79.

56 McClenon, *Wondrous Events*, 151.

Epilogue: Problematizing the Category of 'Demonic Possession'

1 See, for example, Mariscal, *Contradictory Subjects*. Mariscal specifically takes issue with Burckhardt, via Foucault (170). For a preemptive answer to positions such as Mariscal's which leave little room for notions such as the 'subject' or 'agency,' see John Mowitt's 'Avoiding the Subject' in his foreword to Smith, *Discerning the Subject*, ix–xvi.

2 Garrett, *Spirit Possession and Popular Religion*, 2–3.

3 Knox, *Enthusiasm*, 588–9.

4 Burton, *The Anatomy of Melancholy*, 174.

5 Bright, *A Treatise of Melancholy* (London, 1586); see also Babb, *The Elizabethan Malady*, 49; and McGee, *The Elizabethan Hamlet*, 103.

6 James VI of Scotland and I of England, *Daemonologie*, 32.

7 Scot, *The Discouerie of Witchcraft*, 508.

8 Gaspare Marcucci, *Quadripartitum melancholicum* (Rome: Andreas Phaeus, 1645). The chapter on 'Whether Melancholy Can Come from a Daemon' (pt. I, chapter 25) is cited in Schleiner's *Melancholy, Genius, and Utopia*, 54. The chapter discussing the *bacchantes*, sibyls, and *vates* is entitled 'Whether Melancholics Prophesy' (pt. I, ch. 18, cited in ibid., 55).

9 Klibansky, Panofsky, and Saxl, *Saturn and Melancholy*, 'Melancholy as Heightened Self-Awareness,' 228–40.

10 See Screech, *Montaigne and Melancholy*.

11 Ibid., 10.

12 Ibid., 33.

13 Schleiner, *Melancholy, Genius, and Utopia*, 165.

14 Ibid., 206.

15 Screech, *Montaigne and Melancholy*, 10. See also his *Ecstasy and the Praise of Folly*, 53.

16 'While all raptures are ecstasies, not all ecstasies are raptures. Generally speaking, rapture is a higher boon than ecstasy, but some do use the words interchangeably' (Screech, *Ecstasy and the Praise of Folly*, 57).

17 See Weber, 'Between Ecstasy and Exorcism.'

18 Cervantes, *The Devil in the New World*, 101. For a striking illustration of this principle, see plate 23, 'The Devil's role in salvation: St. Rose of Lima in Satan's arms' (113).

19 Screech, *Montaigne and Melancholy*, 8.

20 Screech, *Ecstasy and the Praise of Folly*, xvii ff.

21 Michael Heyd, '"Be Sober and Reasonable,"' 2, 21.

22 See 'Descartes and the Cartesian Philosophy: A Manifestation of Enthusiasm?' chapter 4 of Heyd, '"Be Sober and Reasonable."'

23 See Carvallo, *Cisne de Apolo*, 370.

24 Curtius, *European Literature and the Latin Middle Ages*, 145.

25 See Walker, *Spiritual and Demonic Magic from Ficino to Campanella*.

26 For other antecedents to this magic, see Fanger, *Conjuring Spirits*.

27 'Poetry demands a man with a special gift ... or a touch of madness' (Aristotle, *Poetics*, 1455a, quoted in Burwick, *Poetic Madness*, 1).

28 'No sane-minded poet could ever enter Helicon' (Democritus, as quoted in Cicero, *De divinatione*, 1.80, quoted in Burwick, ibid.).

29 'By some divine force the poet's mind is raised above the ordinary' (Seneca the Younger, *Epistulae Morales*, 84.1–7, quoted in Burwick, ibid.).

30 Burwick, *Poetic Madness*, 8.

31 Epilepsy was called 'the sacred disease' by the Greeks. We still call epileptic fits 'seizures' because of the etymological connection to demonic possession. See Kail, *The Medical Mind of Shakespeare*, 87.

32 For the first printed discussion of tarantism as a form of mad dancing caused by a poisonous spider's bite, see Zuccollo da Cologna, *La pazzia del ballo*.

33 I refer to 'The Baroque Symptom,' a paper on stigmatics presented by Lowell Gallagher at 'Together Apart: Community, Concealment, and Communion,' a conference which took place 23–4 February 2001 at the William Andrews Clark Memorial Library and was sponsored by the UCLA Center for Seventeenth and Eighteenth Century Studies. Stigmatics could experience convulsions similar to those of demoniacs and were often 'pricked' to check the numbness of their stigmatic wounds. This test was similar to those performed on both witches and demoniacs.

34 The Stoic Seneca suffered from asthma and reported that Roman doctors treated it as a momentary departure of the soul from the body, or a practice for death (see Screech, *Ecstasy and the Praise of Folly*, 82).

35 MacDonald, *Mystical Bedlam*, 210.

36 Walker, *Spiritual and Demonic Magic*, 45–6.

37 Acts 2:13.

38 John 8:48, 10:20.

Bibliography

General Sources

Allen, Thomas B. *Possessed: The True Story of an Exorcism*. New York: Doubleday, 1993.

Arnold, Clinton E. *Three Crucial Questions about Spiritual Warfare*. Grand Rapids, MI: Baker, 1997.

Arnold, N. Scott. *Marx's Radical Critique of Capitalist Society: A Reconstruction and Critical Evaluation*. New York: Oxford University Press, 1990.

Aristotle. *Poetics*. Trans. Leon Golden and O.B. Hardison, Jr. Englewood Cliffs, NJ: Prentice-Hall, 1968.

– *Politica: The Basic Works of Aristotle*. Trans. Richard McKeon. New York: Random House, 1941.

– *Politics* 1341b32–1342a15. Trans. in *Education and Culture in the Political Thought of Aristotle*, Carnes Lord. Ithaca and London: Cornell University Press, 1982.

Ashton, John. *The Devil in Britain and America*. York: Ward and Downey, 1896.

Augustine, St, Bishop of Hippo. *Confessions*. Trans. William Watts (1631). 2 vols. Cambridge, MA.: Harvard University Press, 1950.

Baker, Roger. *Binding the Devil: Exorcism Past and Present*. New York: Hawthorn, 1975.

Bakhtin, M. M. 'Discourse in the Novel.' In *The Dialogic Imagination*, ed. Michael Holquist, trans. Caryl Emerson and Michael Holquist, 259–422. Austin: University of Texas Press, 1981.

– 'Epic and Novel.' In *The Dialogic Imagination*, ed. Michael Holquist, trans. Caryl Emerson and Michael Holquist, 3–40. Austin: University of Texas Press, 1981.

– *Rabelais and His World*. Trans. Helene Iswolsky. Bloomington: Indiana University Press, 1984.

Barker, Francis. *The Tremulous Private Body: Essays on Subjection*. London: Methuen, 1984.

Barstow, Anne Llewellyn. *Witchcraze: A New History of the European Witch Hunts.* New York: Pandora, 1994.

Barthes, Roland. 'The Structuralist Activity.' In *European Literary Theory and Practice: From Existential Phenomenology to Structuralism,* ed. Vernon W. Gras, 157–63. New York: Delta, 1973.

Baumann, Richard, and Charles L. Briggs. 'Poetics and Performance as Critical Perspectives on Language and Social Life.' *Annual Review of Anthropology* 19 (1990): 59–88.

Bettelheim, Bruno. *The Uses of Enchantment.* New York: Vintage Books, 1989.

Biow, Douglas. Mirabile Dictu: *Representations of the Marvelous in Medieval and Renaissance Epic.* Ann Arbor: University of Michigan Press, 1996.

Blum, C. 'Le diable comme masque: L'évolution de la représentation du diable à la fin du Moyen Age et au début de la Renaissance.' In *Diable, diables, et diableries au temps de la Renaissance,* ed. M.T. Jones-Davies, 155–61. Paris: Jean Touzot, 1988.

Bourguignon, E. 'Spirit Possession, Belief, and Social Structure.' In *The Realm of the Extra-Human: Ideas and Actions,* ed. A. Bharati, 17–26. Ninth International Congress of Anthropological and Ethnological Sciences (1973). Chicago: Mouton, 1976.

Briggs, Robin. *Witches and Neighbors: The Social and Cultural Context of European Witchcraft.* New York: Viking, 1996.

Bristol, Michael. *Carnival and Theater: Plebeian Culture and the Structure of Authority in Renaissance England.* New York: Methuen, 1985.

Brownlee, Kevin, and Marina Scordilis. *Romance: Generic Transformation from Chrétien de Troyes to Cervantes.* Hanover: University Press of New England, 1985.

Bruno de Jésus-Marie, ed. *Satan.* New York: Sheed and Ward, 1952.

Burckhardt, Jacob. *The Civilization of the Renaissance in Italy.* Vol. 2. Trans. S.G.C. Middlemore. New York: Harper and Row, 1958.

Burwick, Frederick. *Poetic Madness and the Romantic Imagination.* University Park: Pennsylvania State University Press, 1996.

Caciola, Nancy. 'Discerning Spirits: Sanctity and Possession in the Later Middle Ages.' PhD dissertation, University of Michigan, 1994.

Camporesi, Piero. *The Fear of Hell: Images of Damnation and Salvation in Early Modern Europe.* Trans. Lucinda Byatt. University Park: Pennsylvania State University Press, 1990.

Cantor, Norman F. *Inventing the Middle Ages: The Lives, Works, and Ideas of the Great Medievalists of the Twentieth Century.* New York: William Morrow, 1991.

Chaytor, H.J. *From Script to Print: An Introduction to Medieval Vernacular Literature.* Cambridge: W. Heffer and Sons, 1950.

Clark, Stuart. *Thinking with Demons: The Idea of Witchcraft in Early Modern Europe.* Oxford: Clarendon, 1997.

Cope, Jackson I. *Dramaturgy of the Daemonic: Studies in Antigeneric Theater from Ruzante to Grimaldi.* Baltimore: Johns Hopkins University Press, 1984.

Curtius, Ernst Robert. *European Literature and the Latin Middle Ages.* Trans. Willard R. Trask. Princeton: Princeton University Press, 1953.

Daston, Lorraine. 'Marvelous Facts and Miraculous Evidence in Early Modern Europe.' *Critical Inquiry* 18 (1991): 93–124.

Derrida, Jacques. *Of Grammatology.* Trans. Gayatri Chakravorty Spivak. Baltimore: Johns Hopkins University Press, 1997.

– *Writing and Difference.* Trans. Alan Bass. Chicago: University of Chicago Press, 1978.

Deutch, Richard. *Exorcism: Possession or Obsession?* London: Bachman and Turner, 1975.

Douglas, Mary. *Purity and Danger: An Analysis of the Concepts of Pollution and Taboo.* New York: Praeger, 1966.

Ebon, Martin. *The Devil's Bride: Exorcism, Past and Present.* New York: Harper and Row, 1974.

Edmundson, Mark. *Literature against Philosophy, Plato to Derrida: A Defence of Poetry.* Cambridge: Cambridge University Press, 1995.

Eisenstein, Elizabeth. *The Printing Press As an Agent of Change: Communications and Cultural Transformations in Early Modern Europe.* 2 vols. Cambridge: Cambridge University Press, 1979.

El Saffar, Ruth. *Novel to Romance.* Baltimore: Johns Hopkins University Press, 1974.

Eliade, Mircea. *The Myth of the Eternal Return: or, Cosmos and History.* Trans. W. Trask. Princeton: Princeton University Press, 1971.

– *The Sacred and the Profane: The Nature of Religion.* Trans. Willard R. Trask. New York: Harcourt, Brace, 1959.

Fanger, Claire, ed. *Conjuring Spirits: Texts and Traditions of Medieval Ritual Magic.* University Park: Pennsylvania State University Press, 1998.

Fine, Elizabeth C., and Jean Haskell Speer. *Performance, Culture, and Identity.* Westport, CT: Praeger, 1992.

Fisher, Philip. *Wonder, the Rainbow, and the Aesthetics of Rare Experience.* Cambridge, MA.: Harvard University Press, 1998.

Flint, Valerie I. J. *The Rise of Magic in Early Medieval Europe.* Princeton: Princeton University Press, 1991.

Foucault, Michel. *Discipline and Punish: The Birth of the Prison.* Trans. Alan Sheridan. New York: Vintage, 1995.

– *Madness and Civilization: A History of Insanity in the Age of Reason.* New York: Vintage, 1988.

– *The Order of Things: An Archaeology of the Human Sciences.* Ed. R.D. Laing. New York: Vintage, 1970.

– 'What Is an Author?' In *Textual Strategies*, ed. Josué V. Harari, 141–60. Ithaca: Cornell University Press, 1979.

Frye, Northrop. *The Anatomy of Criticism.* Princeton: Princeton University Press, 1957.

- 'Literature as Therapy.' In *The Eternal Act of Creation: Essays, 1979–1990*, ed. Robert D. Denham, 21–36. Bloomington: Indiana University Press, 1993.
- *The Secular Scripture: A Study of the Structure of Romance*. Cambridge, MA.: Harvard University Press, 1976.

Gallagher, Catherine, and Stephen Greenblatt. *Practicing New Historicism*. Chicago: University of Chicago Press, 2000.

Garrett, Clarke. *Spirit Possession and Popular Religion from the Camisards to the Shakers*. Baltimore: Johns Hopkins University Press, 1987.

Gassner, John. 'Catharsis and the Modern Theater.' In *Aristotle's 'Poetics' and English Literature*, ed. Elder Olson, 108–113. Chicago: University of Chicago Press, 1965.

Gauchet, Marcel. *The Disenchantment of the World: A Political History of Religion*. Trans. Oscar Burge. Princeton: Princeton University Press, 1997.

Gilbert, Allan H. *Literary Criticism: Plato to Dryden*. Detroit: Wayne State University Press, 1962.

Gillet, Joseph. 'The Autonomous Character in Spanish and European Literature.' *Hispanic Review* 24.3 (1956): 179–90.

Ginzburg, Carlo. *Ecstasies: Deciphering the Witches' Sabbath*. Trans. Raymond Rosenthal. New York: Pantheon, 1991.

Girard, René. *The Scapegoat*. Trans. Yvonne Freccero. Baltimore: Johns Hopkins University Press, 1986.

Golden, Leon. 'Aristotle, Frye, and the Theory of Tragedy.' *Comparative Literature* 27 (1975): 47–58.
- 'Catharsis.' *Transactions of the American Philological Association* 93 (1962): 51–60.

Goodman, Felicitas. *How about Demons? Possession and Exorcism*. Bloomington: Indiana University Press, 1988.

Grassi, Ernesto, and Maristella Lorch. *Folly and Insanity in Renaissance Literature*. Binghamton, NY: Medieval and Renaissance Texts and Studies, 1986.

Greenblatt, Stephen. *Marvelous Possessions: The Wonder of the New World*. Chicago: University of Chicago Press, 1991.
- *Renaissance Self-Fashioning: From More to Shakespeare*. Chicago: University of Chicago Press, 1980.
- 'Towards a Poetics of Culture.' In *The New Historicism*, ed. H. Aram Veeser, 1–14. New York: Routledge, 1989.

Greene, Thomas. 'The Flexibility of the Self in Renaissance Literature.' In *The Disciplines of Criticism: Essays in Literary Theory, Interpretation, and History*, ed. Peter Demetz, Thomas Greene, and Lowry Nelson, Jr, 241–64. New Haven: Yale University Press, 1968.

Gregory the Great. *Dialogues*. Trans. Odo John Zimmerman. New York: Fathers of the Church, 1959.

Gregory, Brad S. *Salvation at Stake: Christian Martyrdom in Early Modern Europe*. Cambridge, MA: Harvard University Press, 1999.

Greimas, Algirdas Julien. 'Comparative Mythology.' In *On Meaning: Selected Writings in Semiotic Theory*, trans. Paul J. Perron and Frank H. Collins, 3–16. Minneapolis: University of Minnesota Press, 1987.

Guillén, Claudio. 'Literature As System.' In *Literature as System: Essays Toward the Theory of Literary History*, 375–419. Princeton: Princeton University Press, 1971.

Hanks, W.F. 'Text and Textuality.' *Annual Review of Anthropology* 18 (1989): 95–127.

Hardison, O.B., Jr. *The Enduring Monument: A Study of the Idea of Praise in Renaissance Literary Theory and Practice*. Westport, CT: Greenwood, 1973.

– 'Three Types of Renaissance Catharsis.' *Renaissance Drama* n.s. 2 (1969): 3–22.

Hathaway, Baxter. *Marvels and Commonplaces: Renaissance Literary Theory*. New York: Random House, 1968.

Hegel, G.W.F. *On Tragedy*. Ed. Anne and Henry Paolucci. New York: Harper, 1975.

Heyd, Michael. *'Be Sober and Reasonable': The Critique of Enthusiasm in the Seventeenth and Early Eighteenth Centuries*. Leiden: E.J. Brill, 1995.

Hornby, Richard. *Drama, Metadrama, and Perception*. Lewisburg, PA: Bucknell University Press, 1986.

Howard, Jean E. 'The New Historicism in Renaissance Studies.' In *Renaissance Historicism: Selections from* English Literary Renaissance, ed. Arthur F. Kinney and Dan S. Collins, 3–33. Amherst: Massachusetts University Press, 1987.

Hume, David. 'Of Miracles.' In *Enquiries Concerning Human Understanding and Concerning Principles of Morals*, ed. L.A. Selby-Bigge and P.H. Nidditch, 109–31. Oxford: Clarendon, 1975.

Hunt, Lynn, ed. *The New Cultural History*. Berkeley: University of California Press, 1989.

Jacoby, Mario, Verena Kast, and Ingrid Riedel. *Witches, Ogres, and the Devil's Daughter: Encounters with Evil in Fairy Tales*. Boston: Shambhala, 1992.

James, Henry. 'Emergence of Character.' In *The Theory of the Novel*, ed. Philip Stevick, 63. New York: Free Press, 1967.

Jameson, Fredric. 'Magical Narratives: On the Dialectical Use of Genre Criticism.' In *The Political Unconscious: Narrative as a Socially Symbolic Act*, 103–50. Ithaca: Cornell University Press, 1981.

– *The Prison House of Language: A Critical Account of Structuralism and Russian Formalism*. Princeton: Princeton University Press, 1972.

Johns, Adrian. 'The Physiology of Reading and the Anatomy of Enthusiasm.' In *Religio Medici: Medicine and Religion in Seventeenth-Century England*, ed. Ole Peter Grell and Andrew Cunningham, 136–70. Brookfield, VT: Scolar Press, 1996.

Kaiser, Walter. *Praisers of Folly*. Cambridge, MA: Harvard University Press, 1963.

Kantorowicz, Ernst H. *The King's Two Bodies: A Study in Medieval Political Theology*. Princeton: Princeton University Press, 1957.

Kaufmann, Walter. *Tragedy and Philosophy*. Garden City, NY: Anchor, 1969.

Kawin, Bruce F. *The Mind of the Novel: Reflexive Fiction and the Ineffable*. Princeton: Princeton University Press, 1982.

Kernan, Alvin. *The Cankered Muse*. New Haven: Yale University Press, 1950.

Kieckhefer, Richard. *Forbidden Rites: A Necromancer's Manual of the Fifteenth Century.* Stroud, Gloucestershire: Sutton, 1997.

– *Magic in the Middle Ages*. Cambridge: Cambridge University Press, 1990.

Klibansky, Raymond, Erwin Panofsky, and Fritz Saxl. *Saturn and Melancholy: Studies in the History of Natural Philosophy, Religion, and Art*. New York: Basic Books, 1964.

Knight, G. Wilson. *The Christian Renaissance: The Influence of the Bible and the Dogmas of Christianity on the Works of Shakespeare, Dante, Goethe, and Other Poets*. New York: Norton, 1963.

Knox, R.A. *Enthusiasm: A Chapter in the History of Religion, with Special Reference to the Seventeenth and Eighteenth Centuries*. New York: Oxford University Press, 1950.

Kristeller, Paul Oskar, and John Herman Randall, Jr. General Introduction to *The Renaissance Philosophy of Man*, ed. Ernst Cassirer, Paul Oskar Kristeller, and John Herman Randall, Jr, 1–20. Chicago: University of Chicago Press, 1948.

Laín Entralgo, Pedro. *The Therapy of the Word in Classical Antiquity*. Ed. and trans. L.J. Rather and John M. Sharp. New Haven: Yale University Press, 1970.

Lévi-Strauss, Claude. 'The Science of the Concrete.' In *European Literary Theory and Practice: From Existential Phenomenology to Structuralism*, ed. Vernon W. Gras, 133–56. New York: Delta, 1973.

– 'The Structural Study of Myth.' In *European Literary Theory and Practice: From Existential Phenomenology to Structuralism*, ed. Vernon W. Gras, 289–316. New York: Delta, 1973.

Lewis, C.S. *The Discarded Image: An Introduction to Medieval and Renaissance Literature*. Cambridge: Cambridge University Press, 1994.

Lewis, I.M. *Ecstatic Religion: An Anthropological Study of Spirit Possession and Shamanism*. Middlesex, England: Penguin, 1971.

'Longinus.' *On the Sublime*. Trans. W. Hamilton Fyfe. Loeb Classical Library. Cambridge, MA: Harvard University Press, 1973.

Lucas, F.L. *Tragedy: Serious Drama in Relation to Aristotle's Poetics*. New York: Collier, 1965.

Lukács, Georg. *The Theory of the Novel*. Trans. Anna Bostock. Cambridge, MA: MIT Press, 1971.

Maggi, Armando. *Satan's Rhetoric: A Study of Renaissance Demonology*. Chicago: University of Chicago Press, 2001.

Marx, Karl. *Capital: A Critical Analysis of Capitalist Production*. Trans. Samuel Moore and Edward Aveling. Ed. Frederick Engels. New York: International Publishers, 1947.

McClenon, James. *Wondrous Events: Foundations of Religious Belief*. Philadelphia: University of Pennsylvania Press, 1994.

M'Clintock, John, and James Strong. 'Exorcism, Exorcist.' *Cyclopaedia of Biblical, Theological and Ecclesiastical Literature.* New York: Arno, 1969.

Minnis, A.J. *Medieval Theory of Authorship: Scholastic Literary Attitudes in the Later Middle Ages.* London: Scolar Press, 1984.

Mirollo, James. 'The Aesthetics of the Marvelous: The Wondrous Work of Art in a Wondrous World.' In *The Age of the Marvelous,* ed. Joy Kenseth. Hanover, NH: Hood Museum of Art and Dartmouth College, 1991.

Montrose, Louis A. 'Professing the Renaissance: The Poetics and Politics of Culture.' In *The New Historicism,* ed. H. Aram Veeser, 15–36. New York: Routledge, 1989.

Nauman, St Elmo. *Exorcism Through the Ages.* New York: Philosophical Library, 1974.

Newman, Barbara. 'Possessed by the Spirit: Devout Women, Demoniacs, and the Apostolic Life in the Thirteenth Century.' *Speculum* 73 (1998): 733–70.

Nicola, John J. *Diabolical Possession and Exorcism.* Rockford, IL: Tan, 1974.

Nietzsche, Friedrich. *The Birth of Tragedy.* Trans. Walter Kaufmann. New York: Vintage, 1967.

Nischan, Bodo. 'The Exorcism Controversy and Baptism in the Late Reformation.' In *Articles on Witchcraft, Magic and Demonology.* Vol. 9, *Possession and Exorcism,* ed. Brian P. Levack, 161–82. New York: Garland, 1992.

Oesterreich, T.K. *Possession, Demoniacal and Other: Among Primitive Races, in Antiquity, the Middle Ages, and Modern Times.* New York: University Books, 1966.

Petronius. *The Satyricon.* Trans. J.P. Sullivan. London: Penguin, 1986.

Propp, Vladimir. 'Fairy Tale Transformations.' Trans. C.H. Severens. In *Readings in Russian Poetica: Formalist and Structuralist Views,* ed. Ladislav Matejka and Krystyna Pomorska, 94–114. Ann Arbor: University of Michigan Press, 1978.

– 'The Structural and Historical Study of the Wondertale.' In *Theory and History of Folklore,* trans. Ariadna Y. Martin and Richard P. Martin, ed. Anatoly Liberman. Vol. 5, *Theory and History of Literature,* 67–81. Minneapolis: University of Minnesota Press, 1984.

Reed, Walter L. *An Exemplary History of the Novel: The Quixotic versus the Picaresque.* Chicago: University of Chicago Press, 1981.

Ricoeur, Paul. 'The Critique of Religion.' In *The Philosophy of Paul Ricoeur: An Anthology of His Work,* ed. Charles E. Reagan and David Stewart, 213–22. Boston: Beacon, 1978.

– *Figuring the Sacred: Religion, Narrative, and Imagination.* Trans. David Pellauer. Ed. Mark I. Wallace. Minneapolis: Fortress, 1995.

– *The Symbolism of Evil.* Trans. Emerson Buchanan. Boston: Beacon, 1967.

Robbins, R.H. *The Encyclopedia of Witchcraft and Demonology.* New York: Crown, 1959.

Rodewyk, Adolf. *Possessed by Satan: The Church's Teaching on the Devil, Possession, and Exorcism.* Trans. Martin Ebon. Garden City, NY: Doubleday, 1975.

Rose, Mark. 'The Author as Proprietor: Donaldson vs. Becket and the Genealogy of Modern Authorship.' *Representations* 23 (1988): 51–85.

Russell, Bertrand. 'Demonology and Medicine.' In *Religion and Science*, 82–109. London: Oxford University Press, 1953.

Russell, Jeffrey Burton. *Lucifer: The Devil in the Middle Ages*. Ithaca: Cornell University Press, 1984.

– *Mephistopheles: The Devil in the Modern World*. Ithaca: Cornell University Press, 1986.

– *The Prince of Darkness: Radical Evil and the Power of Good in History*. Ithaca: Cornell University Press, 1988.

Rykner, Arnaud. 'Théâtre et exorcisme: Les écorchés de la parole.' *Poetique* 26.102 (1995): 153–62.

Saussure, Ferdinand de. *Course in General Linguistics*. Trans. Wade Baskin. Ed. Charles Bally and Albert Sechehaye with Albert Reidlinger. New York: Philosophical Library, 1959.

Schechner, Richard. *Between Theater and Anthropology*. Philadelphia: University of Pennsylvania Press, 1985.

Schmitt, Charles B. *Aristotle and the Renaissance*. Cambridge: Harvard University Press, 1983.

Scholes, Robert, 'The Mythographers: Propp and Lévi-Strauss.' In *Structuralism in Literature*, 60–73. New Haven: Yale University Press, 1974.

Scholes, Robert, and Robert Kellogg. *The Nature of Narrative*. New York: Oxford University Press, 1966.

Screech, M.A. *Ecstasy and the Praise of Folly*. London: Duckworth, 1980.

Sewall, Richard B. *The Vision of Tragedy*. New Haven: Yale University Press, 1970.

Shattuck, Roger. *Forbidden Knowledge: From Prometheus to Pornography*. New York: St Martin's, 1996.

Sheed, F.J., ed. *Soundings in Satanism*. New York: Sheed and Ward, 1972.

Sieber, Harry. *The Picaresque*. London: Methuen, 1977.

Silverstein, Michael, and Greg Urban. *Natural Histories of Discourse*. Chicago: University of Chicago Press, 1996.

Smith, James Harry, and Edd Winfield Parks, eds. *The Great Critics: An Anthology of Literary Criticism*. 3rd ed. New York: Norton, 1967.

Smith, Paul. *Discerning the Subject*. Minneapolis: University of Minnesota Press, 1988.

Spingarn, Joel Elias. *A History of Literary Criticism in the Renaissance*. 2nd ed. New York: Columbia University Press, 1963.

Squarzina, Luigi. 'Total Theatre: Cruelty, Exorcism, Psychodrama.' *Mosaic: A Journal for the Interdisciplinary Study of Literature* 1.4 (1968): 95–107.

Stallybrass, Peter, and Allon White. *The Politics and Poetics of Transgression*. Ithaca: Cornell University Press, 1986.

Steiner, George. *After Babel: Aspects of Language and Translation*. Oxford: Oxford University Press, 1992.

– *The Death of Tragedy*. New York: Hill and Wang, 1966.

Stephens, Walter. *Demon Lovers: Witchcraft, Sex, and the Crisis of Belief.* Chicago: University of Chicago Press, 2002.

Thomas, Keith. *Religion and the Decline of Magic: Studies in Popular Beliefs in Sixteenth- and Seventeenth-Century England.* New York: Charles Scribner's Sons, 1971.

Thompson, Craig R. 'Erasmus, More, and the Conjuration of Spirits: The Possible Source of a Practical-Joke.' *Moreana* 24 (1969): 45–50.

Thornton, Lawrence. 'Conrad, Flaubert, and Marlow: Possession and Exorcism.' *Comparative Literature* 34.2 (1982): 146–56.

Treip, Mindele Anne. *Allegorical Poetics and the Epic: The Renaissance Tradition to Paradise Lost.* Lexington: University Press of Kentucky, 1994.

Turner, Victor. *The Anthropology of Performance.* New York: *Performing Arts Journal,* 1988.

Veeser, H. Aram, ed. *The New Historicism.* New York: Routledge, 1989.

Verdon, Timothy, and John Henderson. *Christianity and the Renaissance: Image and Religious Imagination in the Quattrocento.* Syracuse, NY: Syracuse University Press, 1990.

Vickers, Brian. 'Epideictic and Epic in the Renaissance.' *New Literary History* 14 (1982–3): 497–537.

Vickery, John B. 'Myth Criticism.' In *The New Princeton Encyclopedia of Poetry and Poetics,* ed. Alex Preminger and T.V. Brogan. Princeton: Princeton University Press, 1993.

Walker, Daniel Pickering. *The Decline of Hell: Seventeenth-Century Discussions of Eternal Torment.* Chicago: University of Chicago Press, 1964.

– 'Demonic Possession Used As Propaganda in the Later 16th Century.' In *Articles on Witchcraft, Magic and Demonology.* Vol. 9, *Possession and Exorcism,* ed. Brian P. Levack, 283–95. New York: Garland, 1992.

– *Spiritual and Demonic Magic from Ficino to Campanella.* London: The Warburg Institute and University of London, 1958; Nendeln: Kraus Reprint, 1976.

– *Unclean Spirits: Possession and Exorcism in France and England in the Late Sixteenth and Early Seventeenth Centuries.* Philadelphia: University of Pennsylvania Press, 1981.

Ward, Benedicta, trans. *Apophthegmata patrum* (The Wisdom of the Desert Fathers). Oxford: Sisters of the Love of God Press, 1981.

Watt, Ian. *Myths of Modern Individualism: Faust, Don Quixote, Don Juan, Robinson Crusoe.* Cambridge: Cambridge University Press, 1996.

Weber, Henri. 'L'exorcisme à la fin du XVIe siècle, instrument de la Contre Réforme et spectacle baroque.' *Nouvelle revue du seizième siècle* 1 (1983): 70–101.

Wicks, Ulrich. 'The Nature of Picaresque Narrative: A Modal Approach.' *PMLA* 89 (1974): 240–9.

– *Picaresque Narrative, Picaresque Fictions.* New York: Greenwood, 1989.

Wimsatt, W.K. 'Poetry and Christian Thinking.' In *The Verbal Icon,* 267–79. Lexington: University of Kentucky Press, 1954.

Wittkower, Rudolf, and Margot Wittkower. *Born Under Saturn. The Character and Conduct of Artists: A Documented History from Antiquity to the French Revolution.* New York: Random House, 1963.

Woodmansee, Martha. 'The Genius and the Copyright: Economic and Legal Conditions of the Emergence of the "Author."' *Eighteenth-Century Studies* 17 (1983–4): 425–48.

Primary Sources: English

Baxter, Richard. *The certainty of the worlds of spirits and, consequently, of the immortality of souls: of the malice and misery of the devils and the damned: and of the blessedness of the justified, fully evinced by the unquestionable histories of apparitions, operations, witchcrafts, voices &c. Written, as an addition to many other treatises for the conviction of Sadduces and infidels ...* London: T. Parkhurst and J. Salisbury, 1691.

Bee, Jesse. *The Most Wonderfull and True Storie of a Certain Witch named Alse Gooderige of Stephen Hill ... As also a True Report of the Strange Torments of Thomas Darling, a Boy of Thirteene Yeres of Age, that was Possessed by the Devill.* Ed. J. Denison. London: Iohn Oxenbridge, 1597.

Blagrave, Joseph. *Blagrave's Astrological Practice of Physick, Discovering, The true way to Cure all kinds of Diseases and Infirmities which are Naturally incident to the Body of Man* (1671). London: Obadiah Blagrave, 1689.

A briefe narration of the possession of William Sommers: and of some proceedings against Iohn Dorrell. [Amsterdam]: [secret press], 1598.

Bright, Timothy. *A Treatise of Melancholy.* London: Thomas Vautrollier, 1586.

The Bugbears. Ed. James D. Clark. New York: Garland, 1979.

Burton, Robert. *The Anatomy of Melancholy* (1621). London: J.M. Dent, 1961.

Butler, Samuel. *Hudibras.* Ed. John Wilders. Oxford: Clarendon, 1967.

Casaubon, Meric. *A Treatise Concerning Enthusiasme* (1655). Facs. of the 2nd ed., 1656. Intro. Paul J. Korshin. Gainesville, FL: Scholars' Facsimiles and Reprints, 1970.

Codrington, Robert, trans. *Ignoramus: a comedy as it was several times acted with extraordinary applause before the Majesty of King James: with a supplement which, out of respect to the students of the common law, was hitherto wanting.* London: For W. Gilbertson, 1662.

Cowley, Abraham. 'Preface to *Poems*' (1656). In *English Literary Criticism: The Renaissance*, ed. O.B. Hardison, Jr, 318–29. New York: Appleton-Century-Crofts, 1963.

[Darrell, John]. *A Briefe Apologie Proving the Possession of William Sommers.* [Middelburg]: [R. Schilders], 1599.

– *A Briefe Narration of the possession, dispossession, and repossession of William Sommers.* [Amsterdam]: n.p., 1598.

– *A Detection of that Sinnful Shamful, Lying, and Ridiculous Discours of Samuel Harshnet.* [London]: [English secret press]: 1600.

- *The Replie of John Darrell to the Answer of John Deacon, and John Walker, concerning demoniakes.* [London]: [English secret press?]: 1602.
- *A Survey of Certain Dialogical Discourses: written by J. Deacon, and J. Walker, concerning divels.* [London]: [English secret press], 1602.
- *A True Narration of the strange and grevous Vexation by the Devil, of seven persons in Lancashire, and William Somers of Nottingham. Wherein the Doctrine of Possession and Dispossession of Demoniakes Out of the word of God is particularly applyed unto Somers ...* [London]: [English secret press], 1600.
- *A True Relation of The grievous handling of William Sommers of Nottingham, Being possessed with a Devill, Shewing How he was first taken, and how lamentably from time to time he was tormented and afflicted.* London: Tho. Harper, 1641.

Darrell, John, James Balmford, and Richard Schilders. *The Triall of Maist. Dorrell, or A Collection of Defences against Allegations not yet suffered to receiue convenient answere.* [Middelburg]: [R. Schilders], 1599.

Deacon, Iohn, and Iohn Walker. *Dialogicall Discourses of Spirits and Divels. Declaring their proper essence, natures, and dispositions: with other the appendantes, peculiarly appertaining to those speciall points. Verie conducent, and pertinent to the timely procuring of some Christian conformitie in iudgement: for the peaceable compounding of the late sprong controuersies concerning all such intricate and difficult doubts.* London: Geor. Bishop, 1601.

Dryden, John. 'The Author's Apology for Heroic Poetry and Poetic License' (1677). In *Essays of John Dryden*, ed. W.P. Ker, 1:178–90. New York: Russell and Russell, 1961.
- *An Essay of Dramatic Poesy* (1668). In *The Great Critics: An Anthology of Literary Criticism*, ed. James Harry Smith and Edd Winfield Parks, 305–60. 3rd ed. New York: Norton, 1967.
- 'Of Heroic Plays, an Essay' (1672). In *Essays of John Dryden*, ed. W.P. Ker, 1:148–59. New York: Russell and Russell, 1961.

D'Urfey, Thomas. *The Comical History of Don Quixote, as it is acted at the Queens Theatre in Dorset-Garden, by their Majesties Servants.* Parts I and II. London: Samuel Briscoe, 1694.

Gammer Gurton's Needle (1575). In *Three Sixteenth-Century Comedies:* Gammer Gurton's Needle *by Mr. S.*, Roister Doister *by Nicholas Udall*, The Old Wife's Tale *by George Peele*, ed. Charles Watters Whitworth, 1–88. New York: W.W. Norton, 1984.

Harsnett, Samuel. *A Declaration of Egregious Popish Impostures.* In *Shakespeare, Harsnett, and the Devils of Denham*, by F.W. Brownlow, 191–416. London and Toronto: Associated University Presses, 1993.
- *A Discovery of the Fraudulent Practices of One John Darrel Bachelor of Arts.* London: [J. Windet for] J. Wolfe, 1599.

Heliodorus. *Aethiopica.* 1587 English translation by Thomas Underdowne as *An Aethiopian History.* London: David Nutt, 1895.

Heywood, Thomas. *An Apology for Actors* (1612). In *Literary Criticism: Plato to Dryden*, ed. Allan H. Gilbert, 552–64. Detroit: Wayne State, 1962.

Heywood, Thomas, and Richard Broome. *The late Lancashire Witches: A Well Received Comedy.* London: Thomas Harper, 1634; Ed. Laird H. Barber. New York: Garland, 1979.

Hobbes, Thomas. *Leviathan* (1651). Ed. Richard Tuck. Cambridge: Cambridge University Press, 1996.

James VI of Scotland and I of England. *Basilikon doron, or, King James's instructions to his dearest sonne, Henry the Prince* (1603). London: M. Flesher for Joseph Hindmarsh, 1682.

– *Daemonologie, in Forme of a Dialogue.* Edinburgh: Robert Walde-graue, 1597.

Jollie, Thomas. *The Surey Demoniack: or an Account of Satans Strange and Dreadful Actings, In and about the Body of Richard Dugdale of Surey, near Whalley in Lancashire; And how he was Dispossest by Gods Blessings on the Fastings and Prayers of divers Ministers and People. The Matter of Fact attested by the Oaths of Several Credible Persons, before some of His Majesties Justices of the Peace in the said County.* London: Jonathan Robinson, 1697.

Jonson, Ben. *The Devil is an Ass.* In *Four Jacobean City Comedies.* Ed. Gamini Salgado. Harmondsworth: Penguin, 1985.

– *The Poetaster* (1602). Manchester, UK, and New York: Manchester University Press and St Martin's Press, 1995.

– *Volpone.* Ed. Philip Brockbank. New York: Hill and Wang, 1969.

Jorden, Edward. *A Briefe Discourse of a Disease Called the Suffocation of the Mother. Written uppon occasion which hath beene of late taken thereby, to suspect possession of an euill spirit, or some such like supernaturall power. Wherin is declared that diuers strange actions and passions of the body of man, which in the common opinion are imputed to the Diuell, haue their true naturall causes, and do accompanie this disease.* London: Iohn Windet, 1603.

Lavater, Lewis. *Of Ghostes and Spirites Walking by Nyght.* Trans. R. H[arrison]. London: H. Benneyman for R. Watkyns, 1572.

Lodge, Thomas. *The Diuel Coniured.* London: Adam Islip for William Mats, 1596.

Marston, John. *The Malcontent.* Ed. George K. Hunter. London: Methuen, 1975.

Marvell, Andrew. *Mr. Smirke: Or, the Divine in Mode* (1676). In *The Complete Works of Andrew Marvell*, ed. Alexander B. Grousart, 4:1–90. New York: AMS, 1966.

Massinger, Philip. *The Roman Actor* (1626). In *Literary Criticism: Plato to Dryden*, ed. Allan H. Gilbert, 568–73. Detroit: Wayne State University Press, 1962.

Michaelis, S. *The Admirable Historie of the Possession and Conversion of a Penitent Woman.* Trans. W.B. London: William Aspley, 1613.

Middleton, Thomas. *A Game at Chess.* Ed. J.W. Harper. New York: Hill and Wang, 1967.

– *The Phoenix.* Ed. John Bradbury Brooks. New York: Garland, 1980.

– *The Witch.* Ed. Edward J. Esche. New York: Garland, 1993.

Milton, John. *Of That Sort of Dramatic Poem Which Is Call'd Tragedy* [Preface to *Samson Agonistes*] (1671). In *John Milton: Complete Poems and Major Prose*, ed. Merritt Y. Hughes, 549–50. Indianapolis: Odyssey, 1980.

More, George. *A True Discourse concerning the certaine possession and dispossession of 7 persons in one familie in Lancashire, which also may serve as part of an Answere to a fayned and false Discoverie which speaketh very much evill, as well of this, as of the rest of those great and mightie workes of God which be of the like excellent nature.* By George More, Minister and Preacher of the Worde of God, and now (for bearing Witnesse unto this, and for justifying the rest) a prisoner in the Clinke, where he hath continued almost for the space of two yeares. [Middelburg]: [R. Schilders], 1600.

More, Henry. *Enthusiasmus Triumphatus* (1662). Intro. M.V. DePorte. Augustan Reprint Society, no. 118. Los Angeles: Clark Memorial Library, 1966.

Nashe, Thomas. *Pierce Penniless His Supplication to the Devil* (1592). In *The Renaissance in England: Nondramatic Prose and Verse of the Sixteenth Century.* Ed. Hyder E. Rollins and Herschel Baker. Lexington, MA: D.C. Heath, 1954.

Plautus. *Menaechmi.* Trans. William Warner. London: Tho. Creede, 1595. In *Narrative and Dramatic Sources of Shakespeare.* Vol. 1, *Early Comedies, Poems, Romeo and Juliet,* ed. Geoffrey Bullough, 12–39. New York: Columbia University Press, 1961.

Potts, Thomas. *Pott's Discovery of witches in the county of Lancaster, reprinted from the original ed. of 1613.* Rev. Edward Bromley. Ed. James Crossley. Manchester: The Chetham Society, 1845.

Ribadeneyra, Pedro de. *The lives of the saints vvith other feasts of the year according to the Roman calendar.* St Omers: Ioachim Carlier, 1669.

Ruggle, George. *Ignoramus: comoedia coram rege Jacobo et Totius Angliae magnatibus per academicos Cantabrigienses habita: cum eorum supplemento quae, causidicorum municipalium reverentia, hactenus desiderabantur* (1615). 3rd ed. London: R.D., 1658.

– *Ignoramus* (manuscript facsimile). Introduction by E.F.J. Tucker. Hildesheim: Georg Olms, 1987.

Scot, Reginald. *The Discouerie of Witchcraft. With A Discourse upon divels and spirits, and first of philosophers opinions, also the maner of their reasoning hereupon; and the same confuted.* London: William Brome, 1584.

Shadwell, Thomas. *The Lancashire-Witches, and Tegue o Divelly the Irish Priest.* Ed. Judith Bailey Slagle. New York: Garland, 1991.

Shakespeare, William. *Works. The Riverside Shakespeare.* Ed. G. Blakemore Evans. Boston: Houghton Mifflin, 1974.

Shelley, Percy Bysshe. 'A Defence of Poetry.' In *The Selected Poetry and Prose of Percy Bysshe Shelley,* ed. Carlos Baker. New York: The Modern Library, 1951.

Sidney, Philip. *The Defense of Poesie.* In *Literary Criticism: Plato to Dryden,* ed. Allan H. Gilbert, 406–61. Detroit: Wayne State, 1962.

Spenser, Edmund. *The Faerie Queene* (1596). Ed. Thomas P. Roche. Harmondsworth: Penguin, 1978.

Steele, Richard. *The Spectator,* No. 14. 11 August 1711. Ed. Donald F. Bond. 2:58. Oxford: Clarendon, 1965.

Taylor, Zachary. *The devil turn'd casuist, or, The cheats of Rome laid open in the exorcism of a despairing devil, at the house of Thomas Pennington in Orrel in the Parrish of Wigan and County of Lancaster.* London: E. Whitlock, 1694.

A Yorkshire Tragedy. Ed. A.C. Cawley and Barry Gaines. Manchester: Manchester University Press, 1986.

Secondary Sources: English

Andreasen, Nancy J.C. 'The Artist As Scientist: Psychiatric Diagnosis in Shakespeare's Tragedies.' *Journal of the American Medical Association* 235.17 (26 April 1976): 1868–72.

Andrews, John F. 'The Purpose of Playing: Catharsis in *Hamlet.*' In *Poetry and Drama in the English Renaissance: In Honour of Professor Jiro Ozu,* ed. Koshi Nakanori and Yasuo Tamaizumi, 1–19. Tokyo: Kenkyusha, 1980.

Anglo, Sydney. 'Reginald Scot's *Discoverie of Witchcraft*: Scepticism and Sadduceeism.' In *The Damned Art: Essays in the Literature of Witchcraft,* ed. Sydney Anglo. London: Routledge and Kegan Paul, 1977.

Armistead, J.M. 'Occultism in Restoration Drama: Motives for Revaluation.' *Modern Language Studies* 9.3 (1979): 60–7.

Babb, Lawrence. *The Elizabethan Malady: A Study of Melancholia in English Literature from 1580 to 1642.* East Lansing: Michigan State College Press, 1951.

– 'Hamlet, Melancholy, and the Devil.' *Modern Language Notes* 59.2 (1944): 120–2.

Baldwin, T.W. *William Shakspere's Small Latine & Lesse Greeke.* 2 vols. Urbana: University of Illinois Press, 1944.

Barber, C.L. *Shakespeare's Festive Comedy: A Study of Dramatic Form and Its Relation to Social Custom.* Princeton: Princeton University Press, 1959.

Battenhouse, Roy W. 'The Ghost in Hamlet: A Catholic "Linchpin"?' *Studies in Philology* 48.2 (1951): 161–92.

Bawcutt, N.H. 'Middleton's *The Phoenix* As a Royal Play.' *Notes and Queries* 201 (1956): 287–8.

Bay, J. Christian. *The Origin and Development of Shakespeare's Hamlet.* Metuchen, NJ: American Book Collector, 1931.

Bennett, Josephine Waters. 'The Storm Within: The Madness of Lear.' *Shakespeare Quarterly* 13.2 (1962): 137–55.

Berry, Herbert. 'The Globe Bewitched and *El Hombre Fiel.*' *Medieval and Renaissance Drama in England* 1 (1984): 211–30.

Bishop, T.G. *Shakespeare and the Theatre of Wonder.* Cambridge: Cambridge University Press, 1996.

Borgman, Albert S. *Thomas Shadwell: His Life and Comedies.* New York: New York University Press, 1928.

Bowers, Fredson T. 'Hamlet As Minister and Scourge.' *PMLA* 70.3 (1955): 740–9.

Bradbrook, Muriel C. 'The Kingdom of Fools.' In *Shakespeare: The Poet in His World,* 188–201. New York: Columbia University Press, 1978.

Braddy, Haldeen. *Hamlet's Wounded Name.* El Paso: Texas Western Press, 1964.

Braden, Gordon. *Renaissance Tragedy and the Senecan Tradition: Anger's Privilege.* New Haven: Yale University Press, 1985.

Bradley, A.C. *Shakespearean Tragedy.* 2nd ed. London: Macmillan, 1905.

Briggs, K.M. *Pale Hecate's Team: An Examination of the Beliefs on Witchcraft and Magic among Shakespeare's Contemporaries and His Immediate Successors.* London: Routledge, 1962.

Brownlow, F.W. 'John Shakespeare's Recusancy: New Light on an Old Document.' *Shakespeare Quarterly* 40 (1989): 186–91.

– 'Samuel Harsnett and the Meaning of Othello's "Suffocating Streams."' *Philological Quarterly* 58 (1979): 107–15.

– *Shakespeare, Harsnett, and the Devils of Denham.* London: Associated University Presses, 1993.

– Review of *Darkness and Devils: Exorcism and* King Lear by John L. Murphy. *Philological Quarterly* 65 (1986): 131–3.

Bruster, Douglas. *Quoting Shakespeare: Form and Culture in Early Modern Drama.* Lincoln: University of Nebraska Press, 2000.

Bucknill, John Charles. *The Mad Folk of Shakespeare.* London and Cambridge: Macmillan, 1867.

Bullough, Geoffrey, ed. *Narrative and Dramatic Sources of Shakespeare.* Vol. 7, *Major Tragedies: Hamlet, Othello, King Lear, Macbeth.* New York: Columbia University Press, 1973.

Butler, Guy. 'Jacobean Psychiatry: Edgar's Curative Stratagems.' *Shakespeare in South Africa* 2 (1988): 15–30.

Cauthen, I.B. 'The Foule Flibbertigibbet.' *Notes and Queries* n.s. 5 (1958): 98.

Cawley, A.C. *English Domestic Drama:* A Yorkshire Tragedy. *An Inaugural Lecture.* Leeds: Leeds University Press, 1966.

– 'A Yorkshire Tragedy and Two Most Vnnaturall and Bloodie Murthers.' In *The Morality of Art: Essays Presented to G. Wilson Knight by His Colleagues and Friends,* ed. D.W. Jefferson, 102–18. London: Routledge, 1969.

– 'A Yorkshire Tragedy Considered in Relation to Biblical and Moral Plays.' In *Everyman and Company: Essays on the Theme and Structure of the European Moral Play,* ed. Donald Gilman, David Bevington, and Robert Potter, 155–68. New York: AMS, 1989.

Clark, Stuart. 'King James's *Daemonologie:* Witchcraft and Kingship.' In *The Damned Art:*

Essays in the Literature of Witchcraft, ed. Sydney Anglo, 156–81. London: Routledge and Kegan Paul, 1977.

Clum, John M. 'Shakespeare and Psychiatry.' *Journal of the American Medical Association* 236.11 (13 September 1976): 1239.

Coddon, Karin S. '"Suche Strange Desygns": Madness, Subjectivity, and Treason in *Hamlet* and Elizabethan Culture.' *Renaissance Drama* n.s. 20 (1989): 51–75.

Corbin, Peter, and Douglas Sedge. Introduction to their edition of *Three Jacobean Witchcraft Plays: The Tragedy of Sophonisba, The Witch, The Witch of Edmonton*. Manchester: Manchester University Press, 1986.

Coursen, Herbert. *Christian Ritual and the World of Shakespeare's Tragedies*. Lewisburg, PA: Bucknell University Press, 1976.

Cox, John D. *The Devil and the Sacred in English Drama, 1350–1642*. Cambridge: Cambridge University Press, 2000.

Craig, Terry Ann. 'Petruchio As an Exorcist: Shakespeare and Elizabethan Demonology.' *Selected Papers from the West Virginia Shakespeare and Renaissance Association* 2.3 (1978): 1–7.

Cunningham, James V. *Woe or Wonder*. Denver: University of Denver Press, 1951.

Curry, Walter Clyde. 'The Demonic Metaphysics of *Macbeth*.' *Studies in Philology* 30.3 (1933): 395–426.

Davidson, Clifford. '*The Phoenix*: Middleton's Didactic Comedy.' *Papers on Language and Literature* 4 (1968): 121–30.

Desai, R.W. 'The Minister of God to Take Vengeance.' *English Language Notes* 31.2 (1993): 22–6.

Dessen, Alan C. 'Middleton's *The Phoenix* and the Allegorical Tradition.' *Studies in English Literature 1500–1900* 6 (1966): 291–308.

Dodson, Daniel B. 'King James and *The Phoenix* – Again.' *Notes and Queries* 203 (1958): 434–7.

Dollimore, Jonathan. *Radical Tragedy: Religion, Ideology and Power in the Drama of Shakespeare and His Contemporaries*. New York: Harvester, 1989.

– 'Transgression and Surveillance in *Measure for Measure*.' In *Political Shakespeare: New Essays in Cultural Materialism*, ed. Jonathan Dollimore and Alan Sinfield, 72–87. Ithaca: Cornell University Press, 1985.

Draper, John W. *The Humors and Shakespeare's Characters*. Durham: Duke University Press, 1945.

Edgar, Irving. *Shakespeare, Medicine and Psychiatry*. New York: Philosophical Library, 1970.

Eliot, T.S. 'Hamlet and His Problems.' In *Critical Theory Since Plato*, rev. ed. Hazard Adams, 764–6. New York: Harcourt Brace, 1992.

Elton, William R. King Lear *and the Gods*. Lexington: University Press of Kentucky, 1988.

Empson, William. *Milton's God*. Cambridge: Cambridge University Press, 1981.

England, Eugene. 'Shakespeare as a Renaissance Therapist.' *Literature and Belief* 11 (1991): 27–39.

Erlich, Avi. *Hamlet's Absent Father*. Princeton: Princeton University Press, 1977.

Estes, Leland L. 'Reginald Scot and His *Discoverie of Witchcraft*: Religion and Science in the Opposition to the European Witch Craze.' *Church History* 52 (1983): 444–56.

Evans, Robert C. 'Contemporary Contexts of Jonson's *The Devil is an Ass*.' *Comparative Drama* 26.2 (1992): 140–76.

Findlay, Alison. '*Hamlet*: A Document in Madness.' In *New Essays on Hamlet*, ed. Mark Thornton Burnett and John Manning, 189–208. New York: AMS, 1994.

Fitzgerald, James D. *The Sources of the Hamlet Tragedy*. Glasgow: Royal Philosophical Society, 1909.

Flatter, Richard. *Hamlet's Father*. New Haven: Yale University Press, 1949.

Fleissner, Robert F. 'Subjectivity As an Occupational Hazard of "Hamlet Ghost" Critics.' *Hamlet Studies* 1.1 (1979): 23–33.

Frye, Roland Mushat. *The Renaissance Hamlet: Issues and Responses in 1600*. Princeton: Princeton University Press, 1984.

Frye, Susan. *Elizabeth I: The Competition for Representation*. New York: Oxford University Press, 1993.

Gibson, J. Paul S.R. *Shakespeare's Use of the Supernatural* (1907). New York: AMS, 1974.

Gilchrist, Fredericka Beardsley. *The True Story of Hamlet and Ophelia*. Boston: Little, Brown, 1889.

Gollancz, Israel. *The Sources of Hamlet, with an Essay on the Legend* (1926). London: Cass, 1967.

Gottschalk, Paul. *The Meanings of Hamlet: Modes of Literary Interpretation since Bradley*. Albuquerque: University of New Mexico Press, 1972.

– 'The Universe of Madness in *King Lear*.' *Bucknell Review* 19.3 (1971): 51–68.

Greenblatt, Stephen. '*King Lear* and Harsnett's "Devil Fiction."' *Genre* 15.1–2 (1982): 239–42.

– 'Loudun and London.' *Critical Inquiry* 12.2 (1986): 326–46.

– *Shakespearean Negotiations: The Circulation of Social Energy in Renaissance England*. Berkeley: University of California Press, 1988.

Grell, Ole Peter, and Andrew Cunningham, eds. *Religio Medici: Medicine and Religion in Seventeenth-Century England*. Brookfield, VT: Scolar Press, 1996.

Gurr, Andrew. '*Hamlet* and the Distracted Globe.' Edinburgh: for Sussex University Press by Scottish Academic Press, 1978.

Gutierrez, Nancy A. 'Exorcism by Fasting in *A Woman Killed with Kindness*: A Paradigm of Puritan Resistance?' *Research Opportunities in Renaissance Drama* 33.1–2 (1994): 43–62.

Haigh, Christopher. *Elizabeth I*. London: Longman, 1988.

Hallett, Charles A. 'The Satanic Nature of Volpone.' *Philological Quarterly* 49.1 (1970): 41–55.

Halpern, Richard. *The Poetics of Primitive Accumulation: English Renaissance Culture and the Genealogy of Capital.* Ithaca: Cornell University Press, 1991.

Hamilton, Donna B. *Shakespeare and the Politics of Protestant England.* Lexington: UP of Kentucky, 1992.

Heinemann, Margot. 'How Brecht Read Shakespeare.' In *Political Shakespeare: New Essays in Cultural Materialism,* ed. Jonathan Dollimore and Alan Sinfield, 202–30. Ithaca: Cornell University Press, 1985.

Herbert, T. Walter. 'Shakespeare Announces a Ghost.' *Shakespeare Quarterly* 1.4 (1950): 247–54.

Hill, Thomas D. 'When God Blew Satan Out of Heaven: The Motif of Exsufflation in *Vercelli Homily XIX* and Later English Literature.' *Leeds Studies in English* n.s. 16 (1985): 132–41.

Hoeniger, F. David. *Medicine and Shakespeare in the English Renaissance.* Newark: University of Delaware Press, 1992.

Hughes, Peter. '"Playing with Grief": Hamlet and the Rituals of Mourning.' *Comparative Criticism* 9 (1987): 111–34.

Hunt, Maurice. 'Shakespeare's Tragic Homeopathy.' In *Shakespeare: Text, Subtext, and Context,* ed. Ronald Dotterer, 77–84. Selinsgrove, PA: Susquehanna University Press, 1989.

Jack, Jane H. 'Macbeth, King James, and the Bible.' In *Twentieth Century Criticism: The Major Statements,* ed. William J. Handy and Max Westbrook, 387–402. New York: The Free Press, 1974.

Jones-Davies, M.T. 'Le diable gagnant ou perdant sur la scène jacobèenne?' In *Diable, diables, et diableries au temps de la Renaissance,* ed. M.T. Jones-Davies, 81–96. Paris: Jean Touzot, 1988.

Joseph, Miriam. 'Discerning the Ghost in *Hamlet.*' *PMLA* 76.2 (1961): 493–502.

– '*Hamlet,* a Christian Tragedy.' *Studies in Philology* 59.2 (1962): 119–40.

Kahn, Victoria. *Machiavellian Rhetoric from the Counter-Reformation to Milton.* Princeton: Princeton University Press, 1994.

Kail, Aubrey C. *The Medical Mind of Shakespeare.* Balgowlah, NSW: Williams and Wilkins, 1986.

Kallendorf, Hilaire. 'Intertextual Madness in *Hamlet:* The Ghost's Fragmented Performativity.' *Renaissance and Reformation / Renaissance et Réforme* 22.4 (1998): 69–87.

Kamps, Ivo. 'Ruling Fantasies and the Fantasies of Rule: *The Phoenix* and *Measure for Measure.*' *Studies in Philology* 92.2 (1995): 248–73.

Kaula, David. 'Othello Possessed: Notes on Shakespeare's Use of Magic and Witchcraft.' *Shakespeare Studies* 2 (1966): 112–32.

Kernan, Alvin. *Shakespeare, the King's Playwright: Theater in the Stuart Court, 1603–1613.* New Haven: Yale University Press, 1995.

Kistner, A.L., and M.K. '*The Family of Love* and *The Phoenix*: Early Developments of a Theme.' *Essays in Literature* 7 (1980): 179–90.

Kittredge, G.L. 'King James I and *The Devil is an Ass*.' *Modern Philology* 9.2 (1911): 195–209.

Latham, Jacqueline E.M. '*The Tempest* and King James's *Daemonologie*.' *Shakespeare Survey* 28 (1975): 117–23.

Latham, Minor White. *The Elizabethan Fairies: The Fairies of Folklore and the Fairies of Shakespeare*. New York: Columbia University Press, 1930.

Law, T.G. 'Devil-Hunting in Elizabethan England.' *The Nineteenth Century* 35 (1894): 397–411.

Levin, Harry. *The Question of Hamlet*. London: Oxford University Press, 1970.

Lewis, Charlton M. *The Genesis of Hamlet*. New York: H. Holt, 1907.

Lewis, C.S. *Hamlet: The Prince or the Poem?* Annual Shakespeare Lecture of the British Academy, 1942. London: H. Milford, 1942.

Lidz, Theodore. *Hamlet's Enemy: Madness and Myth in Hamlet*. New York: Basic Books, 1975.

MacDonald, Michael. *Mystical Bedlam: Madness, Anxiety, and Healing in Seventeenth-Century England*. Cambridge: Cambridge University Press, 1981.

MacDonald, Michael, ed. *Witchcraft and Hysteria in Elizabethan London: Edward Jorden and the Mary Glover Case*. New York: Routledge, 1991.

Maclean, Norman. 'Episode, Scene, Speech, and Word: The Madness of Lear.' In *Critics and Criticism*, ed. R.S. Crane, 94–116. Chicago: University of Chicago Press, 1970.

Mahood, M.M. '*A Midsummer Night's Dream* as Exorcism.' In *Essays on Shakespeare in Honour of A.A. Ansari*, ed. T.R. Sharma, 136–49. Meerut, India: Shalabh Book House, 1986.

Manvell, Roger. 'The Portrayal of Insanity in the Elizabethan and Jacobean Theatre.' *New Humanist* 96 (1981): 16–22.

Marcus, Leah. *The Politics of Mirth: Jonson, Herrick, Milton, Marvell and the Defence of Old Holiday Pastimes*. Chicago: Chicago University Press, 1986.

Marsden, Jean I. 'Ideology, Sex, and Satire: The Case of Thomas Shadwell.' In *Cutting Edges: Postmodern Studies in Eighteenth-Century Satire*, ed. James Gill, 43–58. Tennessee Studies in Literature 37. Knoxville: University of Tennessee Press, 1995.

Matei Chesnoiu, Monica. *William Shakespeare: Knowledge and Truth*. Constanta, Romania: Pontica, 1997.

Maxwell, Baldwin. 'Middleton's *The Phoenix*.' In *Joseph Quincy Adams Memorial Studies*, ed. James G. McManaway, Giles E. Dawson, and Edwin E. Willoughby, 743–53. Washington, D.C.: Folger Shakespeare Library, 1948.

McConica, James. 'Humanism and Aristotle in Tudor Oxford.' *English Historical Review* 94 (1979): 291–317.

McGee, Arthur. *The Elizabethan Hamlet*. New Haven: Yale University Press, 1987.

McLaughlin, Ann L. 'The Journey in *King Lear.' American Imago* 29.4 (1972): 384–99.

Mebane, John S. *Renaissance Magic and the Return of the Golden Age: The Occult Tradition and Marlowe, Jonson, and Shakespeare.* Lincoln: University of Nebraska Press, 1989.

Merchant, W. Moelwyn. 'His Fiend-Like Queen.' *Shakespeare Survey* 19 (1966): 75–81.

Milward, Peter. 'Shakespeare and Elizabethan Exorcism.' *Sophia University: Studies in English Literature and Language* 17 (1981): 33–45.

– *Shakespeare's Religious Background.* London: Sidgwick and Jackson, 1973.

Miola, Robert S. *Shakespeare and Classical Comedy: The Influence of Plautus and Terence.* Oxford: Oxford University Press, 1994.

Moorman, F.W. 'The Pre-Shakespearean Ghost.' *Modern Language Review* 1.3 (1906): 85–95.

– 'Shakespeare's Ghosts.' *Modern Language Review* 1.2 (1906): 192–201.

Muir, Kenneth. 'Appendix 7: Samuel Harsnett and *King Lear.'* In *King Lear*, ed. Kenneth Muir. *The Arden Edition of the Works of William Shakespeare.* London: Methuen, 1975.

– 'Samuel Harsnett and *King Lear.' Review of English Studies* 2 (1951): 11–21.

– *The Sources of Shakespeare's Plays.* New Haven: Yale University Press, 1978.

Mullaney, Steven. 'Apprehending Subjects, or the Reformation in the Suburbs.' In *The Place of the Stage: License, Play and Power in Renaissance England*, 88–115. Ann Arbor: University of Michigan Press, 1988.

Munns, Jessica. '"The Golden Days of Queen Elizabeth": Thomas Shadwell's *The Lancashire Witches* and the Politics of Nostalgia.' *Restoration: Studies in English Literary Culture, 1660–1700* 20.2 (1996): 195–216.

Murphy, John L. *Darkness and Devils: Exorcism and* King Lear. Athens: Ohio University Press, 1984.

Neely, Carol Thomas. '"Documents in Madness": Reading Madness and Gender in Shakespeare's Tragedies and Early Modern Culture.' *Shakespeare Quarterly* 42.3 (1991): 315–38.

Notestein, Wallace. *A History of Witchcraft in England from 1558 to 1718.* New York: Thomas Y. Crowell, 1968.

O'Meara, John. *Otherworldly Hamlet.* Montreal: Guernica, 1991.

Orgel, Stephen. 'Shakespeare and the Kinds of Drama.' *Critical Inquiry* 6 (1979): 107–23.

Oxford Shakespeare Concordances. King Lear: *A Concordance to the Text of the First Folio.* Oxford: Clarendon, 1971.

Pinciss, Gerald M., and Roger Lockyer. *Shakespeare's World: Background Readings in the English Renaissance.* New York: Continuum, 1989.

Platt, Peter G. *Reason Diminished: Shakespeare and the Marvelous.* Lincoln: University of Nebraska Press, 1997.

Pollen, J.H. 'Supposed Cases of Diabolical Possession in 1585–86.' *The Month* 117 (1911): 449–64.

Power, William. 'The Phoenix, Raleigh, and King James.' Notes and Queries 203 (1958): 57–61.

Puhvel, Martin. 'The Perplexing Ghost of Banquo: Ambiguity and Its Roots.' Neuphilologische Mitteilungen 94 (1993): 287–96.

Pye, Christopher. 'Macbeth and the Politics of Rapture.' In The Regal Phantasm: Shakespeare and the Politics of Spectacle, 142–72. New York: Routledge, 1990.

Reed, Robert Rentoul, Jr. Bedlam on the Jacobean Stage. Cambridge, MA: Harvard University Press, 1952.

– The Occult on the Tudor and Stuart Stage. Boston: Christopher, 1965.

Rickert, Corinne. The Case of John Darrell, Minister and Exorcist. Gainesville: University of Florida Press, 1962.

Rose, Mark. 'Conjuring Caesar: Ceremony, History, and Authority in 1599.' In True Rites and Maimed Rites: Ritual and Anti-Ritual in Shakespeare and His Age, ed. Linda Woodbridge and Edward Berry, 256–69. Urbana: University of Illinois Press, 1992.

Rosen, Barbara, ed. Witchcraft in England, 1558–1618. Amherst: University of Massachusetts Press, 1991.

Rosenberg, Marvin. The Masks of Hamlet. Newark: University of Delaware Press, 1992.

Salingar, Leo. 'King Lear, Montaigne, and Harsnett.' Aligarh Journal of English Studies 8 (1983): 124–66.

Salkeld, Duncan. Madness and Drama in the Age of Shakespeare. Manchester: Manchester University Press, 1993.

Sanders, Julie. 'A Parody of Lord Chief Justice Popham in The Devil is an Ass.' Notes and Queries n.s. 44.4 (1997): 528–30.

Schleiner, Winfried. 'The Feste-Malvolio Scene in Twelfth Night against the Background of Renaissance Ideas about Madness and Possession.' Deutsche Shakespeare Gesellschaft West: Jahrbuch (1990): 48–57.

– Melancholy, Genius, and Utopia in the Renaissance. Wiesbaden: Otto Harrassowitz, 1991.

Schmitt, Charles B. John Case and Aristotelianism in Renaissance England. Kingston and Montreal: McGill-Queen's University Press, 1983.

Semper, I.J. 'The Ghost in Hamlet: Pagan or Christian?' The Month n.s. 9:4 (1953): 222–34.

Sharpe, James. The Bewitching of Anne Gunter: A Horrible and True Story of Deception, Witchcraft, Murder, and the King of England. New York: Routledge, 2000.

– Instruments of Darkness: Witchcraft in Early Modern England. Philadelphia: University of Pennsylvania Press, 1996.

Siegel, P.N. 'Discerning the Ghost in Hamlet.' PMLA 78 (1963): 148–9.

Simmons, J.L. 'A Source for Shakespeare's Malvolio: The Elizabethan Controversy with the Puritans.' Huntington Library Quarterly 36.3 (1973): 181–201.

Skulsky, Harold. 'Cannibals vs. Demons in *Volpone*.' *Studies in English Literature 1500–1900* 29.2 (1989): 291–308.

Slagle, Judith Bailey. 'Thomas Shadwell's Censored Comedy, *The Lancashire-Witches*: An Attack on Religious Ritual or Divine Right?' *Restoration and Eighteenth Century Theatre Research* series 2, 7.1 (1992): 54–63.

Soens, A.L. '*King Lear* III.iv.62–65: A Fencing Pun and Staging.' *English Language Notes* (September 1968): 19–24.

Spalding, Thomas Alfred. *Elizabethan Demonology: In Illustration of the Belief in the Existence of Devils, and the Powers Possessed by Them, As It Was Generally Held During the Period of the Reformation, and the Times Immediately Succeeding; With Special Reference to Shakspere and His Works*. London: Chatto and Windus, Piccadilly, 1880.

Spearing, A.C. *Medieval to Renaissance in English Poetry*. Cambridge: Cambridge University Press, 1985.

Stabler, A.P. 'Melancholy, Ambition, and Revenge in Belleforest's Hamlet.' *PMLA* 81.1 (1966): 207–13.

Stampfer, J. 'The Catharsis of *King Lear*.' *Shakespeare Survey* 13 (1970): 1–10.

Sternlicht, Sanford. 'Hamlet – The Actor As Prince.' *Hamlet Studies* 4.1 (1982): 19–32.

Stevens, Robert L. 'Exorcism of England's Gothic Demon.' *Midwest Quarterly* 14 (1973): 151–64.

Stevenson, Robert. 'Shakespeare's Interest in Harsnett's *Declaration*.' *PMLA* 67.3 (1952): 898–902.

Strutt, Joseph. *The Sports and Pastimes of the People of England* (1802). Ed. William Hone. London: Chatto and Windus, 1876.

Taylor, Marion A. *A New Look at the Old Sources of Hamlet*. The Hague: Mouton, 1968.

Ternbach, Herman. *Shakespeare y su 'Hamlet.'* Buenos Aires: Rosario, 1955.

Tschischwitz, Benno. *Shakspere's Hamlet in seinem Verhältniss zur Gesammtbildung, namentlich zur Theologie und Philosophie der Elisabeth-Zeit*. Halle: Waisenhaus, 1867.

Tucker, Edward F.J. '*Ignoramus* and Seventeenth-Century Satire of the Law.' *Harvard Library Bulletin* 19.3 (1971): 314–30.

Tulip, James. 'The Contexts of *Volpone*.' *Imperfect Apprehensions: Essays in English Literature in Honour of G. A. Wilkes*. Ed. Geoffrey Little. Sydney, Australia: Challis, 1996. 74–87.

– 'The Intertextualities of Ben Jonson's *Volpone*.' *Sydney Studies in English* 20 (1994–5): 20–35.

Valesio, Paolo. 'The Language of Madness in the Renaissance.' *Yearbook of Italian Studies* (1971): 199–234.

Van Gundy, Justin Loomis. '*Ignoramus*': *Comoedia Coram Regia Maiestate Jacobi Regis Angliae. An Examination of Its Sources and Literary Influence with Special Reference to Its Relation to Butler's 'Hudibras.'* Lancaster, PA: New Era, 1906.

Waith, Eugene M. Review of *Hamlet's Enemy: Madness and Myth in 'Hamlet'* by Theodore Lidz. *Hamlet Studies* 1.1 (1979): 62.

Waldock, A.J.A. *Paradise Lost and Its Critics.* Cambridge: Cambridge University Press, 1947.

Waters, D. Douglas. 'Shakespeare's *Timon of Athens* and Catharsis.' *Upstart Crow* 8 (1988): 93–105.

Wentersdorf, Karl P. 'The Motif of Exorcism in the Summoner's Tale.' *Studies in Short Fiction* 17 (1980): 249–54.

West, Robert. 'King Hamlet's Ambiguous Ghost.' *PMLA* 70.4 (1955): 1107–17.

Wheatley, Christopher J. *Without God or Reason: The Plays of Thomas Shadwell and Secular Ethics in the Restoration.* Lewisburg, PA: Bucknell University Press, 1993.

Williamson, Marilyn L. '*The Phoenix*: Middleton's Comedy *de Regimine Principum.*' *Renaissance News* 10 (1957): 183–7.

Wills, Garry. *Witches and Jesuits: Shakespeare's Macbeth.* New York: New York Public Library and Oxford University Press, 1995.

Wilson, J. Dover. *What Happens in Hamlet.* New York: Macmillan, 1936.

Yamada, Yumiko. '*Volpone* and *The Devil is an Ass*: Damnation and Salvation through Metamorphosis.' *Studies in English Literature* (Tokyo) 58.2 (1981): 195–211.

Primary Sources: Spanish

Almansa y Mendoza, Andrés de. *Relacion del auto publico de la fè que se celebro en esta corte domingo 21. de enero de 1624.* Madrid: Diego Flamenco, 1624.

Aqui se contiene un caso nueuo que trata de como vn estudiante se fingio duende en vn meson. Madrid: Maria de Quiñones, 1653.

Auto publico de fee celebrado en Sevilla domingo 29 de março 1648. Sevilla: Francisco de Lyra, 1648.

Avellaneda, Alonso Fernández de. *El ingenioso hidalgo don Quijote de la Mancha.* Ed. Agustín del Saz. Barcelona: Juventud, 1980.

La Biblia. Antigua versión de Casiodoro de Reina (1569). Rev. ed. Nashville: Holman, 1988.

Calderón de la Barca, Pedro. *Las cadenas del demonio.* 1684 facsimile in *Comedias*, vol. 17. Ed. D.W. Cruickshank and J.E. Varey. London: Tamesis, 1973.

– *La dama duende.* Ed. Ángel Valbuena Briones. Madrid: Cátedra, 1990.

– *El mágico prodigioso.* Ed. Ángel Valbuena. Madrid: Espasa-Calpe, 1963.

Calderón de la Barca, Pedro, Juan de Zavaleta, and Jerónimo Cáncer. *La margarita preciosa.* Ed. Juan Eugenio Hartzenbusch. In Biblioteca de autores españoles, vol. 14, *Comedias de Don Pedro Calderón de la Barca*, vol. 4, 517–36. Madrid: Atlas, 1945.

Carvallo, Luís Alfonso de. *Cisne de Apolo* (1602). Ed. Alberto Porqueras Mayo. Kassel: Reichenberger, 1997.

Cascales, Francisco. *Tablas poéticas* (1617). Ed. Benito Brancaforte. Madrid: Espasa-Calpe, 1975.

Castañega, Martín de. *Tratado muy sotil y bien fundado de las supersticiones y hechicerías y vanos conjuros y abusiones: y otras cosas al caso toca[n]tes y dela posibilidad y remedio dellas.* Logroño: Miguel de Eguía, 1529; Ed. Agustín G. de Amezúa. Madrid: Sociedad de Bibliófilos Españoles, 1946.

Cervantes, Miguel de. *El casamiento engañoso* y *El coloquio de los perros. Novelas ejemplares II.* Ed. Harry Sieber. Madrid: Ediciones Cátedra, 1992.

– *El celoso extremeño. Novelas ejemplares II.* Ed. Harry Sieber. Madrid: Ediciones Cátedra, 1992.

– *La cueva de Salamanca* (1615). In *Entremeses*, ed. Nicholas Spadacinni. Madrid: Cátedra, 1995.

– *Don Quijote de la Mancha.* Ed. Francisco Rico and Joaquín Forradellas. 2 vols. Barcelona: Instituto Cervantes, 1998.

– *La Galatea. Obras completas.* Vol. 2. Ed. Rodolfo Schevill and Adolfo Bonilla. Madrid: Bernardo Rodríguez, 1914.

– *El ingenioso hidalgo Don Quijote de la Mancha.* Ed. Celina S. Cortázar, Isaías Lerner, et al. 2 vols. Buenos Aires: Editorial Universitaria, 1969.

– *El ingenioso hidalgo Don Quijote de la Mancha.* Ed. Vicente Gaos. 3 vols. Madrid: Gredos, 1987.

– *El ingenioso hidalgo Don Quijote de la Mancha.* Ed. Luís Andrés Murillo. 2 vols. Madrid: Castalia, 1987.

– *El ingenioso hidalgo Don Quijote de la Mancha.* Ed. Rodolfo Schevill and Adolfo Bonilla. 4 vols. Madrid: Gráficas Reunidas, 1928.

– *Novelas ejemplares I.* Ed. Harry Sieber. Madrid: Ediciones Cátedra, 1992.

– *El rufián dichoso.* Ed. Jenaro Talens and Nicholas Spadaccini. Madrid: Cátedra, 1986.

– *Los trabajos de Persiles y Sigismunda.* Ed. Juan Bautista Avalle-Arce. Madrid: Castalia, 1989.

– 'El viejo celoso.' In *Teatro completo*, ed. Florencio Sevilla Arroyo and Antonio Rey Hazas, 826–42. Barcelona: Planeta, 1987.

Ciruelo, Pedro. *A treatise reproving all superstitions and forms of witchcraft: very necessary and useful for all good Christians zealous for their salvation* (1530). Seville: Andrés de Burgos, 1547. Trans. Eugene A. Maio and D'Orsay W. Pearson. Rutherford, NJ: Fairleigh Dickinson University Press, 1977.

Concepción, Fray Luís de la. *Práctica de conjurar* (1673). Facs. ed. with preliminary note by Alexandre Venegas. Barcelona: Editorial Humanitas, 1983.

Covarrubias Orozco, Sebastián de. *Tesoro de la lengua castellana o española* (Madrid: Luís Sánchez, 1611). Ed. Felipe C.R. Maldonado. Rev. Manuel Camarero. Madrid: Castalia, 1995.

Cueva, Juan de la. *Ejemplar poético* (1606). Ed. Francisco A. de Icaza. Madrid: Espasa-Calpe, 1953.

Dávila Padilla, Agustín. *Historia de la fundación y discurso de la provincia de Santiago de México, de la orden de predicadores, por las vidas de sus varones insignes, y casos notables de Nueva España* (1596). Brussels: Ivan de Meerbeque, 1625.

De Bujanda, J.M., ed. *Index de l'inquisition espagnole 1551, 1554, 1559*. In *Index des livres interdits*, vol. 5. Geneva: Librairie Droz, 1984.

– *Index de l'inquisition espagnole 1583, 1584*. In *Index des livres interdits*, vol. 6. Geneva: Librairie Droz, 1993.

Del Río, Martín Antonio. *Disquisitionum magicarum libri sex* (1599). Lyon: Horatius Cardon, 1608.

– *Disquisitionum magicarum libri sex* (1599). Mainz: Johannes Albinus, 1612.

– *Disquisitionum magicarum libri sex* (1599). Coloniae Agrippinae: Thomas and Henry Theodore von Collen, 1720.

– *Disquisitionum magicarum libri sex* (1599). Book 2. Trans. Jesús Moya as *La magia demoníaca*. Madrid: Hiperion, 1991.

Entremés famoso de la endemoniada fingida y chistes de Bacallao (17th century). Attributed to Francisco de Quevedo. Perhaps by Félix Persio Bertizo. In *Obras de Don Francisco de Quevedo Villegas*, ed. Florencio Janer, 501–7. Biblioteca de autores españoles vol. 69. Madrid: Imprenta de los Sucesores de Hernando, 1920.

'El exorcista Calabrés.' Attributed (probably falsely) to Francisco de Quevedo. In *Obras de Don Francisco de Quevedo Villegas*. Vol. 3, *Poesías*, ed. Florencio Janer, 527–8. Biblioteca de autores españoles vol. 69. Madrid: Imprenta de los Sucesores de Hernando, 1920.

Feijóo y Montenegro, Benito. 'Duendes y espíritus familiares.' In *Obras escogidas*. Ed. Vicente de la Fuente, 103–7. Biblioteca de autores españoles vol. 56. Madrid: M. Rivadeneyra, 1863.

– *Teatro crítico universal*. Vol. 3. Ed. Agustín Millares Carlo. Madrid: Espasa-Calpe, 1955.

Fita, Fidel, ed. 'La Inquisición toledana. Relación contemporánea de los autos y autillos que celebró desde el año 1485 hasta el de 1501.' *Boletín de la Real Academia de la Historia* (1887): 289–321.

Gómez Lodosa, Diego. *Iugum ferreum Luciferi, seu exorcismi terribiles, contra malignos spiritus possidentes corpora humana, & ad quaevis maleficia depellenda, & ad quascumque infestationes Daemonum deprimendas*. Valencia: Heirs of Jerónimo Vilagrasa, 1676.

Heliodorus. *Aethiopica*. 1615 Spanish translation by Fernando de Mena as *Historia etiópica de los amores de Teágenes y Cariclea*. Ed. F. López Estrada. Madrid: Aldus, 1954.

Huarte de San Juan, Juan. *Examen de ingenios para las ciencias*. Ed. Guillermo Serés. Madrid: Cátedra, 1989.

López, Juan, Bishop of Monópolis. 'De la vida marauillosa del santo fray Christoual de la Cruz.' In *Historia general de la Orden de Sto. Domingo, y de su Orden de Predicadores*

(1563). Part 4. Chapters 27–30. Reprinted in *Los rufianes de Cervantes: 'El rufián dichoso' y 'El rufián viudo,'* ed. Joaquín Hazañas y la Rua, 53–81. Seville: Imprenta de Izquierdo, 1906.

López Pinciano, Alonso. *Philosophia antigua poética.* Ed. Alfredo Carballo Picazo. 3 vols. Madrid: Consejo Superior de Investigaciones Científicas and Instituto 'Miguel de Cervantes,' 1973.

Loyola, Ignatius of. *Spiritual Exercises.* Trans. Anthony Mottola. New York: Doubleday, 1989.

Luna, Juan de. *Segundo Lazarillo* (1620). Ed. Pedro M. Piñero. Madrid: Cátedra, 1988.

Mira de Amescua, Antonio. *El esclavo del demonio.* Ed. Ángel Valbuena Prat. Madrid: Espasa-Calpe, 1943.

Moreto, Agustín. *Entremés de las brujas.* In *Autos sacramentales y al nacimiento de Christo.* Madrid: Antonio Francisco de Zafra, 1675.

Noydens, Benito Remigio. *Practica de exorcistas y ministros de la Iglesia. En que con mucha erudicion, y singular claridad, se trata de la instruccion de los Exorcismos para lançar, y ahuyentar los demonios, y curar espiritualmente todo genero de maleficio, y hechizos* (1660). Barcelona: Antonio la Cavallería, 1688.

Quevedo y Villegas, Francisco de. *El alguacil alguacilado.* In *Obras de Don Francisco de Quevedo Villegas,* vol. 1, ed. Aureliano Fernández-Guerra y Orbe. Biblioteca de autores españoles, vol. 23. Madrid: Atlas, 1946.

– *Discurso de todos los diablos o infierno enmendado.* In *Obras completas,* vol. 1, ed. Felicidad Buendía. Madrid: Aguilar, 1966.

– *Epistolario.* Mexico City: Consejo Nacional para la Cultura y las Artes, 1989.

– *La hora de todos.* Ed. Luisa López-Grigera. Madrid: Castalia, 1979. Cuadro 11.

– *Poesía original completa.* Ed. José Manuel Blecua. Barcelona: Planeta, 1996.

– *Sueños y discursos.* Ed. James O. Crosby. Madrid: Castalia, 1993.

– *Sueños y discursos* (2-vol. critical edition). Vol. 2. Ed. James O. Crosby. Madrid: Castalia, Nueva Biblioteca de Erudición y Crítica, 1993.

– *Vida del buscón Don Pablos.* Ed. Guillermo Díaz-Plaja. Mexico City: Porrúa, 1986.

– *The Visions of Dom Francisco de Quevedo Villegas, Knight of the Order of St. James.* Trans. R.L. [Roger L'Estrange]. 3rd ed. London: H. Herringman, 1668.

Relacion del auto publico de la fè que se celebro en esta corte domingo 21. de enero de 1624. Madrid: Diego Flamenco, 1624.

Salazar Treviño, Pedro de. *Relacion de vn caso raro, en que fueron expelidos de vna muger casada muchos demonios, en la villa de Madrilejos, a los 14. dias del mes de Otubre deste año passado de 1607.* N.p.: n.p., 1608.

San Román, Alonso de. *Consuelo de penitentes, ò Mesa Franca de spirituales manjares.* Part 2, *Vidas de los célebres Misioneros de Méjico, llamados los Nueve de la Fama.* Tratado IV, *Summa de la vida del sancto varón Fray Christóual de la Cruz, de la Orden de Sancto Domingo de la Nueva España.* Seville: Andrea Pescioni y Iuan de Leon, 1585. Reprinted in

Jean Canavaggio. 'Para la génesis del *Rufián dichoso*: El *Consuelo de penitentes* de Fray Alonso de San Román.' *Nueva revista de filología hispánica* 38.2 (1990): 470–6.

Segundo Lazarillo (1555). Ed. Pedro M. Piñero. Madrid: Cátedra, 1988.

Timoneda, Juan de. *Los menemnos*. In *Obras completas de Juan de Timoneda I*. Marcelino Menéndez Pelayo. Valencia: Est. Tip. Domenech, 1911.

Torquemada, Antonio de. *Jardín de flores curiosas*. In *Obras completas*, vol. 1, ed. Lina Rodríguez Cacho, 495–904. Madrid: Turner, 1994.

Tragicomedia alegórica del parayso y del infierno (1539). In *Teatro español del siglo XVI*. Vol. 1, ed. Urban Cronan, 269–318. Madrid: Sociedad de Bibliófilos Madrileños, 1913.

Vega, Alonso de la. *La duquesa de la rosa*. In *Tres comedias de Alonso de la Vega*, ed. Marcelino Menéndez Pelayo. Dresden: Gedruckt für die Gesellschaft für Romanische Literatur, 1905.

Vega Carpio, Lope de. 'Conjura un culto y hablan los dos de medio soneto abajo.' In *Obras escogidas II: Poesías líricas-poemas-prosa-novelas*, ed. Federico Carlos Sainz de Robles, 222. Madrid: Aguilar, 1964.

– *El divino africano*. In *Obras de Lope de Vega*, vol. 9, *Comedias de vidas de santos*, ed. Marcelino Menéndez Pelayo, 311–62. Biblioteca de autores españoles 177. Madrid: Atlas, 1964.

– *Entremés duodécimo de la endemoniada*. In *Las comedias del famoso poeta Lope de Vega Carpio*. Ed. Bernardo Grassa. Valladolid: Iuan de Bostillo, 1609.

– *Entremés duodécimo: de la endemoniada*. In *Colección de entremeses, loas, bailes, jácaras y mojigangas desde fines del siglo XVI á mediados del XVIII*. Vol. 1, ed. Emilio Cotarelo y Mori. Madrid: Bailly/Bailliére, 1911.

Vélez de Guevara, Luís. *El diablo cojuelo* (1641). Ed. Enrique Rodríguez Cepeda. Madrid: Cátedra, 1984.

Vélez de Guevara, Luís, Francisco de Rojas Zorrilla, and Antonio Mira de Amescua. *El pleyto que tuvo el diablo con el cura de Madrilejos*. Madrid: Imprenta de A. Sanz, 1759. In *Comedias varias*, part 13 (binder's title for collection of printed *sueltas*). University of Pennsylvania Comedia Collection. Spanish Drama of the Golden Age No. 667. Research Publications. Microfilms.

La vida de Lazarillo de Tormes. Ed. Guillermo Díaz-Plaja. Mexico City: Porrúa, 1986.

Zamora, Antonio de. *El hechizado por fuerza*. Ed. Alva V. Ebersole. Valencia: Albatros, 1991.

Secondary Sources: Spanish

Allen, John J. '*Don Quixote* and the Origins of the Novel.' In *Cervantes and the Renaissance*, ed. Michael D. McGaha, 125–40. Easton, PA: Juan de la Cuesta, 1980.

Alonso, José A. 'Ortodoxia y heterodoxia en *Los trabajos de Persiles y Sigismunda*.' PhD dissertation, University of Washington, 1975.

Amezúa, Agustín G. de. 'Prólogo' to Martín de Castañega. *Tratado muy sotil y bien fundado de las supersticiones y hechicerías y vanos conjuros y abusiones: y otras cosas al caso toca[n]tes y dela posibilidad y remedio dellas*. Madrid: Sociedad de Bibliófilos Españoles, 1946.

Amezúa y Mayo, Agustín G. de. *Cervantes creador de la novela corta española*. Vol. 1. Madrid: Consejo Superior de Investigaciones Científicas/Instituto 'Miguel de Cervantes,' 1982.

Andrés, Christian. 'Erotismo brujeril y hechicería urbana en *Los trabajos de Persiles y Sigismunda*.' *Anales cervantinos* 33 (1995–7): 165–75.

Anibal, C.E. 'Voces del cielo – A Note on Mira de Amescua.' *Romanic Review* 1 (1910): 57–70.

Arco y Garay, Ricardo del. 'Cervantes y las supersticiones.' *Boletín de la Biblioteca de Menéndez-Pelayo* 26 (1950): 338–66.

Asensio, Eugenio. *Itinerario del entremés: Desde Lope de Rueda a Quiñones de Benavente*. 2nd ed. Madrid: Gredos, 1971.

Avalle-Arce, Juan Bautista. 'Don Quijote, o la vida como obra de arte.' *Cuadernos Hispano-Americanos* 242 (1970): 247–80.

– *Enciclopedia cervantina*. Alcalá de Henares: Centro de Estudios Cervantinos, 1997.

– '*La Galatea*.' In *Historia y crítica de la literatura española*, gen. ed. Francisco Rico. Vol. 2, *Siglos de Oro: Renacimiento*, ed. Francisco López Estrada, 627–30. Barcelona: Editorial Crítica, 1980.

Baker, Edward. *La biblioteca de Don Quijote*. Madrid: Marcial Pons, 1997.

Barrett, Linton Lomas. 'The Supernatural in the Spanish Non-Religious *Comedia* of the Golden Age.' PhD dissertation, University of North Carolina, Chapel Hill, 1938.

Bataillon, Marcel. *Erasmo y el Erasmismo*. Barcelona: Editorial Crítica, 1977.

– *Erasmo y España*. Mexico City: Fondo de Cultura Económica, 1966.

– *Novedad y fecundidad del* Lazarillo de Tormes. Trans. Luís Cortés Vázquez. Salamanca: Anaya, 1968.

Bataillon, Marcel, and Alexander A. Parker. 'Fundamentos ideológicos de la picaresca.' In *Historia y crítica de la literatura española*, gen. ed. Francisco Rico. Vol. 3, *Siglos de Oro: Barroco*, ed. Bruce W. Wardropper, 474–9. Barcelona: Editorial Crítica, 1983.

Bergúa, José. '*Índice analítico' de* El ingenioso hidalgo Don Quijote de la Mancha *por Miguel de Cervantes*. Mexico City: Porrúa, 1977.

Blasco, Javier. *Cervantes, raro inventor*. Guanajuato, Mexico: University of Guanajuato Press, 1998.

Brioso y Mayral, Julio V. de. 'La brujería aragonesa en la literatura.' In *Brujología*. Congreso de San Sebastián, ponencias y comunicaciones, 233–40. San Sebastián: Seminarios y Ediciones, 1972.

Buendia, Felicidad. 'Índice de obras apócrifas.' In *Don Francisco de Quevedo Villegas, Obras completas*, ed. Felicidad Buendia. Vol. 2. Madrid: Aguilar, 1966.

Calcraft, R.P. 'Fabia et l'ouevre du diable dans *Le chevalier d'Olmedo* de Lope de Vega.' In *Diable, diables, et diableries au temps de la Renaissance*, ed. M.T. Jones-Davies, 29–38. Paris: Jean Touzot, 1988.

Canavaggio, Jean. *Cervantès dramaturge: un théâtre à naître*. Paris: Presses Universitaires de France, 1977.

– 'La conversión del rufián dichoso: fuentes y recreación.' In *On Cervantes: Essays for L.A. Murillo*, ed. James A. Parr, 11–19. Newark, DE: Juan de la Cuesta, 1991.

– 'Para la génesis del *Rufián dichoso*: El *Consuelo de penitentes* de Fray Alonso de San Román.' *Nueva revista de filología hispánica* 38.2 (1990): 461–76.

Cardaillac, Louis. 'A propos de 'Criado de Señor Endemoniado' (Quevedo, *La hora de todos*, Tableaux XI).' *Co-textes* 2 (1981): 19–25.

Caro Baroja, Julio. *Las brujas y su mundo*. Madrid: Alianza Editorial, 1966.

– *Las formas complejas de la vida religiosa: Religión, sociedad y carácter en la España de los siglos XVI y XVII*. Madrid: Akal, 1978.

– 'El *Quijote* y la concepción mágica del mundo.' In *Vidas mágicas e Inquisición*, 1:167–83. Madrid: Taurus, 1967.

– *Teatro popular y magia*. Madrid: Revista de Occidente, 1974.

– *Vidas mágicas e Inquisición*. Vol. 2. Madrid: Católica, 1977.

– *The World of the Witches*. Trans. O.N.V. Glendinning. Chicago: University of Chicago Press, 1964.

Carreter, Fernando Lázaro. *'Lazarillo de Tormes' en la picaresca*. Barcelona: Ariel, 1983.

Casalduero, Joaquín. *Sentido y forma de 'Los trabajos de Persiles y Sigismunda.'* Buenos Aires: Editorial Sudamericana, 1947.

– *Sentido y forma del teatro de Cervantes*. 2nd ed. Madrid: Gredos, 1974.

Cascardi, Anthony J. 'Cervantes's Exemplary Subjects.' In *Cervantes's 'Exemplary Novels' and the Adventure of Writing*, ed. Michael Nerlich and Nicholas Spadaccini, Hispanic Issues 6, 49–72. Minneapolis: Prisma Institute, 1989.

– 'Secularization and Literary Self-Assertion in *Don Quijote*.' In *Cultural Authority in Golden Age Spain*, ed. Marina S. Brownlee and Hans Ulrich Gumbrecht, 209–33. Baltimore: Johns Hopkins University Press, 1993.

Case, Thomas E. 'Metatheater and World View in Lope's *El divino africano*.' *Bulletin of the Comediantes* 42.1 (1990): 129–42.

Castro, Américo. 'Cervantes y la Inquisición.' In *Hacia Cervantes*, 267–91. Madrid: Taurus, 1957.

– 'La estructura del "Quijote."' In *Hacia Cervantes*, 267–91. Madrid: Taurus, 1957.

– 'El *Quijote*, taller de existencialidad.' *Revista de Occidente* 8 (1967): 1–33.

Cervantes, Fernando. *The Devil in the New World: The Impact of Diabolism in New Spain*. New Haven: Yale University Press, 1994.

Checca, Peter Anthony. 'The Role of the Devil in Golden Age Drama.' PhD dissertation, Pennsylvania State University, 1975.

Chow, Sue-Lin. 'Another Source for Timoneda's *Menemnos*.' *Bulletin of the Comediantes* 21 (1969): 52–6.

Christian, W.A. *Apparitions in Late Medieval and Renaissance Spain*. Princeton: Princeton University Press, 1981.

– *Local Religion in Sixteenth-Century Spain*. Princeton: Princeton University Press, 1981.

Cilveti, Angel L. *El demonio en el teatro de Calderón*. Valencia: Albatros Ediciones, 1977.

Ciocchini, Héctor E. 'Quevedo y la construcción de imágenes emblemáticas.' *Revista de filología española* 48.4 (1965): 393–405.

Cisneros, Luís Jaime. *El* Lazarillo de Tormes. Buenos Aires: Kier, 1946.

Comfort, William J. Review of *Un gran inspirador de Cervantes: El Doctor Juan Huarte de San Juan y su 'Examen de Ingenios'* by Rafael Salillas. *Modern Language Notes* 21 (1906): 30–2.

Cortázar, Celina S. de. 'El infierno en la obra de Quevedo.' *Sur* 350–1 (1982): 189–209.

Cotarelo Valledor, Armando. *Cervantes lector*. Discurso leído ante el Instituto de España en la Fiesta Nacional del Libro, 23 abril 1940. Madrid: Publicaciones del Instituto de España, 1943.

Cotarelo y Mori, Emilio. *Colección de entremeses, loas, bailes, jácaras y mojigangas desde fines del siglo XVI á mediados del XVIII*. Vol. 1. Nueva biblioteca de autores españoles vol. 17. Madrid: Bailly/Bailliére, 1911.

Crawford, J.P. Wickersham. 'The Devil as a Dramatic Figure in the Spanish Religious Drama Before Lope de Vega.' *Romanic Review* 1 (1910): 302–83.

Creel, Bryant L. 'Theoretical Implications in Don Quixote's Idea of Enchantment.' *Cervantes* 12.1 (1992): 19–44.

Crosby, James O. 'Al margen de los manuscritos de los *Sueños*: La huella del lector contemporáneo.' *Nueva revista de filología hispánica* 24 (1975): 364–75.

Cruz Casado, Antonio. 'Auristela hechizada: Un caso de maleficia en el *Persiles*.' *Cervantes* 12.2 (1992): 91–104.

De Armas, Frederick A. 'Evoking Apuleius' Mysteries: Myth and Witchcraft in Céspedes y Meneses' *El soldado Píndaro*.' In *Studies in Honor of Donald W. Bleznick*, ed. Delia V. Galván and Anita K. Stoll, 1–16. Newark: Juan de la Cuesta, 1995.

– 'Literature's Occult Art in the Spanish Golden Age: A Preface.' *Crítica Hispánica* 15.1 (1993): 5–16.

De Cesare, Giovanni Battista. '"El rufián dichoso" como experimento.' In *La comedia de magia y de santos*, ed. F.J. Blasco, E. Caldera, J. Álvarez Barrientos, and R. de la Fuente, 107–22. Madrid: Ediciones Júcar, 1992.

Defourneaux, Marcelin. *Daily Life in Spain in the Golden Age*. Trans. Newton Branch. Stanford: Stanford University Press, 1979.

Del Arco, Ricardo. 'Cervantes y las supersticiones.' *Boletín de la Biblioteca de Menéndez Pelayo* 26 (1950): 338–61.

Descouzis, Paul. *Cervantes, a nueva luz.* Vol. 1, *El 'Quijote' y el Concilio de Trento.* Analecta Romanica 19. Frankfurt: V. Klostermann, 1966.

– *Cervantes, a nueva luz.* Vol. 2, *Con la Iglesia hemos dado, Sancho.* Madrid: Ediciones Iberoamericanas, 1973.

Díaz Migoyo, Gonzalo. 'Desendemoniando *El aguacil endemoniado*: La inversión significante entre texto y contexto.' *Mester* 9.2 (1980): 55–70.

Díez Fernández, José-Ignacio, and Luisa-Fernanda Aguirre de Cárcer. 'Contexto histórico y tratamiento literario de la "hechicería" morisca y judía en el *Persiles*.' *Cervantes* 12.2 (1992): 33–62.

Dowling, John. 'La farsa al servicio del naciente siglo de las luces: *El hechizado por fuerza* (1697), de Antonio de Zamora.' In *El teatro español a fines del siglo XVII: Historia, cultura y teatro en la España de Carlos II*, ed. Javier Huerta Calvo, Harmden Boer, and Fermín Sierra Martínez, 2:275–86. Amsterdam and Atlanta: Diálogos Rodopi, 1989.

Dümchen, Sybil. 'The Function of Madness in *El Licenciado Vidriera*.' In *Cervantes's 'Exemplary Novels' and the Adventure of Writing.* Hispanic Issues 6, ed. Michael Nerlich and Nicholas Spadaccini, 99–124. Minneapolis: The Prisma Institute, 1989.

Egido, Aurora. 'Sobre la demonología de los burladores (De Tirso a Zorrilla).' *Iberoromania* 26 (1987): 19–40.

El Saffar, Ruth. *Beyond Fiction: The Recovery of the Feminine in the Novels of Cervantes.* Los Angeles: University of California Press, 1984.

– 'The Truth of the Matter: The Place of Romance in the Works of Cervantes.' In *Romance: Generic Transformation from Chrétien de Troyes to Cervantes*, ed. Kevin Brownlee and Marina Scordilis Brownlee, 238–52. Hanover: University Press of New England, 1985.

Elliott, J.H. 'Quevedo and the Count-Duke of Olivares.' In *Spain and Its World, 1500–1700*, 189–212. New Haven: Yale University Press, 1992.

Ettinghausen, Henry. *Francisco de Quevedo and the Neostoic Movement.* Oxford: Oxford University Press, 1972.

Ferrán, Jaime. 'Algunas constantes en la picaresca.' In *La picaresca: Orígenes, textos y estructuras.* Actas del I Congreso Internacional sobre la Picaresca, ed. Manuel Criado de Val, 53–64. Madrid: Fundación Universitaria Española, 1979.

Flecniakoska, Jean-Louis. 'Les rôles de Satan dans les autos de Lope.' *Bulletin Hispanique* 66 (1964): 30–43.

Flores Arroyuelo, Francisco J. *El diablo en España.* Madrid: Alianza Editorial, 1985.

– *El diablo y los españoles.* Murcia: Universidad de Murcia, 1976.

Flynn, Maureen. 'The Spanish *Auto de fe*.' *Sixteenth Century Journal* 22 (1991): 281–97.

Forcione, Alban K. *Cervantes and the Mystery of Lawlessness.* Princeton: Princeton University Press, 1984.

– *Cervantes, Aristotle, and the* Persiles. Princeton: Princeton University Press, 1970.

– *Cervantes' Christian Romance: A Study of* Persiles y Sigismunda. Princeton: Princeton University Press, 1972.

– 'Cervantes's Secularized Miracle: *La fuerza de la sangre.*' In *Cervantes and the Humanist Vision*, 317–97. Princeton: Princeton University Press, 1982.

García de la Concha, Víctor. 'La estructura ternaria del *Lazarillo de Tormes.*' In *Historia y crítica de la literatura española*, gen. ed. Francisco Rico. Vol. 2, *Siglos de Oro: Renacimiento. Primer suplemento*, ed. Francisco López Estrada, 178–82. Barcelona: Editorial Crítica, 1980.

– 'La intención religiosa del *Lazarillo.*' *Revista de filología española* 55.3–4 (1972): 243–77.

García Rodero, Cristina. *Festivals and Rituals of Spain*. Text by J.M. Caballero Bonald. New York: Harry N. Abrams, 1992.

Gillespie, Ruth C. 'Don Quijote and the *"pecados mortales."'* *Hispania* 42 (1959): 40–1.

Gilman, Stephen. 'The Death of Lazarillo de Tormes.' *PMLA* 81.3 (1966): 149–66.

– *The Novel According to Cervantes*. Berkeley and Los Angeles: University of California Press, 1989.

Gómez-Quintero, Ela. 'La crítica social en *El aguacil endemoniado*, de Quevedo.' In *Homenaje a Humberto Piñera*, 88–96. Madrid: Playor, 1979.

González Palencia, Angel. *Un curandero morisco del siglo XVI: Román Ramírez y las fuentes de la comedia 'Quien mal anda en mal acaba' de Don Juan Ruiz de Alarcón*. Madrid: Tipografía de Archivos, 1930.

Granjel, L.S. *La medicina española del siglo XVII*. Salamanca: Universidad de Salamanca, 1978.

Green, Otis H. 'El "Ingenioso" Hidalgo.' *Hispanic Review* 25 (1957): 175–93.

Greer, Margaret Rich. *The Play of Power: Mythological Court Dramas of Calderón de la Barca*. Princeton: Princeton University Press, 1991.

Guillén, Claudio, and Fernando Lázaro Carreter. 'Constitución de un género: la novela picaresca.' In *Historia y crítica de la literatura española*, gen. ed. Francisco Rico. Vol. 3, *Siglos de Oro: Barroco*, ed. Bruce W. Wardropper, 468–73. Barcelona: Editorial Crítica, 1983.

Hanrahan, Thomas. '*Lazarillo de Tormes*: Erasmian Satire or Protestant Reform?' *Hispania* 66.3 (1983): 333–9.

Harrison, Stephen. 'Magic in the Spanish Golden Age: Cervantes's Second Thoughts.' *Renaissance and Reformation / Renaissance et Réforme* n.s. 1 (1980): 47–64.

– 'Milagros, astrología y racionalización de la magia.' In *La composición de* Los trabajos de Persiles y Sigismunda. Madrid: Pliegos, 1993.

Hasbrouck, Michael D. 'Posesión demoníaca, locura y exorcismo en el *Quijote.*' *Cervantes* 12.2 (1992): 117–26.

Heiple, Daniel L. 'Renaissance Medical Psychology in *Don Quijote.*' *Ideologies and Literature* 2 (1979): 65–72.

Herr, Richard. *The Eighteenth-Century Revolution in Spain*. Princeton: Princeton University Press, 1958.

Huerga, Alvaro. 'La picaresca de las beatas.' In *La picaresca: Orígenes, textos y estructuras*. Actas del I Congreso Internacional sobre la Picaresca, ed. Manuel Criado de Val, 141–8. Madrid: Fundación Universitaria Española, 1979.

Huergo, Humberto. 'Bajo el peso de la ley: Impureza y maternidad en la obra satírica de Quevedo.' PhD dissertation, Princeton University, 1993.

Hughes, Gethin. '"Lazarillo de Tormes": The Fifth "Tratado."' *Hispanófila* 61 (1977): 1–9.

Imirizaldu, Jesús, ed. *Monjas y beatas embaucadoras*. Madrid: Editora Nacional, 1977.

Jauss, Hans Robert. 'Ursprung und Bedeutung der Ich-Form im *Lazarillo de Tormes*.' *Romanistisches Jahrbuch* 8 (1957): 290–311.

Johnson, Carroll B. *Madness and Lust: A Psychoanalytical Approach to Don Quixote*. Berkeley and Los Angeles: University of California Press, 1983.

– 'Of Witches and Bitches: Gender, Marginality and Discourse in *El casamiento engañoso* and *Coloquio de los perros*.' *Cervantes* 11.2 (1991): 7–25.

Kagan, Richard. *Lucrecia's Dreams: Politics and Prophecy in Sixteenth-Century Spain*. Berkeley: University of California Press, 1990.

Kallendorf, Hilaire. 'The Diabolical Adventures of Don Quixote, or Self-Exorcism and the Rise of the Novel.' *Renaissance Quarterly* 54.1 (2002): 193–223.

Kallendorf, Hilaire, and Craig Kallendorf. 'Conversations with the Dead: Quevedo and Statius, Annotation and Imitation.' *Journal of the Warburg and Courtauld Institutes* 63 (2000): 131–68.

Kamen, Henry. *Inquisition and Society in Spain in the Sixteenth and Seventeenth Centuries*. Bloomington: Indiana University Press, 1985.

– *The Spanish Inquisition: A Historical Revision*. New Haven: Yale University Press, 1998.

Lapesa, Rafael. 'En torno a *La española inglesa* y el *Persiles*.' In *De la Edad Media a nuestros días*. Madrid: Gredos, 1967.

Lima, Robert. *Dark Prisms: Occultism in Hispanic Drama*. Lexington: University of Kentucky Press, 1995.

– 'Spanish Drama of the Occult through the Eighteenth Century: An Annotated Bibliography of Primary Sources.' *Crítica Hispánica* 15.1 (1993): 117–38.

Lisón Tolosana, Carmelo. *La España mental I: Demonios y exorcismos en los Siglos de Oro*. Madrid: Ediciones Akal, 1990.

Llamas Martínez, Enrique. *Santa Teresa de Jesús y la Inquisición española*. Madrid: Consejo Superior de Investigaciones Científicas, 1972.

López Poza, Sagrario. 'Quevedo, humanista cristiano.' In *Quevedo a nueva luz: Escritura y política*, ed. Lía Schwartz Lerner and Antonio Carreira, 59–81. Málaga: Universidad de Málaga, 1997.

Maldonado, C.R. 'Algunos datos sobre la composición y dispersión de la biblioteca de

Quevedo.' In *Homenaje a la memoria de don Antonio Rodríguez-Moñino, 1910–1970,* 405–28. Madrid: Castalia, 1975.

Maldonado de Guevara, Francisco. 'La renuncia a la magia en el *Quijote* y en el *Fausto.' Anales cervantinos* 2 (1952): 1–109.

Mancini, Guido. *Gli entremeses nell'arte di Quevedo.* Pisa: Libreria Goliardica Editrice, 1955.

Maravall, José Antonio. *Utopia and Counterutopia in the 'Quixote.'* Trans. Robert W. Felkel. Detroit: Wayne State University Press, 1991.

Mariscal, George. *Contradictory Subjects: Quevedo, Cervantes, and Seventeenth-Century Spanish Culture.* Ithaca: Cornell University Press, 1991.

Márquez Villanueva, Francisco. 'Crítica social y crítica religiosa en el "Lazarillo": la denuncia de un mundo sin caridad.' In *Historia y crítica de la literatura española,* gen. ed. Francisco Rico. Vol. 2, *Siglos de Oro: Renacimiento,* ed. Francisco López Estrada, 374–7. Barcelona: Editorial Crítica, 1980.

– *Espiritualidad y literatura en el siglo XVI.* Madrid: Alfaguara, 1968.

– 'Planteamiento de la literatura del "loco" en España.' *Sin Nombre* 10.4 (1980): 7–25.

Martinengo, Alessandro. *La astrología en la obra de Quevedo: Una clave de lectura.* Madrid: Alhambra, 1983.

Mendeloff, Henry. 'Exorcism in Blatty and Berceo.' *Comparative Literature Studies* 11 (1974): 218–25.

Menéndez Pelayo, M. *Historia de las ideas estéticas en España,* ed. Fernando Lázaro Carreter. *Menéndez Pelayo: Su época y su obra literaria.* Vol. 2. Salamanca: Anaya, 1962.

– *Historia de los heterodoxos españoles.* 8 vols. Madrid: Consejo Superior de Investigaciones Científicas, 1963.

Mitchell, Timothy J. *Violence and Piety in Spanish Folklore.* Philadelphia: University of Pennsylvania Press, 1988.

Molho, Mauricio. '"El sagaz perturbador del género humano": Brujas, perros embrujados y otras demonomanías cervantinas.' *Cervantes* 12.2 (1992): 21–32.

Muñoz Iglesias, Salvador. *Lo religioso en el 'Quijote.'* Toledo: Estudio Teológico de San Ildefonso, 1989.

Nadler, Steven. 'Descartes's Demon and the Madness of Don Quixote.' *Journal of the History of Ideas* 58.1 (1997): 41–55.

Nolting-Hauff, Ilse. *Visión, sátira y agudeza en los 'Sueños' de Quevedo.* Trans. Ana Pérez de Linares. Madrid: Gredos, 1974.

Norton, F.J. *A Descriptive Catalogue of Printing in Spain and Portugal, 1501–1520.* Cambridge: Cambridge University Press, 1978.

Olmos García, Francisco. 'La Inquisición en la época y en la obra de Cervantes.' In *Cervantes en su época,* 11–117. Madrid: Ricardo Aguilera, 1968.

O'Reilly, Terence. 'The Erasmianism of *Lazarillo de Tormes.'* In *Essays in Honour of Robert Brian Tate from His Colleagues and Pupils,* ed. Richard A. Cardwell, 91–100. Nottingham: University of Nottingham Press, 1984.

Ortega y Gasset, José. *Meditations on Quixote*. Ed. Julián Marías. Trans. Evelyn Rugg and Diego Marín. New York: W.W. Norton, 1963.

Parker, Alexander A. *Literature and the Delinquent: The Picaresque Novel in Spain and Europe, 1599–1753*. Edinburgh: Edinburgh University Press, 1967.

– *The Theology of the Devil in the Drama of Calderón*. London: Blackfriars, 1958.

Parr, James A. 'La estructura satírica del *Lazarillo*.' In *La picaresca: Orígenes, textos y estructuras*. Actas del I Congreso Internacional sobre la Picaresca, ed. Manuel Criado de Val, 375–84. Madrid: Fundación Universitaria Española, 1979.

Passafari, Clara. 'El dominio del fuego y la Noche de San Juan en las tradiciones populares de Argentina.' *Folklore americano* 53 (1992): 141–50.

Pavia, Mario N. *Drama of the Siglo de Oro: A Study of Magic, Witchcraft, and Other Occult Beliefs*. New York: Hispanic Institute in the United States, 1959.

Piero, Raúl A. del. 'Algunas fuentes de Quevedo: I. Los herejes del *Sueño del infierno*.' *Nueva revista de filología hispánica* 12.1 (1958): 36–52.

Pinta Llorente, Miguel de la. *Aspectos históricos del sentimiento religioso en España*. Madrid: Consejo Superior de Investigaciones Científicas, 1961.

Portuondo, Augusto A. *Diez comedias atribuidas a Lope de Vega: Estudio de su autenticidad*. Charlottesville: Biblioteca Siglo de Oro, 1980.

Predmore, Richard. 'La función del encantamiento en el mundo del *Quijote*.' *Anales cervantinos* 5 (1955–6): 61–78.

Pring-Mill, Robert D.F. 'Some Techniques of Representation in the *Sueños* and the *Criticón*.' *Bulletin of Hispanic Studies* 45 (1968): 270–84.

Read, Malcolm K. *Visions in Exile: The Body in Spanish Literature and Linguistics, 1500–1800*. Philadelphia: John Benjamins, 1990.

– 'The Word Made Flesh: Magic and Mysticism in Erasmian Spain.' In *The Birth and Death of Language*, 97–135. Madrid: Porrúa-Studia Humanitatis, 1983.

Redondo, Augustin. 'Gayferos: De caballero a demonio (o del romance al conjuro de los años 1570).' *Nueva revista de filología hispánica* 36.4 (1982): 997–1009.

Redondo, Augustin, and André Rochon, eds. *Visages de la folie, 1500–1650, domaine hispano-italien*. Colloque tenu a la Sorbonne les 8 et 9 mai 1980. Paris: Sorbonne, 1981.

Reed, Walter. '*Don Quixote*: The Birth, Rise and Death of the Novel.' *Indiana Journal of Hispanic Literatures* 5 (1994): 263–78.

Rennert, Hugo Albert. *The Life of Lope de Vega (1562–1635)*. New York: Benjamin Blom, 1968.

– *The Spanish Stage in the Time of Lope de Vega*. New York: Dover, 1963.

Rico, Francisco. 'Brujería y literatura.' In *Brujología*. Congreso de San Sebastián, ponencias y comunicaciones, 97–118. San Sebastián: Seminarios y Ediciones, 1972.

Riley, E.C. *Cervantes's Theory of the Novel*. Oxford: Oxford University Press, 1962.

– '"Romance" y novela en Cervantes.' In *Cervantes: Su obra y su mundo*. Actas del I Congreso Internacional Sobre Cervantes, ed. Manuel Criado de Val, 5–13. Madrid: Edi-6, 1981.

Robert, Marthe. *The Old and the New: From* Don Quixote *to Kafka.* Trans. Carol Cosman. Berkeley and Los Angeles: University of California Press, 1977.

Rodríguez Marín, Francisco. 'Las supersticiones del *Quijote.*' In *Estudios cervantinos*, 621–35. Madrid: Atlas, 1947.

Romero, Carlos. *Introduzione al 'Persiles' di Miguel de Cervantes.* Venice: Consiglio Nazionale delle Ricerche, Distribuisce Libreria Universitaria, 1968.

Roth, Cecil. *The Spanish Inquisition.* New York: Norton, 1964.

Roux, Lucette Elyane. *Du logos à la scène: Ethique et esthétique. Dramaturgie de la comédie de saints dans l'Espagne du Siècle d'Or (1580–1630).* 2 vols. Lille: Université de Lille III, Service de Reproduction des Thèses, 1975.

Sánchez, Alberto. 'Conexiones temáticas de la comedia cervantina *El rufián dichoso.*' In *Filología y crítica hispánica: Homenaje al Prof. Federico Sánchez Escribano*, ed. Alberto Porqueras Mayo y Carlos Rojas, 121–41. Madrid: Ediciones Alcalá/Emory University, 1969.

Schevill, Rodolfo, and Adolfo Bonilla. Introducción to ed. of Miguel de Cervantes, *Persiles y Sigismunda.* Madrid: Bernardo Rodríguez, 1914.

Schwartz, Lía. 'Figuras del Orco y el infierno interior en Quevedo.' In *Hommage à Robert Jammes*, ed. Francis Cerdan, 3:1079–88. 3 vols. Toulouse: Presses Universitaires du Mirail, 1994.

Schwartz Lerner, Lía. 'En torno a la enunciación en la sátira: Los casos de *El Crotalón* y los *Sueños* de Quevedo.' *Lexis* 9.2 (1985): 209–27.

– 'Formas de la poesía satírica en el siglo XVII: Sobre las convenciones del género.' *Edad de Oro* 6 (1987): 215–34.

– 'Golden Age Satire: Transformations of Genre.' *Modern Language Notes* 105.2 (1990): 260–82.

Scott Soufas, Teresa. *Melancholy and the Secular Mind in Spanish Golden Age Literature.* Columbia: University of Missouri Press, 1990.

Sevilla, Florencio. 'Del "Quijote" al "Rufián dichoso": Capítulos de teoría dramática cervantina.' *Edad de Oro* 5 (1986): 217–45.

Sieber, Harry. *Language and Society in* La vida de Lazarillo de Tormes. Baltimore: Johns Hopkins University Press, 1978.

– 'Literary Continuity, Social Order, and the Invention of the Picaresque.' In *Cultural Authority in Golden Age Spain*, ed. Marina S. Brownlee and Hans Ulrich Gumbrecht, 143–64. Baltimore: Johns Hopkins University Press, 1993.

– 'The Narrators in Quevedo's *Sueños.*' In *Quevedo in Perspective: Eleven Essays for the Quadricentennial*, ed. James Iffland, 101–16. Newark, DE: Juan de la Cuesta, 1982.

Spencer, Forrest Eugene, and Rudolph Schevill. *The Dramatic Works of Luís Vélez de*

Guevara: Their Plots, Sources, and Bibliography. Berkeley: University of California Press, 1937.

Stapp, William. 'Dichoso por confiado.' *Anales cervantinos* 25–6 (1987–8): 413–52.

Stegmann, Tilbert Diego. *Cervantes' Musterroman 'Persiles.' Epentheorie und Romanpraxis um 1600 (El Pinciano, Heliodor, 'Don Quijote').* Hamburg: Hartmut Lüdke, 1971.

Sullivan, Henry W. 'The Beyond in the Here-and-Now: Passing Through Purgatory in *Don Quixote,* Part Two.' *Crítica Hispánica* 15.1 (1993): 63–84.

– *Grotesque Purgatory: A Study of Cervantes's* Don Quixote, *Part II.* University Park: Pennsylvania State University Press, 1996.

Truman, Ronald W. *Spanish Treatises on Government, Society and Religion in the Time of Philip II. The 'De Regimine Principum' and Associated Traditions.* Leiden: E.J. Brill, 1999.

Urbina, Eduardo. *Principios y fines del* Quijote. Potomac, MD: Scripta Humanistica, 1990.

Varas, Patricia. 'El *Rufián dichoso*: Una comedia de santos diferente.' *Anales cervantinos* 29 (1991): 9–19.

Vilanova, Antonio. 'Lázaro de Tormes, pregonero de su propia deshonra.' In *Historia y crítica de la literatura española,* ed. Francisco Rico. Vol. 2, *Siglos de Oro: Renacimiento. Primer suplemento,* ed. Francisco López Estrada, 183–7. Barcelona: Editorial Crítica, 1980.

Wardropper, Bruce. 'Cervantes' Theory of the Drama.' *Modern Philology* 52 (1954–5): 217–21.

Weber, Alison. 'Between Ecstasy and Exorcism: Religious Negotiation in Sixteenth-Century Spain.' *Journal of Medieval and Renaissance Studies* 23.2 (1993): 221–34.

– 'Cuatro clases de narrativa picaresca.' In *La picaresca: Orígenes, textos y estructuras.* Actas del I Congreso Internacional sobre la Picaresca, ed. Manuel Criado de Val, 13–18. Madrid: Fundación Universitaria Española, 1979.

Weiger, John. *The Individuated Self: Cervantes and the Emergence of the Individual.* Athens, Ohio: Ohio University Press, 1979.

Williamsen, Amy R. *Co(s)mic Chaos: Exploring* Los trabajos de Persiles y Sigismunda. Newark, DE: Juan de la Cuesta, 1994.

Willis, Raymond S. 'Lazarillo and the Pardoner: The Artistic Necessity of the Fifth *Tractado.*' *Hispanic Review* 27 (1959): 267–79.

Wilson, Diana de Armas. 'The Histrionics of Exorcism: Isabela Castrucha.' In *Allegories of Love: Cervantes's* Persiles and Sigismunda, 223–47. Princeton: Princeton University Press, 1991.

Zamora Vicente, Alonso. 'El cautiverio en la obra de Cervantes.' In *Homenaje a Cervantes,* ed. Francisco Sánchez-Castañer, 2:237–56. Valencia: Editorial Mediterráneo, 1950.

Zimic, Stanislav. 'La caridad "jamás imaginada" de Cristóbal de Lugo (estudio de *El rufián dichoso* de Cervantes).' *Boletín de la Biblioteca de Menéndez Pelayo* 56 (1980): 85–171.

Primary Sources: Italian

Bandello, Matteo. *Novelle*. Ed. Gioachino Brognoligo. 5 vols. Bari: Laterza, 1910–12.
Boccaccio, Giovanni. *The Decameron*. Trans. Mark Musa and Peter Bondanella. New York:
   Mentor, 1982.
– *Elegia di Madonna Fiammetta*. Ed. Maria Pia Mussini Sacchi. Milan: Mursia,
   1987.
Bruno, Giordano. 'De gli eroici furori.' In *Opere di Giordano Bruno e di Tommaso
   Campanella*, ed. Augusto Guzzo and Romano Amerio, 569–658. Milan and Naples:
   Riccardo Ricciardi, 1956.
Campanella, Tommaso. 'Anima immortale.' In *Opere di Giordano Bruno e di Tommaso
   Campanella*, ed. Augusto Guzzo and Romano Amerio, 790. Milan/Naples: Riccardo
   Ricciardi, 1956.
– 'XVII: La religione nel poema.' In *Poetica* (1596), ed. Luigi Firpo, 144–8. Rome: Reale
   Accademia d'Italia, 1944.
Castelvetro, Lodovico. *The Poetics of Aristotle Translated and Annotated* (1570) (excerpts).
   Trans. Allan H. Gilbert. In *Literary Criticism*, ed. Gilbert, 304–57.
Giacomini, Lorenzo. *Sopra la purgazione della tragedia* (1586). In *Trattati di poetica e
   retorica del Cinquecento*. Vol. 3, ed. Bernard Weinberg, 347–71. Bari: Gius. Laterza &
   Sons, 1972.
Gilbert, Allen H., ed. *Literary Criticism: Plato to Dryden*. Detroit: Wayne State University
   Press, 1962.
Grazzini, Giovanni. *Teatro di Grazzini*. Bari: Laterza, 1953.
Guarini, Giambattista. *The Compendium of Tragicomic Poetry* (1599) (excerpts). Trans.
   Allan H. Gilbert. In *Literary Criticism*, ed. Gilbert, 504–33.
Mazzoni, Jacopo. *On the Defense of the Comedy of Dante* (1688) (excerpts). Trans. Allan H.
   Gilbert. In *Literary Criticism*, ed. Gilbert, 359–403.
Menghi, Girolamo. *Flagellum Daemonum, Exorcismos Terribiles, Potentissimos, &
   efficaces, Remediaque probatissima, ac doctrinam singularem in malignos spiritus expellen-
   dos, facturasque & maleficia fuganda de obsessis corporibus complectens, cum suis benedic-
   tionibus, & omnibus requisitis ad eorum expulsionem* (1577–8). Venice: P. Balleonius,
   1697.
Minturno, Antonio. *L'arte poetica* (1564) (excerpts). Trans. Allan H. Gilbert. In *Literary
   Criticism*, ed. Gilbert, 275–303.
Petrarca, Francesco. 'Canzone CXXXVI.' In *Antologia della letteratura italiana*. Vol. 1, ed.
   Attilio Momigliano, 296–7. Milan: Giuseppe Principato, 1967.
Pico della Mirandola, Giovanni. 'Oration on the Dignity of Man.' Trans. Elizabeth Liver-
   moore Forbes. In *The Renaissance Philosophy of Man*, ed. Ernst Cassirer, Paul Oskar
   Kristeller, and John Herman Randall, Jr, 223–54. Chicago: University of Chicago Press,
   1948.

Tasso, Torquato. *Discourses on the Heroic Poem* (1594) (excerpts). Trans. Allan H. Gilbert. In *Literary Criticism*, ed. Gilbert, 466–503.
– *Le lettere di Torquato Tasso*. Ed. Cesare Guasti. 5 vols. Florence: Le Monnier, 1875.
– *Risposta del S. Torquato Tasso al discorso del Sig. Oratio Lombardelli intorno a i contrasti, che si fanno sopra la Gierusalemme liberata*. Ferrara: G. Vasalini, 1586.
Weinberg, Bernard, ed. *Trattati di poetica e retorica del Cinquecento*. 4 vols. Bari: Gius. Laterza and Sons, 1970.
Zuccollo da Cologna, Simeon. *La pazzia del ballo*. Padua: Giacomo Fabriano, 1549.

Secondary Sources: Italian

Aguzzi-Barbagli, Danilo. 'Humanism and Poetics.' In *Renaissance Humanism: Foundations, Forms and Legacy*. Vol. 3: *Humanism and the Disciplines*, ed. Albert Rabil Jr, 85–170. Philadelphia: University of Pennsylvania Press, 1988–91.
Baldassarri, Guido. '*Inferno' e 'cielo': tipologia e funzione del 'meraviglioso' nella 'Liberata.'* Rome: Bulzoni, 1977.
Clark, Stuart. 'Tasso and the Literature of Witchcraft.' In *The Renaissance in Ferrara and Its European Horizons*, ed. J. Salmons and Walter Moretti, 3–21. Cardiff: University of Wales Press, 1984.
Clubb, Louise G. *Giambattista della Porta: Dramatist*. Princeton: Princeton University Press, 1965.
Gentilcore, David. *From Bishop to Witch: The System of the Sacred in Early Modern Terra d'Otranto*. Manchester: Manchester University Press, 1992.
Ginzburg, Carlo. 'Folklore, magia, religione.' In *Storia d'Italia*. Vol. 1, *I caratteri originali*, 603–79. 3rd ed. Turin: Giulio Einaudi, 1972.
Hathaway, Baxter. *The Age of Criticism: The Late Renaissance in Italy*. Ithaca: Cornell University Press, 1962.
Kallendorf, Craig. 'From Virgil to Vida: The *Poeta Theologus* in Italian Renaissance Commentary.' *Journal of the History of Ideas* 56.1 (1995): 41–62.
– *In Praise of Aeneas*. Hanover, NH: University Press of New England, 1989.
Leo, Ulrich. 'Staunen und Wunder' (Kapitel 2). In *Torquato Tasso: Studien zur Vorgeschichte des Secentismo*, 101–12. Bern: A. Francke Ag., 1951.
Montgomery, Robert L., Jr. 'Allegory and the Incredible Fable: The Italian View from Dante to Tasso.' *PMLA* 81 (1966): 45–55.
Nencioni, Enrico. 'Le tre pazzie (Orlando, Lear, Don Quijote).' In *Saggi critici di letteratura italiana*, 143–73. Florence: Suc. de Le Monnier, 1898.
Niccoli, Ottavia. *Prophecy and People in Renaissance Italy*. Trans. Lydia G. Cochrane. Princeton: Princeton University Press, 1990.
Raimondi, Ezio. 'Tra grammatica e magia.' In *Rinascimento inquieto*, 161–88. Palermo: Manfredi, 1965.

Rebhorn, Wayne. *Foxes and Lions: Machiavelli's Confidence Men.* Ithaca: Cornell University Press, 1988.

Roche, Thomas P., Jr. 'Tasso's Enchanted Woods.' In *Literary Uses of Typology from Late Middle Ages to Present,* ed. Earl Miner, 49–78. Princeton: Princeton University Press, 1977.

Sozzi, Bortolo Tommaso. 'Il magismo nel Tasso.' In *Studi sul Tasso,* 303–36. Pisa: Nistri-Lischi, 1954.

Spoerri, Theophil. *Renaissance und Barock bei Ariost und Tasso.* Bern: Paul Haupt, 1922.

Weinberg, Bernard. 'Castelvetro's Theory of Poetics.' In *Critics and Criticism,* ed. R.S. Crane, 146–68. Chicago: University of Chicago Press, 1970.

– *A History of Literary Criticism in the Italian Renaissance.* 2 vols. Chicago: University of Chicago Press, 1974.

Primary Sources: Northern European

Erasmus, Desiderius. 'Exorcism, or the Spectre' (1524). In *The Colloquies of Erasmus.* Trans. Craig R. Thompson. Chicago: University of Chicago Press, 1965.

– *Praise of Folly.* Trans. Betty Radice. In *Collected Works of Erasmus,* ed. A.H.T. Levi, vols 27–8. Toronto: University of Toronto Press, 1986.

Krämer, Henry, and James Sprenger. *Malleus maleficarum* (1486). Trans. Montague Summers. Bungay, Suffolk: John Rodker, 1928. Reprint, New York: Dover, 1971.

Luther, Martin. *Tischreden.* Ed. Ulrich Köpf and Helmar Junghans. 6 vols. Weimar: Böhlaus Nachfolger, 1912.

Malleus Maleficarum, maleficas et earum haeresim framea conterens, ex variis auctoribus compilatus, & in quatuor Tomos iustè distributus, Quorum duo priores vanas daemonum versutias, praestigiosas eorum delusiones, superstitiosa strigimagarum caeremonias, horrendos etiam cum illis congressus, exactam denique tam pestifera secta disquisitionem, & punitionem complectuntur. Tertius praxim Exorcistarum ad Daemonem, & Strigimagarum maleficia de Christi fidelibus pellenda; Quartus verò Artem Doctrinalem, Benedictionalem, & Exorcismalem continent. Editio nouissima, infinitis penè mendis expurgata; cuique accessit Fuga Daemonum & Complementum artis exorcisticae. Lyon: Claude Bourgeat, 1669.

Pithoys, Claude. *La descouvertvure des faux possedez.* Ed. P.J.S. Whitmore. In *A Seventeenth-Century Exposure of Superstition: Select Texts of Claude Pithoys (1587–1676),* ed. Whitmore, 1–44. The Hague: Martinus Nijhoff, 1972.

Peucer, Caspar. *Commentarius de praecipuis divinationum generibus* (1553). Frankfurt: Typis Wechelianis apud Claudium Marnium et haeredes Ioan. Aubrii, 1607.

Saint-Évremond, Seigneur de [Charles Marguetel de Saint Denis]. *Of Tragedy, Ancient and Modern* (1672) (excerpts). Trans. Mr. des Maizeaux and Allan H. Gilbert. In *Literary Criticism,* ed. Gilbert, 659–63.

Weyer, Johan. *De praestigiis daemonum* (1563). Ed. George Mora et al. Trans John Shea. Binghamton, NY: Center for Medieval and Early Renaissance Studies, 1991.

Secondary Sources: Northern European

Chomarat, Jacques. 'Erasme et le Diable.' In *Diable, diables, et diableries au temps de la Renaissance*, ed. M.T. Jones-Davies, 131–48. Paris: Jean Touzot, 1988.

Dinzelbacher, Peter. *Heilige oder Hexen? Schicksale auffälliger Frauen in Mittelalter und Frühneuzeit*. Zürich: Artemis and Winkler, 1995.

Midelfort, H.C. Erik. *Mad Princes of Renaissance Germany*. Charlottesville: University Press of Virginia, 1994.

Schnierer, Peter Paul. *Entdämonisierung und Verteufelung: Studien zur Darstellungs- und Funktionsgeschichte des Diabolischen in der englischen Literatur seit der Renaissance*. Tübingen: Max Niemeyer, 2002.

Screech, M.A. *Montaigne and Melancholy: The Wisdom of the Essays*. Selinsgrove, PA: Susquehanna University Press, 1983.

Index